Speech Science Primer

**Physiology, Acoustics,
and Perception of Speech**

Speech Science Primer
Physiology, Acoustics, and Perception of Speech

Gloria J. Borden, Ph.D.

Department of Speech
Temple University
Philadelphia, Pennsylvania
and
Haskins Laboratories
New Haven, Connecticut

and

Katherine S. Harris, Ph.D.

Department of Speech & Hearing Sciences
The Graduate School,
City University of New York
New York, New York
and
Haskins Laboratories
New Haven, Connecticut

WILLIAMS & WILKINS
Baltimore/London

Copyright ©, 1980
Williams & Wilkins
428 E. Preston St.
Baltimore, Md. 21202, U.S.A.

Made in the United States of America

Reprinted 1981
Reprinted 1982
Reprinted 1983

Library of Congress Cataloging in Publication Data

Borden, Gloria J.
   Speech science primer.

   Includes bibliographies and index.
   1. Speech—Physiological aspects. 2. Hearing. 3. Speech perception. I. Harris, Katherine S., joint author. II. Title. [DNLM: 1. Acoustics. 2. Speech perception. 3. Speech—Physiology. WV501 B728s]
QP306.B72   612′.78   79-11286
ISBN 0-683-00941-9

Composed and printed at the
Waverly Press, Inc.
Mt. Royal and Guilford Aves.
Baltimore, Md. 21202, U.S.A.

Dedication

To our students,
past, present, and future.

Preface

The reason for writing this text was to try to satisfy a need for a comprehensive but elementary book on speech science. We have faced the dilemma of lacking a satisfactory text for undergraduate or graduate speech science courses; several books might suffice, but any one of the available books was either too restricted in scope or too advanced. The need was for a text that is easy to understand and that integrates material on production, acoustics, and perception of speech.

Courses in speech science in the 1950s were often focused on speech production and hearing, the content being primarily anatomy and physiology. During the 1960s, the study of the acoustics of speech was added to many course curricula. Now, the most comprehensive courses include speech perception, thus completing coverage of the communicative process from the speaker to the listener. In most college speech departments, a separate course pursues the areas of cognition, language, and memory, leaving the production and perception of the speech signal itself to speech science, allowing for some overlap. No presently available text covers this expanded speech science curriculum in an elementary way.

The primary audience to which this text is addressed are the students of speech pathology and audiology. The material should also be interesting to students of medicine, psychology, education, and linguistics. Typically, these disciplines cover various aspects of the material presented in this text and such readers may be interested in a comprehensive treatment. This book is clearly introductory, but it could serve as a graduate text for students who never had a survey course in speech science as undergraduates. Students drawn to the study of speech pathology and audiology by an interest in helping those with communicative disorders find that information is lacking on normal communication processes with which to compare the pathologies. As more is learned, through research, about the normal processes involved in speech, continued study of speech science helps to fill that need.

Speech science as a self-contained discipline is a relatively recent development, although facets of it have a long history. Acoustics has long been an aspect of physics and engineering, speech physiology a part of biology, speech perception an outgrowth of both biology and sensory psychology, and speech in its relation to language in general has long been included in the study of linguistics. This book embraces each of these facets and attempts to unify them.

When we undertake a course of study, we are often led gently to the subject by some introductory readings and lectures, and after the main body of the course, are again eased to the end of the term with some concluding remarks and provocative discussions. It is not unlike a traditional play in which the author sets the stage, unfolds the drama, and ends with the dénouement. The relative size of the chapters in this text reflects some such organization, with the middle three chapters, 3, 4, and 5, dealing with acoustics, production, and perception, the chief substance of the course. The first chapter sets speech in the larger framework of language. Chapter 2 samples the history of speech science by describing a few pioneers in acoustics, phonetics, speech pathology, speech engineering, and perception. The scientists were selected by us to serve as examples of the diversity of approach used by workers in this field. Having introduced the subject and dealt with a bit of its history, the first two chapters are then followed by the main body of the book.

The fact that speech is audible mandated the study of sound as a prerequisite to the understanding of the production and perception of speech sounds. Chapter 3, on acoustics, lays the foundation upon which the real stuff of speech science, Chapters 4 and 5, are built. Chapter 4, "Speech Production," describes the dynamics of speech with the emphasis on physiology rather than anatomy. A serious attempt is made to integrate physiology and acoustics, as we have found that speech production physiology is better remembered when the sound-producing mechanisms are strongly associated with the acoustic output.

In Chapter 5 on speech perception, an account of how the ear works is followed by a discussion of acoustic cues used by listeners and some experimental results which hint at how speech may be decoded by listeners.

Chapter 6 on research tools emphasizes the instruments generally available in small college laboratories as these are the instruments that students are most apt to have experience in using. Mention is made of instrumentation available in larger speech science laboratories as well, so that students will recognize these research tools when they appear in journal articles.

Finally, a comprehensive text on speech could not omit consideration of its evolution. Theories on this subject in Chapter 7 are followed by some relevant experimental evidence in an attempt to reconstruct what we can never directly verify, but what will continue to be a provocative subject.

Chapters 6 and 7, then, form the dénouement of the text. Chapter 7 serves particularly well as a final chapter because a consideration of speech evolution not only puts speech back into a larger framework, but demands knowledge of some neurophysiology and of the source-filter functions of the vocal tract, topics considered in Chapters 4 and 5.

Since the book serves as an introduction to a large body of information, we do not presume to have covered every topic of importance nor to have dealt with the topics included in depth. A selected bibliography concludes each chapter, however, to encourage the student to pursue each subject further and to fill in the necessary gaps. As an undergraduate course, the text may be used as presented; as a graduate course many of the references might be added as required readings.

Gloria J. Borden
Katherine S. Harris

Acknowledgments

Most helpful in the writing of this book were comments made by the many students who have used this text in various stages of its completion. In addition, our colleagues have critically read parts or all of the book. They include Fredericka Bell-Berti, Jane Collins, Franklin Cooper, Bonnie Engel, Carol Gelfer, Arlene Greenstein, Reinhardt Heuer, Gary Kuhn, Nancy McGarr, Gary Milsark, Mary Joseph Osberger, Lawrence Raphael, Claude Simon, and Michael Weiss. Their carefully considered comments and suggestions were gratefully received. Throughout, we have been advised and encouraged by Jean Lovrinic.

Most of the original figures for the book were drafted by Agnes McKeon to whom we are indebted. We want to thank Cully Miller for the photographs in Chapter 6, Stephen Crump from Kay Elemetrics for producing most of the sound spectrograms in the text, and Miye Shakne for making several charts. Jolie Bookspan's efforts in compiling the glossary have enriched the text for future students, and the careful supervision of the typing of the many drafts of this manuscript provided by Dorothy Mewha has been invaluable. In addition to Dorothy Mewha's staff, we were aided in proofing the text by Jolie Bookspan, Elly Knight, and Abigail Peterson Reilly.

We have been supported in our writing by our respective universities, Temple University and the City University of New York, both in the encouragement we have received and in the use of facilities. The chairmen of our respective departments, Murray Halfond of the Department of Speech at Temple and Irving Hochberg of the Program in Speech and Hearing Sciences at the Graduate Center of the City University of New York have been particularly generous. We probably would not have written the text in its present form had we not had the common experience of working at Haskins Laboratories in New Haven, where research in speech production and speech perception are viewed as natural complements of one another.

We are grateful to our husbands and children for cheering us on: to John, Becky, Julie, Tom, and Sam Borden and to George, Maud, and Louise Harris. Finally, our many questions have been answered with patience by our editor, Ruby Richardson, whom we thank as we turn the text over to her.

Gloria J. Borden
Katherine S. Harris

Contents

Preface vii
Acknowledgments ix

Chapter 1.
SPEECH, LANGUAGE, AND THOUGHT 1

Speech 1
Language 2
Thought 3
   Thought without Language
   Thought and Language
   Language and Speech as a Carrier for Thought
Development of Language and Speech 5
   Learning Theory and Language
   Innateness Theory
   Linguistic Competence
From Thought to Speech 8
Bibliography 15

Chapter 2.
PIONEERS IN SPEECH SCIENCE 17

Hermann von Helmholtz:
Acoustics of Speech 17
Henry Sweet:
Descriptive Phonetics 19
Alexander Graham Bell:
Teaching the Deaf 19
Homer W. Dudley:
Electronic Synthesis of Continuous Speech 21
Franklin Cooper, Alvin Liberman, and Pierre Delattre:
Speech Perception and the Pattern

Playback 22
Since Then 24
Bibliography 25

Chapter 3.
ACOUSTICS 27

A Pure Tone: An Example of Simple Harmonic Motion 27
   The Swing Analogy: An Example of Velocity Gradation in Simple Harmonic Motion
   Particle Movement in Sound
   Pressure Wave Movement in Sound
   Essential Constituents of Sound
   Interference Patterns
Complex Tones 35
   Harmonics: Characteristic of Periodic Complex Tones
   Aperiodic Complex Signals
Frequency and Pitch 38
The Decibel: A Measure of Relative Intensity 39
Intensity and Loudness 41
Velocity of Sound through Space . . . 42
Wavelength 42
Resonance 43
Acoustics and Speech 45
Bibliography 45

Chapter 4.
SPEECH PRODUCTION 47

Neurophysiology of Speech 48
   The Brain
   The Neuron
   Central Nervous System Control of Speaking

Spoonerisms: Evidence for Preplanning

Respiration   58
Modification of Airstream for Speech Sounds
Negative Pressure Breathing
The Respiratory Mechanism
Inspiration
  Quiet
  For Speech
Expiration
  For Sustained Voicing
  For Speech

Phonation   74
Conversion of Air Pressure into Sound
Myoelastic Aerodynamic Theory of Phonation
Framework of the Larynx
Vocal Fold Adjustments during Speech
  Voiceless Consonants
  Voiced Speech Sounds
Subglottal Air Pressure
Bernoulli Effect
Vocal Fold Vibration
Fundamental Frequency
Voice Quality
Relationship between Frequency and Intensity
Summary

Articulation and Resonance   89
The Vocal Tract: Variable Resonator and Sound Source
  Sounds Produced
  Combined Sounds
Landmarks of the Tract
  Oral Cavity
  The Velum
  The Tongue
  The Lips
Acoustic Theory of Vowel Production
  Resonance of Tube Open at One End
  Resonance of Male Vocal Tract Vowels: /i/, /ɑ/, and /u/
  The Vowel Triangle
  Relationship between Acoustics and Physiology
  Tense-Lax Vowels
Diphthong Production
Semivowel Production
Velopharyngeal Port: Vocal Tract Modifier

Nasal Production
Vocal Tract as Sound Source
  Stops or Plosives
  Fricatives
  Affricates

English Speech Sounds   124
Sound Influence
  Adaptation
  Assimilation
  Coarticulation
Suprasegmentals
  Stress
  Intonation
  Duration and Juncture

Feedback Mechanisms in Speech . . .   131
Auditory Feedback
Tactile Feedback
Proprioceptive Feedback
Internal Feedback
Developmental Research on Feedback Mechanisms

Models of Speech Production   138
Peterson and Shoup: Physiological and Acoustic Phonetics
Chomsky and Halle: Distinctive Features
Liberman: The Speech Code
Speech Goals: Target Theory and Auditory Theory
Timing Models
Feedback Models

Production of a Sentence   145
Bibliography   156

Chapter 5.
SPEECH PERCEPTION 161

The Listener   161
Hearing   162
The Outer Ear
The Middle Ear
The Inner Ear
The Auditory Nerve
Perception of Speech   171
Acoustic Cues in Speech Perception
  Vowels
  Diphthongs
  Semivowels
  Nasal Consonants
  Stops
  Fricatives and Affricates
  Cues for Manner, Place, and Voicing

Suprasegmentals
Context Dependence
Categorical Perception
  Within-language and Cross-language Studies in Adults
  Infant Studies
  Animal Studies
  Auditory and Phonetic Analysis
  Adaptation Studies
  Categorical Perception and Learning
  Production and Perception
Neurophysiology of Speech Perception
  Cerebral Lateralization
  Memory and Speech Perception
  Neurophysiological Development and Perception
Theories of Speech Perception
  Active Theories
  Passive Theories
  Quantal Theory
Bibliography 209

Tape Splicing
Listening Station
Use of Computers in Experimental Phonetics
Bibliography 242

Chapter 7.
EVOLUTION OF LANGUAGE AND SPEECH 245

Social Framework 246
  Fossil Hominids
  Cognitive Prerequisites
  Why Speech?
Psychological Framework 252
  Chimpanzee Language
  Bird Song
  Child Language
Biological Framework 256
  Brain Organization
  Lateralization
  Vocal Tract Changes
A Likely Tale 262
Conclusion 264
Bibliography 265

Appendix 1.
The Phonetic Alphabet for American English 267

Appendix 2.
Cranial Nerves Important for Speech and Hearing 269

Appendix 3.
Spinal Nerves Important for Speech 271

Glossary 273

Index 285

Chapter 6.
RESEARCH TOOLS IN SPEECH SCIENCE 215

Observational and Experimental Research 215
Some Instruments 216
  Acoustic Phonetics
    Recording Speech
    Waveform Analysis
    Spectral Analysis
  Physiological Phonetics
    Respiratory Analysis
    Laryngeal Function
    Supralaryngeal Movement
    Muscle Activity
  Speech Perception

CHAPTER 1

Speech, Language, and Thought

O chestnut tree, great rooted blossomer,
Are you the leaf, the blossom or the bole?
O body swayed to music, O brightening glance,
How can we know the dancer from the dance?

W. B. Yeats "Among School Children"
1928

This book is about speech. It is about spoken English in particular. It is not a book about language or thought. We do want to consider speech in its context, however, before we consider it separately and rather arbitrarily removed from its source. If we were to study grapes used for wine without mentioning vineyards, it would be a little like the study of speech with no recognition of its cognitive origin. Also, speech is the manifestation of only one of many kinds of languages. A study of speech with no mention of language would be a little like a study of one particular grape with no acknowledgment of the many others used for winemaking.

First of all, speech is only one method of *communication*. A female ape assumes a sexually submissive and presumably inviting posture to communicate the fact that she will accept intercourse with a male. A dog with hackles raised growls at an intruder to communicate his determination to prevent further intrusion. The animal kingdom offers countless examples of signs which communicate various condi-

tions within and across species. We human beings alone demonstrate many methods of communication. We signal to others by waving flags, by Morse code, by television and radio transmission, by raising an eyebrow, by writing a newspaper column, by singing, by putting hands on hips, by swearing, by painting a picture, by sticking out tongues, by playing a musical instrument, by kissing, by blushing, by dancing, by throwing a plate through the air, and finally, we speak. We speak in our homes, at work, at school, and at play. We speak to our babies, to our pets, and to ourselves. What is speech? How does it relate to language and to thought? If you have ever known an adult who has suffered brain damage sufficient to impair speech, you have probably observed that the speech impairment is accompanied by some effects upon language and upon some aspects of thought. Speech, language, and thought are closely related, but they can be considered separately, because they are qualitatively different.

SPEECH

If you have ever been to a foreign country and heard all those around you speaking a language which you do not understand, especially a language unrelated to your own, you are apt to have had two impressions. The first impression is that the spoken language seems like long spurts

of a complex and constantly changing stream of sound without separations. You have no way of knowing the end of one word and the beginning of the next. The second general impression is that this strange tongue is extremely difficult. The speakers seem to talk much faster than

1

speakers of your own language. Yet, even small children can do it with ease. How intelligent they must be!

These impressions of a foreign tongue are more accurately a description of speech than are the impressions we have of our own speech. We take our own speech for granted. It seems simple, but the sounds change quickly, requiring complex articulatory gymnastics on the part of the speaker. It is no simple matter, yet our children are quite good at it by 3 or 4 years of age. Although some children may have difficulties later in learning to read, all normal children learn to speak. They are natural language learners, and they develop language by hearing the speech of others. Speech is audible. It can be described in terms of its loudness, its pitch, and its duration. It is meaningful sound strung out in time. Speech is only one way in which we use our language, however. We also write, read, and listen to others speak.

LANGUAGE

The reason, of course, that we fail to understand the strange speech of an unknown language is that, although we can hear the speech, we do not know the words, the sounds, the rules of the language. A particular *language* is a rule-governed communication system composed of meaningful elements, which can be combined in many ways to produce sentences, some of which are novel. Our knowledge of English permits us to say and understand something as prosaic as:

It's hot as Hades this afternoon.

This sentence has undoubtedly been said many times because of laziness of mind, but our language also permits us to say and understand something completely new, something we have never heard said before, such as this quotation from a Tom Robbins novel:

In any case, and whichever the ever, upon a sweaty but otherwise nondescript afternoon in early August 1960, an afternoon squeezed out of Mickey's mousy snout, an afternoon carved from mashed potatoes and lye, an afternoon scraped out of the dog dish of meteorology, an afternoon that could lull a monster to sleep, an afternoon that normally might have produced nothing more significant than diaper rash, Sissy Hankshaw stepped from a busted-jaw curbstone on Hull Street in South Richmond and attempted to hitchhike an ambulance.

Tom Robbins, *Even Cowgirls Get the Blues.* Boston: Houghton Mifflin Co., 1976, p. 37.

We understand this sentence, although it is completely original with Robbins, because we share with the author the knowledge of the rules of a language. The rules of *semantics* enable us to associate words or phrases with meanings. We and the author have a common understanding of 'diaper rash.' The rules of *syntax* enable us to have common expectations of word order. As readers, we were kept waiting until the words 'Sissy Hankshaw' for the subject of the sentence. When the verb 'stepped' arrived, our mutual *phonological* rules dictated that it have an '-ed' ending to agree with the previous verbs in the past tense. Robbins and his readers know the same rules; they share a language. Users of language can be creative. They can create sentences never heard before.

Language, unlike speech, is intangible. It is knowledge of a creative communication system, and that knowledge is in the mind. How is language related to speech? Noam Chomsky of Massachusetts Institute of Technology writes about this knowledge of language as *linguistic competence* to distinguish it from the use of language, *linguistic performance.* Speech is the conversion of language into sound. There are other languages besides vocal ones, however. There are gestural languages; American Sign Language (Ameslan), used by the deaf, is an example.

The syntactic rules of Ameslan differ from English. Word order is often determined by the chronology of events or by stressed words. For example, in Ameslan one would sign "Sun this morning. I saw. Beautiful." rather than "It was a beautiful sun I saw this morning." If the word to be stressed in "I like the movies" is 'movies,' an Ameslan user would sign "Movies I like." The semantic rules are, of course, entirely different, as the Ameslan user associates meanings with signs made by the hands, face, and arms. The shape of the sign, its movement or how it changes, and its position relative to the rest of the body are all meaningful. Again, the knowledge or competence one has in the system can be called language, in contrast to the use of it, which is called performance. As with speech, performance usually falls short of the user's competence. Signs are sometimes indicated quickly and incompletely.

Mistakes are made, but the user's competence remains. In speaking, we often use fragments of sentences rather than sentences. We think of something else in mid-sentence, and start a new sentence before we have completed the first. Yet, when a teacher says, 'Put your answer in a complete sentence,' the student knows how to do it. He or she knows the language, even though it is rarely reflected fully in speech. How does this linguistic knowledge relate to thought?

THOUGHT

Thought may be defined as an internal representation of experiences. Jerome Bruner of Harvard suggests that the representation can be in the form of images, of action, or of language. We presumably use all available representations of our experiences, but some people report the use of some forms more than others. We may think via internal images, vaguely visual, when we are solving a problem, such as how many suitcases we think we can fit into the trunk of a car. Architects and artists often think in visual images. Thought can be represented, too, by internal action or muscle imagery. In solving the problem of the direction and force needed to place a tennis shot out of reach of an opponent, we think in terms of action. Choreographers, athletes, and some physicists think this way. Albert Einstein, in describing his understanding of how he thought, wrote:

> The words of the language, as they are written or spoken, do not seem to play any role in my mechanism of thought. The psychical entities which seem to serve as elements in thought are certain signs and more or less clear images which can be "voluntarily" reproduced and combined. . . . But taken from a psychological viewpoint, this combinatory play seems to be the essential feature in productive thought — before there is any connection with logical construction in words or other kinds of signs which can be communicated to others. The above mentioned elements are, in my case, of visual and some of muscular type.

> Ghiselin, B., *The Creative Process*, New York: Mentor Books, 1955, p. 43.

Representation of thought in some language, whether it be verbal or mathematical, seems important in the mental activities of language users. Although it is apparent that we can think without knowledge of any formal language, as evidenced by deaf children and by some people with aphasia, it is equally apparent that those who do know a language, use it to aid thinking. We shall first consider thought without language and then thought with language.

Thought without Language

We have all had the experience of having an idea which we find difficult to verbalize. Indeed, words often seem inadequate. Our ideas expressed seem but a rough sketch of our thinking. People with *aphasia*, language impairment due to brain damage, demonstrate the independence of thinking and language. Often an aphasic will seem to have an idea to express, but lack the language to embody the thought.

Some deaf children, who have not been exposed to sign language, are quite delayed in learning the language of their community, because of the difficulties they encounter in learning oral speech. Hans Furth has shown, however, that the cognitive abilities of these children develop almost normally. Helen Keller, the well-known author, who was blind and deaf from the age of 18 months, writes that she did not understand the first important concept of language learning, the idea that symbols stand for elements of our experience, until she was 9 years old. When her teacher was communicating the word 'water' by having the child feel her face with one hand as she said the word, and feel the water with the other hand, the child suddenly made the association. Helen quickly learned the 'names' of everything soon after. Language learning had begun, yet Helen surely was not an unthinking child before that experience. Her thinking must have been represented in images.

The Swiss psychologist, Jean Piaget, concluded from his observations of normal children, that cognition develops on its own. Language interacts with it and certainly reflects the child's thinking, but language does not determine the thinking. According to his view, it does no good to train a child in language in order to develop cognition. Rather, he sees the stages of cognitive development as reflected in the child's use of language.

Lev Vygotsky, a Russian, also observed evidence of nonverbal thought in children. Infants demonstrate their understanding of relationships and their problem-solving abilities independently of their use of language, just as they also make speech-like babbling sounds, which seem to lack intellectual content. Later in the child's development, speech and thought unite.

Thought and Language

Vygotsky's great contribution was his idea of "inner speech." Although he viewed early language as being essentially communicative, he maintained that some use of early language was egocentric: the child communicates with himself. From about 3 to 7 years of age, the vocal egocentric speech gradually becomes subvocal "inner speech," which is a way of internally talking to oneself. It is neither thought nor speech, but something in between. When we think in language, we think in linguistic fragments, in abbreviated phrases, the words fading quickly or only partly formed.

Piaget agreed with Vygotsky's description of inner speech, having observed its beginnings in the egocentric speech of the children in his studies. Preschool children echo words and phrases they hear around them (echolalia) and incorporate them into their own monologues. They talk about what they are doing, the toys they are playing with, the picture they are painting. A whole room of kindergarten children can be talking, sometimes taking turns as in conversation, but each one is talking about his own experiences, in a collective monologue. The point that Piaget emphasized was that this use of language reflected a stage of thinking in which children seldom include the point of view of others. They see things primarily from their own viewpoint, hence the egocentric speech. Gradually, the frequency of the egocentric speech decreases as the frequency of socialized speech increases. If in some sense we 'speak' to ourselves as as well as speak to others, does this inner speech aid in thinking?

Language and Speech as a Carrier for Thought

Thoughts are not always sequential. Sometimes a thought is formed as an association internally 'seen' as a whole. We necessarily distort it, when we string it out on the time line of language and speech. Despite this distortion, there are many advantages in using language to represent thought. Language helps in making an idea or an experience available. By expressing the thought verbally or by a mathematical formula, it can be elicited more easily for further consideration. Language also aids thinking by providing a frame to hold information in memory. It enables us to express ideas about people, places, or things which are not present.

In all of this discussion, language has been viewed as a vessel for thought and as a reflection of thought, but not as something which determines thought. Linguistic determinism was advanced by the linguist Edward Sapir, however, and even more strongly by his student, Benjamin Whorf. The Whorfian hypothesis in its strongest version — that language determines thinking — is not generally accepted today. It was based on comparative linguistic data which show that languages differ in the number of terms for such things as color or snow. The reasoning was that people with many words for snow actually perceived distinctions which people with one word failed to perceive. Language determined their experiences and their thinking. A weak version of this idea is that it may be easier for an Eskimo to talk about snow than it is for a Guatemalan, but there is no significant difference in their perceptions or ability to think about snow. The interests and needs of one language group may simply differ from those of another— hence the differences in vocabulary.

Instead of comparing languages, one can look at a particular language and observe differences based upon social group membership. Basil Bernstein, a sociolinguist, used cultural differences as an explanation of linguistic differences he observed between middle class and working class children in Great Britain. When children were asked to describe a picture, for example, the typical middle class child would be fairly explicit, using many nouns. One would not need to see the picture being described to imagine it. The typical working class child, in describing the same picture, would use far fewer nouns, substituting such words as 'he,' 'it,' or 'they,' so that it would be difficult to imagine the picture from the description alone. Bernstein attributed this difference to cultural differences; the working class family in England has a strong hierarchy so that children are not expected to be explicit but to listen to the head of the family, while the middle class family is less authoritarian and each member has a say. In addition, the working class family member usually talks about shared experiences, so the context is understood, whereas the middle class family member is more apt to talk about experiences of his own and does not assume so much knowledge on the part of the listener. Bernstein's choice of terms, *restricted code* (in the working class case) and *elaborated code* (in the middle class

case) is unfortunate, as it connotes classist ideas, which Bernstein disavows. His studies, however, do point out the influence of cultural habits, if not differences in thinking, upon language.

Despite small differences in the use of language by different people who share a language, and despite the larger differences among the various languages of the world in their structure and vocabularies, there may be some universal features of all human languages. To the extent that this is true, one ought to be able to learn something about the human mind, as Chomsky suggests, by studying the rules of human language.

> There are any number of questions that might lead one to undertake a study of language. Personally, I am primarily intrigued by the possibility of learning something, from the study of language, that will bring to light inherent properties of the human mind.
>
> Chomsky, N., *Language and Mind* (enlarged edition). New York: Harcourt Brace Jovanovich, Inc., 1972, p. 103.

If language is conceived as a set of rules by which an infinite number of sentences can be generated, using a stock of words which constantly expands to cover all concepts one may choose to express, then humans are the only creatures yet known to have a command of language. Another factor which seems to be unique to human beings is that they can talk about their languages. Homo sapiens may well be the only creature on Earth who uses the brain in an attempt to understand brains and uses language in an attempt to understand languages. The interaction of thinking, language, and speech may seem clearer if we look further at language development in normal children.

DEVELOPMENT OF LANGUAGE AND SPEECH

Normal children have, at birth, the potential to walk and to talk, although as babies they can do neither. They are genetically endowed with the appropriate neurophysical systems, but time is needed for these systems to develop and mature. The brain is approximately 40% the size it will attain by adulthood; the more peripheral areas, the vocal tract and the legs, await the anatomical change and the development of motor-sensory associations appropriate to talking and walking. At 6 months, children sit up and *babble* in meaningless vocal play. By the arrival of the first birthday, they may have started to walk and to name things. By the second birthday, they may be putting two words together for rudimentary telegraphic sentences, and by the fourth, they will have mastered the essential rules of the language of their elders. The rapidity and apparent ease with which children learn language is a phenomenon of childhood and can never be repeated with such ease by adults. Many adults learn new languages, especially those who already know several languages, but the time most conducive to learning languages is before puberty. Wilder Penfield, the Canadian neurophysiologist, put the cut-off age at about 15. The best time for learning language, however, is during the first 4 years.

What children universally accomplish with spontaneity and speed, psychologists, linguists, and speech scientists have laboriously analyzed with only moderate success. The question they ask is: how do children acquire language? Theorists on this subject can be generally divided into two groups. One group of theorists analyzes language development in terms of learning principles. The other group analyzes language development in terms of an innate propensity for language. Perhaps the most currently popular view is that only the details or individual items of a particular language are learned, while the structural and creative underpinnings universal to all languages are inherited.

Learning Theory and Language

Learning in the classical sense is the formulation of a new bond or association between a stimulus and a response. The classic experiment, performed by Ivan Petrovich Pavlov in Russia in the 1920s, resulted in an association or bond between the sound of a bell and a dog's salivation. This bond was new and therefore considered to be 'learned,' because before the experiment, the dog did not salivate at the sound of a bell. The learned behavior, or *conditioned response* (CR), was produced by pairing an *unconditioned stimulus* (UCS), in this case, meat powder, with the *conditioned stimulus* (CS), the bell. Since meat powder reflexively causes increased salivation (an automatic physiological response to food), the contiguous presenta-

tion of meat powder and the bell sound produced a neural bond between the two, so that finally the bell alone would produce salivation.

1. UCS (meat powder) ⟶ UCR (salivation)
2. UCS (meat powder) ⟶ UCR (salivation)
   CS (bell) ⟶
3. CS (bell) ⟶ CR (salivation)

In classic conditioning, the unconditioned response is involuntary (perspiration, heart rate change, salivation) and its cause is known (an object of fear, food). There is another model of learning in which the unconditioned response is under voluntary control (the subject pushes a lever or makes a sound) and the cause is not evident. In this case, the learning is effected, not by the pairing of stimuli, but by reinforcement or reward, a method called *operant conditioning*. If the operant response is rewarded with food, praise, or some other positive experience, the behavior is strengthened, but if it is punished with electric shock, criticism, or some negative experience, the behavior is weakened. The operant conditioning model was developed by B. F. Skinner. The application of his theory to language learning is detailed in his book *Verbal Behavior*. Skinner writes that language is learned by selective reinforcement provided to the child as he uses language to operate upon his environment.

Another learning theorist, O. H. Mowrer, has suggested that the reinforcement or reward may not always produce an observable response but that responses may occur within the child. In the observable instance, the association of the utterance 'mama' with the rewarding presence of the mother with food and comfort establishes 'mama' as a learned response. In the case of an internal response the child finds that just the word 'mama' produces positive feelings, or rewards, even if the word is not said aloud. In what Mowrer has termed his *autistic* theory, children may rehearse, subvocally in their cribs, some new words they have heard which set up sufficient internal rewards that the words become learned or conditioned behavior. This theory accounts for children suddenly revealing learned words which we have never heard them say.

Certainly, learning theories are consistent with facts about much of children's semantic acquisition, the learning of word meanings. They may even explain the initial stages of adopting the syntax or word order of the particular language. The shaping of the correct sounds of speech may also be dependent upon the reward of being understood and perhaps obeyed. If a child who has said /tuti/ 'tootie' to no avail finds that /kuki/ 'cookie' produces the desired delicacy, he or she is amply rewarded and will use 'cookie' in the future.

Innateness Theory

There is much about language development, however, that learning theories cannot explain. Human language users are creative in their use of the system. They both understand and produce sentences they have never heard before, and therefore, could never have learned. Children, after hearing sufficient utterances of their language, pick up the rules and can use these stored rules to understand new sentences and to generate original sentences. They may learn an irregular verb form such as 'ran' by conventional learning methods, but once they have figured out the rule for regular past tense, they are apt to say 'runned,' as their rule-seeking instinct overpowers the items they have learned. Many psycholinguists think that this ability to abstract the rules of the language is innate, and some think that aspects of linguistic structure are innnate.

Linguistic Competence

Noam Chomsky has written most persuasively on this subject. As we have seen, he is careful to distinguish between the competence one has in a language, the set of rules with which one produces language, and the performance, which consists of the speech, however fragmented, that we utter. One has only to contrast a skilled speaker with an inarticulate one to realize the differences which exist in performance. However, basic linguistic competence seems to be accessible to all normal individuals, and it is this fundamental

linguistic knowledge which linguists think humans are born able to acquire.

Eric Lenneberg presents physiological evidence of linguistic competence in the human family. Not only is language potential hereditary, but it is posited to be species-specific, that is, it is realized only in Homo sapiens.

Thinking provides a foundation for language; children can only talk about what they know, but they may know more than they can express with their incompletely developed language. Psycholinguists find that children are pattern-seekers. Based on the language they hear around them, they seem to form hypotheses about linguistic rules and apply them in their own way. The language of children appears not to be a poor imitation of adult language, but rather a different language with its own rules. The syntactic rule system, vocabulary, and phonology of child language are each comparatively undifferentiated. Children's rules for the negative may include the use of 'no' with an affirmative sentence 'No go home,' despite the fact that they never hear adults saying it that way. Children's meanings for 'doggie' may include all four-legged animals; only later will they differentiate the term further. Children's sound systems may use stops whenever stops, fricatives, or consonant clusters appear in adult speech, so that they might pronounce 'two,' 'Sue,' and 'stew' all something like /tu/ 'two.'

As they develop their language systems, they are enlarging their knowledge of *semantics*, the meanings associated with words and phrases, and at the same time, are discovering the rules by which their particular language is governed. The rules are of three sorts: *syntactic* rules which account for the structure of sentences, including transformations of simple declarative sentences into questions or passives; *morphological* rules which account for changes in meaning brought about by changing sounds (cat, cats) or by intonation (Yes. Yes?); and *phonological* rules, thought to account for the sounds of the speech stream. Many linguists consider morphological rules to be redundant with syntactic rules on the one hand and phonological rules on the other.

A simple sentence may suffice as an

example of how these rules are used in linguistic analysis: 'The eggs are taken by the girl.'

neme,' then, is used when one wishes to refer to the function of a sound family in the language to signal differences in mean-

SYNTAX (structure)

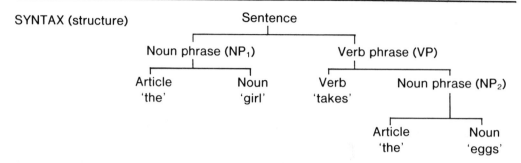

Transformation rule for changing active sentence to passive:

$T_{passive}$: NP_2 be + verb + en by NP_1

'The eggs are taken by the girl'
(NP_2) (be) (verb) (by) (NP_1)

PHONOLOGY (sounds)

'eggs' = /ɛgz/

Progressive assimilation: the voiced /g/ changes the following /s/ to voiced /z/: /ɛgz/

A *morpheme* is the smallest linguistic segment which means something. The word 'cats,' then, is composed of two morphemes 'cat' and '-s' which means 'more than one.' A *phoneme* is a family of sounds which functions in a language to signal a difference in meaning. The fact that 'pat' and 'bat' differ in meaning, demonstrates that /p/ and /b/ are phonemes in English. A phoneme, by itself, is meaningless. It cannot be described as a sound either, for a phoneme can be actualized as one of several different sounds. Thus, the sounds of /p/ in 'paper,' 'spoon,' and 'top' differ from one another, with the first produced with a burst of air, the second without the burst, and the third often with no lip opening at all. These variants of the phoneme are often called *allophones*, and the sounds themselves *phones*. The term 'pho-

ing, while the term 'phone' is used when one wishes to refer to a particular sound. Slashed lines indicate phonemes, /p/, and brackets indicate phones [p]. Ordinary alphabetics will identify many sounds unambiguously, but for other sounds, we need a way of specifying them unambiguously. The most commonly used system for transcribing the sounds of speech, the International Phonetic Alphabet, appears in Appendix 1.

Spoken language arises from knowledge of meanings (semantics) formalized into structure (syntax, morphemes, phonemes) that is finally encoded into the sounds of speech. We shall conclude this chapter with a model of the interactions and conversions, as we view them, in going from thought to speech.

FROM THOUGHT TO SPEECH

Two young women in Philadelphia's Museum of Art pause before a painting by Henri Matisse entitled "Odalisque Jaune." One woman says to the second, "Look at this picture. There's something about the faces, and the patterns that reminds me of some Japanese prints I saw in a museum

in New York." We cannot presume to know how this utterance was derived from the young woman's linguistic knowledge and originally from her thought processes, but we must assume that some reference was made to stored visual experiences of Japanese prints and that associations were

Figure 1.1. A Matisse painting. Matisse: "Odalisque Jaune." Philadelphia Museum of Art: Samuel S. White, III and Vera White Collection.

Figure 1.2. A Japanese woodcut. Kiyonaga: ''Shigeyuki Executing Calligraphy,'' 1783. Philadelphia Museum of Art: Given by Mrs. John D. Rockefeller.

made between the highly patterned areas of the Japanese woodcuts (Fig. 1.2) and the juxtaposition of patterns in the Matisse painting (Fig. 1.1). Entering into the process in some way must have been a sense of pleasure and a positive attitude for the effects produced.

A model of thought, language, and speech conversions is presented in Figure 1.3. The circles overlap to suggest both the interrelationships involved and their simultaneity. The young woman's visual and aesthetic experiences, both in the present and the past, relate to ideas she has about their similarities and to her feelings about the pictures. The woman chose to represent her thought in language in order to communicate her response to the pictures to her companion.

There are a number of ways in which the woman could have framed her ideas and feelings, but based on certain semantic, syntactic, and morphophonological decisions, she expressed her thought in the utterance quoted above. She was constrained by the rules of her language and by the rules of her speech-producing mechanism. We shall make no attempt to suggest how the meaning is converted into a form ready for speaking. We recognize, too, that the delivery of the message could have been in writing or in some gestural language as well as in speech. Choosing speech, however, the young woman somehow readied for delivery the message which her friend eventually heard.

It seems probable that chunks of the message are briefly stored in a buffer (temporary storage) ready for output. The chunks are perhaps of sentence length or phrase length. Evidence for this storage comes from slips of the tongue. The fact that people make mistakes such as 'He cut the knife with the salami,' Victoria Fromkin's example, indicates the existence of such a buffer in order for the speaker to have substituted what should have been the last word for the fourth-to-the-last word.

Timing and *prosodic* aspects of the utterance are viewed in our model as superimposed upon the message as it is converted into speech. For example, the prosody, which includes the intonation pattern and the stress pattern of the phrase, remains constant despite slips of the tongue. Stress is placed upon the last word whether the speaker says 'He cut the salami with the KNIFE' or 'He cut the knife with the SALAMI,' indicating separate instructions for word order and for prosody. Also, the utterance can be said at a variety of rates, from fast to slow, indicating somewhat separate timing commands.

There must be a transformation on the speech level from a relatively abstract representation of the speech to the actual neuromotor activity which controls the muscle activity, cavity changes, and air pressure modifications heard as 'speech.' Alvin Liberman and Franklin Cooper have made a case for conversions in speech which are reminiscent of the deep to surface structure conversions suggested by Chomsky. In the language conversions, linguistic rules are used; in the speech conversions, neuromotor, myomotor, and articulatory rules are used, omitting for the sake of simplicity any mention of sensory control mechanisms. Figure 1.4 schematizes the conversions viewed as important in processing speech. The *phonetic* information with its component *features* means that speech sounds (phonetic transcription) which the speaker intends to deliver and the distinctive aspects of these sounds (features) such as voicing, nasality, or place of production, are represented rather abstractly in what we have described as the buffer. From the figure, four conversions are detailed; from the internal speech representation to nerve impulses, from nerve impulses to muscle contractions, from muscle contractions to vocal tract shape and air pressure changes, and from these changes to an acoustic waveform. Figure 1.5 shows that these conversions result in an acoustic signal in which the phonetic features overlap and the abstract phonemes as separate entities no longer exist.

In our model the same speech rules are applied. They are seen to occur simultaneously and to relate to one another.

In the buffer, the utterance exists as an internal representation of the speaker's acoustic goal (see Nooteboom later in "Models of Speech Production," Chapter

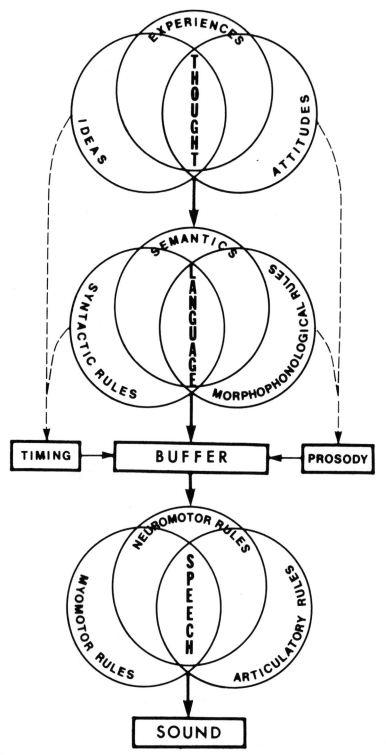

Figure 1.3. A model showing contributions of various factors to output at the thought, language, and speech stages.

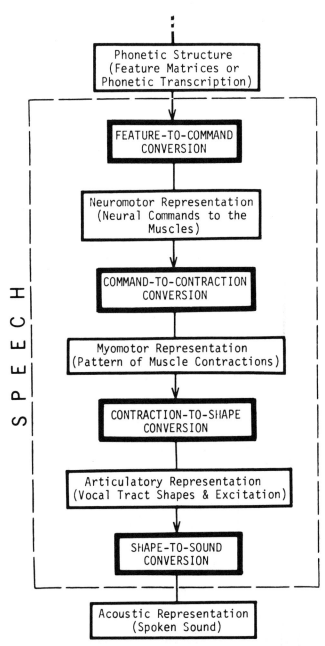

Figure 1.4. A model of the speech production process. It is assumed that each speech sound can be represented as a complex of abstract phonetic features. The features are actualized as neural commands to the articulatory muscles, which shape the vocal tract. The vocal tract shape determines the output speech acoustic signal. (Reprinted from F. S. Cooper: How Is Language Conveyed by Speech. In *Language by Ear and by Eye*, edited by J. F. Kavanagh and I. G. Mattingly, by permission of the M. I. T. Press, Cambridge, Mass. © 1972, p. 34.)

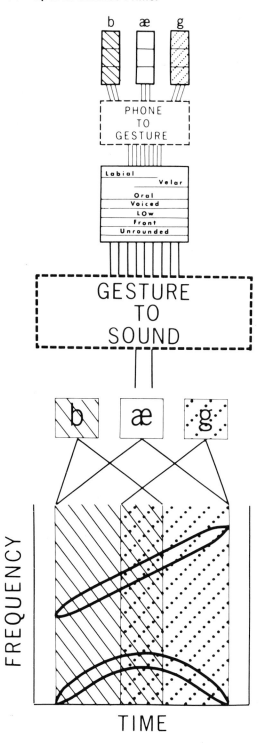

4) and as an internal representation of the physiology of speech production in terms of its three-dimensional space coordinates (see MacNeilage in the same section). The speaker knows the intended sounds and what has to be done to produce them. She unconsciously 'knows' what cavity shapes and air pressure changes are required to go from the end of 'Japanese' to the beginning of 'prints' and from the /n/ to the /i/ in /dʒæpənɪz/, 'Japanese.' Applying the rules of speech, a stream of sound is produced.

We are far from understanding how this works. Neither do we understand how a listener processes speech to arrive at the intent of the speaker. Speech science is the study of these issues: the production of speech, the acoustics of the signal, and the perception of speech by a listener. If the buffer is considered to hold the intended message, speech scientists concern themselves with everything downstream of that stage. The transformations from an intended phrase to its acoustic realization by a speaker, and the transformations from acoustics of speech to the decoding of the intended phrase by a listener, are within the province of investigation by the speech scientist.

Figure 1.5. A representation of the encoding occurring in the speech signal. Each phone is conceived as a matrix of features. The matrix is transformed into a series of gestures, and into sound. In the sound representation, the features of the phones overlap temporally. This figure will be discussed at greater length in Chapter 4. (Reprinted from A. M., Liberman: *Cognitive Psychology. 1*, 1970, 314.)

BIBLIOGRAPHY

Bernstein, B., A Socio-linguistic Approach to Socialization: With Some Reference to Educability. In *Directions in Sociolinguistics*. J. J. Gumperz and D. Hymes (Eds.) New York: Holt, Rinehart & Winston, 1972, pp. 465–497.

Bruner, J. S., *Studies in Cognitive Growth*. New York: Wiley & Sons, 1966.

Carroll, J. B., *Language and Thought*. Englewood Cliffs, N. J.: Prentice-Hall, 1964.

Cherry, C., *On Human Communication*, 2nd Ed. Cambridge, Mass.: M. I. T. Press, 1966.

Chomsky, N., *Language and Mind* (enlarged edition). New York: Harcourt Brace Jovanovich, Inc., 1972.

Cooper, F. S., How Is Language Conveyed by Speech? In *Language by Ear and by Eye*. J. F. Kavanagh and I. G. Mattingly (Eds.) Cambridge, Mass.: M. I. T. Press, 1972, pp. 25–45.

Cutting, J. E., and Kavanagh, J. F., On the Relationship of Speech to Language. *ASHA 17*, 1975, 500–506.

Dale, P. S., *Language Development: Structure and Function*, 2nd Ed. New York: Holt, Rinehart & Winston, 1976.

Fromkin, V., and Rodman, R., *An Introduction to Language*. New York: Holt, Rinehart & Winston, 1974.

Furth, H., *Thinking Without Language: Psychological Implications of Deafness*. New York: The Free Press, 1966.

Lenneberg, E. H., *Biological Foundations of Language*. New York: Wiley & Sons, 1967.

Liberman, A. M., The Grammars of Speech and Language. *Cognitive Psychol. 1*, 1970, 301–323.

Mowrer, O. H., *Learning Theory and Personality Dynamics*. New York: Ronald Press, 1950.

Penfield, W., and Roberts, L., *Speech and Brain Mechanisms*. Princeton, N. J.: Princeton University Press, 1959.

Piaget, J., *The Language and Thought of the Child*. Atlantic Highlands, N. J.: Humanities Press, 1959. (Translation of *Le Langage et la Pensée chez L'Enfant*. Neuchâtel and Paris: Delachaux et Niestlé, 1923).

Skinner, B. F., *Verbal Behavior*. New York: Appleton-Century-Crofts, 1957.

Slobin, D. I., *Psycholinguistics*. Glenview, Ill.: Scott, Foresman & Co., 1971.

Vygotsky, L. S., *Thought and Language*. Cambridge, Mass.: M. I. T. Press, 1962.

Whorf, B. L., *Language, Thought, and Reality*. Cambridge, Mass.: M. I. T. Press and New York: Wiley & Sons, 1956.

CHAPTER 2

Pioneers in Speech Science

History is the essence of innumerable biographies.

Thomas Carlyle, *On History*

There have been so many people instrumental in the development of speech science that it would be more confusing than helpful to name them, even were we to limit ourselves to the most influential. Rather than attempt to outline a history of speech science, we have chosen to demonstrate the diversity of approach inherent in this discipline, by describing the contributions of a few of the pioneers in different aspects of the field. A pioneer, then, is not necessarily the most important person but is rather one of the first to use a given approach.

Speech science is the study of the physiology of speech production, the acoustical characteristics of speech, and the processes by which listeners perceive speech. The discipline has attracted the interest of linguists, psychologists, engineers, and speech pathologists. The linguists are primarily interested in descriptive phonetics, in the phonological description of various languages, and in the prosodic rules of the languages. The psychologists are primarily interested in psychoacoustics, the perceptual cues of speech, measurement of speech intelligibility, and the ways in which the human brain processes the speech signal. The engineers are primarily interested in the analysis of the sounds of speech, the transmission of speech in communication systems, the development of visual speech displays, and the development of speech synthesizers and machines that will recognize speech and individual speakers. The speech pathologists are primarily interested in speech production including its inception in the central nervous system, its control mechanisms, its muscle activity, movements, and results in air pressure changes and sound. In practice, however, the linguist, psychologist, engineer, and speech pathologist often share common interests and work together in one laboratory.

HERMANN VON HELMHOLTZ: ACOUSTICS OF SPEECH

The human ear has been a valuable instrument in the study of the acoustics of speech, long before the electronic age brought with it electrical frequency analyzers and the computers of the 20th century. Hermann Ludwig Ferdinand von Helmholtz, born near Berlin in 1821 of English, German, and French ancestry, was to use his ears extensively in the study of the acoustics of the human voice and the resonances of the vocal tract cavities. A man of wide interests, living before the age of specialization, he studied mathematics, physics, and medicine, and contributed to the fields of physiology, optics, acoustics, mathematics, mechanics, and electricity through his university teaching, and his research. His published papers and books numbered over 200. His father was a teacher of philology and philosophy. His mother was a descendent of William Penn on her father's side and of French ancestry on her mother's side. A sickly child, von Helmholtz had trouble with grammar, history, and vocabulary and was confused in distinguishing left from right, but he was widely read and showed an early curiosity and love of nature. After studying medicine at the University of Berlin and working as a surgeon in the army, he became a professor, first at Königsberg, then Bonn, and finally in Heidelberg and Berlin. Helmholtz always combined teaching with research. He thought it was important to experiment and to demonstrate to himself the principles to be taught in the lecture hall. He studied the sense of hearing, both in its physiology, and in various aspects of sensation, pure tone sensation, and the hearing of combination tones. He worked out the mathematics of resonance. Noting that blowing across bottles with more or less water in them produced different sounds, he found he could make one bottle sound like /u/ and two bottles, sounded simultaneously, resemble /o/. Refer to Appendix 1 for the sounds produced.

Using hollow glass globes with two openings, later known as Helmholtz resonators (Fig. 2.1), he developed a technique to analyze the frequency components of complex tones. First, he would coat the smaller nipple-shaped end with sealing wax and obtain an air-tight fit into his ear canal. Each globe was made to be tuned to a different tone. Stopping up his other ear with more sealing wax, he would listen to complex sounds. The resonator would dampen most sounds except those of its own natural frequency. Thus, he analyzed the fundamental frequency and harmonics of the human voice and the major resonances of the cavities above the larynx.

Wondering why a particular vowel has a distinctive quality whether said or sung, and whether said by men, women, or children, Helmholtz held tuning forks of different frequencies in front of his mouth and those of other people, with oral cavities shaped for a particular vowel. He found that different shapes had different

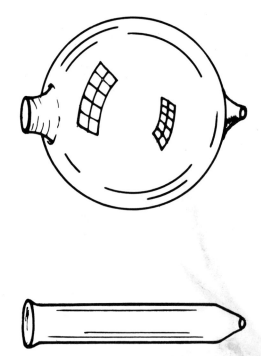

Figure 2.1. Helmholtz resonators. (Adapted from an illustration in *On the Sensations of Tone as a Physiological Basis for the Theory of Music,* 1863.)

resonant frequencies. Thus, Helmholtz determined what he thought were the absolute resonances of each vowel; later, however, the resonances were found to be relative for different size vocal tracts. In 1863, he published his great work on acoustics of speech and on harmonic theory: *On the Sensations of Tone as a Physiological Basis for the Theory of Music.*

Helmholtz is described as a calm, reserved scholar. He liked to go mountain climbing, and claimed that thoughts often came to him when he was hiking. Married twice, he had two children by his first wife who died when he lived in Heidelberg. His daughter married the son of Werner von Siemens, the founder of the Physico-Technical Institute near Berlin. Helmholtz was the first director of the institute. One of his students was Heinrich Hertz, who later demonstrated electromagnetic waves and was to have the unit for cycles per second (Hz) named after him. Besides his scholarly activities Helmholtz thought it was important to deliver popular lectures on scientific subjects to the public, which was unusual in Germany at that time. Helmholtz would undoubtedly be surprised to know he is being described as a pioneer in speech science, as his interests were much more far ranging. For example, he invented the ophthalmoscope and provided mathematical proof of the conservation of energy. Nonetheless, Helmholtz helped us understand some of the most important principles of the acoustics and physics of speech: that the puffs of air escaping through the vocal folds are the acoustic source of the voice, that the harmonics of the voice are resonated in the pharynx and oral cavities, and that vowels are recognized because of these distinctive resonances.

HENRY SWEET: DESCRIPTIVE PHONETICS

When Henry Sweet was born in England in 1845, Helmholtz was 24 years old and had already published his first paper on the connection between nerve cells and fibers. Sweet was to come to the study of speech by an entirely different route, by an interest in languages and in phonetics. He was a teacher of English pronunciation, and was the model for George Bernard Shaw's Henry Higgins in the play *Pygmalion,* later to be adapted as Lerner and Loewe's musical *My Fair Lady.* Sweet graduated from Balliol College at Oxford, but partly because he obtained only a fourth in 'Greats,' the examinations, he was never made a professor in philology and was more appreciated in Germany than in his own country. Influenced by the German school of philology, by the impressive work in phonetics done in India, and by a system of visible speech, developed by Alexander Melville Bell for educating the deaf, Sweet developed a phonetic system called 'Broad Romic' in which each symbol represented a group of similar sounds. The idea that a family of sounds, operating together in a language, may be distinguished from the individual sounds as spoken was new. Thus, he may be said to have been the first to hit upon the concept of the phoneme, although the word itself was not coined by him. Sweet's symbol system eventually led to the International Phonetic Alphabet listed in Appendix 1. With the publication of one of his books, *Handbook of Phonetics* in 1877, he established England as the European birthplace of the science of phonetics. Despite his obvious preeminence in England in the field of phonetics, Sweet was not appointed in 1876 to the Chair of Comparative Philology at University College, London and was passed over again in 1885 as a candidate for Merton Professorship of English Language and Literature at Oxford. The final blow came in 1901 when he was denied the Professorship of Comparative Philology at Oxford. Linguistic scholars in Europe were astonished at the lack of academic recognition given Sweet in England. He was merely appointed a Reader in Phonetics at Oxford.

Unlike the calm, reserved Helmholtz, Sweet was bitter and sarcastic. His scholarship and writings continued at full pace, despite his disappointments, and he published *A History of English Sounds* in 1874, revised in 1888, and *A Primer of Phonetics* with descriptions of each articulation in 1890. An early member of the Philological Society in London, the Society finally recognized his great contribution to the study of descriptive phonetics in the presidential address given by Christopher L. Wrenn in 1946, 34 years after Sweet's death.

ALEXANDER GRAHAM BELL: TEACHING THE DEAF

In 1847, only 2 years after the birth of Henry Sweet in England, Alexander Graham Bell was born in Edinburgh. Later to be world renowned as the inventor of the telephone, he always considered himself to be a scientist and inventor by avocation, but a teacher of the deaf by vocation. His father, Melville Bell, was a speech teacher and elocutionist who lectured at the University of Edinburgh and wrote pamphlets and books on elocution. Melville's greatest achievement was the development of Visible Speech (Fig. 2.2), originally a system of symbols representing the physiology behind each speech sound. The tongue was represented by a horseshoe-shaped symbol, its position indicating the most active part of the tongue. With symbols for lips and voice, any speech sound could be represented visually. Alexander Graham Bell spent much of his life instructing teachers in the use of his father's system for describing speech production.

As a child, Alexander, then called Aleck, was extremely musical and curious about nature, but uninterested in formal studies. At 15, Aleck was called to London to live with his 70-year-old Grandfather Bell, who was a teacher of public speaking, teaching pupils who stammered and suffered with other impediments of speech. Under the guidance of his grandfather, Aleck learned how to apply himself to serious study, to be independent in the control of his own finances, to recite passages from Shakespeare's plays, and to dress 'like a gentleman.'

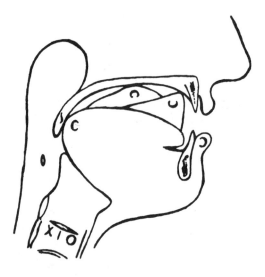

ʇʞ ɑʄʊ ʊʃ ʊʃɜ.

I caught the thief.

Figure 2.2. Adapted from a figure in A. G. Bell's *English Visible Speech in Twelve Lessons*, 1895. Bell wrote this book to popularize his father's transcription system.

Back in Edinburgh a year later, he started his long career of teaching while he was still a student, first at Weston House at Elgin, then at Edinburgh University. Unaware that he was repeating the experiments of Helmholtz, Aleck discovered the resonances of the vocal tract cavities by snapping his finger against his throat and cheeks as he assumed various vocal tract positions. He also repeated the experiment of determining the frequencies of the resonators by vibrating tuning forks in front of his mouth as he assumed different vowel positions.

Having lost Aleck's two brothers to illness, the family emigrated to Canada for Melville's retirement when Aleck was 23. In Great Britain, Aleck had gained a reputation as an outstanding teacher of speech to the deaf, using his father's Visible Speech method. In America, he continued teaching the deaf and trained teachers in schools for the deaf to use the system. He came into contact with the scientific community in Boston, started work on his many ideas for inventions, and in 1876, shouted the famous sentence: "Mr. Watson, come here — I want to see you." which his assistant, Thomas Watson, heard and understood through the receiver of the first telephone, installed between Bell's laboratory and his bedroom down the hall.

In 1877, Bell married Mabel Hubbard, the deaf daughter of Gardiner Hubbard, one of his partners in the newly established Bell Telephone Company. They returned briefly to England to promote the telephone and Visible Speech for the deaf, but the family, which eventually included two daughters, settled in Washington during the winters and at their large estate in Nova Scotia during the summers. Although Bell made many profitable inventions, he always considered his work for the deaf to be paramount. He established the Volta Bureau, a center of information about deafness, developed the audiometer for testing hearing, and continued to promote Visible Speech. Throughout his life, he had been sleepless by night, preferring to sleep late into the morning. By working at night, he could be alone and more productive during his most active years. Basically a solitary man himself, Alexander Graham Bell helped other people commu-

nicate with one another, even those who could not hear.

HOMER W. DUDLEY: ELECTRONIC SYNTHESIS OF CONTINUOUS SPEECH

The science of speech has benefited from the contribution of a psychophysicist in Helmholtz, a linguist in Sweet, a speech pathologist in Bell, and an electrical engineer in the person of Homer Dudley. Dudley was a pioneer in speech synthesis, making machines that could produce

speech-like sounds. In the 18th and 19th centuries, speech had been produced artificially by mechanical manipulation of artificial heads and mechanisms designed to simulate the lungs, larynx, and vocal tract of a speaker, but speech synthesis, as we know it, had to await the 20th century

Figure 2.3. The Bell Telephone demonstration of the Voder at the 1939 World's Fair. (Reproduced with permission of American Telephone and Telegraph Company.)

arrival of electronic circuits. It was Dudley's invention, called the Voder, built in 1937 and 1938 at Bell Laboratories, that first synthesized continuous speech by electric circuits.

Homer Dudley had started his career in Pennsylvania, where his family had moved from Virginia when he was a schoolboy. His father was a preacher and upon moving to Pennsylvania, his parents took in pupils for lessons in the classics and other academic subjects and to study for the ministry. Homer graduated from high school early. On his first teaching assignment, he taught the 5th, 6th, 7th, and 8th grades in one room; his second position was to teach high school students. Finding it difficult to keep discipline in the classroom, Dudley abandoned his plans to teach and started working his way through Pennsylvania State University where electrical engineering courses were being introduced into college curricula at that time. Dudley joined the technical staff of Bell Telephone Laboratories, the engineering laboratory of Western Electric, then located in New York City. He remained working there for over 40 years, much of that time in the telephone transmission division.

Later on, he worked with Robert Riesz and others on the development of the Vocoder. The purpose of the Vocoder was to filter speech into 10 bands in such a way that the information could be transmitted over narrower bandwidths than were previously possible. After transmission, the channel information, along with a noise circuit for consonant sounds and a buzz circuit for voicing, was used to synthesize speech that closely resembled the original, except for some loss in voice quality. The Vocoder was demonstrated at the tercentenniel celebration at Harvard and led to the celebrated "talking machine," the Voder, a Voice Operation Demonstrator. The Voder synthesizer was shown at the 1939 and 1940 World's Fairs. (Fig. 2.3) It made recognizable speech sounds, at least if listeners were cued to know the sort of utterances to expect. The operator pushed a pedal for the voice or hiss source and pressed 10 keys to control the resonances. Special keys simulated the stop consonants such as /p/ or /t/. In the demonstrations, a dialogue would be conducted between a man and the Voder operated by a woman. Over 20 telephone operators were extensively trained to operate the machine during the World's Fair demonstrations. Unlike previous synthesizers, the Voder was based more closely upon the acoustics of speech rather than its articulation. Just as radio transmission is accomplished by modulating a carrier tone by the signal of interest (in FM, the frequency is modulated; in AM, the amplitude is modulated), Dudley conceived of speech as a carrier tone or sound source which is modulated by the movements of the vocal tract.

Homer Dudley, now in his 80s, lives quietly in New Jersey. His contributions to speech science were that he made explicit the carrier nature of speech and he applied the carrier idea to specific principles for speech analysis and synthesis. These ideas underlie modern conceptualizations of the speech process.

FRANKLIN COOPER, ALVIN LIBERMAN, AND PIERRE DELATTRE: SPEECH PERCEPTION AND THE PATTERN PLAYBACK

We have picked a few pioneers in the study of speech production and acoustics, but little systematic work in speech perception was possible until speech scientists knew enough about the acoustics of speech to control acoustic parameters one at a time in testing listeners. The development of the sound spectrograph in the 1940s at Bell Laboratories by Ralph Potter and his colleagues provided an instrument that allowed investigators to conveniently analyze the frequencies represented in speech across time, producing a visual display called a spectrogram. With it came a sudden increase in information about the acoustics of speech. Speech perception questions remained: what aspects of the complex sound pattern of speech are important in listening to speech, and what aspects are less important? In order to find out, an engineer, a psychologist and a linguist joined their talents at Haskins Laboratories, then in New York, to investigate the perception of speech.

Potter had conceived of the reverse of the sound spectrograph as a machine which could input a visual pattern and convert it to sound. Franklin Cooper at Haskins saw that the development of such a pattern playback would provide a powerful instrument for the study of speech perception. Cooper, born and educated in Illinois, had received his doctorate in physics from Massachusetts Institute of Technology in 1936. After a few years with General Electric Research Laboratories, in 1939, Cooper became Associate Research Director of Haskins Laboratories, where he remained as its president and director for 20 years, and where he now serves as an associate director. As part of his efforts

to develop a reading machine for the blind, Cooper constructed the Pattern Playback synthesizer (Fig. 2.4).

Alvin Liberman, a psychologist who received his bachelor and master of arts degrees at the University of Missouri and his doctorate at Yale, is a member of the psychology department at the University of Connecticut and is an adjunct professor at Yale. Joining Haskins Laboratories in 1944 and currently its president, Liberman, along with Cooper, used the Pattern Playback to systematically vary the acoustic parameters of speech to determine the cues used in speech perception.

At the invitation of Cooper and Liberman, Pierre Delattre, a Frenchman by birth, joined the experimental work in speech perception conducted at Haskins

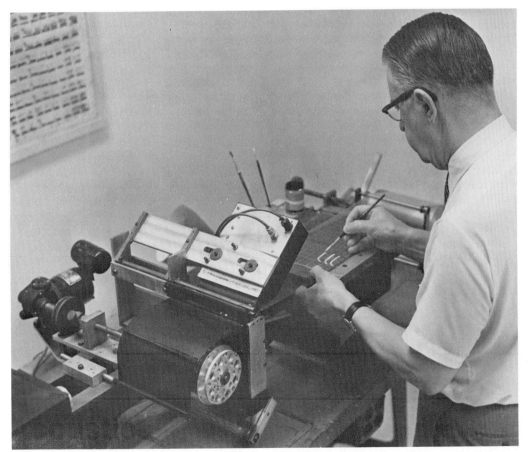

Figure 2.4. F. S. Cooper painting a syllable on the Pattern Playback synthesizer. Speech was synthesized by converting patterns painted on acetate film loops into acoustic signals by a photoelectric system (Haskins Laboratories).

during the 1950s. Delattre was an expert in French linguistics whose specialty was in teaching foreigners to master French phonetics. For 16 years he directed the French phonetics program held during summers at Middlebury College in Vermont. During much of this time, he was a member of the faculty at the University of Pennsylvania. He had a good eye for painting playback patterns and the patience to listen to their acoustic effects. He learned the rules for painting patterns for such sentences as 'Oh, my aching back,' and even composed a piece of synthesized music which he entitled 'Scotch Plaid.'

The collaboration of Cooper, Liberman, and Delattre lasted until Delattre's death and produced most of the early work in speech perception. The value of the Pattern Playback as an instrument for speech perception remained unsurpassed until computer-controlled synthesizers became available. The experimenter could see at a glance the whole acoustic pattern, could hear how it sounded repeatedly, and could easily modify it. Systematically varying an acoustic dimension thought to be important in perception, the investigators had listeners compare and label the synthesized stimuli. By such means, the Haskins group, which included many other investigators, demonstrated the role of linguistic experience upon speech perception and the role of context in the perception of individual phonemes. While Haskins Laboratories pioneered in the systematic study of speech perception, we cite it chiefly because it is a good example of the point we are trying to emphasize: that the roads to speech science are many and varied. At Haskins today, there are engineers, linguists, speech pathologists, and psychologists, all of them interested in experimental phonetics or speech science.

SINCE THEN

In general, the experimental study of the acoustics of speech is ahead of the study of speech physiology. Based upon spectrographic analysis, that is, the analysis of the speech signal according to the various sound frequencies in its composition, and upon systematic synthesis of speech, we now know a substantial amount about the acoustics of speech. This knowledge has made synthetic speech or talking machines possible. We know less about speech physiology from experimental studies, but work in this area is increasing rapidly through the efforts of many speech scientists at universities and laboratories throughout the United States and abroad. Speech perception research is currently branching out in many directions: infant and animal perception, the role of the cerebral hemispheres in perception, the role of context and linguistic experience in perception, the role of memory and attention, and investigations of the stages of processing involved in the perception of speech.

There are two overlapping methods of sharing research information in speech. One method is to attend and participate in conventions organized by professional organizations. The largest common meeting ground is at the fall and spring meetings of the Acoustical Society of America (ASA). Research papers are presented at these meetings and ideas are exchanged. Another arena for professional exchange is at the annual convention of the American Speech-Language-Hearing Association (ASHA). Speech scientists belong to many other professional organizations, state, national, and international. An attempt to consolidate the various disciplines represented has been made in the establishment of the American Association of Phonetic Sciences. Their meetings are held concurrently or immediately after the ASA meeting. A prominent international association is the International Congress of Phonetic Sciences which meets in a different country every 4 years.

The second forum for exchange of ideas and research is in the journals published by ASHA and ASA, the above mentioned national associations. ASA publishes the *Journal of the Acoustical Society of America*, usually called *JASA*. ASHA publishes one basic research journal, the *Journal of Speech and Hearing Research*, and another journal of clinical research, the *Journal of Speech and Hearing Disorders*. The *Journal of Phonetics* is a relatively new publication with emphasis on experimental phonetics. Many other journals include research on speech production, acoustics of speech, and speech perception. *Speech and Language, Brain and Language, Perception and Psychophysics, Phonetica,* and *Folia Phoniatrica* are names of but a few of these journals. Theoretical articles are sometimes published in *Psychological Review,* and a few innovative research studies appear in the journal of the American Association for the Advancement of Science, *Science.* Individual scientists often will send copies of their own articles on written request.

Speech laboratories exchange progress reports or working papers as another means of information dissemination. Widely read are the *Quarterly Progress Report* issued by the Research Laboratory of Electronics at Massachusetts Institute of Technology in Cambridge, Massachusetts, the *Speech Transmission Quarterly Progress and Status Report* issued by the Royal Institute of Technology (KTH) in Stockholm, Sweden; and the *Status Report on Speech Research* issued by Haskins Laboratories in New Haven, Connecticut. Many universities also distribute working papers in speech science written by faculty and students.

The future of speech science lies in work that will aim to show the ways in which speech production and speech perception may interact and in work that will lead to automatic speech recognition as well as synthesis. In the following three chapters, we shall survey some of what is now known about acoustics, speech production, and speech perception.

BIBLIOGRAPHY

Bell, A. G., *The Mechanism of Speech.* New York: Funk & Wagnalls Co., 1908.

Bell, A. G., *English Visible Speech in Twelve Lessons.* Washington, D. C.: Volta Bureau, 1895.

Bell, M., *Visible Speech: The Science of Universal Alphabetics: or Self-Interpreting Physiological Letters for the Printing and Writing of all Languages in one Alphabet; elucidated by Theoretical Explanations, Tables, Diagrams, and Examples.* London: Simpkin, Marshall, & Co., 1867.

Bronstein, A. J., Raphael, L. J., and Stevens, Cj. (Eds.), *Biographical Dictionary of the Phonetic Sciences.* New York: The Press of Lehman College, 1977.

Bruce, R. V., *Bell: Alexander Graham Bell and the Conquest of Solitude.* Boston: Little, Brown & Co., 1973.

Delattre, P. C., Liberman, A. M., and Cooper, F. S., Acoustic Loci and Transitional Cues for Consonants. *J. Acoust. Soc. Am. 27,* 1955, 769–773.

Dudley, H., The Carrier Nature of Speech. *Bell Syst. Tech. J. 19,* 1940, 495–515. Reprinted in Flanagan, J. L., and Rabiner, L. R. (Eds.), *Speech Synthesis: Benchmark Papers in Acoustics.* Stroudsburg, Pa.: Dowden, Hutchinson & Ross, Inc., 1973, pp. 22–42.

Dudley, H., Reisz, R. R., and Watkins, S. A., A Synthetic Speaker. *J. Franklin Inst. 227,* 1939, 739–764.

Helmholtz, H. L. F., *Die Lehre von den Tonempfin-*

dungen als physiologische Grundlage für die Theorie der Musik. Braunschweig: F. Vieweg und sohn, 1863. Translated, *On the Sensations of Tone as a Physiological Basis for the Theory of Music.* 2nd English translation from the 4th German edition of 1877 by A. S. Ellis. New York: Dover Publications, 1954.

Liberman, A. M., Cooper, F. S., Shankweiler, D. P., and Studdert-Kennedy, M., Perception of the Speech Code. *Psychol. Rev.* 74, 1967, 431–461. Also in David, E. E., Jr., and Denes, P. B. (Eds.), *Human Communication: A Unified View.* New York: McGraw-Hill, 1972, pp. 13–50.

McKendrick, J. G., *Hermann Ludwig Ferdinand von Helmholtz.* New York: Longmans, Green & Co., 1899.

Sweet, H., *Handbook of Phonetics.* Oxford: Clarendon Press, 1877.

Sweet, H., *History of English Sounds,* Revised. Oxford: Clarendon Press, 1888.

Sweet, H., *A Primer of Phonetics.* Oxford: Clarendon Press, 1890.

Wrenn, C. L., Henry Sweet: Presidential Address delivered to the Philological Society on Friday, 10th May, 1946. Reprinted in Sebeok, T. A. (Ed.), *Portraits of Linguists.* Bloomington, Ind.: Indiana University Press, 1966, pp. 512–532.

CHAPTER 3

Acoustics

"Holla your name to the reverberate hills,
And make the babbling gossip of the air
Cry out."

William Shakespeare, *Twelfth Night*

The study of sound is called acoustics. Since speech is a continuously changing stream of sound, it is necessary to have a clear understanding of the nature of sound in general, before one can fully understand either the production of speech sounds by speakers or the reception of speech sounds by listeners.

The first thing to understand about sound is that it has no substance; it is not a thing. It has no mass or weight, but it is rather a set of movements or a disturbance. A sound wave can exist as a disturbance in a gas such as air, in liquid such as water, or in a solid such as a pipe or railroad track. The medium of transmitting speech sounds is usually air; therefore, sound in air will be emphasized in this chapter.

One of the problems in the first attempt at understanding sound is the fact of its invisibility. Since the molecules of air are not visible to the human eye, the waves of disturbance moving through air cannot be seen. A second problem in understanding sound is the fact that most sounds are complex. This results in a complex pattern of air particle disturbance. To surmount these barriers of understanding, one must make visible the invisible and one must start with the simplest of all sound patterns, the pure tone.

A PURE TONE: AN EXAMPLE OF SIMPLE HARMONIC MOTION

One seldom hears a pure tone in the world of sounds. Most of the sounds we hear, the street noises, the sounds of speech, and even the sounds of music are complex in that they consist of many tones or frequencies heard simultaneously. A *pure tone* has only one frequency of vibration. It is the result of a vibration which repeats itself at a constant number of cycles per second. The number of cycles per second is termed its *frequency*. Some musical instruments are narrowly tuned and vibrate at few frequencies, but to achieve the effect of only one frequency, special metal tuning forks (Fig. 3.1) are forged which will vibrate mainly at a specified frequency. This vibration produces essen-

tially a pure tone, the simplest of all sounds and therefore the easiest to describe.

The tuning fork, when struck and set into vibration, moves in *simple harmonic motion*. The tines, or prongs, of the fork move back and forth a fixed number of times per second no matter how hard it is struck to set it into motion. The initial impact will force both tines of the fork to move away from the state of rest. Because of the elasticity of the material, however, the tines will come back to their original position. *Elasticity* is the restoring force which causes particles in an elastic medium to bounce back when displaced. Push your finger into the fatty part of your arm or leg and you will find that the tissue

27

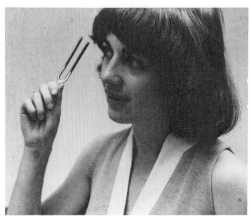

Figure 3.1. A tuning fork will produce a pure tone (Temple University).

restores itself quickly. In simple harmonic motion, however, the movement does not stop with the elastic recoil of the particles, or tines of the tuning fork in this case. The vibrator continues to move through the resting place due to inertia. *Inertia* is the tendency for motion or lack of motion to continue. If something is not moving, it takes less energy for it to remain motionless than to start moving because of inertia. On the other hand, if something is moving, it is easier for it to keep moving than to stop, again because of inertia. When we continue to watch television after a program which interests us is finished, even though the following program is uninteresting, we are demonstrating a behavioral form of inertia. The tines of the tuning fork continue to move after their elastic recoil to their original positions, but they continue only so far, for the velocity gradually decreases because of resistance. Then they return once more to the resting point due again to elasticity, and the cycle repeats itself.

We have described one cycle of vibration in simple harmonic motion, but it needs to be illustrated further for clarity. Figure 3.2 illustrates the steps taken during one and one-half cycles of tuning fork vibration.

The Swing Analogy: An Example of Velocity Gradation in Simple Harmonic Motion

Consider the simple harmonic motion (SHM) of a swing hanging from the branch of a tree. When you displace the swing from its resting position by pulling it back, it not only returns to its original position but goes past it. This back and forth movement, although different in some respects, is somewhat analogous to the movement of air particles when set into vibration during the transmission of a sound.

The example of the swing illustrates an important property of simple harmonic motion, which is the continuous manner in which the displaced object changes velocity. *Velocity* is the speed, in a certain direction, of the swing, in this case. In Figure 3.3, the spot on the ground over which the swing hangs when at rest is labeled 2. Consider that a given force will displace the swing to 3; then it will swing back and forth toward 1 and 3 until it dies down. While swinging, the velocity changes, gradually diminishing as it approaches 1 and 3, where it drops for an instant to 0 before changing direction. Maximum velocity is reached each time the swing passes over the resting place. Since the swing comes to a momentary standstill at each end of the excursion, the maximum *acceleration*, which is the rate of change in velocity, is at these extreme points where the swing changes direction.

If the movement of the swing were graphed as it changes position in time, it would look like Figure 3.4.

The velocity is graded with zero velocity and maximum acceleration at B, D, F, H, J, and L and maximum velocity at the zero crossing C, E, G, I, and K. Notice, too, that the motion is dying down gradually due to loss of energy from friction. This decrease in the amplitude of displacement is called *damping*. Although the excursion of the swing is dying down, the frequency remains constant. Frequency is the number of cycles per second, and as shown in Figure 3.4, the time it takes for the swing to go back and forth one complete cycle (A to E) is equal to the time it takes to complete the second cycle (E to I). The time taken for each cycle is termed the *period*. If the frequency were 20 cps (cycles per second), then the period would be 1/20th of a second or 50 msec. The graph of a simple harmonic motion is the same as a graph of a *sine wave*. The pattern is simple because there is only one frequency

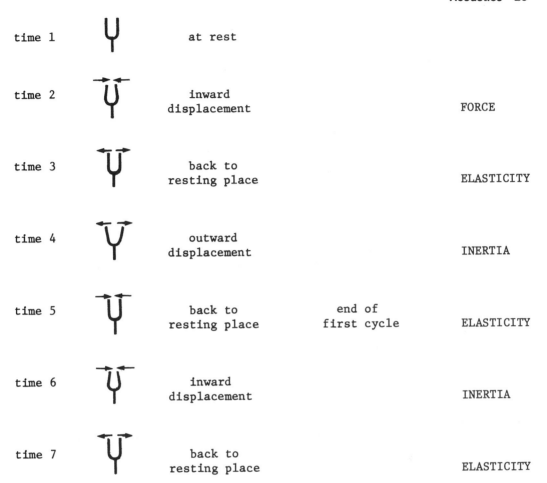

time 1   at rest

time 2   inward
displacement   FORCE

time 3   back to
resting place   ELASTICITY

time 4   outward
displacement   INERTIA

time 5   back to
resting place   end of
first cycle   ELASTICITY

time 6   inward
displacement   INERTIA

time 7   back to
resting place   ELASTICITY

Figure 3.2 Tuning fork displacements in one and one-half cycles of vibration.

of vibration. It repeats itself until it damps out and is therefore *periodic*.

Particle Movement in Sound

In the sound of a pure tone, the individual air particles move in response to a pure tone vibrator in SHM. They do not, however, move along an arc as a pendulum or swing does. Air particles moving in response to a pure tone vibrator move in SHM but in the direction of the wave propagation, as we shall illustrate further on in the chapter.

Practice moving in SHM. Place your pencil or finger on the middle circle marked B of Figure 3.5a. Move it to C, then A, then C, and continue at a fixed relatively slow frequency without stopping. Try moving your finger at the same fre-quency but with a larger excursion from the resting place using Figure 3.5b to set the range.

The movements you make with your pencil could be displayed as an amplitude by time graph called a *waveform* (Fig. 3.6).

Return to Figure 3.5 and practice SHM at a constant frequency for both a and b, but this time make the movements at a relatively high frequency (an increased number of cycles per second). The waveforms would then look more like Figure 3.7.

These movements back and forth over the resting place are magnified versions of the movement of a single air particle when a pure tone is sounded. If a tuning fork specified to vibrate at 440 cps (the A above middle C on the piano) were sounded in the middle of the room, every molecule of

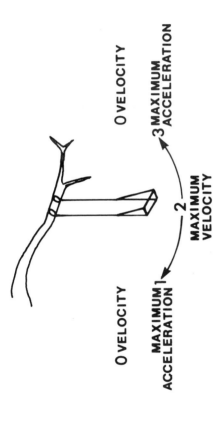

Figure 3.3. Simple harmonic motion (SHM) of a swing. The swing is at zero (0) velocity at the extremes of its excursion, as it changes direction and at maximum velocity at 2, the middle of the excursion.

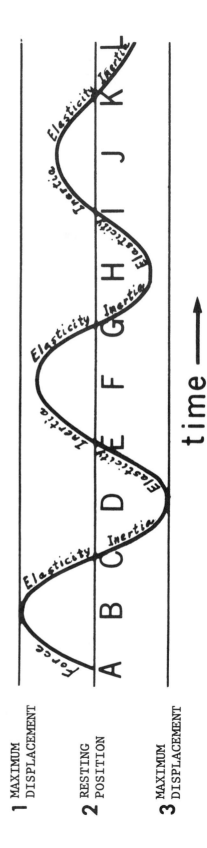

Figure 3.4. Waveform produced by graphing SHM of a swing.

air in the room would soon move in place. Each particle would initially move away from the tuning fork (due to the force against it from a neighboring particle), then back to the resting place (due to elasticity), then further toward the fork (due to inertia), then back to the resting place (elasticity), and so on as long as the vibration lasted. Each particle would complete 440 of these cycles during each second.

Pressure Wave Movement in Sound

We have been analyzing the movement of individual particles during a pure tone stimulus. If each particle is moving in place, how does the disturbance move from one location to another? Particles surrounding the vibrator start moving before particles further away from the sound source. The molecules of air oscillating in SHM disturb adjacent molecules and thus the disturbance is transmitted away from the source. This disturbance takes the form of a pressure wave radiating outward, much as the ripples seen emanating from a point in still water after a pebble has been tossed. Since the pure tone is periodic, the pressure wave is repeated and is followed by evenly spaced pressure waves.

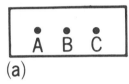 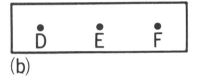

Figure 3.5. Simulate SHM by moving finger rhythmically from *B* to *C* to *A* to *C*, oscillating with gradually and continuously changing velocity. Repeat with *EFDF* at same frequency.

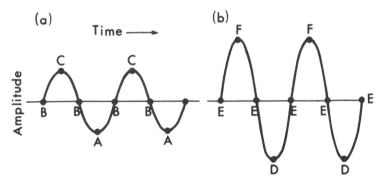

Figure 3.6. Waveform of SHM traced in Fig 3.5; *a* and *b* differ in amplitude but are equal in frequency.

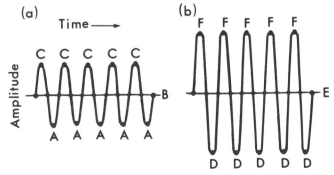

Figure 3.7. Waveforms of a higher frequency than represented in Fig 3.6; *a* and *b* differ in amplitude but are equal in frequency.

Figure 3.8 is a schematic representation of 10 individual air molecules. At Time 1, before the pure tone vibrator is set into motion, the particles are at rest, equidistant from one another. At Time 2, the outward movement of one of the tines of the tuning fork has forced Particle A to move away from the fork approaching Particle B. At Time 3, Particle A has bounced back to its resting place due to the fact that air is an elastic medium, but Particle B has been displaced by the influence (during Time 2) of the impinging Particle A. Notice that as time proceeds, areas of *compression,* in which molecules are closer together, alternate with areas of *rarefaction,* in which molecules are further apart. For example, in Time 7 a high pressure area formed by the juxtaposition of Particles B, C, and D, is surrounded by relatively low pressure areas. By Time 10, the first pressure wave has moved further away from the sound source and now consists of Particles E, F, and G. At the same time, a second pressure wave is emanating from the vibrator and consists of Particles A, B, and C.

It is helpful to visualize compression waves moving through a medium by a simple demonstration using coiled wire. A toy currently on the market called Slinky serves well. Spreading the coil along a table top between your hands, hold one hand steady and move the other back and forth in SHM until waves can be seen to flow through the coil. Observe that the waves move in the same direction as the hand movement. This type of wave, in which particle movement is in the same direction as wave movement, is called a *longitudinal wave.* Sound waves are longitudinal whether in air or in liquid. Waves seen radiating from tossing a stone or dipping a finger into water are called *transverse waves,* because although the waves move out from the source of the disturbance, the water particles move at right angles to the wave: up and down, as any cork-watching fisherman will attest.

If all the air molecules in a room were colored green, a tuning fork vibrating in the center of the room would be surrounded by a globe of relatively dark green (an area of compression of air particles) which would move away from the vibrator. Although each particle moves back and forth in place, the disturbance moves throughout the room. Each compression area is followed by a pale green area (rarefaction area) which in turn is followed by another compression area (see Fig. 3.9). The pressure waves move out from the vibrator in all directions.

The pressure waves can be graphed as a sine wave in somewhat the same way that we represented individual particle motion. Figure 3.10 shows the relationship.

Waveforms are common representations of sound signals. A waveform is an amplitude by time display and therefore represents particle motion as in Figure 3.10*a*, but it is understood that it also represents the pressure variation in the medium as a whole as in Figure 3.10*b*.

A cathode ray oscilloscope is an instrument which can display any sound as a waveform. Remember that the movement of any particular particle, were it visible, would not look like that waveform. Rather, the waveform is an abstract representation of the displacement from rest which the particle undergoes during a certain time

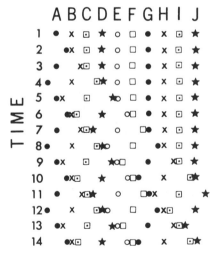

Figure 3.8. Schematic drawing of 10 air particles in SHM at 14 moments in time. The sound source is conceived to be to the *left.* Pressure waves move to the *right.* Time runs from *top* to *bottom.* Notice that although the pressure wave, indicated by a clustering of three adjacent particles, moves from *left* to *right,* each individual particle moves relatively little in SHM.

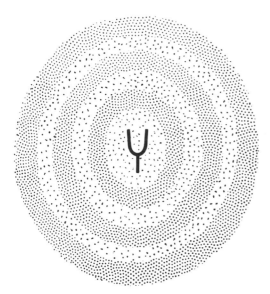

Figure 3.9. Pressure wave emanating from a sound source. (The areas of compression should encircle the vibrator as a globe, a representation not indicated in this two-dimensional figure.)

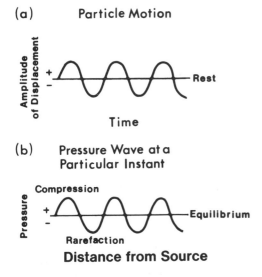

(a)   Particle Motion

**(b)   Pressure Wave at a
            Particular Instant**

Figure 3.10. The waveform of a pure tone (a) and a graph of pressure variations as a function of distance from the source (b). The waveforms correspond.

scissa (X or horizontal axis) again by convention.

Essential Constituents of Sound

Are these periodic pressure waves sound? It's the old 'tree in the forest' question. If a tree falls in a forest with no one about to hear it, is there a sound? We know that a sound must have as prerequisites something moving and a medium (in our examples, air) through which the disturbance can travel. To complete the definition of sound, the disturbance must be audible. It must be capable of producing corresponding vibrations in some receiving ear, but the ears of different creatures are tuned to different sounds. Bats hear sounds of extremely high frequencies which are inaudible to the human ear. Although some dictionaries limit the definition of sound to those vibratory disturbances audible to man, this seems unnecessarily restrictive. Yet, there are some vibrations which are inaudible to any creature on Earth due to their extremely low or high frequency or extremely low intensity. Can the disturbances which result from these vibrations be called sound? That too seems extreme.

Let us arbitrarily define *sound*, then, as an audible disturbance of a medium produced by a source. The source could be a guitar string energized by the pluck of a finger or human vocal folds energized by air from the lungs. The medium could be gas, liquid, or solid; any elastic medium can carry an acoustic signal. The disturbance must be such that it could cause corresponding vibrations in a receiver. The receiver could be the auditory system of any creature for which the signal is audible. According to our definition, then, the falling tree created an audible disturbance, which, even if it were not heard, could be called a sound.

Interference Patterns

It is remarkable that the air can be filled with many sounds, all of which can be transmitted simultaneously. Because air molecules vibrate in place, they can be responsive to many signals at once. It does happen, however, that signals of the same frequency can interfere with one another.

span. The *amplitude* of displacement indicates the intensity or power of the sound, and by convention, the *ordinate* of a waveform often indicates units of intensity. Time is represented along the *ab-*

This occurs when the frequency is generated from two sources or, more often, when the signal is reflected from a barrier such as a wall to compete, in a sense, with itself.

The waveforms of two signals having a common frequency sum in a straightforward way. The resulting summation waveform depends upon the phase relationship between the signals. In order to understand phase relationships, it helps to conceive of a cycle of vibration as a circle. Every circle has a total of 360° (degrees), so that one-half of a cycle would be 180°, one-fourth of a cycle would be 90°, and three-fourths, 270°. A sine wave can be viewed as a circle twisted open in the middle in order to represent time as at the top of Figure 3.11.

If two signals of the same frequency are *in phase,* their pressure waves crest and trough at the same time, and the sum of the signals will have double the amplitude. Figure 3.11 illustrates pure tone signals which are in phase, 90° out of phase, and 180° out of phase. When signals are 90° out of phase, one signal is one-fourth of a cycle ahead of the other. At each instant, the amplitudes of the two waveforms are simply added. When two acoustic signals having the same frequency of vibration are 180° out of phase, the result is silence, for each particle receives two equal forces in opposite directions. Each particle then remains at rest.

The problem of interference patterns is especially acute in the design of concert halls, requiring people trained in architectural acoustics. Unless halls are designed with acoustic considerations, sounds produced in them will reflect from the hard walls in such a way that they will *reverberate,* which means the sound is prolonged as it bounces back and forth. This

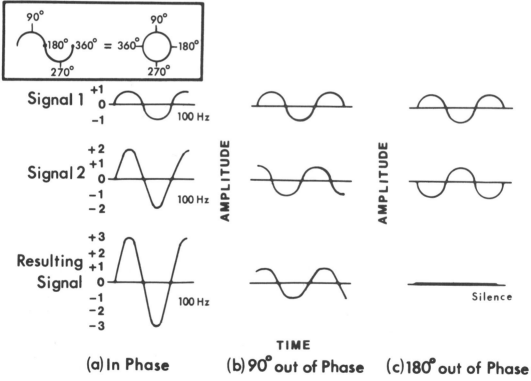

Figure 3.11. Results of adding two pure tones (*Signal 1* and *Signal 2*) differing in phase and amplitude, but of the same frequency. In all cases, the *Resulting Signal* will be a pure tone of the same frequency, but phase and amplitude will vary. The addition of two pure tones of the same frequency and amplitude but 180° out of phase will produce silence, as shown in *Column c*.

prevents listeners from adequately hearing the next sound. The sounds will be louder in some places and softer in others due, also, to the interference patterns. The presence of a large audience dressed in sound-absorbing clothes helps the situation, as do absorbent materials used as wall and ceiling coverings, floor coverings, and chair upholstery. On the other hand, too much absorption dulls the power of the sounds. The right balance is difficult to achieve, yet none of us wants to have the misfortune of sitting in an acoustically dead spot in an auditorium where interference patterns due to reflected sound and sound absorption cause partial sound cancellation.

COMPLEX TONES

Most sound sources, unlike the tuning fork, produce vibrations which are complex. Rather than vibrating in SHM, they move in a complex manner which consists of more than one frequency. When these movements are graphed, a more complex waveform replaces the sine wave of the pure tone. To understand the derivation of a *complex tone,* simply add two sine waves of different frequencies. It is important to remember that many sounds of the same frequency and in phase may be added (as in Fig. 3.11), but the result will always be a sine wave: a representation of a pure tone. If two or more pure tones of different frequencies are added, however, the result will be a complex tone. Figure 3.12 shows an instance of the addition of pure tones to form a complex tone. There are two kinds of complex sounds, those in which the pattern of vibration, however complex, repeats itself (periodic) and those in which the vibration is random and has no repeatable pattern (*aperiodic*).

Play a note on the piano or sing 'ah' and the resulting sounds will be complex but periodic in their waveforms. Drop a book on the floor or hiss through your teeth and the resulting sounds will be complex (more than one frequency) but aperiodic (no repeatable pattern) in their waveforms.

Harmonics: Characteristic of Periodic Complex Tones

Periodic complex vibrations produce signals in which the component frequencies are integral multiples of the lowest frequency of pattern repetition, or *fundamental frequency.* Figure 3.13 represents a waveform of a complex periodic sound wave similar to that produced when a woman says 'ah', shown in comparison with a pure tone waveform of 200 cps. It is clear that both patterns repeat themselves at the same frequency. This first *harmonic* is called the fundamental frequency (abbreviated f_o). The higher frequencies are multiples of the f_o. The second harmonic is 2 times 200, or 400 cps; the third harmonic is 3 times 200, or 600 cps, and so forth. In physics, the f_o is considered to be the first harmonic, whereas in music the first multiple (2 times the f_o) is called the first harmonic, a tradition which has caused some confusion. We will follow the convention of physics.

A waveform offers amplitude and time information. It is not easy, in general, to estimate the amplitude of the individual harmonics from a complex waveform. Frequency information can be obtained by counting how many times the pattern is repeated each second. For a pure tone, this process is easy, but for a complex tone it is difficult because only the f_o can be counted easily.

A second type of display for vibrating patterns is called a line spectrum or *amplitude spectrum* (plural: *spectra*) in which the ordinate (the vertical line) represents the amplitude of the signal as before, but the abscissa (the horizontal line) represents frequency. Any complex periodic signal can be mathematically analyzed into its component frequencies, a discovery made by J. B. Fourier in France during the first quarter of the 19th century.

A review of the waveforms previously presented but now paired with their corresponding spectra in Figure 3.14 will serve to distinguish the two displays.

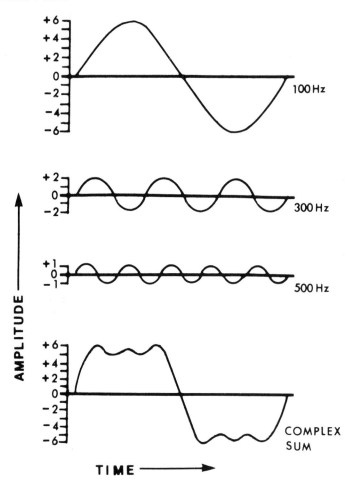

Figure 3.12. Waveform of a complex tone derived from three pure tones of differing frequency.

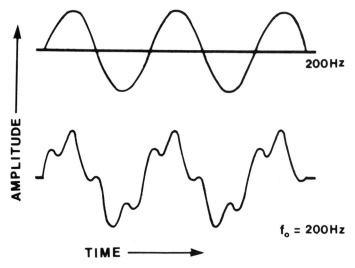

Figure 3.13. Waveforms of a pure tone and a complex tone, each with a fundamental frequency of 200 Hz.

Aperiodic Complex Signals

The sounds of a book dropping or a hiss made between the teeth are complex as they consist of more than one frequency, but the frequencies are not harmonically related as they are for periodic sounds. In both cases, the air is set into random excitation with multiple frequencies of vibration as a result. The waveforms are *aperiodic* as there is no repetition of a displace-ment pattern. The book slam is *transient*, however, producing a burst of noise of short duration, whereas the hiss is continuous for as long as the airstream is set into turbulence by passing through a narrow constriction. Amplitude spectra can be made for aperiodic as well as periodic signals. Figure 3.15 shows the waveforms and spectra of typical aperiodic sound signals.

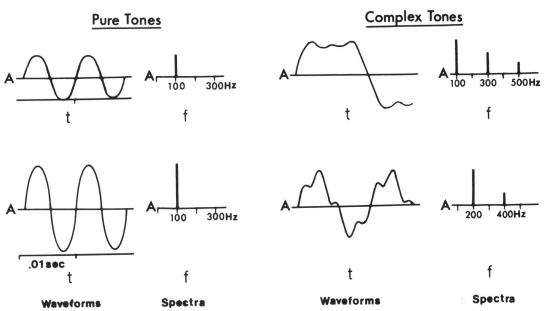

Figure 3.14. Waveforms and corresponding spectra. The two signals on the *left* are vibrations at a single frequency (pure tones) whereas the two signals on the *right* represent different complex vibrations, analyzed as a fundamental frequency and higher harmonics.

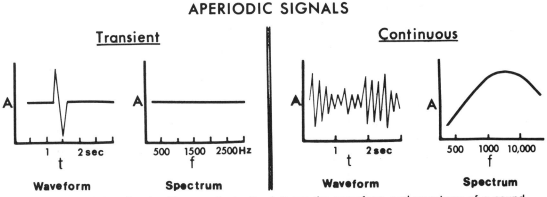

Figure 3.15. Noise signals. The graphs to the *left* are the waveform and spectrum of a sound similar to a book dropping. Since the frequencies are many and random, an average amplitude is indicated rather than individual frequencies. The graphs to the *right* are the waveform and the spectrum of a hissing noise. The envelope of the amplitude as a function of frequency is indicated.

FREQUENCY AND PITCH

We have stated that frequency is the number of vibratory cycles per second. The notations 100 cps, 100 ~, and 100 Hz (hertz) all mean the same thing: 100 cycles per second. The unit Hz is preferred. People differ in the frequency range to which their ears are tuned, but in general, young, healthy, human ears can detect vibrations as low as 20 Hz and as high as 20,000 Hz. Vibrations too low in frequency to be audible are called subsonic, those too high, ultrasonic. We may not hear extremely low frequencies as sound, but we can often feel them. The frequencies important in the speech signal are within the 100- to 5000-Hz range. Contrasting this frequency range with that used by bats which emit sound between 20,000 and 100,000 Hz, one can see that sound is used for different purposes. Human beings use sound to communicate thoughts and feelings, whereas bats use sound to locate insects for prey. Whether sound emission is used for localization or for communication, however, it is important that the frequency response of the auditory system be matched to the frequency characteristics of the sound-producing mechanism. Human vocal folds normally vibrate between 80 Hz and about 500 Hz during speaking situations, but some of the speech noises made in the mouth contain frequencies which extend to several thousand cycles per second. The human auditory system then is responsive to these frequencies of vibration.

Frequency relates directly to *pitch*. Pitch is a sensation. In general, when frequency of vibration is increased, we hear a rise in pitch, but when frequency is decreased, we hear a lowering of pitch. The relationship is not linear, however. A constant interval of frequency increase does not result in a constant change in pitch. Frequency is a fact of physics, an event which can be measured by instruments: the number of cycles in a specified time. Pitch, in contrast, is a psychological phenomenon. It is the way in which frequency changes are perceived by the listener. It can be measured only by asking listeners to make judgments.

The human auditory system is more responsive to some frequency changes than to others. In the low frequencies (below 1000 Hz) perceived pitch is fairly linear in its relationship to frequency, but as the frequencies get higher, it takes a larger change in frequency to effect a change in the sensation of pitch. The relationship between the physical property of frequency and the psychological sensation of pitch is illustrated in Figure 3.16. The units of frequency are cycles per second; the units of pitch are *mels*. Testing listeners at various frequencies, the pitch of a 1000 Hz tone is used as a reference and is arbitrarily called 1000 mels. Whatever frequency is judged to be half that pitch is called 500 mels, twice that pitch is called 2000 mels. The mel curve shown by the *solid line* in Figure 3.16 is the result of this scaling procedure.

It can be seen that the word frequency refers to cycles per second and the word pitch is reserved for the perception of frequency. The mel scale was plotted by having listeners judge the pitch of pure tones. What about complex tones? How do lis-

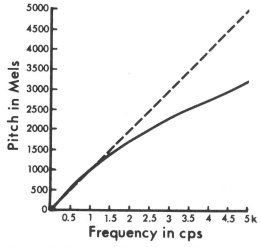

Figure 3.16. A replotting of the Stevens and Volkmann mel scale. The *solid line* indicates the way in which pitch (mels) increases with frequency in cycles per second (Hz). The *dashed line* shows the relationship if correlation were perfect. (Adapted from S. S. Stevens *et al.*: *Journal of the Acoustical Society of America. 8,* 1937.)

teners judge the pitch of a sound containing more than one frequency? The pitch of a complex periodic tone is judged by listeners to correspond to the fundamental frequency of the harmonic series. Surprisingly, the auditory system compensates for the loss of the lower harmonics and 'hears' the f_o even when it is absent. For example, a complex tone composed of the frequencies 600, 900, and 1200 Hz is judged to have a pitch of 300 Hz, because that is the largest divisor. Judgments of pitch for aperiodic sounds are more generally influenced by the center of the frequency band or the frequency at which the amplitude is highest.

THE DECIBEL: A MEASURE OF RELATIVE INTENSITY

We have referred to the fact that the amplitude of vibration, the extent of particle displacement, is an indication of the intensity or power of the sound. In order to describe the relative intensity of two sounds, we use a unit of measurement called a *decibel* (dB), literally one-tenth of a Bel, in honor of Alexander Graham Bell (1847–1922), the American inventor of the telephone and educator of the deaf. The decibel scale of intensity is an example of a logarithmic scale. In a *linear scale* such as a measuring stick, there is a zero, and each increment is equal to the next, so you can sum units by addition. A *logarithmic scale,* as you can see on the chart below, is based on "exponents" of a given number called the base. For decibels, the base is 10, and the scale is constructed with increments which are not equal but represent increasingly large differences.

Linear scale

1,000	
	>diff. = 1,000
2,000	
	>diff. = 1,000
3,000	
	>diff. = 1,000
4,000	

Logarithmic scale

$10^2 =$	100	
		>diff. = 900
$10^3 =$	1,000	
		>diff. = 9,000
$10^4 =$	10,000	
		>diff. = 90,000
$10^5 =$	100,000	

10 = base; 2, 3, 4, and 5 are logarithms

Why use a logarithmic scale for sound intensity? There are two reasons for this system. The first reason is that the human ear is sensitive to a large intensity range, as many as 10^{13} (10,000,000,000,000 or 10 trillion) units of intensity in a linear scale. That would be too many numbers to handle, but on a condensed logarithmic scale, the number is reduced to 130 decibels.

The second reason is that the logarithmic scale more nearly approximates the way human ears judge loudness. It has been known since the 19th century writings of German scientists Ernst Weber (1834) and Gustav Fechner (1860) that equal increases in sensation (in this case loudness) are obtained by multiplying the stimulus by a constant factor. This principle does not work for all the intensities of sound to which the ear is sensitive, but is accurate enough to be practical. Each step in the decibel scale, then, corresponds roughly to an equal growth in loudness, even though the sound power differences are large.

The power of a sound is proportional to the square of the pressure, or to put it in reverse, the pressure is the square root of the power. Just as an inch or a centimeter is a unit of measurement used for length, the units of measurement used in acoustics are *watts* (for power) and *dynes* (for pressure). In physics, *intensity level* refers to the power of the signal as measured in watts per square centimeter. In the acoustics of speech and hearing, *sound pressure level* has customarily been used as the measure, and the pressure unit is dynes per square centimeter. Either power or pressure units can be converted to decibels.

You may have heard that a certain airplane takes off with a sound level of 100 dB *SPL* (sound pressure level), or that the average intensity of conversational speech is about 60 dB *IL* (intensity level). The first measure used pressure as the reference; the sound pressure of the airplane noise was 10^5 more than a barely audible sound (100,000:1 ratio). Had it been measured by using a power reference, it would still be 100 dB, but the intensity ratio would be 10^{10} to 1 (10,000,000,000:1), since the power increments are the square of the pressure increments. The second measure, the speech intensity, used a power reference. This relationship between power and pressure makes it necessary to use separate formulas to compute the decibel, one when using a power reference (watts) and the other for use with a pressure reference (dynes).

The important thing to remember about measuring the intensity of a sound is that there is always a standard. The decibel is a unit of intensity which is really a ratio, a comparison of the sound in question with a reference sound. The power reference is 10^{-16} watts/cm^2 and the pressure reference is 0.0002 dynes/cm^2, both signals at the threshold of human audibility. The formula for decibels using an intensity (power) reference is:

$$dB\ IL = 10\left(log_{10}\ \frac{W_o}{W_r}\right)$$

where IL = intensity level (reference is 10^{-16} watts/cm^2), W_o = output power in watts (power of signal to be measured), W_r = reference power in watts (power of the reference signal 10^{-16} watts/cm^2), and log_{10} = logarithm of the ratio W_o/W_r. The base is 10. The log is the exponent. For example, if the ratio were 100:1, the log would be 2 because $10^2 = 100$ and the exponent is 2.

The formula used to compute decibels using a sound pressure level reference for comparison is:

$$dB\ SPL = 20\left(log_{10}\ \frac{P_o}{P_r}\right)$$

In this formula, P_o represents the pressure you wish to measure (output) and P_r the pressure you use for comparison (reference). For example, if the sound of interest

were to have a pressure level of 20 dynes/cm^2, that sound would be 100,000 times the reference pressure.

$$\frac{20\ dynes/cm^2}{0.0002\ dynes/cm^2} = \frac{100,000}{1}$$

Since the ratio is 100,000:1, the logarithm to the base 10 of the ratio is 5. (Simply count the zeros.) The formula instructs us to multiply the log of the ratio by 20. Since $20 \times 5 = 100$, the answer is 100 dB SPL.

Remember that the $\boxed{log_{10}\ \dfrac{P_o}{P_r}}$ is one small number, the exponent, in this case, 5.

To take another example, if a sound with 10 times as much pressure as a barely audible sound were to be measured, how many decibels SPL would it be? The log of 10 is 1 (only one zero) and $20 \times 1 = 20$; therefore, it would be 20 dB SPL.

You should also be able to compute the ratio or the pressure in dynes when given the decibels. A 60 dB SPL conversation, as an instance, is how much more sound pressure than what is barely audible?

$$60\ dB\ SPL = 20x\ \left(x = log_{10}\ \frac{P_o}{P_r}\right)$$

$$x = 3$$

Since the log is 3, the ratio must be 1,000:1 (3 zeros).

So the sound of an average conversation is 1,000 times more sound pressure than barely audible sound pressure, or to be exact, 0.2 dynes/cm^2.

$$\begin{array}{r} 0.0002\ dynes/cm^2 \\ \times\ 1,000 \\ \hline 0.2000\ dynes/cm^2 \end{array}$$

What does 0 dB mean? If a sound is measured to have an intensity of 0 dB, does it mean that there is no sound? Not at all.

$$dB = 20\ (log\ of\ the\ ratio)$$
$$0\ dB = 20 \times 0$$

The log is zero. Since there are no zeros in the ratio, the ratio is equal to 1, which means that the output is equal to the reference pressure.

Ratio	Log	dB (20 × log of ratio)
1,000:1	3	60 dB SPL
100:1	2	40 dB SPL
10:1	1	20 dB SPL
1:1	0	0 dB SPL

All sound within a few feet of the listener:

0 dB	Threshold of hearing
20 dB	Rustling of leaves
30 dB	Whisper (3 feet)
35 dB	Residential area at night
45 dB	Typewriter
60 dB	Conversation
75 dB	Shouting, singing (3 feet)
100 dB	Approaching subway train, for people on waiting platform
120 dB	Jet airplane, for man on runway Amplified rock music (6 feet)
130 dB	Painfully loud sound

Thus, it can be seen that 0 dB means the sound in question is equal to the reference sound rather than silence.

The sound pressure levels of certain familiar sounds are approximated below:

INTENSITY AND LOUDNESS

Intensity or sound pressure, like frequency, is a physical property of the acoustic signal which can be measured by an instrument called a sound level meter. The intensity of a signal is directly related to its loudness. As intensity is increased, the sound is judged by listeners to be louder. *Loudness* is the subjective, psychological sensation of judged intensity. Like frequency and pitch, intensity and loudness are not in perfect correlation. Again,

the human auditory system acts on the signal, so that sensations of equal loudness for different frequencies require very different intensities.

A *phon* is a unit of equal loudness. Figure 3.17 is a plot of equal loudness levels at different frequencies. The *heavy line* is the important *absolute threshold of audibility*, the intensities at each frequency which are just audible by young, healthy ears. It is clear that the human auditory

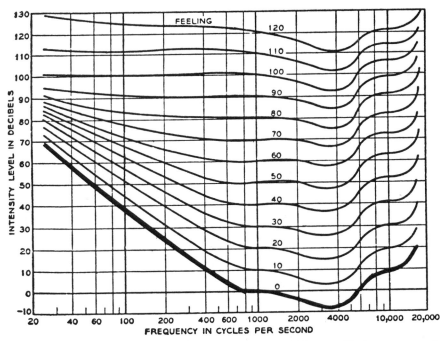

Figure 3.17. Loudness level contours derived by Fletcher and Munson. Each *curve* sounds equally loud at all frequencies. The loudness in phons is indicated on each curve. (Adapted from H. Fletcher and W. A. Munson: *Journal of the Acoustical Society of America. 5,* 1933.)

system is designed to receive the middle frequencies (1000 to 6000 Hz) with much less intensity than is needed for the extremely low and high frequencies. This information is used in the specifications for manufacturing audiometers: instruments used to test hearing, to compare a person's threshold with that of young healthy ears. The zero setting on an audiometer is simply the *heavy line* in Figure 3.17 which is straightened out on the graph paper used to chart the test, the audiogram.

The *lighter lines* are the phon curves of equal loudness. The 20-phon line is equally loud at all frequencies to a 1000-Hz tone at 20 dB, whereas a 70-phon line is equal in loudness at all frequencies to a 1000-Hz tone at 70 dB. At low loudness levels, there is a large difference between the middle and the extreme frequencies in the amount of intensity needed to effect equal loudness judgments, but at higher loudness levels, the large intensity differences disappear.

When listeners are asked to judge relative loudness (half as loud, twice as loud) in a scaling procedure similar to that used to obtain the mel scale for pitch, the unit of loudness is called a *sone*, with 1 sone equal in loudness to a 1000-Hz tone at 40 dB. By this method, it can be determined that the sensation of loudness increases more slowly than the actual increase in intensity.

Physical properties	Psychological properties		
Frequency Hz	Pitch	Mel	(Scaling)
Intensity dB	Loudness	Sone	(Scaling)
		Phon	(Equal)

VELOCITY OF SOUND THROUGH SPACE

Velocity is simply speed in a certain direction. Light travels faster than sound or has greater velocity as we know from our experience with lightning and thunder. We see the flash before we hear the crash. At normal atmospheric conditions, sound travels through air at about:

344 meters per second

or

1130 feet per second

or

758 miles per hour

It travels much faster through liquids and the fastest along solids, because the elasticity and density of the medium affect the velocity of conduction. Velocity is independent of pressure as long as the temperature remains the same. A faint sound will travel just as fast as a loud sound. The soft sound will not travel as far due to the *Inverse Square Law* (intensity varies inversely as the square of the distance from the source), but it will travel as fast as a loud sound. Temperature does make a difference, however, and sounds will travel faster on a hot summer day than on a wintry day.

Velocity of particle movement must not be confused with velocity of sound wave propagation. Particles vibrating in SHM constantly change velocity, moving with maximum velocity over their resting places. Velocity of the sound wave moving through space, the speed with which the disturbance moves from one spot to another, is, by contrast, a constant (refer back to Fig. 3.8).

WAVELENGTH

The length of a sound wave is the distance in space which one cycle occupies. One can measure from any point in one cycle to the corresponding point in the next cycle. The symbol used to denote *wavelength* is the Greek letter lambda (λ). Figure 3.18 illustrates the wavelength of complex and pure tone signals.

Wavelength depends upon two factors, the frequency of the vibration and the velocity of sound wave propagation in the medium.

Observe wavelength changes by taking a small pan of water and dipping your finger into the water repeatedly, first at a slow frequency then at a higher frequency. Notice that the distance between the crests of the ripples in the lower frequency condition is greater than in the higher frequency condition. High frequency sounds occupy less space per cycle, have a shorter wavelength, than do low frequency sounds.

The second factor, that of the medium, is also important. We have seen that sound waves are conducted through solids at a higher velocity than through liquids, and through liquids at a higher velocity than through gases. Given that wavelength (λ) equals the constant velocity (c) divided by the frequency (f),

$$\lambda = \frac{c}{f}$$

a sound of a certain frequency would have a longer wavelength in water, for example, than in air.

Imagine the wavelength of certain familiar speech sounds. Say 'ah' at a comfortable pitch. If you are a woman, the fundamental frequency of that complex sound is likely to be around 200 Hz; if you are a man, around 100 Hz. The man's voice would have a 3-meter wavelength, whereas the woman's would be almost 2 meters. Each meter corresponds to some 3 inches more than a yard.

$\lambda = \dfrac{c}{f}$

$\lambda = \dfrac{344 \text{ meters per second}}{200 \text{ Hz}}$ = about 1.75 meters or 67 inches (5'7")

$\lambda = \dfrac{344 \text{ meters per second}}{100 \text{ Hz}}$ = 3.4 meters or 11'3"

When saying 'sh' to quiet someone, the high energy frequencies are closer to 2500 Hz, which would make a wavelength as short as 14 cm (between 5 and 6 inches).

$$\lambda = \frac{34,400 \text{ cm per sec}}{2,500 \text{ Hz}} = \sim 14 \text{ cm}$$

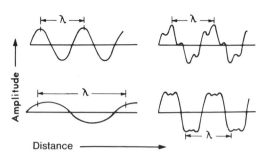

Figure 3.18. Wavelength (λ) is the distance occupied by one complete cycle of vibration.

Sounds of high frequency and short wavelengths are more directional than low frequency sounds. Longer wavelengths radiate more and go around corners more easily.

That explains why bats emit such high frequency sounds (ultrasonic). The bat is interested in catching small flying insects. The sound from the bat reflects from any object in its path with more intensity than from neighboring objects, thereby localizing the prey for the kill. Only a signal with short wavelength and little radiation could localize such a small target. Bats, even if blind, can analyze the reflected sound for information on size and distance of either obstacles or food.

Variation in wavelength also explains why we often hear voices in an adjoining room quite clearly but fail to understand what they are saying. Speech contains both high and low frequency components. The low frequency sounds with longer wavelengths diffract around the wall and enter through the door. The higher frequency components of speech having shorter, more directional wavelengths, radiate less widely and are largely lost. Receiving only part of the signal, we listeners cannot understand what was said.

RESONANCE

If you have ever pushed a child in a swing, you know that you must time each push to coincide with the harmonic motion of the swing. If you were to run forward and push the swing at some central point in its swing toward you, instead of waiting for it to reach the maximum distance in its excursion, you would simply shorten its arc. It is also possible that you would be knocked to the ground. The frequency with which the swing completes a cycle during 1 second is the *natural resonant frequency* of the swing. This frequency is independent of amplitude. Push a child with less force, then with more force; the arcs will vary in amplitude, but the frequency will be the same. What if the swing broke and a piece of weak rope were removed from each side, making the swing shorter? Would the natural resonant frequency of the shorter-roped swing be the same as the swing with longer ropes? We know by experience that this new swing would have a higher natural frequency (more cycles per second) than the previous swing. In general, smaller things vibrate at higher frequencies than larger versions of the same thing.

Everything which vibrates has a natural frequency, or in many cases, frequencies of vibration when left to vibrate freely (*free vibration*). A machine could be attached to the swing forcing it to vibrate at any frequency (*forced vibration*), but even under these circumstances, the swing would vibrate at maximum amplitude only if forced to vibrate at its own natural resonant frequency. The *resonance* of a vibrator depends upon its physical charac-

teristics as we know from the design of tuning forks.

Everything vibrates and can therefore resonate, whether audible or not. A *resonator* is something which is set into vibration by the action of another vibration. Resonators do not initiate the sound energy. A sound is created elsewhere and the resonator will vibrate in sympathy with it if the sound from the source is at or near the resonant frequencies of the resonator.

Take the damper off a piano string by pressing the key gently down so there is no sound, then loudly sing the note which corresponds with the depressed key, and you will demonstrate sympathetic resonance for yourself as the string vibrates in response to your singing. The piano string, the swing, and the tuning fork are examples of mechanical resonators. An *acoustic resonator* is something which contains air. A body of air will resonate in response to sound containing frequencies which match the natural resonant frequencies of the volume of air. We can understand this

¼ WAVE RESONATOR

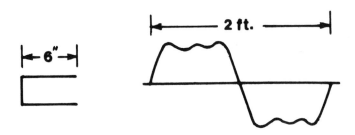

Given tube 6" long
open at one end

$$f = \frac{c \text{ (constant velocity)}}{4 \cdot 1 \text{ (length of tube)}}$$

$$f = \frac{1130 \text{ ft}}{4 \cdot 1/2 \text{ ft}} = \frac{1130}{2} = 565 \text{ Hz}$$

$$3f = 1695 \text{ Hz}$$
$$5f = 2825 \text{ Hz}$$

Figure 3.19. A tube open at one end, closed at the other, will resonate at odd multiples of its lowest resonant frequency. The lowest frequency has a wavelength that is 4 times the length of the tube.

principle by thinking about the construction of musical instruments. It is not enough to have strings mounted on a board to achieve the quality of sound associated with a violin, a cello, or a guitar. Although the energy for the sound is provided by a bow or a pluck, and the source of the sound is in the vibration of the strings, the air-filled boxes behind the strings also serve to resonate certain frequencies which make the instruments distinctive. A small volume of air will naturally vibrate at higher frequencies than a large volume of air.

As you add water to a bottle, notice the sound increases in frequency as the air space gets smaller. If the frequency of the air volume at the top of the bottle were matched to the frequency of a tuning fork by adding water until they would correspond, one could tilt the bottle, altering the shape of the air container, but the air would continue to resonate in response to the tuning fork. The shape of the air cavity is not as important as the volume.

An acoustic resonator which relates to speech because it is analogous to the resonance of the vocal tract and the ear canal is an air-filled tube which is open at one end and closed at the other end. The air within the tube vibrates at certain frequencies depending on the length of the tube. The wavelength of the fundamental resonance in such a tube is 4 times the length of the tube. To put it another way, only $\frac{1}{4}$ of the wave can fit into the tube at any one pass. Figure 3.19 contrasts the resonator length with the waveform of the resonant frequencies. Quarter wave resonators only vibrate at odd multiples of the fundamental due to the closure at one end. These resonators will be discussed more fully in later chapters.

Sharply tuned resonators, those which vibrate at a narrow band of frequencies, continue to vibrate longer with less damping than a broadly tuned resonator which vibrates at many frequencies but builds and dies out quickly. A tuning fork or a narrowly tuned musical instrument will vibrate longer than, for example, a door will vibrate when you knock on it.

ACOUSTICS AND SPEECH

This chapter will serve as a foundation for much of the rest of the book. The marvel of speech is the way in which the distinctive sounds which can be produced by the human vocal folds and vocal tract are varied and combined with one another to serve as a code for communication. In the next chapter, the general way in which humans make these significant sounds will be outlined.

BIBLIOGRAPHY

Textbook Treatments of Acoustics:

Benade, A. H., *Horns, Strings, and Harmony.* Anchor Books, Garden City, N. Y.: Doubleday, 1960.

Denes, P., and Pinson, E., *The Speech Chain.* New York: Doubleday, 1973.

Ladefoged, P., *Elements of Acoustic Phonetics.* Chicago: University of Chicago Press, 1962.

Pierce, J. R., and David, E. E., Jr., *Man's World of Sound.* Garden City, N. Y.: Doubleday, 1958.

Stephens, R. W. B., and Bate, A. E., *Acoustics and Vibrational Physics.* New York: St. Martin's Press, 1966.

Van Bergeijk, W. A., Pierce, J. R., and David E. E., Jr., *Waves and the Ear.* Anchor Books, Garden City, N. Y.: Doubleday, 1960.

Wood, A., *Acoustics.* New York: Dover Publications, 1966.

Classic References:

Fletcher, H., and Munson, W. A., Loudness, Its Definition, Measurement, and Calculation. *J. Acoust. Soc. Am. V,* 1933, 82–108.

Fourier, J. B. J., *Théorie Analytique de la Chaleur.* Paris: F. Didot, 1822.

Rayleigh, J. W. S., *Theory of Sound.* New York: Dover Publications, 1960. First published by Macmillan in London, 1878.

Stevens, S. S., Volkmann, J., and Newman, E. B., A Scale for the Measurement of the Psychological Magnitude Pitch. *J. Acoust. Soc. Am. 8,* 1937, 185–190.

CHAPTER 4

Speech Production

The advice of the Duchess to Alice is well founded. Under ordinary circumstances, a speaker is conscious of the meaning of his message, of his search for appropriate words to express that meaning, and perhaps of his feelings about the topic or listener. Only under circumstances of change or novelty, attempting new words, or speaking with a new dental appliance, does the speaker become conscious of the processes involved in sound production. Beginning students of phonetics are surprised at their inability to describe what they are doing when they produce certain speech sounds. The fact that skilled speakers can effortlessly produce such a complex and rapidly changing acoustic stream beguiles some students into the assumption that the study of phonetics must be equally effortless. If speech is so easy, should not the study of speech be easy?

The higher we look into the nervous system, however, the less we know. We know a substantial amount about the sounds which emerge from the mouth of a speaker, and from acoustic analyses, have derived information on production. We know something about the movements of parts of the speaker's body, and we are currently learning about the muscle activity accompanying some of these movements. We can infer from information on muscle activity something about the nerve impulses which fire the muscles. We know little, however, about the organization and coordination of these impulses in the brain and even less about how these impulse

patterns are derived from stored linguistic knowledge and ultimately from thought.

We will not attempt to explore the mysterious realms of decision-making, conceptualization, memory, nor the many linguistic choices which are made either by volition or by habit as a speaker prepares to say something: choices in semantics, syntax, and phonology. Even though we are restricting ourselves in considering the act of speech with its linguistic head severed from it, we have a wealth of topics to consider: the neurophysiology of speech production, the physics of respiration for speech, the dynamics of phonation, the articulation of speech sounds, the resonance of the vocal tract, the feedback mechanisms used to monitor speech, and some of the theories of how the speech production mechanisms work. In all sections of this chapter, the emphasis will be on physiology, the dynamics of speech production. Anatomy will be kept to a minimum; only the most important nerves, muscles, cartilages, and bones will be mentioned.

The goal in producing speech is to make certain meaningful sound combinations. It is an acoustic goal. To effect that goal, the speaker uses air to make a variety of sounds (in English, some 40 different sounds), which are further modified when they are produced in context with one another. The sounds are produced by regulating the airstream as it passes from the lungs to the atmosphere. This regulation is brought about by movements of jaw, lips, tongue, soft palate, pharynx and vocal folds to alter the shape of the vocal tract. The movements are mainly the result of muscle contractions, which are due to nerve impulses, and of course the whole process is controlled in the nervous system. Figure 4.1 shows the flow of motor activity for speech in its several states.

NEUROPHYSIOLOGY OF SPEECH

The brain and the nerve fibers which extend from the brain are constantly active. As long as there is life, nervous impulses are fired throughout the system. Unlike a computer, it is always turned on. When a signal, such as a sound, is received by the brain, the activity in certain areas sharply increases. There is increased activity, too, as a person prepares to do something. The nervous system is a network of specialized cells called *neurons*. The neurons are supported by other protective and nourishing cells and are oxygenated by a generous blood supply.

The nervous system can be divided into the central nervous system (*CNS*), consisting of the brain and the spinal cord, and the peripheral nervous system (*PNS*), consisting of the nerves which emerge from the base of the brain (*cranial nerves*) to serve the head region and from the spinal cord (*spinal nerves*) to serve the rest of the body. (See Fig. 4.2.) Some neurons are motor or *efferent*, which means that they carry impulses from the central nervous system to the periphery. Other neurons are sensory or *afferent*, which means they carry information from the peripheral sense organs to the CNS. For example, when a person decides to close his lips, efferent neurons, or *motor* nerve fibers carry the impulses to the lip muscles which contract. When the lips close, touch receptors near the surface of the skin are stimulated carrying *sensory* information that the lips have touched along afferent neurons to the brain. The courses of nerve fibers through the spinal cord and throughout the body are linear in direction and can therefore be classified as afferent or efferent, but the nerve fibers which make up the higher centers of the brain itself are interconnected in a compact, three-dimensional mesh and are not easily classified as either afferent or efferent. The peripheral nervous supply is best left for later discussion, along with the muscles and receptors which it serves, but the role of the CNS in speech production should be mentioned first, since it is the brain which initiates and controls all of the motor events which take place during speech.

The Brain

The brain is formed by a central *brain stem* on top of the spinal cord with the *cerebellum* positioned behind it and two *cerebral hemispheres,* which partly obscure the brain stem, on top. The higher brain stem includes the *thalamus* and the *basal ganglia.* The lower brain stem includes the *pons* and *medulla oblongata.* The medulla narrows into the spinal cord. Figure 4.3 is a lateral view of one hemisphere, showing the position of the brain stem underneath the cover of the cerebrum. The human brain weighs approximately 1.5 kg (kilograms) or about 3 pounds. The surface of the cerebrum called the *cortex* is made up of billions of cell bodies of individual nerve cells. It is the general function of nerve cells, or neurons, to which we now turn our attention.

The Neuron

Neurons assume many shapes and lengths, but they always have a cell body and extensions which receive and transmit impulses. Each neuron leads its own independent biological life and upon adequate stimulation, generates its own elec-

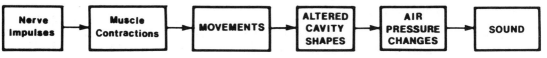

Figure 4.1. The chain of events leading to speech sound production.

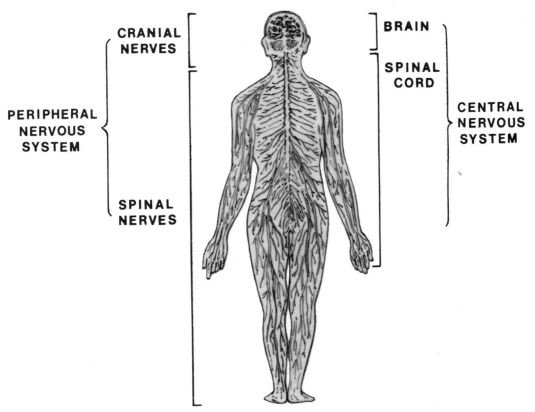

Figure 4.2. The divisions of the nervous system.

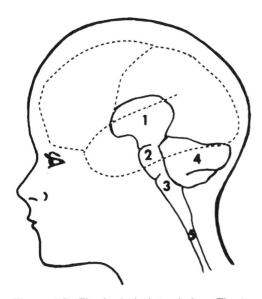

Figure 4.3. The brain in lateral view. The two cerebral hemispheres are shown as *dotted structures* lying over the higher brain stem (*1*), pons (*2*), cerebellum (*4*), and medulla (*3*). The medulla narrows into the spinal cord (*5*).

trical activity. A type of neuron is illustrated in Figure 4.4. Nervous activity approaches the cell body of the neuron via *dendrites*. The impulse leaves the cell body by way of the *axon*. The nervous system works under an *all-or-none principle* of firing. In order for an impulse to be conducted along an axon, the first part of the axon beyond the cell body must be stimulated to its threshold. If the stimulation falls below the particular threshold for that neuron, the axon does not fire at all. If it reaches its threshold, however, the axon fires at full capacity no matter how high the stimulation. (See Fig. 4.5.) A strong group of impulses arriving at the cell body can increase frequency of impulses but not the amplitude of each impulse. Within the nervous system, intensity is coded in terms of frequency.

If a neuron fires, what actually happens? The excitation is conducted along the axon leading from the cell body. The critical change which takes place at the

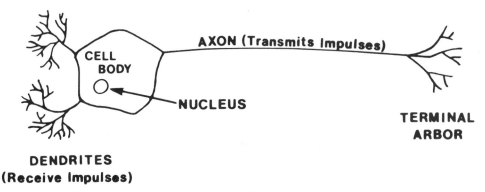

Figure 4.4. A single neuron. Impulses travel from *left* to *right*.

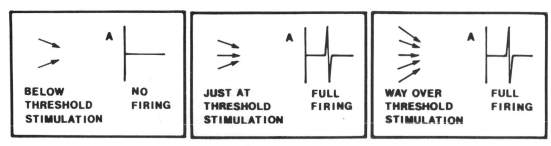

Figure 4.5. The all-or-none principle. The three panels show stimulation of a nerve at below threshold, threshold, and above threshold levels. If the neuron fires, it fires with a fixed amplitude (*A*).

point of excitation is an increased permeability of the membrane which encases the axon or nerve fiber. At the point of stimulation, a momentary increase in permeability of the membrane allows an exchange of ions which depolarizes the nerve fiber for an instant.

Imagine a cross-section of an axon. The interior of the nerve fiber is filled with a jelly-like substance rich in potassium ions (K^+). Outside the membrane which sheaths the axon is a seawater-like fluid rich in sodium ions (Na^+). Most of the sodium ions are excluded from the axon by the nature of the membrane itself and by complex metabolic interactions. Potassium ions, however, are free to cross the membrane.

At rest, the interior of the nerve fiber is negative by some 50–80 millivolts (mV; thousandths of a volt) relative to the electrical charge outside the neuron.

When a stimulation which reaches the threshold for that neuron arrives, the membrane surrounding the axon becomes more permeable allowing the sodium ions

(Na^+) to enter. Potassium ions (K^+) then start to leave the neuron, and for that instant, about 0.5 msec, the interior of the axon is more positively charged than the exterior by about 30–50 mV. Immediately after the moment of firing, the chemistry of the neuron is restored to that of the resting state until another nerve impulse comes along. Figure 4.6 schematizes this electrochemical event.

A particular point along the axon is depolarized which stimulates the next point and the next. Once fired, the neuron is self-stimulating. It is interesting to note that although the nervous impulse travels along the nerve fiber longitudinally, the actual movement of particles is across the membrane and therefore is perpendicular to the nerve fiber (Fig. 4.7).

The velocity with which each impulse travels along the nerve fibers depends upon the diameter of the nerve fiber and upon its myelinization. Conduction velocity in mammals is proportional to about 6 times the diameter of the neuron. For example a small neuron of 10 μ (microns)

AT REST   AT MOMENT OF FIRING   AFTER FIRING

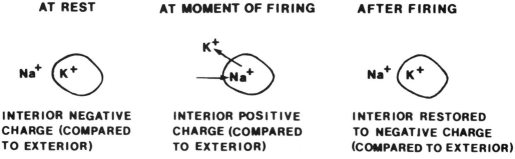

INTERIOR NEGATIVE
CHARGE (COMPARED
TO EXTERIOR)

INTERIOR POSITIVE
CHARGE (COMPARED
TO EXTERIOR)

INTERIOR RESTORED
TO NEGATIVE CHARGE
(COMPARED TO EXTERIOR)

Figure 4.6. Electrochemical events at the cell membrane before, during, and after a nerve cell fires.

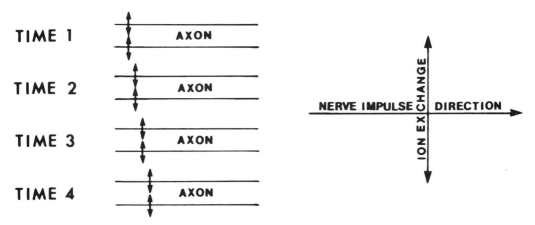

Figure 4.7. The transmission of an impulse along an axon. On the *left,* the position of ion exchange is shown at successive moments in time. The nerve impulse travels in a direction perpendicular to the direction of ion exchange, as shown on the *right.*

diameter will conduct an impulse approximately 60 meters per second, whereas a 20-μ neuron, the largest in the human body, will conduct at a velocity of about 120 meters per second. Another factor which increases the rate of nerve impulse conduction is the presence of *myelin* encasing most human nerve fibers. Its fatty whitish appearance accounts for the term *white matter* for parts of the nervous system. The myelin coats each axon, with interruptions spaced along the neuron exposing the axon. The nervous impulse skips along from one exposed area to the next at high velocities. The cell bodies, by contrast, are not coated with a myelin sheath and are therefore referred to as *gray matter.*

Conduction from one neuron to another involves the release of chemicals at the *synapse,* the juncture of the neurons. The chemicals act to bridge the small space between nerve fibers. There are approximately 1,000 billion such synapses in the human brain (Fig. 4.8).

Some chemicals facilitate the firing of the next cell, while other chemicals inhibit the firing of the next cell. Many neurons can converge to fire a single neuron, and conversely a single neuron can stimulate many other neurons simultaneously. This arrangement of convergences and divergences of neurons combines with the chemical variations which can inhibit or facilitate synaptic transmission to account for the enormous flexibility of the nervous system. A myriad of different three-dimensional patterns of nerve fiber networks can be established in both the central nervous system and the peripheral nervous system.

A bundle of neuron fibers is called a *nerve.* Each neuron fires independently,

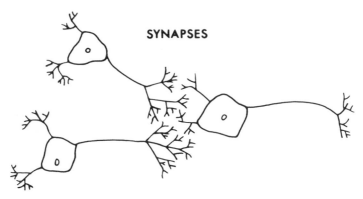

SYNAPSES

Figure 4.8. Schematic drawing of three neurons. The two at the *left* synapse with the one at the *right*. Impulses travel from *left* to *right*.

but a nerve often serves a particular area of the body. The auditory nerve, as an instance, is a bundle of some 30,000 fibers, most of them sensory, carrying information from the inner ear to the brain.

Frequency of neuronal firing is limited by the fact that an axon must restore itself after each firing to its state of rest before it can fire again. Some neurons can fire about 200 times a second, or as in some highly specialized nerve cells, over 1,000 times a second.

With this basic review of nerve fiber function as a background, let us consider what is known about how the central nervous system controls spoken language.

Central Nervous System Control of Speaking

Although we are far from understanding the nerve networks which may govern speech, we have obtained information about certain general areas of the brain which are related to the production of speech. It has long been known that when a gunshot wound or other trauma is inflicted on the brain, or when a person suffers a stroke—damage to the cells of the brain caused by a ruptured blood vessel or a blood clot (*cerebral vascular accident* or *CVA*)—language disturbances often result. The language impairment, termed *aphasia,* can take many forms: disabilities in forming what to say, in comprehension, in articulation, in writing, in reading, in naming things, or in multiple combinations of these disabilities in varying degrees of severity.

Long known, too, is the fact that the left cerebral hemisphere of the brain controls movement and sensation on the right side of the body, whereas the right cerebral hemisphere controls movement and sensation on the left side of the body. Thus, a victim of a CVA or stroke in the right hemisphere might be partially or completely paralyzed on his left side depending upon the location and extent of the brain damage.

It was as recently as 1861, however, that the Parisian neurosurgeon and anthropologist, Paul Broca, discovered by autopsy of a formerly aphasic patient that speech production was controlled in the third convolution of the *frontal lobe* of the left cerebral hemisphere. (See Fig. 4.9.) Not long after, in 1874, Carl Wernicke localized the understanding of speech in the first convolution of the left *temporal lobe.* Such strict localization of function has given way in recent times to a view of the brain as more flexible in its assignment of function. Neurologists agree, however, that the left hemisphere is dominant for the control of speech in almost all right-handed people and the majority of left-handed people, that the critical area of the cerebrum for language in general is the area around the temporal-parietal juncture, and that, although the exact site known as Broca's area can, in some cases, be removed without affecting speech, the production of the motor impulses for speech muscles involves some portion of the posterior inferior area of the left frontal lobe.

Broca and Wernicke performed autopsies on a few patients to develop and sub-

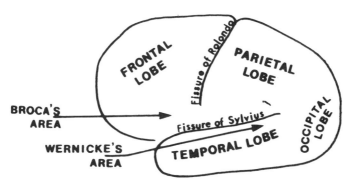

Figure 4.9. Lateral view of the cerebral cortex with the major divisions marked. The lateral surface of the cortex is divided into four lobes; the frontal, parietal, temporal, and occipital. The Fissure of Rolando divides the frontal lobe from the parietal, while the Fissure of Sylvius separates the temporal lobe from them. The areas believed by Broca and Wernicke to be implicated in speech production and speech understanding are indicated.

stantiate their theories, but their theories have been confirmed in part and the important areas of the cerebral cortex for speech have been further delineated by Wilder Penfield, a neurosurgeon in Montreal, using an entirely different approach. While treating epilepsy by surgical methods, Penfield and Lamar Roberts, Penfield's colleague and former student, stimulated the exposed areas of the brains of over 70 patients, in order to map the cortex before surgery. The stimulations were used to locate the areas contributing to the epileptic seizures, but as a by-product, the surgeons learned a great deal about brain function.

Since the brain contains no pain receptors, electrical stimulation can be conducted without general anesthesia, permitting patients to be fully conscious and to speak. A small current was applied via a fine wire touching the exposed cortical cells at many locations. The patient would respond by a muscle contraction at one location, by reporting a tingling sensation at another location, by vocalizing, by reexperiencing auditory and visual events of the past, or by sudden inability to speak. Locations for each response were numbered by dropping tiny pieces of paper on the site and the numbered cortex was photographed. Figure 4.10A shows a photograph of a mapped cortex with the positive responses to each stimulation numbered. The schematic drawing *below* (Fig. 4.10B) indicates the area in relation to the entire side of the cerebrum.

A glance at Figure 4.9 or 4.10B shows the *Fissure of Rolando* creating a vertical division between the frontal and *parietal lobes*. Stimulations to the left of this fissure, when applied to the posterior portion of the frontal lobe, usually resulted in motor responses: muscle contractions and movements. This area is referred to as the motor strip, although a few of the responses were sensory. To the right of the Rolandic fissure, almost all of the responses to stimulation were sensory. In both motor and sensory strips of the cortex, the body is represented upside down as illustrated in a cross-section of the motor strip in the right hemisphere (Fig. 4.11). Notice the way in which the motor responses of the toes and lower limbs are represented at the top of the cortex, whereas the motor responses of the head are represented on the inferior surface of the frontal lobe. Remarkable is the extent of cortical representation assigned to the lips, tongue, jaw, and laryngeal mechanism in both the motor and sensory areas of the cerebrum. Along with the hand, the body parts implicated in speech have the highest representation of associated gray matter along the motor and sensory strips of both cerebral hemispheres. It is as if most of the rest of the body were meant to nourish and transport the head and hands, which act upon and receive information from the environment.

Although some of the strictly motor and sensory aspects of speech production mechanisms seem to be controlled from

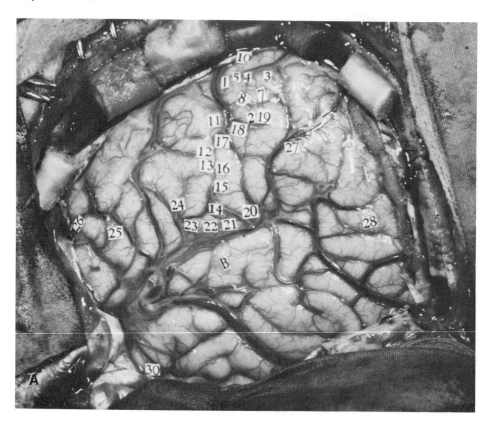

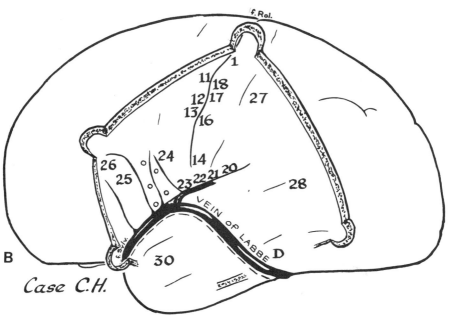

Figure 4.10. (*A*) Photograph of the left cortical surface of Case CH after speech mapping. *Numbers* indicate points stimulated. (*B*) Penfield's drawing of Case CH on a standard chart. Aphasia (aphasic arrest) was produced by the stimulating electrode placed at *Points 26, 27,* and *28.* Anarthria (motor speech arrest) was produced at *Points 23* and *24.* (From Wilder Penfield and Lamar Roberts: *Speech and Brain-Mechanisms,* © 1959 by Princeton University Press. Reprinted by permission of Princeton University Press.)

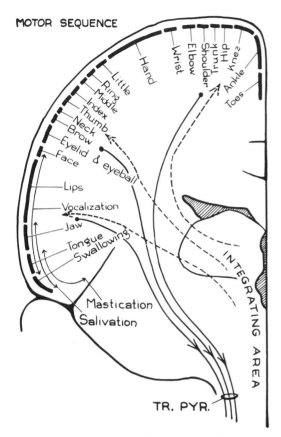

MOTOR SEQUENCE

TR. PYR.

INTEGRATING AREA

Figure 4.11. Cross-section through the motor strip of the right hemisphere, showing the location of response to electrical stimulation. *TR. PYR.* refers to the pyramidal tract. (From Wilder Penfield and Lamar Roberts: *Speech and Brain-Mechanisms,* © 1959 Princeton University Press. Reprinted by permission of Princeton University Press.)

both hemispheres, the overall control of organized spoken language resides in one hemisphere, usually the left. When Penfield stimulated certain regions of the cortex, patients were unable to name pictures or answer questions. At other sites, they spoke but with slurred articulation. It was possible, upon a single stimulation in the temporal-parietal region to elicit a sequential auditory and visual experience. One patient reported that she was in her kitchen and could hear the sounds of the neighborhood outside. It was more than a memory of an event. The subject relived and reheard the event while simultaneously being conscious of being in Montreal with Dr. Penfield. These experiences

could, on occasion, be elicited several times by consecutive stimulation. Another stimulation in the temporal-parietal region interrupted the naming of pictures. When a picture of a butterfly was shown to the subject, he could not elicit its name. After the stimulation stopped, the patient reported that when he failed to recall 'butterfly,' he tried to elicit the word for 'moth' but could not recall that word either.

Figure 4.12 summarizes the areas found by Penfield and Roberts to be important for speech based upon stimulation evidence. The anterior area in the lower frontal lobe coincides with Broca's area and stimulation here most often resulted in slurred speech or temporary *dysarthria*. The posterior area is large, including part of the temporal lobe, an extension of the area known as Wernicke's area, and part of the parietal lobe. Penfield considers this region to be most critical for language and speech. Stimulations in this region not only produced sequential experiences of past events but would interrupt the ability to use language. The patient sometimes could not say what he wanted to say or failed to understand what was spoken to him, thus simulating aphasia. The superior speech cortex was considered to be least important but supplemental to the motor area. It should be noted that although three general areas could be indicated, the functions of the areas were not as discrete as Penfield and Roberts had expected. They attribute the overlaps to subcortical connections among the areas. They were careful to point out that an electrical stimulus would disrupt whole systems and networks, implicating nerve cells far from the site of the stimulating electrode.

The Penfield and Roberts evidence is rich in implications for us about the central nervous system control of speech, of language, of sequential memory, and even of thought. It is worth our attention that the simple responses of vocalization or movement of speech muscles were bilaterally induced, whereas the more complex responses of recounting experiences or aphasic interruptions of speech were lateralized to one side of the brain. No stimulation resulted in a spoken word. At no point did a stimulation result in the patient involuntarily saying something like 'chair.'

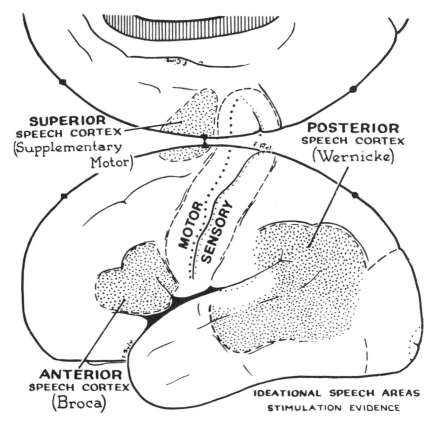

SUPERIOR
SPEECH CORTEX
(Supplementary
Motor)

POSTERIOR
SPEECH CORTEX
(Wernicke)

MOTOR
SENSORY

ANTERIOR
SPEECH CORTEX
(Broca)

IDEATIONAL SPEECH AREAS
STIMULATION EVIDENCE

Figure 4.12. Summary map of the areas of the surface of the left cerebral hemisphere found by Penfield to be important for speech. The *lower drawing* shows the lateral surface, while the *upper drawing* shows the continuation of the areas on the medial cortical surface. (From Wilder Penfield and Lamar Roberts: *Speech and Brain Mechanisms,* © 1959 by Princeton University Press. Reprinted by permission of Princeton University Press.)

Speech involves simultaneous action in many parts of the brain and is apparently too complex to be elicited by a single stimulus, although its production can be interrupted.

With the knowledge that one hemisphere of the cerebrum is dominant for speech, the Montreal group developed what is known as the *Wada Test* to establish which side is dominant for a particular person. Physicians are reluctant to operate on the brain unless they know which areas control language. Medical decisions on the extent of the operation depend on assessing the relative importance of tumor removal and disrupting the patient's ability to communicate. A physician can remove more extensive tissue on the side of the cerebrum which is not dominant for speech.

To obtain this information, sodium amytal is injected into the carotid artery on one side of the neck at a time. The *carotid artery* conducts the blood supply to the brain, and the sodium amytal will produce a temporary effect upon the side in which it is injected. Normal function returns quickly, so there is little time for elaborate testing. The patient often lies upon a table with his arms extended toward the ceiling and his knees flexed. The effect of the injection is immediate and dramatic. The leg and the arm on the side opposite the affected cerebral hemisphere collapse. The patient is asked to count, to name pictures, and to answer questions. The whole procedure is then repeated on the other side. Usually, sodium amytal injection has a much more disruptive effect on speech and language for one side of the brain than for the other. Brenda Milner of McGill University in Montreal found that among 140 right-handed and 122 left-handed people, 96% of the right handers had speech represented on the left side of the brain, and 70% of the left handers also had left hemisphere dominance. When speech was represented bilaterally, as it was in a few subjects, naming was stronger on one side and the ability to order words on the other.

All of the evidence for lateralization of speech production, whether from the autopsies performed by Broca or Wernicke, from the electrical stimulation work by Penfield and Roberts, or from the sodium amytal test as described by Wada and Rasmussen, is taken from the cerebral hemispheres. Many neurophysiologists view the cerebrum as the source of voluntary motor activity. Penfield, in contrast, views the motor cortex as merely a platform at which voluntary motor impulses arrive, having originated in the higher brain stem. From the motor cortex, in any case, they course down the *pyramidal* (cortico-spinal) *tract* to the muscles. Damage or dysfunction at the cortical level can result in *spasticity,* often observed among victims of *cerebral palsy.* Muscles contract but fail to relax. Damage in the higher brain stem can result in uncontrolled addition of movement to voluntary acts (*athetosis*), another common symptom of cerebral palsy, or in the hypokinesis or rigidity common in Parkinson's disease. Overall damage or oxygen deprivation can result in *mental retardation* which decreases the level of language ability, among other things, according to the degree of the damage. More discrete CNS disorders can produce a variety of learning disabilities, such as the inability to attend to something, problems in reading (*dyslexia*), inability to attach meaning to the sound patterns of speech (*auditory agnosia*), various and complex disorders in language (*developmental aphasia*) or problems not only with language but with communication and human relationships in general (*autism*). When there is a lack of coordination and integration of movement, the disorder may reside in the cerebellum.

The cerebellum, posterior to and below the cerebrum, has long been known to coordinate the timing and regulation of complex skilled movements. John Eccles has made the study of the cerebellum a chief concern and proposes that the cerebellum has been programmed to execute automatically the most complex skilled tasks. He gives as an example the command to 'write your name.' The command originates, according to Eccles, in the cerebrum, while the cerebellum automatically controls the timing, intensity, and interaction of the multitude of muscle commands from the cerebrum. The muscles contract and relax in a set pattern without the need for the person's voluntary control over each segment of the signature. Motor impulses from the cerebrum are simultaneously relayed to the opposite lobe of the cerebellum. Within a few hundredths of a second, the cerebellum is thought to be directing the complex flow of impulses from the motor cortex, which it continues to do during the action. The cerebellum receives position and movement information from muscles and joints and has many connections with the spinal cord as well as the cerebrum. While Wilder Penfield would say that the command to write or speak originates in the higher brain stem rather than the cerebrum, as in Eccles' account, neurologists agree that the cerebrum, cerebellum, and basal ganglia interact in any skilled voluntary activity such as speaking, albeit in ways not yet understood.

Spoonerisms: Evidence for Preplanning

William A. Spooner, an English clergyman and dean of New College at Oxford at the turn of the century, is less famous for his lectures than for his humorous speech reversals. Instead of saying "You've missed my history lectures," he would say "You've hissed my mystery lectures," a confusion now known as a '*spoonerism.*' "*Work* is the curse of the *drink*ing class," he is reputed to have said. Word reversals and phoneme reversals do suggest that speakers hold a complete phrase in some stage of readiness for speech. Otherwise, the transposition of a word or sound from the end of the intended phrase to the beginning would not occur. Speech errors, and there are other kinds of error in addition to spoonerisms, reveal something about speech production. The chart in Table 4.1 lists examples of speech sound errors collected by Victoria Fromkin of UCLA. Notice that consonants and vowels are never interchanged, that the errors are always consistent with the rules of English (optimal is moptimal, never ngoptimal, because /ŋ/ in English never initiates a syllable), and that most errors involve the first syllable, often the first sound, of a word. Interesting, too, is the observation that the stress and intonation of the phrase or sentence remain constant in the face of word changes. In Fromkin's example "Seymour sliced the knife with the salami," the pitch rise and increased intensity which would have been vested in 'knife' in the intended sentence, were incorporated in the production of 'salami.' These errors serve to hint at neurophysiological mechanisms in speech production in the planning stages prior to the transmission of motor impulses to muscles. It is clear that speakers do not normally call forth and speak a sentence one word at a time. Let us consider how a phrase held in readiness for production would in general be made audible and then more specifically what physiological mechanisms would be recruited.

RESPIRATION

Modification of Airstream for Speech Sounds

Regardless of the forms that the planning stages for speech may take, the time must come to produce sounds. Turning our attention to this more accessible activity, let us consider first the general task confronting the speaker. All English speech sounds are the result of manipulation of air from the lungs. The speaker must produce a stream of exhaled air to manipulate and then proceed to manipulate it in ways which are audible to a listener.

While it is a tribute to man's ingenuity to detail the variety of sounds he produces

Table 4.1
Segmental Errors in Speech*

Errors	Examples	
Consonant errors		
Anticipation	A reading list	A leading list
	It's a real mystery	It's a meal mystery
Perseveration	Pulled a tantrum	Pulled a pantrum
	At the beginning of the turn	At the beginning of the burn
Reversals	Left hemisphere	Heft lemisphere
(Spoonerisms)	A two-pen set	A two-sen pet
Vowel errors		
Reversals	Feet moving	Fute meeving
	Fill the pool	Fool the pill
Other errors		
Addition	The optimal number	The moptimal number
Movement	Ice cream	Kise ream
Deletion	Chrysanthemum plants	Chrysanthemum p ants
Consonant	Speech production	Peach seduction
clusters	Damage claim	Clammage dame
split or moved		

* Segmental errors in speech can involve vowels as well as consonants. Some typical types of substitution of sounds are shown. Such errors provide evidence that the discrete phonetic segments posited by linguistic theory exist in the mental grammar of the speaker. Taken from V. A. Fromkin, Slips of the tongue. *Scientific American 229,* 1973, 114.

for the many speech systems used in the languages of the world, limits are clearly set by the speech mechanisms. The speaker only has a few movable parts with which to create sounds: the vocal folds, tongue, jaw, lips, and soft palate. There are only a few cavities to use as resonators: the mouth, pharynx, and nasal cavities being the primary ones. Yet speakers of the world use as phonemes (families of sounds which signal differences in meaning) a multitude of vocalized sounds, produced as the speakers vibrate their vocal folds, and create a large variety of vocal tract shapes to act as resonators, and a large number of noises, hisses, clicks, small explosions of air, grunts, and murmurs. A few sounds are produced on air intake rather than outflow, and in some languages, sounds which are otherwise identical are made distinctive by a change in relative pitch.

In English, there are approximately 40 phonemes. They are listed in Appendix 1. They are all created by making exhaled air audible. The two primary methods used for making the air audible are to *voice* and to create consonant noises. Voicing is the creation of a somewhat periodic sound wave by the rapid opening and closing of the vocal folds. The air from the lungs is thus chopped into tiny puffs of air which are audible. Consonant noise is created by the positioning of parts of the speech mechanism in such a way that aperiodic sounds are created in the vocal tract, mostly in the mouth or *oral cavity*. Both the sounds of voicing and the sounds of consonant noise are resonated in the *vocal tract*.

Say 'ah.' That is an example of a sound with voicing. All English vowels are voiced. The vocal folds are set into vibration producing the source of the sound which gets its characteristic 'ah' quality (as opposed to 'ee,' also voiced) by the acoustic resonance provided in this case by a large oral cavity and a relatively small pharyngeal cavity. Try the sounds 'sh' and 'k.' These sounds are examples of two different kinds of consonant noise. The source of these sounds is not at the vocal folds but in the oral cavity. The 'sh' noise is produced by forcing the airstream through a narrow constriction. The air is stopped completely for 'k,' so that it can be released suddenly to produce a transient burst of sound.

Finally, these two methods can be combined for speech sounds which are really a combination of periodic and aperiodic sound. Try prolonging 's' and then continue the noise but start voicing at the same time. Another speech sound is produced, 'z,' adding another variation in the manipulation of the airstream.

The speech production mechanisms can be likened to a peculiar musical instrument with a variable resonator, capable of producing sounds that are at one moment based on an oscillation and, at the next, on turbulence. The whole system is powered by the air from the lungs. Figure 4.13 diagrams the process.

Negative Pressure Breathing

Preparatory to exhaling air for the production of speech sounds, sufficient air must be inhaled. Under normal circum-

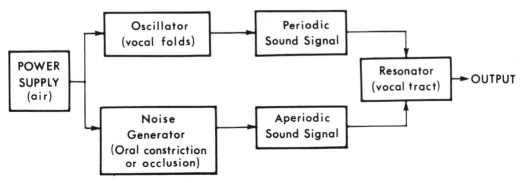

Figure 4.13. Block diagram of the speech production process. Air power is converted into a periodic or an aperiodic acoustic signal, which is modified by the vocal tract.

stances, air is taken into the lungs in much the same way it is taken into an accordion or bellows. Press the keys as hard as you will on an accordion, and no sound will emerge unless you have first expanded the cavity by elongating it. Enlarging the space inside the accordion reduces the air pressure inside the cavity in comparison with the outside atmospheric pressure. The molecules of air which occupied the accordion in its collapsed state have much more room in the enlarged body of the accordion, so that the air pressure is momentarily lowered. (Boyle's law: volume and pressure are inversely related.) This situation of lower pressure inside than outside the accordion does not last, however, because the accordion has an inlet for the outside air. Unequal pressures will always equalize themselves if given a chance; molecules will move from areas of greater density to areas of less density. Since the enlarged volume of air within the accordion is an area of low pressure relative to the outside air, air rushes into the accordion to maintain equalization as it is being enlarged.

Thus, enough pressure is built up in the accordion to enable the musician to play a musical phrase before more air must be taken in. The musician plays the accordion by compressing it, thereby decreasing its volume and increasing the pressure within.

Similarly, the bellows used to stimulate a fire is expanded manually, thus creating a negative pressure (compared to the outside pressure) which is quickly made equal by air coming in from the outside. When the pressures are equalized, compression of the bellows changes the pressure balance, forcing air out to fan the fire. (Boyle's law again: as the volume decreases, the pressure increases.) Figure 4.14 illustrates the volume-pressure relationship.

These examples of pressure-volume relationships are analogous to human breathing. People often think of the lungs as two balloons which are blown up with air as we breathe in. In automatic breathing, this is not the way it works, although that method is used by frogs and when humans receive mouth-to-mouth artificial

ATMOSPHERIC PRESSURE

NEGATIVE PRESSURE COMPARED TO ATMOSPHERE

ATMOSPHERIC PRESSURE RESTORED

Figure 4.14. Air pressure-volume relations in an accordion. When the player enlarges the accordion, pressure falls. Air then enters through an inlet valve, to equalize pressure.

respiration. It is not the case that we breathe in, therefore our lungs and chest expand, and we breathe out, therefore our lungs and chest contract. Rather, it works the other way around; we expand our chest and lungs causing air to flow in to equalize the negative pressure or partial vacuum created, then we contract our chest and lungs causing air to flow out to equalize the positive pressure created by the contraction. It is by changing the volume that we change the pressure.

Thus, air is brought into the lungs via the larynx, trachea, bronchi, bronchioles, the passageways increasingly branching until they reach the small air sacs (alveoli) which compose most of the lungs. It is there that the exchange of oxygen for carbon dioxide from the blood takes place, an exchange which is essential for life.

The Respiratory Mechanism

A surplus of carbon dioxide and a need for oxygen is automatically signaled in the *medulla oblongata*, the reflex seat for respiration in the brain stem. The medulla, in turn, initiates nerve impulses from the brain and spinal cord to various muscles in the *thorax* or chest. The thorax (Fig. 4.15) is bounded by the *vertebrae* in the back and the *sternum* or breast bone in the front. Completing the cylinder are 12 sets of *ribs* which form a skeletal framework from the front to the vertebrae in the back. The ribs are *osseous* (bony) except for the section of each rib contiguous with the sternum. These sections are made of cartilage. The lower ribs share cartilaginous attachments to the sternum, and the lowest two ribs are only attached at the back to the vertebral column.

This barrel-shaped cavity, the thorax, has as its floor a dome-shaped muscle sheet called the *diaphragm*, which simultaneously serves as the ceiling for the abdominal cavity. The lungs rest on the diaphragm and since they are spongy, elastic masses of air cells and lack muscles, they change shape by assuming the form of their container. When the diaphragm lowers or elevates, the lungs go along for the ride. In a similar manner, when the thorax expands or contracts by rib elevation and depression, the lungs also expand and con-

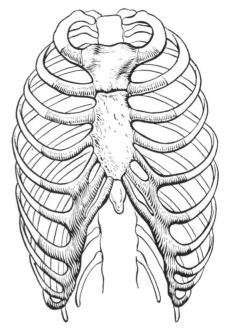

Figure 4.15. The thoracic cage. (Adapted from J. V. Basmajian: *Primary Anatomy,* 6th Ed., The Williams & Wilkins Co. © 1970).

tract due to a linkage which they have with the ribs. The rib cage is lined with a membrane called the *costal* (rib) *pleura* or alternatively, the *parietal pleura*. The lungs are covered by another membrane called the *pulmonary pleura* or sometimes the *visceral pleura*. These two membranes, the costal and pulmonary pleurae, adhere to one another and, at the same time, can slide across one another without friction, due to the presence of a viscous fluid between them. (Similarly, liquid between two thin plates of glass enables the plates to move across each other, while the surface tension of the fluid holds the plates of glass together.) This pleural linkage between the lungs and ribs enables the lungs to expand and contract as the thoracic cage changes volume (Fig. 4.16). Even without movement, the pleural linkage helps to keep the lungs expanded and the ribs compressed.

Inspiration

Quiet

For quiet inspiration (or inhalation), the medulla automatically sends neuronal im-

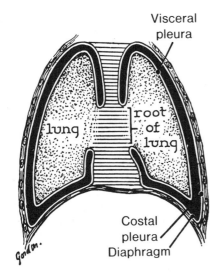

Visceral
pleura

lung   root
of
lung   lung

Costal
pleura
Diaphragm

Figure 4.16. Schematic coronal section of thorax, showing costal and pulmonary plurae. (Adapted from J. V. Basmajian: *Primary Anatomy,* 7th Ed., The Williams & Wilkins Co. © 1976.)

pulses via the spinal cord to the pertinent thoracic muscles. Several nerves emerge from the spinal cord at the level of the neck (*cervical nerves*) and join to form a nerve bundle known as the *phrenic nerve.* The phrenic nerve innervates the diaphragm, the convex sheet of muscle fibers which separates the thoracic and abdominal cavities. When nervous stimulation is sufficient to contract the diaphragm, the muscle fibers shorten, pulling the central part downward toward the edges, which are attached to the lower ribs. The effect is to lower and flatten the diaphragm to some extent. As the diaphragm forms the floor of the thoracic cavity, thoracic volume is increased vertically as the floor is lowered (Fig. 4.17). One can often observe the abdomen protruding upon inspiration, due to the downward pressure of the diaphragm upon the abdominal contents.

At the same time that the diaphragm is lowering, nerve impulses are transmitted via nerves emerging from the spinal cord at the level of the chest (*thoracic nerves*) to innervate muscles which run between the ribs (intercostal muscles: inter = between; costal = ribs). There are 12 ribs on each side of the thorax, allowing for 11 sets of intercostal muscles to connect

them. Furthermore, there are two layers of intercostal muscles, one layer superficial to the other. The *external intercostal muscles* connect the osseous portion of the ribs but do not connect the cartilage sections near the sternum. They lie superficial to the *internal intercostal muscles,* which connect the cartilage and osseous portions of the ribs starting at the front, but do not connect the ribs adjacent to the vertebrae (Fig. 4.18). The external and internal intercostal muscles are opposed in the direction in which the muscle fibers course. The external fibers course obliquely from the vertebrae down and out as they extend toward the sternum, whereas the internal fibers course obliquely in the opposite direction from the sternum down and out, as they extend toward the vertebrae. On a legal size piece of paper, draw a schematic representation of the intercostals as shown in Figure 4.18, which you can wrap around one side of your rib cage.

During inspiration, the external intercostal muscles and the section of the internal intercostals which lies between the cartilaginous portions of the ribs (the *interchondral* part) contract to elevate the ribs. Observe from the muscle representation which you have wrapped around your side that the vertebrae act as the fulcrum for the external intercostals, supplying leverage so that when the muscles shorten, the main effect is to lift the rib below. The same effect can be imagined in the front, where the internal intercostal muscles join the interchondral portions of the ribs. The muscle fibers course down and away from the sternum which gives support to the upper part of each muscle, again supplying the leverage necessary to lift the rib below. This action is aided by the twisting of the cartilages. Elevation of the ribs is thus produced by the joint efforts of the external intercostal muscles and the interchondral parts of the internal intercostal muscles, aided by a slight rotation of the cartilages. The result of these actions is an expansion of the thoracic cavity in both the anterior to posterior dimension and the lateral dimension (Fig. 4.19).

As the volume within the thorax increases with corresponding lung volume increase insured by the pleural linkage, air pressure inside the lungs decreases relative to atmospheric pressure outside. In order to keep the pressure equal, air from the outside moves to the area of less density or lower pressure, within the lungs.

The upper airways serve as the conduit (Fig. 4.20). Air normally enters the nasal cavities, where it is warmed, moistened, and filtered before it proceeds down the pharynx, passes as previously described through the larynx, down the trachea or windpipe, and then enters into increasingly branched tubes (bronchi, bronchioles) until the final multitudinous subdivisions ending at the alveolar sacs of the lungs. Mouth breathing is also possible, but tends to dry out the throat.

For Speech

Inspiration for speech differs from quiet inspiration in three ways. If the speaker knows he is going to need more energy for either a loud or long utterance, the inspiration must be greater in volume. The diaphragm and intercostal muscles can be augmented by any of several muscles capable of sternum and rib elevation: the *sternocleidomastoid*, the *scalenus*, the *subclavius*, and the *pectoralis major* and *minor* muscles in front, the *serratus anterior* muscle at the sides, and the *levatores costarum* muscles, *serratus posterior superior* muscle and *latissimus dorsi* muscle at the back (Fig. 4.21). A second difference is in the degree of automaticity. We breathe in and out, day and night, conscious and unconscious, and the process is under reflexive control, with the rate and depth of volume change dependent upon need. However, we can assume more voluntary control over our breathing. When we are

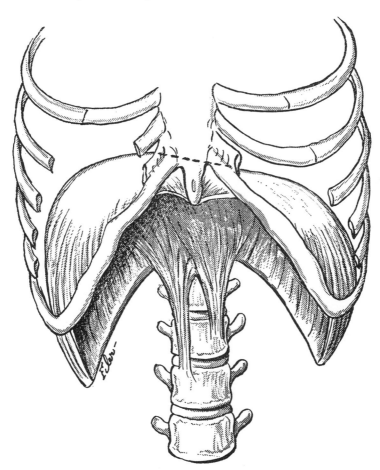

Figure 4.17. The diaphragm in anterior view. (Reprinted with permission from D. R. Dickson and W. M. Maue: *Human Vocal Anatomy,* Charles C. Thomas © 1970.)

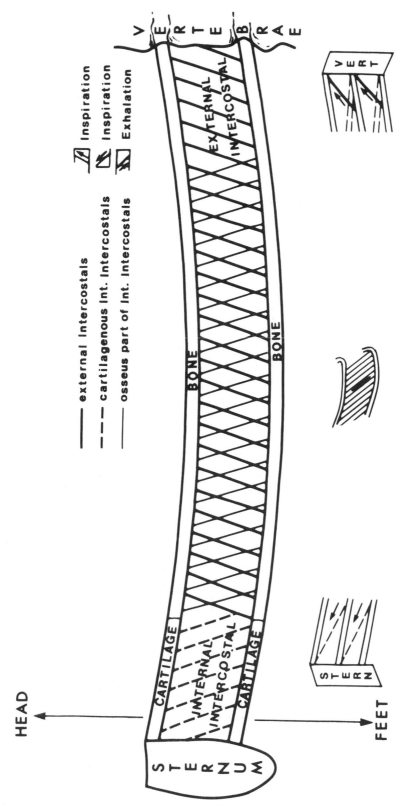

Figure 4.18. Wrap-around representation of the functions of the external and internal intercostal muscles as suggested by Fredericka Bell-Berti. (See text for explanation.)

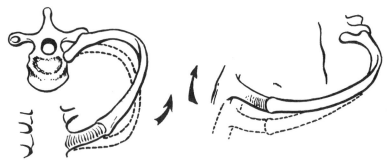

Figure 4.19. The movements of the ribs in inspiration. Inspiration lifts the ribs, increasing the transverse dimension of the chest, and causes the front end of the rib to rise, thus increasing front to back diameter. (Adapted from J. V. Basmajian: *Primary Anatomy,* 7th Ed., The Williams & Wilkins Co. © 1976.)

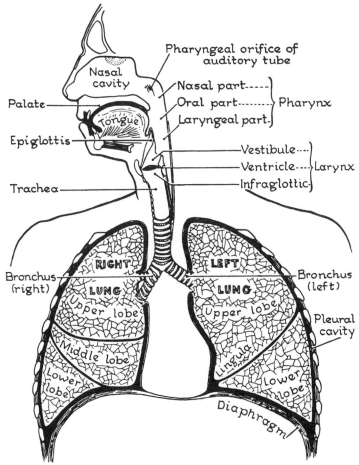

Figure 4.20. The airways of the respiratory system. (Adapted from J. V. Basmajian: *Grant's Method of Anatomy,* 9th Ed., The Williams & Wilkins Co. © 1976.)

reading a poem or singing a song, we are often conscious of making a larger volume change on inspiration in order to have enough air pressure to complete a long phrase without interruption.

Thirdly, inspiration for speech is quicker and comprises less of the total respiratory cycle than during quiet breathing. Time your breaths during rest and during the reading of a paragraph; you may not find

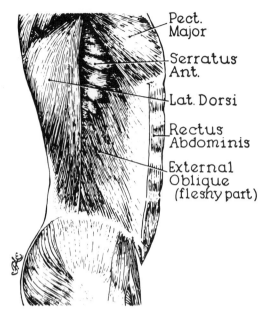

Pect. Major

Serratus Ant.

Lat. Dorsi

Rectus Abdominis

External Oblique (fleshy part)

Figure 4.21. Lateral view of the thorax. Some of the muscles used to elevate the ribs in deep inspiration. (Adapted from J. V. Basmajian: *Primary Anatomy,* 7th Ed., The Williams & Wilkins Co. © 1976.)

a significant difference in breaths per minute, which may range from 12 to 20 a minute, but the ratio between inspiration and expiration will differ markedly. During quiet breathing the ratio is roughly 40% inspiration and 60% expiration whereas for speech it is about 10% inspiration and 90% expiration (Fig. 4.22), although the ratio varies somewhat according to context.

Expiration

When the glottis is open for inspiration, air from the outside enters the lungs; when the inspiratory muscle effort is complete (depending upon the pressure needs of the task ahead), there is a moment of equalized pressure. The pressure in the lungs is equal to the atmospheric pressure. At a relatively high thoracic volume, however, a large inspiratory force is required to maintain the volume. If one were to relax the inspiratory muscles, the air would suddenly rush out due to the lung-rib cage recoil. Try it yourself. Inhale deeply by enlarging your rib cage and lung volume. Then, while holding the volume constant, hold your breath but open the *glottis.* If the

glottis is open, pressure above and below must be equal. If you let the inspiratory muscles relax, the air will rush out due to three passive forces: the *elastic recoil* of the lungs and rib cage (the expanded elastic tissues of the lungs bouncing back to their natural shape), *torque,* the force of the untwisting of the cartilages next to the sternum, and gravity which may aid in lowering the rib cage. These three passive forces suffice to decrease the volume of the rib cage and lungs. According to Boyle's law, the volume decrease increases the pressure within, causing air to flow out. The inspiration-expiration changes of volume and pressure are related in Figure 4.23. Just as for inspiration, it was necessary to increase the thoracic volume to effect a pressure decrease, it is necessary to decrease thoracic volume to effect a pressure increase for expiration.

In quiet expiration, the exchange of air is small (approximately 0.5 liter). With deeper breaths like those which accompany exercise, the volume of air exchanged increases. The amount of air exchanged during ins and outs of quiet respiration is called *tidal volume.* At rest, people take from 12 to 20 breaths per minute and the inspiration phase is only somewhat shorter in duration than the expiration phase. If one were to take a maximum inspiration and then produce a maximum expiration, this volume of air is called one's *vital capacity* (VC). The vital capacity of a person is related to sex, size, and breathing habits. As an average, human vital capacity is approximately 5 liters, but

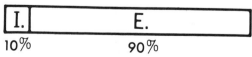

QUIET BREATHING

I.	E.
40%	60%

BREATHING FOR SPEECH

I.	E.
10%	90%

Figure 4.22. Comparison of the inspiratory (*I*) and expiratory (*E*) proportions of the respiratory cycle for quiet breathing and speech.

large male mountain climbers would surely have larger vital capacities than many people. The half a liter exchanged during quiet breathing is only 10% of the exchange one is capable of, and since there is an additional 2 liters of residual air which one is unable to expel, the tidal volume of 0.5 liter is only about 7% of total lung volume. Lung volumes and some of the standardized terminology are given in Figure 4.24.

For Sustained Voicing

The passive expiratory forces of elasticity, torque, and gravity are not sufficient by themselves to sing a note or to speak. Expiration during voicing then differs from that during quiet breathing, and expiration during speech differs from both.

In order to maintain a constant *pressure* to produce a note sung at a constant intensity, the passive recoil force of the rib cage-

lung coupling is used as a background force to which is added active muscle contractions, first inspiratory muscles, then expiratory. If a singer permitted expiratory forces to act unaided, the lungs would collapse suddenly and the note could not be sustained. The purpose of the active inspiratory forces (muscle contractions) is to slow down the outflow. The expiratory muscle forces are recruited later to further decrease thoracic size below the limits set by elastic recoil.

A pressure-volume diagram of the human chest showing the spring-like action of the respiratory system was first presented by Rahn et al. (1946). It shows how pressures vary at different lung volumes (Fig. 4.25). Lung volumes are plotted on the ordinate axis in terms of the percentage of vital capacity. The relaxation pressure curve (P_r) is plotted by asking people to adjust to a certain lung volume and then

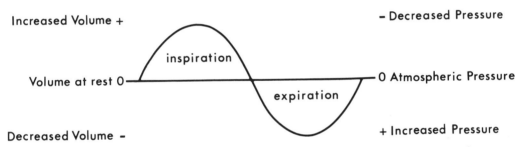

Increased Volume +

inspiration

Volume at rest 0

– Decreased Pressure

0 Atmospheric Pressure

expiration

Decreased Volume –

+ Increased Pressure

Figure 4.23. Changes of lung volume and pressure during inspiration and expiration.

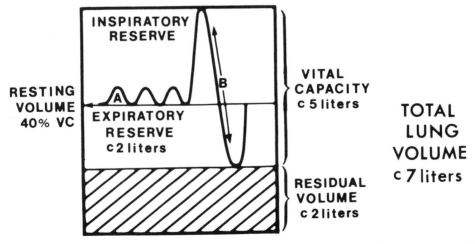

INSPIRATORY RESERVE

RESTING VOLUME 40% VC

EXPIRATORY RESERVE c 2 liters

VITAL CAPACITY c 5 liters

RESIDUAL VOLUME c 2 liters

TOTAL LUNG VOLUME c 7 liters

Figure 4.24. Inspiration and expiration during quiet, or tidal, breathing (*A*) and in a maximum exhalation and inhalation (*B*). Standard terminology for various parts of the total lung capacity is indicated.

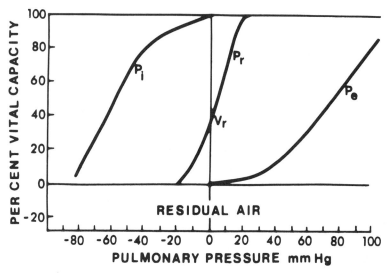

Figure 4.25. The pressure volume diagram. In the figure, P_i indicates the maximum inspiratory pressure curve, P_r indicates the relaxation curve, and P_e indicates the maximum expiratory pressure curve. V_r, residual volume. (See text for explanation.) (Adapted from H. Rahn et al.: *American Journal of Physiology. 146,* 1946.)

open the glottis and relax. At high lung volumes, people exhale upon relaxation, whereas at low lung volumes, they inhale. Pulmonary pressure (on the abscissa) is measured and recorded for each lung volume. At high lung volumes, a positive pressure is recorded upon relaxation; at low lung volumes, a negative pressure. The S-shaped curve which results is an index of average pressures supplied by the *passive* (non-muscular) inspiration and expiration forces.

Take a quiet breath. At the end of the expiration, one reaches a relaxed state in which the tension between the rib cage (which tends to expand) and the lungs (which tend to collapse) are balanced. This happens at about 40% of vital capacity, the *relaxation volume*. At high volumes, as we know from our trial, there is a force created, mostly from the elasticity of the lungs, which is expiratory. Conversely, at low lung volumes, the relaxation pressure of the lungs and rib cage recoil forces is inspiratory. For example, if you exhale all the air that you can and open your glottis, you will have created a large force to assist in inspiration. Let go and you'll see. This relaxation pressure curve then represents a background force of lung elasticity and rib cage elasticity including torque and

gravity which we can use in respiration to assist our muscles in changing lung volume. The *maximum inspiratory pressure* curve to the left of the relaxation curve is the summed forces of the relaxation (or recoil pressure) and inspiratory muscle pressure at different lung volumes. At high lung volumes, there is little more the muscles can add to the recoil forces, but at lower lung volume, the force exerted by inspiratory muscles is great and is added to the passive forces. The *maximum expiratory pressure* to the right of the relaxation curve is also the sum of active and passive forces for expiration at different lung volumes. It can be seen that more expiratory muscle force is possible at high lung volumes.

Figure 4.26 shows a mirror image of the relaxation pressure curve, depicting the active, muscle forces (either inspiratory on the *left* or expiratory on the *right*) which must be produced to balance the passive forces at certain chest volumes.

The pressure-volume relationships are altered somewhat when a person is lying down, since the abdominal contents press upon the diaphragm and increase lung pressure.

Mead, Bouhuys, and Proctor depict the modifications made to this background of recoil force when singers attempt to sustain a tone of low but constant intensity. Maintaining a subglottal pressure of 7 cm of H_2O (air pressure is traditionally measured by how far a column of water or mercury would be moved), the vocalist adds active muscle force of inspiratory muscles (during expiration) for the first half of the tone in order to check the recoil force, and then starts to contract the expiratory muscles with increasingly greater force (Fig. 4.27). For the first part of the tone, the vocalist continues to activate the external intercostal muscles and the inter-

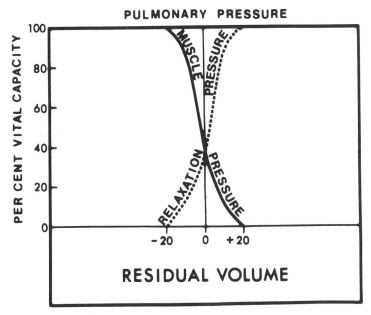

Figure 4.26. Muscle pressures needed at various lung volumes to balance the relaxation pressure supplied by passive forces. (Plotted from data in H. Rahn *et al.*: *American Journal of Physiology. 146*, 1946.)

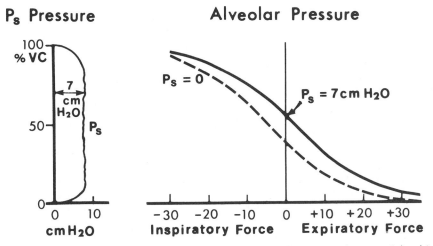

Figure 4.27. Forces required to maintain a constant subglottal pressure for a sustained tone, at varying lung volumes. (Adapted from J. Mead *et al.*: *Annals of the New York Academy of Science. 155*, 1968.) The *dashed line* indicates the relaxation or elastic curve with open glottis. The *solid line* indicates the muscle forces required to maintain subglottal pressure of 7 cm of water.

chondral part of the internal intercostal muscles, only gradually reducing the contractions so that the rib cage and lungs will decrease in volume smoothly. These muscles serve to brake the recoil forces. Thus, inspiratory muscles are used during expiration. As lung volume approaches the state in which the natural output pressure is 7 cm of H_2O, the expiratory muscles prepare to increase activity in order to maintain that pressure at decreasing lung volumes. Mead makes the point that muscle activity must constantly change in order to sustain a constant subglottal pressure at different lung volumes.

For Speech

The continued action of the inspiratory muscles to check the rate of expiration seen in sustaining a tone is also evident during expiration for speech.

The process of respiration is summed up in Table 4.2 by outlining the chain of events from neural impulses to the results in air pressure and air movement.

The expiratory muscles are innervated by spinal nerves. The thoracic nerves (T_1–T_{11}) innervate the internal intercostal muscles, the interosseus portions of which contract to shorten the distance between the ribs by depressing them, thereby reducing thoracic volume. The abdominal muscles are active in extended expiration as their contraction presses in upon the abdominal contents forcing the diaphragm up. The chief abdominal muscles used in expiration are the *rectus abdominis*, the *external and internal obliques*, and the *transversus abdominis* (Fig. 4.28).

Draper, Ladefoged, and Whitteridge recorded muscle activity from inspiratory muscles (external intercostals and diaphragm) and expiratory muscles (internal intercostals and abdominal muscles) while subjects spoke. In Figure 4.29, air pressure and muscle activity are indicated as measured in a subject counting from 1 to 32 at conversational loudness. The technique of electromyography is explained in Chapter 6. Note that the pressure drops gradually. The muscles of inspiration continue to contract, gradually decreasing activity. Aided by the force of the relaxation pressure, or elasticity of the respiratory system, the expiratory muscles are gradually recruited to further reduce lung volume, extending the exhalation.

Expiration for speech differs from expiration for a sustained tone, however, because of the addition of several factors. During speech, intensity is constantly changing because certain sentences, phrases, words, and syllables are given emphasis. In order to increase the intensity of the speech sound, the speaker must increase subglottal pressure. For example, during one expiration a speaker might say 'The *quality* of *mercy* is not *strained* but *droppeth* as the *gentle* *rain* from *heaven* upon the *place* beneath,' and would stress the italicized words or syllables. Stetson was the first phonetician who emphasized the contribution of the respiratory muscles to speaking. He believed that although the larger muscles of the chest and abdomen contributed to exhalation, it was the smaller intercostal muscles (internal intercostals) which would produce the small pulses overlaid on the breath stream. Stetson related the pulses to individual syllables, but if we modify that concept and relate the added internal intercostal contractions to stress, we would find general agreement with him. The abdominal muscles are recruited for added expiratory force in heavily stressed utterances or for long utterances.

Stressed syllables are produced by possible increases in three factors: duration, frequency, and intensity. Intensity of voicing is controlled by subglottal pressure, and it increases as a function of between the 3rd and 4th power of the subglottal air pressure.

$$I = P_s{}^3 \text{ or } P_s{}^4$$

A small change in pressure makes a large intensity difference. If you double the subglottal pressure, the intensity will increase between 8 and 16 times ($2^3 = 8$, $2^4 = 16$), a 9- to 12-dB increase of sound intensity. Ladefoged has shown that a subglottal air pressure increase is not usually associated with particular consonants in English, however, so that the respiratory system continues during speech to supply a fairly constant pressure for a given utterance. It is the opening and closing at the

Table 4.2
Summary Chart of Events during Respiration*

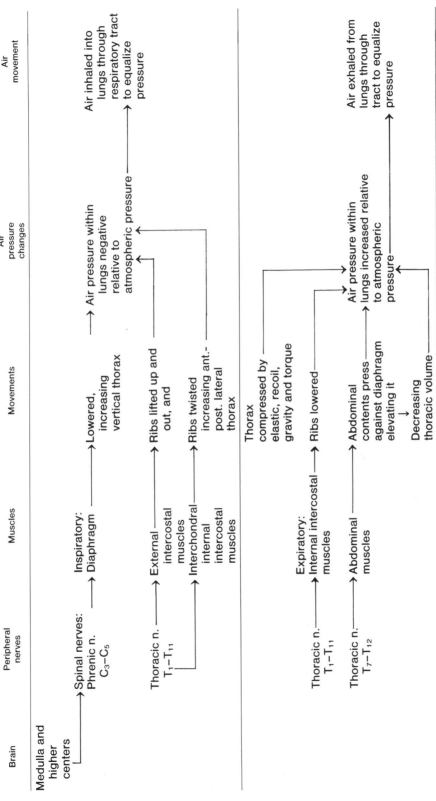

Brain	Peripheral nerves	Muscles	Movements	Air pressure changes	Air movement
Medulla and higher centers	**Inspiratory:** Spinal nerves: Phrenic n. C_3–C_5	Diaphragm	Lowered, increasing vertical thorax	Air pressure within lungs negative relative to atmospheric pressure	Air inhaled into lungs through respiratory tract to equalize pressure
	Thoracic n. T_1–T_{11}	External intercostal muscles	Ribs lifted up and out, and		
		Interchondral internal intercostal muscles	Ribs twisted increasing ant.-post. lateral thorax		
			Thorax compressed by elastic, recoil, gravity and torque		
	Expiratory: Thoracic n. T_1–T_{11}	Internal intercostal muscles	Ribs lowered	Air pressure within lungs increased relative to atmospheric pressure	Air exhaled from lungs through tract to equalize pressure
	Thoracic n. T_7–T_{12}	Abdominal muscles	Abdominal contents press against diaphragm elevating it → Decreasing thoracic volume		

* This chart represents the basic motor (efferent) events for respiration. There is also sensory (afferent) information sent back to the central nervous system. There are automatic feedback mechanisms which signal the need for more oxygen to the medulla. There are also specialized muscle fibers in the respiratory muscles which are responsive to muscle stretch. These along with the sensation of air movement through the respiratory tract enable the breather to consciously or unconsciously control respiration.

glottis and in the vocal tract above which alters the airflow and air pressure as we measure them at the mouth for different speech sounds. The same principle holds for voicing differences. Netsell has demonstrated invariant subglottal air pressure for voiced-voiceless cognates /t/ and /d/. The distinction between them is made at the larynx and in the supraglottal areas rather than in the amount of pressure applied below the larynx. In running speech, stressed syllables then are alternated with

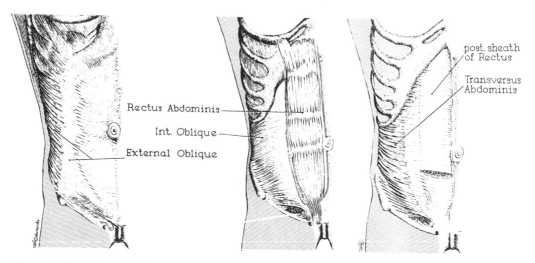

Rectus Abdominis

Int. Oblique

External Oblique

post. sheath of Rectus

Transversus Abdominis

Figure 4.28. A frontal view of the abdominal muscles used in expiration. (Adapted from J. V. Basmajian: *Primary Anatomy*, 6th Ed., The Williams & Wilkins Co. © 1970.)

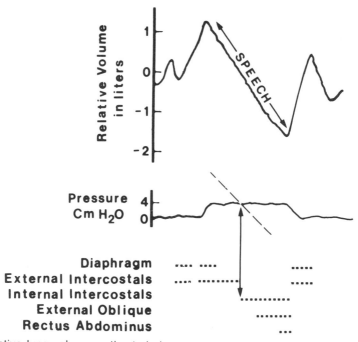

Figure 4.29. Relative lung volume, estimated air pressure and muscle activity during speaking. Muscle activity changes from inspiratory to expiratory as lung volume decreases, to maintain subglottal pressure. Active muscles are indicated below figure. (Adapted from P. Ladefoged: *Three Areas in Experimental Phonetics*, Oxford University Press, © 1967.)

unstressed syllables, and it is by increasing subglottal air pressure via the respiratory system that we produce the added intensity which is one characteristic of stress.

Another difference between expiration for speech and for either sustained phonation or for quiet breathing is that phrase groups determine the duration of the expiration. In saying: "I'm nobody. Who are you? Are you nobody too?", a speaker might use one expiration or perhaps two. The break for a breath is partially determined by the text, however, as Emily Dickinson would surely not have wanted us to interrupt her phrase by taking a breath after 'Who.' Variations in expiratory duration depend upon what is spoken (Fig. 4.30). It results in relatively long durations of the expiratory part of the respiratory cycle. If a speaker wants to finish a long phrase without interruption, he often continues to contract expiratory muscles, using some of his expiratory reserve, even at the expense of his comfort.

A final difference between quiet breathing and breathing for speech is the volume of air expended. During normal relaxed breathing, we use only 10% of our vital capacity. For example, we may inhale up to 55% of VC and then exhale to 40%. Hixon reports that in conversational speech, we typically inspire up to roughly the 60% VC level and do not take another breath until we have reached an appropriate stopping place near resting expiratory level of about 30 to 40% VC. Therefore, we use only about 25% of our vital capacity for conversational speech. During loud speech, we use 40% of vital capacity, the

expiratory phase going from perhaps 80% to 40% VC (Fig. 4.31). It would seem that barring some respiratory ailment, the problems of respiration common to some speech pathologies are not a matter of needing more air energy, since only the middle ¼ of vital capacity is usually used at conversational levels, but more likely are problems in control and modification of the airstream.

In voice disorders, the airstream is often wasted through inefficient use of the energy, rather than lack of air. The irregularities seen in the respiratory patterns of deaf speakers are related to anomalies of vocal fold and vocal tract modifications of the airstream as well as to its initiation. Respiratory irregularities are often seen, too, in the patterns produced by speakers

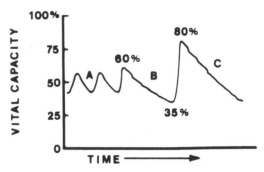

Figure 4.31. Lung volume changes during tidal breathing (*A*), conversational speech (*B*), and loud speech (*C*). (Adapted from "Respiratory Function in Speech" by Thomas J. Hixon in *Normal Aspects of Speech, Hearing, and Language*, edited by Minifie/Hixon/Williams, © 1973, p. 115. Reprinted by permission of Prentice-Hall, Inc., Englewood Cliffs, N. J.)

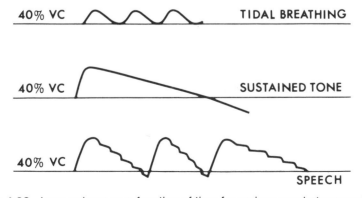

Figure 4.30. Lung volume as a function of time for various respiratory conditions.

with motor disorders (for example, cerebral palsy). Irregularities also appear as a lack of coordination between lower and upper respiratory systems, evidenced during the dysfluent utterances of some speakers who stutter. Again, it is less a problem of inability to change lung volumes sufficiently for pressure changes, but more often, it is a problem in affording proper resistance to the airstream at the vocal folds or in the upper vocal tract. Sometimes, a speaker with a motor dysfunction will contract the abdominal muscles concurrently with the external intercostal muscles as he inhales, a seemingly contradictory maneuver, even though the external intercostals win the battle (he actually inhales). Often, one can observe in less efficient breathers a tendency to spend a great deal of muscular energy lifting the sternum and upper rib cage (clavicular breathing, it is sometimes called) when with the same energy applied to different muscles, one could lift the lower ribs and produce a greater thoracic expansion. People with normal speech, however, seem to vary a great deal in whether the larger movements are at the abdomen-diaphragm region or at the upper chest.

PHONATION

Conversion of Air Pressure into Sound

The power supply for speech is the expired air from the lungs, but it falls to the actions of the upper airways to convert this air supply into audible vibrations for speech. As mentioned before, speakers use two methods of transforming the air into sounds for speech. The first method involves using the air pressure to set the elastic vocal folds which lie in the larynx into vibration, producing a periodic sound wave (with a repeated pattern). The second method involves allowing air to pass through the larynx into the vocal tract (the passages between the vocal folds and the outside air), where various modifications of the airstream result in noises: bursts, hisses, or combinations of these aperiodic sound waves (with no repeated pattern of vibration). The first method is termed *voicing*, and it is this vocal mode and its variation that we now consider.

Myoelastic Aerodynamic Theory of Phonation

The vocal folds are shelf-like elastic protuberances of tendon, muscles, and mucous membrane which lie behind the 'Adams's apple' or thyroid cartilage and run in an anterior-posterior direction. Their tension and elasticity can be varied; they can be made thicker or thinner, shorter or longer; they can be opened wide, closed together, or put into intermediate positions, and they can be elevated or depressed in their vertical relationship to the cavities above. In running speech, all these adjustments occur at very rapid rates. These dynamic variations of vocal fold modes are the result of an evolutionary change from a simple sphincter or valve-like mechanism in lower forms of life to the human larynx, in which the muscles controlling the folds are divided into several groups with specific functions, allowing a wide range of adjustments.

When the vocal folds are together and vibrating, they are in the voicing mode. Before considering the laryngeal structures and their functions in voicing, you can gain an immediate understanding of vocal fold physiology by producing that vibration of the lips known in the United States as the 'Bronx cheer' and in Great Britain as a 'raspberry.' Insure your privacy and then put your lips together in such a way that air pressure from behind sets them into an audible vibration. The sound is that of air escaping in rapid bursts, not the sound of the lips moving. It is apparent that it is the air pressure producing the lip movements, not the lip muscles, and yet the lips have to be put together and with the right amount of tension for it to work. Try it with lips slightly apart, or tightly pursed and you will meet with failure. Although the 'Bronx cheer' is quite easily observed, there was not general agreement until relatively recently that the vocal folds worked in somewhat the same way.

In the middle of the 18th century, it was

generally thought that vocal folds vibrated like strings, thus directly producing vibrations in air. Even as late as 1950, Husson, with the neurochronaxic theory, proposed that the vocal folds vibrated as a consequence of nerve impulses to the vocalis muscle rather than as a consequence of the action of expired air on the vocal folds. The currently accepted theory of phonation, however, is essentially that proposed by both von Helmholtz and Müller in the 19th century and amplified by van den Berg in a series of papers in the 1950s, *the myoelastic aerodynamic theory* of phonation. The key word is aerodynamic. The vocal folds are activated by the airstream from the lungs rather than by nerve impulses. 'Myoelastic' refers to the ways in which the muscles (myo-) change their elasticity and tension to effect changes in frequency of vibration.

The number of times the vocal folds open and close per second is the frequency of vocal fold vibration. The frequency of vocal fold vibration directly determines the lowest frequency (fundamental frequency) of the sound which is produced. Men have voices which have an average fundamental frequency (f_o) of approximately 125 Hz. Women are more apt to voice with a f_o over 200 Hz, and children, over 300 Hz. Size of the vocal folds is one determinant of fundamental frequency. The larger the vibrating mass of the vocal folds, the lower the frequency. Typically men have larger vocal folds than women. They have vocal fold lengths approximating 17 to 24 mm, whereas women's vocal folds are more apt to range between 13 and 17 mm. Given a pair of vocal folds of a particular length and weight, however, a person can increase the frequency of vibration appreciably by lengthening and tensing the folds, thus decreasing the effective mass. Usually, the vocal folds may be stretched by 3 or 4 mm. Singers are trained to have a range of 2 octaves (each octave is a doubling of frequency). A bass voice can go as low as about 80 Hz and a lyric soprano higher than 1 kHz. Muscular action is thus important in the control of voicing. Muscles act to bring the folds together so that they can vibrate, and muscles regulate their thickness and tension to alter the fundamental frequency.

The essential point of the myoelastic theory, however, is that the determinants of the vibratory cycle are aerodynamic. Air pressure from the lungs opens the vocal folds for each vibration. They close again for each vibration due to their inherent elasticity and a sudden pressure drop between the folds (Bernoulli principle) as the air streams through the glottis.

An explanation of the details of phonation requires anatomical knowledge of the larynx. Only the anatomy essential to a basic understanding of vocal fold function for speech will be presented in this text.

Framework of the Larynx

In addition to its use for speech, the larynx is used to control the flow of air into and out of the lungs, providing oxygen to the body, to prevent food, water, or other substances from entering the lungs, to aid in swallowing, and to enable a buildup of pressure within the thorax for such functions as coughing, vomiting, defecation, and lifting heavy objects.

The larynx is suspended from the *hyoid bone* and sits on top of the *trachea* (Fig. 4.32). The trachea, formed by a series of horseshoe-shaped cartilages with the open part at the back, can be located at the base of the neck, whereas the hyoid bone is floating under the jaw and can best be felt by tilting the head back slightly. A small horseshoe-shaped bone, it can be distinguished from the cartilages by its rigidity. The laryngeal framework lies anterior to the lower pharynx which leads to the esophagus and on to the stomach. Therefore, food and liquids must pass over the entrance to the lungs to gain access to the entrance to the stomach, a seemingly inefficient arrangement, which is the cost paid for the adaptation of the larynx as a sound source for speech. During swallowing, a leaf-shaped cartilage, the *epiglottis*, covers the entrance to the larynx. In other animals, the larynx is positioned high in the throat and can be coupled to the nasal airways, in which case food and liquids pass from the mouth around the sides of the larynx and straight into the esophagus, with no danger of entering the windpipe.

The larynx is a tube composed of cartilages connected by ligaments and connect-

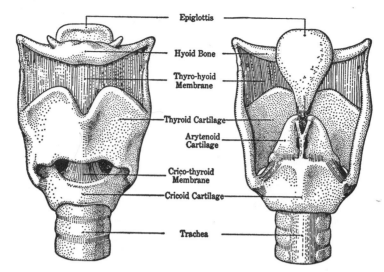

Figure 4.32. Front and back views of the larynx. (Reprinted with permission from V. A. Anderson: *Training the Speaking Voice*, Oxford University Press © 1977.)

ing membranes and covered by mucous membrane. The enclosed area forms an hour glass space (Fig. 4.33) with a vestibule above two sets of folds, the *ventricular folds* or 'false vocal folds,' and the 'true vocal folds' used for voicing. The ventricular folds form a second constriction, just above the true vocal folds. The vertical space between the two sets of folds is called the *laryngeal ventricle* and the horizontal space between the true vocal folds is called the *glottis*. Below the vocal folds the space widens again within the cartilaginous framework.

The cartilages which serve to maintain the laryngeal space and to support the muscles which regulate its changes are the *thyroid*, *cricoid*, and *arytenoid* cartilages. The cricoid cartilage, so named because it is shaped like a signet ring, (Greek, krikos = ring, oid = like) can be considered to be an overgrown tracheal ring. It forms the top ring of the trachea, distinctive because of the large plate (lamina) in the back, a strong contrast to the tracheal rings which are open at the back. The narrow front and sides of the cartilage form the arch, and the broad lamina at the back forms the signet-like part of the ring, which faces posteriorly (Fig. 4.34).

Although the vocal folds are not attached to the cricoid cartilage, the cricoid articulates with three cartilages which do

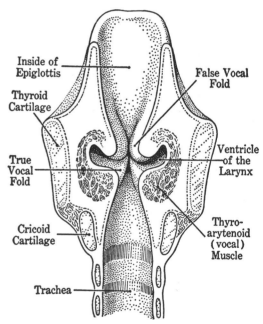

Figure 4.33. Frontal section of the larynx. Notice the constrictions formed by the ventricular folds and the 'true vocal folds' below. (Reprinted with permission from V. A. Anderson: *Training the Speaking Voice*, Oxford University Press © 1977.)

support the vocal folds: the thyroid cartilage and two arytenoid cartilages. The arytenoid cartilages are roughly pyramidal in shape and articulate with the cricoid

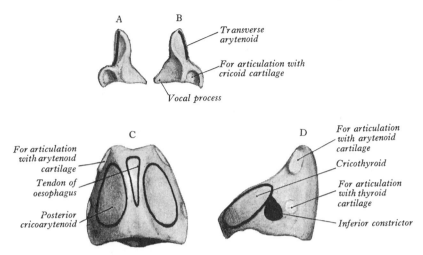

Figure 4.34. The arytenoid and cricoid cartilages. (*A*) The left arytenoid cartilage, medial aspect. (*B*) The right arytenoid cartilage, medial aspect. (*C*) The cricoid cartilage, posterior aspect. (*D*) The cricoid cartilage, left lateral aspect. Muscle attachments are indicated as *heavy lines*. (Reprinted with permission from R. Warwick and P. L. Williams (Eds.): *Gray's Anatomy*, 35th British Edition, Longman Group, Ltd. © 1973.)

cartilage via oval depressions on their inferior surfaces which correspond with convex facets on the top sides of the cricoid lamina. When the arytenoids are in place, a small projection at the base of each cartilage (the vocal process) points anteriorly and is the point of attachment for the vocal ligament with its associated folds. The vocal ligament and the *thyroarytenoid* muscle which adjoins it are stretched between the vocal process of the arytenoid cartilages in the back and the deep angle of the thyroid cartilage in the front (Fig. 4.35). The larger extension of the base of each arytenoid cartilage is called the muscular process, because three muscles important for the positioning of the vocal folds are attached to it. The muscular process extends posteriorly and somewhat laterally.

The largest cartilage, the thyroid cartilage, so named because it is like a shield (Greek, thyreos = large shield), is positioned anterior to the arytenoid cartilages, which its sides enclose, and superior to the cricoid cartilage, the back laminal crest of which it also encloses. It forms an angle in the front which is more acute in men (~90°) than in women (~120°), hence the common term 'Adam's apple' instead of 'Eve's apple.' There is a notch (Fig. 4.36)

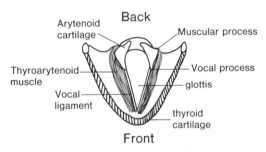

Figure 4.35. The larynx from a superior view, showing the relationships among the thyroid, cricoid, and arytenoid cartilages, and the thyroarytenoid muscle.

where the laminae separate above the angle which can usually be located by feeling along the midline of your throat with your index finger. The plates are widely separated in the back and extend into two superior horns which project toward the cornua (horns) of the hyoid bone above. The two smaller inferior horns articulate with the cricoid cartilage below by fitting into a round facet on each side of the cricoid laminae. The cartilages of the larynx can move in relation to one another to a limited degree. The thyroid and cricoid cartilages can rock back and forth upon each other as will be discussed later in reference to pitch change. The arytenoids

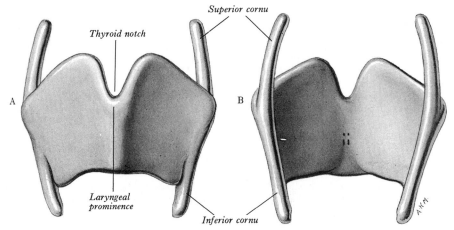

Figure 4.36. The thyroid cartilage. (*A*) Anterior aspect. (*B*) Posterior aspect. (Reprinted with permission from R. Warwick and P. L. Williams (Eds.): *Gray's Anatomy,* 35th British Edition, Longman Group, Ltd, © 1973.)

can rotate and rock on the cricoid cartilage and can slide a bit toward one another. The muscles attached to the muscular process of the arytenoids control these movements, as will be discussed in relation to vocal fold adjustments.

Vocal Fold Adjustments during Speech

The vocal folds at rest are apart, creating a V-shaped glottal space with its apex behind the thyroid cartilage and its widest separation at the back, where the folds attach to the vocal process of the arytenoid cartilages. During running speech, the vocal folds are separated for voiceless speech sounds, such as the consonants /s/ or /t/, are brought together for the voiced sounds, such as the vowels and diphthongs /u/, /i/, and /aɪ/, in the words 'two' /tu/, 'tea' /ti/, and 'tie' /taɪ/, and are less firmly brought together for voiced consonants such as /z/ and /d/ where voicing is needed in addition to large air pressures in the oral cavity (Fig. 4.37).

Voiceless Consonants

The simplest adjustment of the vocal folds for speech is the one taken for voiceless consonants. The folds open wide or *abduct* in order to obtain sufficient air from the lungs to create noises in the oral cavity. As speech proceeds, voiceless con-

sonants are interspersed in the speech stream singly or in clusters, demanding rapid glottal opening to interrupt voicing. The job is done by a pair of large triangular muscles attached by tendons to the top of the muscular process of each arytenoid cartilage; the muscle fibers fan out as they course back and down to attach to the dorsal plates of the cricoid cartilage (Fig. 4.38). Named for their position and attachments, the *posterior cricoarytenoid muscles* (PCA) upon contraction rotate the arytenoid cartilages by pulling the muscular processes down and medially, thereby moving the vocal processes apart. Innervation to this and almost all of the other intrinsic muscles of the larynx is supplied by the *recurrent nerve,* a branch of the Xth cranial nerve, the vagus nerve.

Voiced Speech Sounds

Open vocal folds cannot be set into vibration, so in order to produce the voiced sounds of speech, the normally separated folds must be *adducted* (brought together) or nearly so. To approximate the vocal folds, the arytenoid cartilages must be brought closer together with their vocal processes rocked inward toward one another. A strong band of muscular fibers runs horizontally across the posterior surfaces of the arytenoid cartilages. This muscle, the *transverse arytenoid* muscle is overlaid by some muscular fibers in the

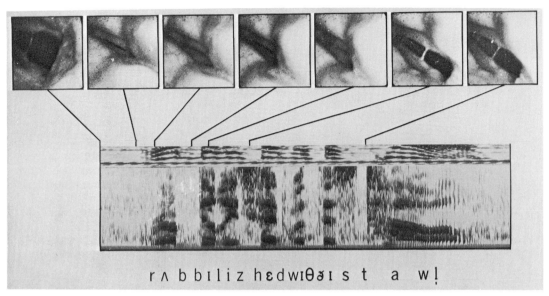

r ʌ b bɪl i z hɛdwɪθəɪ s t a wl̩

Figure 4.37. The glottis, viewed from above with a fiber bundle, at various times in the production of a sentence. The posterior part of the glottal chink is at the *lower right* in each view. Note the open glottis in the first frame for inspiration, the relatively closed glottis in the third frame for a vowel, and the relatively open glottis in the sixth frame for a voiced consonant. (The structure apparently connecting the folds in the *rightmost view* is a bead of mucus.) (Reprinted with permission from M. Sawashima *et al.: Phonetica. 22,* S. Karger AG, Basel, © 1970.)

shape of an X called the *oblique arytenoid* muscles (Fig.4.39). Together, termed the *interarytenoid* muscle (IA), they adduct the arytenoid cartilages and thereby, the vocal folds. The primary adductor is thought to be the interarytenoid muscle. To aid in adduction of the vocal folds, by rocking the muscular process of the arytenoids forward and down, thereby pressing the vocal processes together, are the *lateral cricoarytenoid* muscles (LCA) (Fig. 4.40). For stronger adduction of the folds, as for vowel production, both the IA and LCA are usually used. For speech sounds requiring voicing but also requiring a sound source above the glottis, the vocal folds are often less closely adducted and the interarytenoid muscle is sufficient. Hirose and Gay (Fig. 4.41) have differentiated the function of laryngeal muscles by measuring the electrical activity generated as these muscles contract. The recording method (electromyography or EMG) is explained in Chapter 6.

The vocal folds themselves are composed of (1) the vocal ligaments which are the thickened edges of the *conus elasticus*

membrane rising from the cricoid cartilage, (2) the muscles which are attached to the ligaments, the internal part of the *thyroarytenoid* muscles commonly called the *vocalis* muscles, and (3) the mucous membrane which covers them. The vocal ligaments and the vocalis muscles which form the body of the vocal folds emerge from the projection of the arytenoid cartilage known as the vocal process. Due to the cartilage, they are stiffer at the back and become inceasingly flexible toward the front. When relaxed, the vocal folds are thick and open and close in an undulating manner, the mucous membrane moving somewhat independently like flabby skin on a waving arm. The external part of the thyroarytenoid muscle extends to the muscular process of the arytenoid with some fibers wrapping around the arytenoid, commingling with the interarytenoid muscles. More research is needed to differentiate the role of the internal (vocalis) and external parts of the thyroarytenoid muscles in phonation, but in general they are thought to tense the folds.

The muscle activity needed to adduct

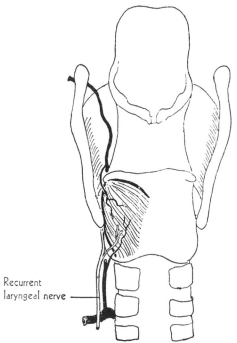

A necessary condition for voicing is that the air pressure below the folds must exceed the pressure above the folds. If the pressure above the folds builds up so that the pressure drop across the glottis necessary for voicing is lost, then voicing ceases. A test of this is to try to prolong a voiced stop consonant such as a [b]. You can voice the sound for only a short time because the lip closure for the [b] results in air pressure building up behind the lip closure until it equals the subglottal air pressure. Since there is no longer more pressure below the folds than above them, voicing is not possible. For speech at conversational level, a subglottal air pressure in the range of 7–10 cm of H_2O (centimeters of water pressure) is sufficient to produce voicing at approximately 60 dB intensity.

The effect of subglottal air pressure sufficient to separate a pair of vocal folds can be seen in Figure 4.42, schematic diagrams made from a movie of a vibrating larynx. The vocal folds open at the bottom first

Figure 4.38. The posterior cricoarytenoid muscle. Posterior view. (Although only one muscle is shown, the muscle is paired.) (Reprinted with permission from D. P. Quiring and J. H. Warfel: *The Head, Neck, and Trunk*, Lea and Febiger © 1967.)

and tense the vocal folds simply readies them for vibration but does not cause the vibration itself. For the 'Bronx cheer,' you had to put your lips together, and that required muscular effort, but the sound itself was produced by aerodynamic forces acting upon the elastic bodies of your lips. The two aerodynamic forces which produce vibration of the vocal folds are the *subglottal air pressure* (P_s) applied to the lower part of the folds, forcing them open, and the negative pressure which occurs as air passes between the folds (the *Bernoulli effect*). These positive and negative pressures set the vocal folds into vibration due to the elasticity of the folds.

Subglottal Air Pressure

Consider first the subglottal air pressure which parts the vocal folds. During each opening, a tiny puff of air escapes and this ballistic array of air bullets sets up a pressure wave at the glottis which is audible.

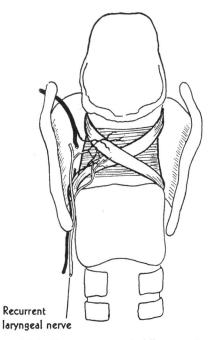

Figure 4.39. Transverse and oblique arytenoid muscles shown in posterior view. Together, these muscles are referred to as the interarytenoid muscle. (Reprinted with permission from D. P. Quiring and J. H. Warfel: *The Head, Neck, and Trunk*, Lea and Febiger © 1967.)

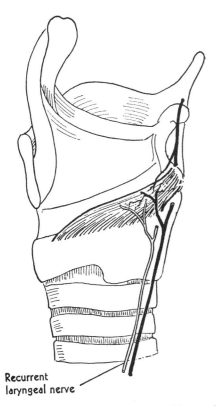

Recurrent
laryngeal nerve

Figure 4.40. The lateral cricoarytenoid muscle; lateral view, with the left side of the thyroid cartilage removed. (Reprinted with permission from D. P. Quiring and J. H. Warfel: *The Head, Neck, and Trunk,* Lea and Febiger © 1967.)

and then the opening proceeds up to the top of the folds. As the top part of the vocal folds opens, the bottom part can be seen to be closing. Thus, there is a vertical phase difference, creating a wave-like motion of the folds, the normal movement during vibration for chest voice. If the speaker speaks or sings in a high falsetto voice, however, the vertical phase difference is lost and each of the taut folds moves as a unit. The closing phase of each cycle is the result of the second aerodynamic phenomenon important to voicing, the pressure drop due to the Bernoulli principle.

Bernoulli Effect

Daniel Bernoulli, mathematician and physician living in Switzerland in the 18th century, whose father and uncle were distinguished scientists and mathematicians,

developed the kinetic theory of gases and liquids, part of which is known as the Bernoulli principle. The Bernoulli effect is based upon the observation that when a gas or liquid current runs through a constricted passage, the velocity (speed in a certain direction) increases. Simply stated, the Bernoulli principle is that such an increase in velocity results in a drop in the pressure exerted by the molecules of moving gas or liquid, the pressure drop being perpendicular to the direction of the flow. Figure 4.43 illustrates the increase in velocity within a narrow portion of a passage and the resulting decrease in pressure against the lateral walls.

The conventional airplane wing is designed to take advantage of the Bernoulli effect to elevate the aircraft. The wing is streamlined on the top surface (Fig. 4.44), permitting a higher velocity of air current than that passing underneath. The higher velocity results in a drop in pressure against the top surface, which creates a difference between the pressures under and over the wings, thereby elevating the plane. You can elevate a piece of paper, using the same principle, by holding one end of it under your lips and blowing air across the top (Fig. 4.45).

We experience the Bernoulli phenomenon constantly. When a draft of air flows through a narrow corridor, the doors opening into rooms off the hall slam shut, because the pressure on the hall side of the doors is lower than that on the room side. If you have ever been in a lightweight car cruising alongside a heavy truck on a highway and felt your car being sucked alarmingly close to the truck, it is because the faster airstream created between your car and the truck has lowered the pressure against the truck side of your car relative to the other side.

Vocal Fold Vibration

During voicing, each cycle of vocal fold vibration is due both to the subglottal air pressure which has built up sufficiently to open the folds and to the Bernoulli principle which, as the air rushes through the glottis at an increased velocity, accounts for a sudden drop in pressure against the inner sides of each fold and sucks them

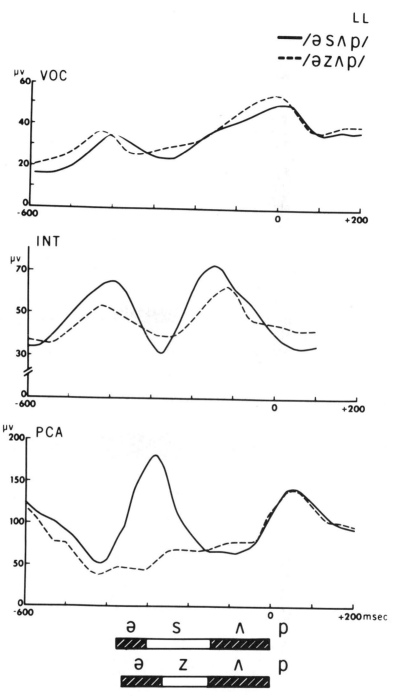

Figure 4.41. Superimposed EMG curves for voiced (z; *dashed line*) and voiceless (s; *solid line*) fricatives in nonsense syllables. Although vocalis muscle (*VOC*) activity is similar for both, for /s/, interarytenoid (*INT*) activity is reduced during the time that posterior cricoarytenoid activity (*PCA*) is greatly increased. (Reprinted with permission from H. Hirose and T. Gay: *Phonetica. 25,* S. Karger AG, Basel, © 1972.)

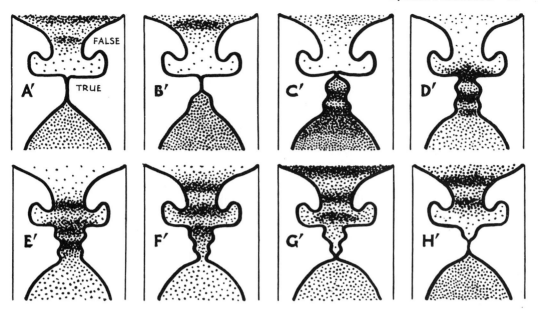

Figure 4.42. Schematic cross-sections of the vocal folds during vibration. It can be seen that the folds open and close from *bottom* to *top*. (From *Singing: the Mechanism and the Technic,* 4th Ed., by William Vennard, © 1967 by Carl Fischer, Inc. All rights reserved. Reprinted by permission of the publisher.)

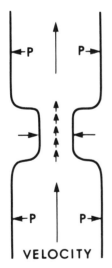

Figure 4.43. Schematic diagram of flow through a constricted passage. In the constriction, velocity is greater, but outward pressure on the sides of the constriction is absent.

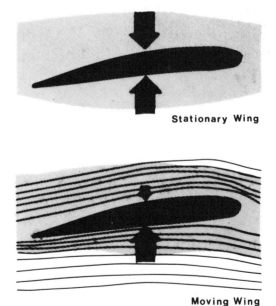

Figure 4.44. Aerodynamic forces on an airplane wing. (See text for discussion.)

together again. The whole process is made possible by the fact that the folds themselves are elastic. Their elasticity not only permits them to be blown open for each cycle, but the elastic recoil force (the force which restores any elastic body to its resting place) works along with the Bernoulli principle to close the folds for each cycle of vibration.

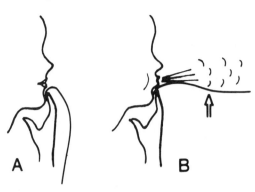

Figure 4.45. Illustration of the Bernoulli principle. When airflow is increased on the top side of the paper by blowing, pressure is lower on the top side than on the bottom side, causing the sheet to rise. (Adapted from *Singing: the Mechanism and the Technic*, 4th Ed., by William Vennard, © 1967 by Carl Fischer, Inc. All rights reserved. Reprinted by permission of the publisher.)

The vocal folds move in a fairly periodic way. During sustained vowels, for example, the folds open and close in a certain pattern of movement which repeats itself. This action produces a barrage of air bursts which sets up an audible pressure wave (sound) at the glottis. The pressure wave of sound is also periodic; the pattern repeats itself. Like all complex periodic sounds, it contains harmonics. It consists of a fundamental frequency and many multiples of that fundamental frequency. The fundamental frequency is the number of glottal openings per second.

The human voice is a low frequency sound compared to most of the sounds of the world, including the other sounds which humans make above the larynx. Since it contains many harmonics, the voice is also a complex sound. We never hear the sound of vocal fold vibration, however, because by the time it has reached the lips of the speaker, it has been changed by the vocal tract. If we were to lower a microphone down to the vocal folds, we would record a sound which has a spectrum resembling Figure 4.46. The lowest frequency, the frequency of the vibration itself, sets up a 2nd harmonic (2 times the f_o), a 3rd harmonic (3 times the f_o), and so forth. Notice that it is characteristic of the human voice that the higher harmonics have less intensity than the

lower harmonics, so that although the voice contains many high frequency components, the emphasis is on the low frequencies. The intensity falls off at about 12 dB per octave (each doubling of the frequency).

A major difference between the sound of a low frequency and a high frequency voice is due to the differences in the spacing of the harmonics. Figure 4.46 shows the difference. Notice how many more harmonics are at low fundamental frequencies. A child with a f_o of 350 Hz would have a 2nd harmonic at 700 Hz, a 3rd at 1050 Hz, and a 4th at 1400 Hz. In contrast, a man with a f_o at 150 Hz would have a 2nd harmonic at 300 Hz, and the 9th harmonic would correspond closely with the child's 4th harmonic. In the same way, a single person adjusting the frequency of his voice also changes the harmonic spacing. Notice, in the figure, that the shape and slope of the spectrum remain similar for man and child.

Fundamental Frequency

The human voice is composed of many frequencies; it is a complex tone. The hu-

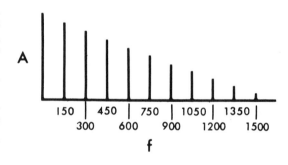

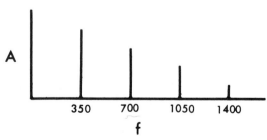

Figure 4.46. Schematic spectra of sounds resulting from vocal fold vibration. The spectra represent two different frequencies of phonation, thus the harmonic spacing is altered.

man listener perceives the lowest frequency, the fundamental frequency, as the speaker's pitch. The fundamental frequency is constantly changing, as we know when we listen for the *intonation* patterns of sentences. 'Are you sure?' has a rising intonation pattern, whereas 'I'm sure' has a falling intonation pattern. The speaker produces these different patterns by altering the fundamental frequency of vocal fold vibration.

According to the myoelastic aerodynamic theory of phonation, frequency of vocal fold vibration is determined by the elasticity, tension, and mass of the vocal folds. More massive folds (longer and thicker) vibrate at naturally lower frequencies than shorter and thinner folds. More elastic folds vibrate at high frequencies because they bounce back faster. Vocal folds vibrate faster when they are tense than when they are slack. The primary way to make a given set of vocal folds more tense is to stretch them.

You may have noted that longer folds contribute to increased mass and lower f_o in one condition and to increased tension and higher f_o in another condition. This is because a longer pair of vocal folds (compared to other speakers) will be more massive and produce a lower frequency voice; men's voices are lower than children's voices. Yet a lengthening of vocal folds (within the same speaker) will stretch out and thin the effective vibrating portion of the vocal folds, adding tension and thereby producing a higher fundamental frequency. The pair of muscles responsible for stretching the vocal folds and thereby controlling f_o change are the *cricothyroid* muscles.

Since the vocal folds lie between the thyroid cartilage and the two arytenoid cartilages, the way to stretch the folds would be to enlarge the distance between these cartilages. The cricothyroid muscles can do just that. Since they are attached to the side of the cricoid ring and rise (part straight up and the other part at an oblique angle) to the thyroid cartilage, their contraction pulls the two cartilages toward one another by lifting the anterior arch of the cricoid cartilage toward the thyroid cartilage. The closing of the space between the cricoid arch and the front of the thy-

roid has been likened to the closing of the visor on a suit of armour. Figure 4.47 shows the location of the cricothyroid muscles on the outside of each side of the larynx. The effect which their contraction has in elevating the front of the cricoid cartilage, is to tip the posterior plate of the cricoid backward. The arytenoid cartilages ride on the cricoid cartilage and the vocal folds are stretched. Van den Berg terms this effect of cricothyroid muscle action longitudinal tension. The innervation of the cricothyroid muscle is from the superior laryngeal nerve (vagus, Xth cranial nerve) unlike all the other intrinsic muscles of the larynx which are innervated by the recurrent nerve (another branch of the vagus nerve).

The addition of longitudinal tension to the vocal folds increases the fundamental frequency at which they vibrate, at least for much of the frequency range used in speech. For extreme frequencies, other mechanisms are thought to be instrumental in pitch control. At high frequencies, such as for falsetto voice, the cricothyroid is used to further increase tension although no further lengthening is possible. The vo-

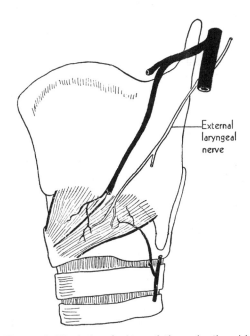

—External laryngeal nerve

Figure 4.47. Lateral view of the cricothyroid muscle. (Reprinted with permission from D. P. Quiring and J. H. Warfel: *The Head, Neck, and Trunk*, Lea and Febiger © 1967.)

cal folds are pulled extremely taut and forego their usual wave-like motion. The vocal ligaments vibrate more like strings.

At extremely low frequencies, the strap muscles of the neck (particularly the *sternohyoid* muscle, Fig. 4.48) assume more responsibility for lowering f_o. You may have noticed the larynx move up slightly in the vertical plane for high frequencies or, more noticeably, move down in the neck for low frequencies. The muscles above the hyoid bone (suprahyoid muscles) elevate the larynx. These movements are thought by some to add vertical tension to the membranes which serve as a lining for the larynx, and for the trachea below. Increased vertical tension in the conus elasticus during laryngeal elevation and decreased vertical tension in the case of laryngeal lowering would affect the vocal folds. The conus elasticus membrane

emerges from the cricoid cartilage and rises in a medial direction to the vocal folds where its thickened border becomes the vocal ligament.

A further source of tension in the vocal folds is the internal tension possible with the contraction of the thyroarytenoid muscles themselves, especially the vibrating portions known as the vocalis muscles. Antagonistic to the cricothyroid muscles, since they shorten rather than lengthen the folds, the vocalis can increase tension to raise f_o and perhaps tune the vocal folds to make the cricothyroid lengthening more effective. Research is needed to clarify the interaction of muscular and non-muscular contributions to frequency change. Atkinson has indicated that the relative contribution may vary within an individual's f_o range.

It seems that fundamental frequency is primarily affected by applying more or less longitudinal tension to the vocal folds via the cricothyroid muscles and secondarily affected by such adjustments as applying more or less vertical tension to the folds via the muscles which can elevate (suprahyoid muscles) or depress (infrahyoid muscles) the larynx, by applying more or less intrinsic tension in the vocalis muscles themselves, or by changing subglottal pressure.

Voice Quality

Much of what distinguishes one voice from another results from the effects of the resonating cavities and structures above the larynx, but part of what is called voice quality or timbre is due to the way in which the vocal folds themselves vibrate. One obvious difference among voices is fundamental frequency, which listeners perceive as pitch. Other differences have to do with how closely the folds are approximated or with irregularities along the edges of the folds. If one or both of the folds are paralyzed, compensations must be made to set up a vibration if possible. Sometimes one vocal fold can be trained to move more than halfway to meet the paralyzed one. If part or all of the larynx has been surgically removed because of cancer, the speaker must learn to vibrate other tissues and muscle masses

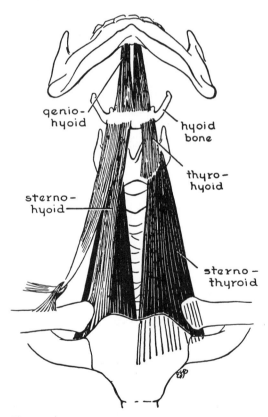

Figure 4.48. The strap muscles of the neck, anterior view from below. (Reprinted with permission from J. V. Basmajian: *Primary Anatomy*, 7th Ed. The Williams & Wilkins Co. © 1976.)

such as scar tissue or the cricopharyngeus muscle. Some alaryngeal speakers (people whose larynges have been removed) have to resort to an artificial sound source which they hold to the outside of the neck. This produces a 'voice' with an artificial, mechanical quality.

Quality differences depend upon various modes of vocal fold vibration. A breathy voice, popular with some movie stars and celebrities in the 1950s, is achieved by failing to adduct the vocal folds sufficiently for full voicing. They are close enough to be vibrated but the sound of continuously released air accompanies the sound wave set up by the air pressure volleys. A hoarse voice is caused by irregularities in the folds. When the vocal folds are irritated and swollen, as they may be during a cold with laryngitis, the voice becomes hoarse. Hoarseness can also be indicative of vocal abuse, either from focusing too much tension in the larynx causing *contact ulcers*, lesions produced by the arytenoid cartilages banging against one another, or from overusing the voice as happens commonly to women and occasionally to men who develop nodules along the edges of the vocal folds. Extremely low frequency phonations, sometimes called *vocal fry* or *creaky* voice (Ladefoged's term) are not to be cultivated but

are instructive as a demonstration of what is happening during voicing, for if you tighten your larynx and voice in an extremely low frequency, you can hear the individual pops of sound set up with each burst of air.

A characteristic of some voices which is related to quality is the way in which some speakers initiate the vibrations. Good use of the voice requires that the initiation of voicing be gradual so that the amplitude of the waveform builds through the first few cycles to the desired intensity. Some speakers initiate voicing with what is called a *glottal attack* (or sometimes harsh glottal attack) when the vocal folds are tightly adducted prior to vibration and the opening cycles of vibration are at full amplitude, creating the air burst of a *plosive*, similar to /b/ or /g/ but produced at the glottis. The symbol for this burst is [ʔ] so that instead of saying or singing 'I' [aɪ], the person produces [ʔaɪ]. Harry Belafonte, a popular singer in the United States, made repeated visits to the hospital during the height of his career to have vocal nodules removed from his vocal folds, nodules caused by glottal attack. Hirose and Gay have shown that glottal attack is accompanied by increase of activity in the lateral cricoarytenoid muscles (Fig. 4.49) which compress the center of the vocal folds.

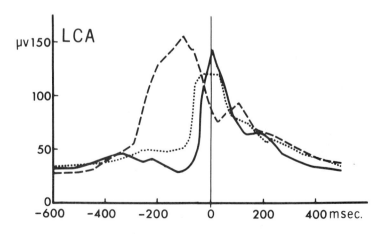

Figure 4.49. Contrasting activity patterns in the lateral cricoarytenoid muscle (*LCA*) for various forms of vocal attack. The onset of the vowel is marked as *0*. Activity is earliest for glottal attack (*dashed line*) later for voiced attack (*dotted line*) and latest for voiceless aspirate attack (*solid line*). (Reprinted with permission from H. Hirose and T. Gay: *Folia Phoniatrica (Basel). 25*, S. Karger AG, Basel, 1973.)

Relationship between Frequency and Intensity

We have seen that by increasing the subglottal air pressure, keeping other things constant, we can increase vocal intensity. However, if subglottal pressure is increased without muscular adjustments of the vocal folds, the fundamental frequency as well as the intensity will increase. If someone is phonating a steady tone and is (gently) punched in the stomach, the tone not only gets louder but increases in pitch. The pitch rise may be due to a reflexive tensing of the vocal folds or to the fact that the increased subglottal air pressure causes the vocal fold closure to occur more quickly because of the Bernoulli effect. When one is speaking, at the end of a breath, the f_o drops naturally along with the intensity by about 2–7 Hz per cm of H_2O decrease. A speaker can reverse this affinity, however. If a singer wants to increase intensity but maintain the f_o, he must lower the resistance to the airflow at the vocal folds, either by relaxing the cricothyroid a bit or by lowering the internal tension by relaxing the thyroarytenoid muscle. Similarly, when asking 'Are you sure?', in order to signal the question with a rising fundamental frequency, the speaker must work against the natural fall in frequency at the end of a breath group by increasing cricothyroid activity, stretching the folds, and at the same time, increasing internal intercostal muscle activity to give added stress to the word 'sure.'

Increased vocal intensity is due to greater resistance (afforded by the vocal folds) against the increased airflow. The vocal folds are blown wider apart, releasing a larger puff of air which sets up a sound pressure wave of greater amplitude. The vocal folds not only move farther apart for each vibratory cycle of increased intensity, but they stay adducted for a larger part of each cycle. In Figure 4.50, the changes in the vocal fold movement are schematized and presented with the resulting change in waveform.

Summary

We have seen that phonation is a dynamic process, varying as it does during

1. Opening
2. Closing
3. Closed

Open from
50–70% Cycle

HIGHER INTENSITY
HIGHER FREQUENCY

Increased P_{sub}

Open from
30–50% cycle
snaps closed faster

Figure 4.50. Schematic of the movement of the vocal folds during voicing. At higher subglottal pressure, the folds remain closed for a greater proportion of the vibratory cycle, and close more rapidly. Thus, frequency tends to increase, as well as intensity.

running speech in intensity, frequency, and quality. The output is a rapidly varying acoustic stream made up of segments of silence, periodic sounds, and noises. The change back and forth between voiced and voiceless states is particularly difficult for speakers. As a result, normal speakers alter the voicing state. For example, we say 'cats' [kæts] with a voiceless [s], but after a voiced stop, it is easier to continue voicing and change the [s] to a [z] as in 'dogs' [dɔgz]. An example where this tendency is unacceptable is in [gæzəlin] for [gæsəlin] in the word 'gasoline.' Another instance of the inherent difficulty in rapidly changing from the voiceless to voicing states during speech is exemplified by speakers who stutter. Much of the difficulty in stuttering is in the smooth coordination of muscle activity necessary to make these transitions. The child who is attempting to say his name 'Sam' might prolong [s: æm] or repeat [s-s-s-s-s], but he is not really stuttering on the [s]. Rather, he produces the [s] very well, but fails to make a smooth transition to the voiced [æ].

Table 4.3
Summary Chart of Events during Voicing*

Peripheral nerves	Muscles	Movements	Air pressure	Air movement
Xth cranial n. (vagus) Recurrent branch ⟶	PCA ⟶	Open vocal folds before thorax enlargement		⟶ Air enters via larynx to lungs
	IA ⟶	Adduction of vocal folds		
	LCA ⟶	Medial compression of vocal folds	P_s builds Pressure drops across glottis, $P_{sub} > P_{supra}$	
	Voc. ⟶	Intrinsic tension	Resistance offered to P_s by vocal fold tension	
Xth cranial n. (vagus) Ext. branch of sup. laryngeal n. ⟶	CT ⟶	Longitudinal tension		
		Vocal folds blown ⟵ open	Subglottal air pressure overcomes vocal fold resistance	
				⟶ Released puff of air
		Folds sucked ⟵ together	Negative pressure *vs.* lateral edges of folds as velocity of air increases (Bernoulli effect)	
				⟶ Airstream cut off
		Vocal folds part ⟵	P_{sub} builds again	Another puff of air ⟶ released

* The abbreviations used in the table are: PCA, posterior cricoarytenoid muscle; IA, interarytenoid muscle; LCA, lateral cricoarytenoid muscle; Voc., vocalis muscle; CT, cricothyroid muscle.

Phonation must be coordinated with respiration. The motor commands to the larynx must be related to those of the respiratory system. To take a breath for speech, the glottis opens quickly before the thorax expands, and when the vocal folds adduct for voicing, the action is simultaneous with expiration. Table 4.3 summarizes the chain of events in vocal fold vibration from neural impulses to the results in air pressure and movements. For muscular adjustments the arrows move from left to right, whereas for aerodynamic forces the arrows move from right to left.

ARTICULATION AND RESONANCE

To recapitulate, air from the lungs can either be exhaled through the open larynx to provide energy for sound production above the larynx, as for the sound /s/, or it can be chopped into bits at the vibrating larynx, setting up the periodic sound of voicing. In either case, whether the sound source is at the glottis or in the mouth, the sounds are further modified by the resonances of the vocal tract. In speech production terminology, *articulation* refers to movements of the tongue, pharynx, palate, lips, and jaw to make speech sounds. Resonance, in this context, refers to the acoustic response of air molecules within the oral, nasal, and pharyngeal cavities to some source of sound; the air can be set into vibration in response to a sound from the larynx or a sound created in the oral cavity. It will be seen that movements of the articulators are necessary both for producing sounds in the vocal tract itself and for altering the acoustic resonance characteristics of the tract.

The Vocal Tract: Variable Resonator and Sound Source

The vocal tract includes all of the air passages above the larynx from the glottis to the lips (Fig. 4.51). The large resonant cavities are the pharyngeal cavity, the oral cavity, and when it is open, the nasal cavity. The air spaces between the lips, between the teeth and the cheeks (*buccal* cavities), and within the larynx and trachea are also resonators. You recall from Chapter 3 that air-filled tubes resonate at certain frequencies depending upon whether they are open at one or both ends, upon the length of the tube, the shape of the tube, and the size of the opening. We

know that musical instruments have resonators to amplify and filter the sound. Stringed instruments are designed with resonating boxes graded in size to impart different qualities to the music. The large resonating cavity of the bass viol emphasizes the low frequencies of a complex sound, whereas the smaller resonating cavity of a violin emphasizes the high frequencies. The remarkable characteristic of the human vocal resonator is that its shape can be varied. The cavity shapes can be altered by movements of the articulators. Tongue elevation and fronting creates a smaller area in the oral cavity but widens the area in the pharyngeal cavity. Conversely, tongue depression and backing enlarge the area in the oral cavity while reducing the pharyngeal area. Lip protrusion lengthens the vocal tract creating a lower frequency resonator.

Sounds Produced

The speech sounds which we know as vowels, diphthongs, semivowels, and nasals are the result of filtering the periodic wave produced at the glottis through the vocal tract, which varies its configuration and thereby its resonant frequencies for each sound. The cavity variations and res-

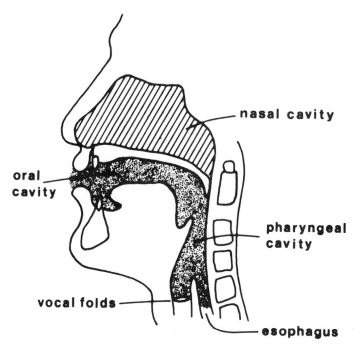

Figure 4.51. A section of the head showing the major cavities of the vocal tract.

onance changes are what make the sounds distinctive. The sounds which emerge at the lips are periodic because of the repetitious movements of the vocal folds.

The vocal tract may also serve as a location for additional speech sound sources. Sounds produced higher in the tract are aperiodic. One class of sounds is the transients created by blocking the airstream and then releasing the built up air pressure suddenly, as in the *stop* consonant /t/. The term plosive is also used for this kind of sound, in recognition of the explosive nature of the air burst.

A second class of aperiodic sounds originating in the vocal tract may be called continuous noises. They are created by forcing the airstream through a constriction, resulting in a noisy turbulence. These sounds last longer than the sharp bursts of the stops. The *fricative* /ʃ/ as in 'shoe' is an example.

Combined Sounds

Speech sound sources can be combined in a variety of ways. A stop closure can be combined with a fricative release, producing an *affricate* /tʃ/. The upper vocal tract sound source of any of the stops, fricatives, or the affricate can be combined with voice, producing such voiced consonants as /d/, /ʒ/, or /dʒ/. These sounds then have two sources; one at the glottis and the other in the oral cavity. In all of these instances of sounds produced in the vocal tract, the cavities of the tract also serve to resonate the sounds. Therefore, the vocal tract is always a resonator and often a source of speech sounds as well (Table 4.4).

Following a description of the vocal tract, we shall consider the sounds of English, starting with the most resonant, open tract sounds (the vowels, diphthongs, and semivowels) and proceeding to the less resonant sounds produced with a more constricted vocal tract (the nasals, stops, and fricatives). For each class of speech sounds, we shall discuss the physiology of its production and the acoustic result.

Landmarks of the Tract

The posterior part of the vocal tract is formed by a tube of muscles known as the *pharynx*. The muscles are divided into three groups according to their position (Fig. 4.52). The *inferior constrictor muscles* are at the level of the larynx, the *middle constrictor muscles* start high in the back and course down to the level of the hyoid bone, and the *superior constrictor muscles* form the back of the pharynx from the level of the palate to the mandible. Contraction of the constrictor muscles narrows the pharyngeal cavity, and relaxation of the muscles widens it. The nasal, oral and laryngeal cavities open into the pharyngeal cavity. The parts of the pharynx behind each cavity are called the nasopharynx, oropharynx, and laryngopharynx, respectively. (See Fig. 4.51.)

Oral Cavity

The oral cavity is bounded in front and along the sides by the teeth set into the *alveolar processes* of the upper jaw or *maxillary bone* (Fig. 4.53) and the lower jaw or *mandible* (Fig. 4.54). The most important teeth for speech are the *incisors,*

Table 4.4
Speech Sound Sources

Source	Resonator	Sound	Manner	Examples
Vocal folds	Vocal tract	Periodic	Vowels	/i/ /u/
			Diphthongs	/ai/ /ou/
			Semivowels	/w/ /y/
			Nasals	/m/ /ŋ/
Vocal tract	Vocal tract	Aperiodic	Stops	/p/ /k/
			Fricatives	/s/ /f/
			Affricate	/tʃ/
Vocal folds and vocal tract	Vocal tract	Mixed periodic and aperiodic	Voiced stops	/b/ /g/
			Voiced fricatives	/z/ /v/
			Voiced affricate	/dʒ/

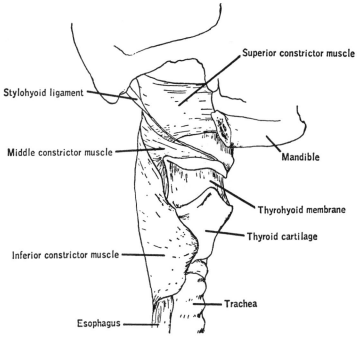

Figure 4.52. The pharyngeal constrictor muscles. Lateral view. (Reprinted with permission from H. M. Kaplan: *Anatomy and Physiology of Speech,* McGraw-Hill Book Co. © 1960.)

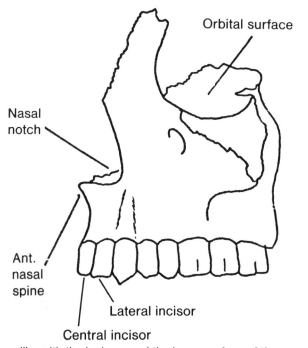

Figure 4.53. The maxilla, with the incisors and the lower surface of the eye socket indicated.

the flat-edged biting teeth in the front of the mouth. There are two central incisors and two lateral incisors in each jaw. They are used with the lower lip, with the tongue, and with each other to create a constriction for such sounds as /f/, /θ/, and /s/. The roof of the oral cavity consists of the *hard palate* (Fig. 4.55) and the soft

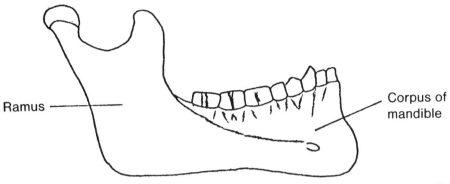

Figure 4.54. The mandible. The two major sections, the ramus and corpus of the mandible, are indicated.

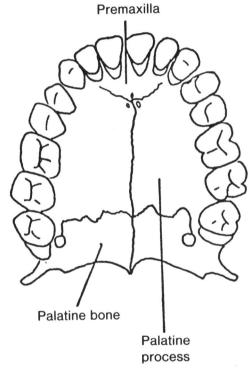

Figure 4.55. The hard palate, with the palatine process of the maxilla and the palatine bone indicated.

palate or *velum*. The anterior ⅔ of the hard palate is formed by the palatine process of the maxillary bone, and the other ⅓ is formed by part of the palatine bone. An important landmark on the hard palate is the posterior portion of the alveolar process called the alveolar ridge. You can feel the alveolar ridge as the ridged shelf behind the upper incisors. Many speech sounds are either generated or resonated as a result of actions of the tongue in

The Velum

The velum or soft palate has one muscle intrinsic to it called the uvular muscle. You can see the *uvula* hanging down in the back of your mouth when you look in a mirror. The greater part of the soft palate, however, consists of a broad muscle entering the sides of the velum from the temporal bones behind and above on each side. These muscles, the *levator palatini* their function is to elevate the soft palate, thus closing the entrance to the nasal cavities above. (Look ahead to Fig. 4.81.) When the levator palatini muscles contract, the soft palate is lifted up and back toward the posterior wall of the pharynx. This action (*velopharyngeal closure*) occurs to some degree for most of the speech sounds in English. The three nasal sounds in English, /m/, /n/, and /ŋ/, require nasal resonance. For these exceptions, the port to the nasal cavities is left open by relaxing the levator palatini muscles.

The Tongue

The floor of the oral cavity is largely formed by the three-dimensional muscle mass, the tongue. The tongue can be moved as a mass in three directions; up and back, down and back, and up and forward. The extrinsic muscles of the tongue are capable of moving the tongue body in the oral and pharyngeal spaces because of their attachments outside of the tongue (Fig. 4.56). The *styloglossus* muscles are attached to the styloid process of each temporal bone. The muscle fibers run down and forward inserting into the sides of the tongue. Contraction of the styloglossus muscles pulls the tongue back and up. This movement is important for sounds such as /u/ as in 'Sue.' The *hyoglossus* muscles are attached to the hyoid bone and the fibers run in a thin sheet up into the lateral base of the tongue. Hyoglossus contraction results in tongue depression and backing. The sounds /ɑ/ and /a/ have low tongue positions. The *genioglossus* muscles are attached to the inside of the mandible at the superior mental spine. The muscle fibers radiate up and back in a fan to insert throughout the length of the tongue down to and including the hyoid bone. Contraction of the genioglossus muscle draws the hyoid bone and tongue root forward, permitting the front of the tongue to move forward and to elevate. High forward tongue placement is important for /i/, as in 'see.'

While the extrinsic muscles determine the gross position of the tongue, the intrinsic muscles of the tongue determine the shape (Fig. 4.57). The *superior longitudinal* muscle consists of many muscle fibers

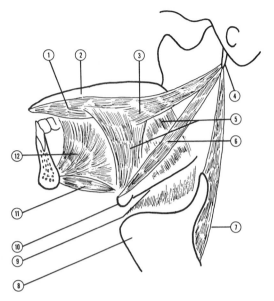

Figure 4.56. A schematic diagram of the extrinsic tongue musculature in lateral view (indicated by * in the following list) and some associated structures. (*1*) The inferior longitudinal muscle (an intrinsic muscle of the tongue); (*2*) dorsum of the tongue; *(*3*) styloglossus muscle; (*4*) styloid process of the temporal bone; *(*5*) hyoglossus muscle; (*6*) stylohyoid muscle (this muscle lifts the hyoid bone up and back; it is not discussed in the text); (*7*) stylopharyngeal muscle (this muscle lifts the larynx; it is not discussed in the text); (*8*) thyroid cartilage; (*9* and *10*) hyoid bone; (*11*) geniohyoid muscle (this muscle stabilizes the hyoid bone; it is not discussed in the text); *(*12*) genioglossus muscle. (Reprinted with permission from W. R. Zemlin: *Speech and Hearing Sciences: Anatomy and Physiology,* Prentice–Hall, Inc. © 1968.)

coursing from the back of the tongue to the tip. Contraction of the superior longitudinal muscle curls the tongue tip up. The *inferior longitudinal* muscles, also running from the root to the tip of the tongue, along the underside of the tongue, act to depress the tongue tip. Between the superior and inferior longitudinal muscles is the major part of the tongue mass. Muscle fibers coursing from top to bottom of the mass (*vertical muscles*) interweave with muscle fibers coursing from the middle of the tongue out to the sides (*transverse muscles*). Together the middle intrinsic muscles of the tongue shape the tongue into a variety of configurations.

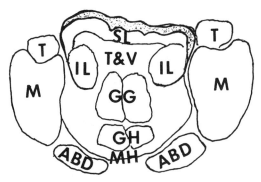

Figure 4.57. The tongue in frontal section. Intrinsic muscles indicated by * in the following list. *SL, the superior longitudinal muscles; *T & V, transverse and vertical muscles; *IL, inferior longitudinal muscles; GG, genioglossus muscles; GH, geniohyoid muscles; MH, mylohyoid muscles; ABD, anterior belly of the digastric muscles; T, teeth; M, mandible.

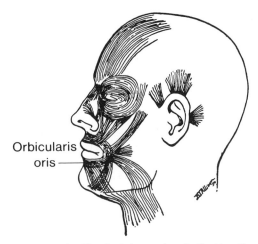

Figure 4.58. The facial muscles, indicating the position of the orbicularis oris. (Adapted from J. V. Basmajian: *Primary Anatomy*, 7th Ed., The Williams & Wilkins Co. © 1976.)

The Lips

Many facial muscles intermingle with the fibers of the major lip muscle, the *orbicularis oris* which encircles the lips (Fig. 4.58). To close the lips for bilabial sounds, /p/, /b/ or /m/, or to protrude the lips for /u/ or /w/, contraction of the orbicularis oris muscle is necessary.

Acoustic Theory of Vowel Production

In 1941, Chiba and Kajiyama wrote a classic monograph on the acoustic derivation of the vowel. Based upon earlier work by von Helmholtz and others, Crandall at Bell Telephone Laboratories had calculated the resonances of the vocal tract for different vowels, by applying acoustic laws of double resonators from equations calculated in 1896 by Rayleigh. Chiba and Kajiyama measured the vocal tract from X-ray photographs and, using Crandall's formulas, calculated the resonant frequencies for single and double resonators of comparable size. When the frequencies as computed coincided with the frequencies of real vowels, the Tokyo group considered that they had gained information on that resonator. The resonances of the vowel /i/ matched those of a single resonator, while those of /u/ and /ɑ/ corresponded with those of double resonators. Fant of Sweden presented a comprehensive study of the acoustics of vowels based upon measurements of the vocal tract taken from X-ray photographs of a Russian speaker during vowel production. His *Acoustic Theory of Speech Production* was published in 1960. It relates a source-filter account of vowel production to the resonances as shown on a sound spectrograph. Fant found the Helmholtz resonator model to be appropriate for only a few vowels. He used a three-parameter model developed by Stevens and House, determining the location of the main tongue constriction, the amount of lip protrusion, and vocal tract cross-sectional areas. For most vowels, it is convenient to consider the vocal tract as a single tube, whereas for consonants a more complex transmission line is a more accurate description.

Resonance of Tube Open at One End

During vowel production, the vocal tract approximates a tube closed at one end and open at the other, because the vocal folds are essentially closed during voicing and the speaker's lips are open. The lowest natural frequency at which such a tube resonates will have a wavelength (λ) 4 times the length of the tube. A male vocal tract, for example, may have a length of approximately 17 cm. The wavelength of the lowest resonant frequency at which the air within such a tube would naturally vibrate, would be 4 × 17 cm or 68 cm. To determine the frequency of vibration (f = velocity/wavelength), one must also consider the velocity of sound in air. If the length of the tube had been measured in terms of feet, the velocity of sound in air in feet (1130 ft/sec) should be used in the formula. Since we have used the metric measure of centimeters, we must compute the velocity in centimeters (344 meters/sec, therefore 34,400 cm/sec).

$$f = \frac{c}{\lambda} = \frac{34{,}400 \text{ cm}}{68 \text{ cm}} = \text{about 506 Hz}$$

where c is used for constant, since in a given medium and at a given temperature, sound travels at a constant velocity. The lowest resonant frequency of such a tube is, thus, about 500 Hz, and it also resonates at odd multiples of that frequency. Why odd multiples? The even multiples are not effective resonant frequencies. Figure 4.59 illustrates the compatibility of the odd multiples with the 500-Hz resonance of the tube. The compression waves and rarefaction waves coincide in direction at the zero crossing, whereas the frequencies which are even multiples of the principle resonant frequency affect the air particles with opposing forces neutralizing one another.

Resonance of Male Vocal Tract

Tubes, then, resonate naturally at certain frequencies when energized, frequencies which depend upon the configuration

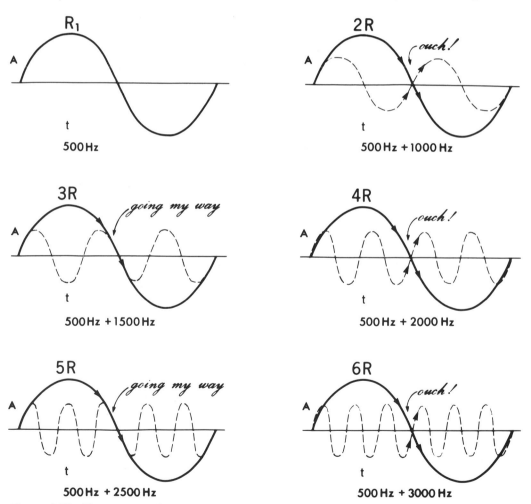

Figure 4.59. The resonant frequencies of a tube open at one end and closed at the other. The even harmonics are not effective resonant frequencies because they are cancelled at the entrance to the tube (''ouch!'') while the odd harmonics are compatible (''going my way'').

and the length of the tube. A human vocal tract is similar to the sort of acoustic resonator we have been describing. There are some differences, largely because unlike the rigid tube, the vocal tract has soft, absorbent walls and is never of absolutely constant cross-sectional area, but the approximation is close enough for our discussion.

Chiba and Kajiyama illustrated the resonances of a tube open at one end, and they related these resonances to those occurring in a vocal tract which is fairly uniform in cross-section (Fig. 4.60). The first resonance of such a tube or tract as schematized in the upper left of the figure, is a frequency which has a wavelength 4 times the length of the tube. Therefore only ¼ of the pressure wave can energize the air within the tube at any one time. The first pressure wave will reach maximum velocity (N_1) at the opening of the tube, or in the case of the human resonator, at the lips. The second frequency at which such resonators vibrate, shown at the lower left of the figure, is 3 times the lowest resonant frequency, as can be seen in the fact that ¾ of the wave fits into the length of the tube. This sets up two points of maximum velocity (N_2 and N_2'). The third resonance (R_3) is a frequency with a wavelength shorter than the tube or vocal tract. It is 5 times the lowest resonance, so $\frac{5}{4}$ of the wave equals the tube length and velocity is maximum at three places. The fourth resonance is 7 times the first, and the maximum velocity occurs in four places. The points of maximum velocity are important, because Chiba shows how the resonances change in frequency if the tract is constricted near a point of maximum velocity or a point of maximum pressure. Remember (Chapter 3 in the discussion of simple harmonic motion) that points of maximum pressure correspond to points of minimum velocity and vice versa. Figure 4.61 may serve to illustrate the inverse relationship between pressure and velocity.

Continuing our consideration of the unconstricted vocal tract, imagine a sound

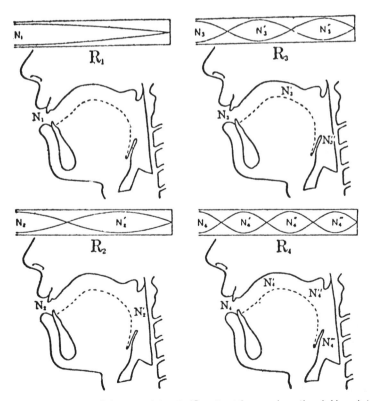

Figure 4.60. The resonances of the vocal tract. (See text for explanation.) *N*, points of maximum velocity; *R*, resonances. (From T. Chiba and M. Kajiyama: *The Vowel: Its Nature and Structure*, Kaiseikan, Tokyo, 1941.)

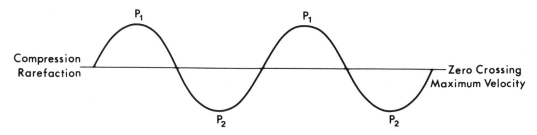

P₁ - maximum positive pressure

P₂ - maximum negative pressure

Figure 4.61. The inverse relationship between pressure and velocity for a sine wave. Pressure is greatest at points P_1 and P_2 for positive and negative values. Velocity is greatest at zero crossings, and at a minimum at P_1 and P_2.

produced at the vocal folds passing through the air-filled cavities of a tract which resonates at frequencies of 500, 1500, and 2500 Hz, about the same resonant frequencies as the 17-cm tube which we discussed in the previous section. Stevens and House and Fant have presented simplified versions of how a sound produced by vibrations of the vocal folds is changed by the resonant response of the vocal tract. The changes which occur can best be understood by comparing the sound at its source at the glottis with the final output at the lips. Whatever acoustic changes might occur, they can be attributed to the effects of transmission through the vocal tract. Figure 4.62 contrasts the waveforms of a vowel sound at its source and at the lips. The source waveform must be inferred, as one would have to lower a microphone into the larynx to record it directly. At first glance, it looks as if the vowel has more high frequency energy than the glottal waveform. The exact nature of the changes undergone in transfer can better be appreciated by contrasting the Fourier spectra. A Fourier analysis, as you recall from Chapter 3, is a process of separating a complex wave into its component frequencies. The spectrum of the sound source (the sound produced at the vocal folds) can be seen to consist of a fundamental frequency (corresponding to the frequency of vocal fold vibration) and many multiples, or harmonics, of the fundamental (Fig. 4.63). These harmonics diminish in intensity as they increase in frequency. If we could hear it, the sound

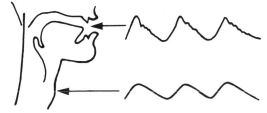

Figure 4.62. A sound wave at the lips and at the glottis. Notice that the waveform is different at the lips, due to the filtering action of the vocal tract.

of voicing would sound like a low-pitch buzz. The middle spectrum is a plot of the resonant frequencies of a neutral vocal tract, which we have computed to be 500, 1500, and 2500 Hz. These are the frequencies at which the air in a tract of that shape and length would vibrate maximally in response to another complex sound. When the sound represented by the first spectrum is transmitted through a vocal tract that resonates at the frequencies indicated in the second spectrum, the resulting sound will be a product of the two. Specifically, the glottal source with its many harmonics is filtered according to the frequency response of the vocal tract. The harmonics of the glottal sound wave which correspond to or are near the resonant frequencies of the vocal tract are amplified, and those distant from the resonant frequencies of the tract lose energy and are thus greatly diminished. The sound which emerges at the end of the tract (the lips) has the same harmonics as the sound at the source (the glottis), but the amplitude of the harmonics has been modified, altering the quality of the sound.

The frequencies which we have described as appropriate for a neutral male tract, a tract shaped to produce the schwa sound [ə] as in the second vowel of 'sofa,' would not be the resonant frequencies for the same vocal tract if it were longer, shorter, or different in its configuration. Speakers differ in size, and a speaker can move his lips, tongue, and jaw creating many different vocal tract sizes and shapes. Any change of vocal tract alters the frequencies at which the cavities resonate. A convincing demonstration of the effect of the vocal tract as a variable resonator is to hum a steady tone and then move the lips and tongue around at random and listen for the changes. The source of the sound at the vocal folds remains constant; the only changes are in the shapes of the resonator. One discovers that simply by changing vocal tract shape, one can make all the vowel sounds.

Vowels /i/, /ɑ/, and /u/

To better understand the derivation of the vowels we hear, let us follow the sounds for /i/, /ɑ/, and /u/, the vowel triangle extremes, from their source at the vocal folds as they are transferred through the vocal tract (which amplifies certain harmonics and attenuates others) until they emerge at the lips. The acoustic result of vocal fold vibration is termed the *source function*, the acoustic result of a certain vocal tract shape and length is termed the *transfer function*, and the output at the lips is a product of the two functions (plus an effect of sound radiation at the lips). The source function is largely independent of the transfer function. For example, you can assume a fixed vocal tract shape and produce that sound with widely different fundamental frequencies. Singing the vowel [i] up the scale, you are conscious of maintaining the appropriate resonator for [i] for each note, whereas the source of the sound is changing. When the source changes, there are two differences: the fundamental frequency is different and the spacing between the harmonics is different, as we discussed previously in connection with phonation. (See Fig. 4.46.)

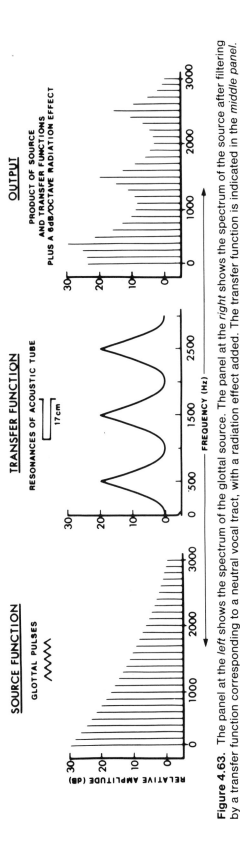

Figure 4.63. The panel at the *left* shows the spectrum of the glottal source. The panel at the *right* shows the spectrum of the source after filtering by a transfer function corresponding to a neutral vocal tract, with a radiation effect added. The transfer function is indicated in the *middle panel*.

Despite these differences, the resonances of the vocal tract remain the same.

High, Front, Unrounded Vowel. The sound /i/ in the word 'key' is distinctive because of the high frequency energy from the resonances in the oral cavity. In order to resonate at such high frequencies, the oral cavity must be made small. That is why the speaker fronts and elevates the tongue toward the alveolar ridge. The tongue mass fills most of the oral cavity, leaving a small volume of air to vibrate (Fig. 4.64). The pharynx, however, enlarges because the posterior part of the tongue, which normally occupies pharyngeal space, moves up and forward. The muscle which is the primary agent for this adjustment is the genioglossus muscle, innervated by the XII cranial nerve, the hypoglossal nerve (Fig. 4.65). Because the tongue is high and fronted and there is no lip protrusion, /i/ is classified as a high, front, unrounded vowel.

If a speaker should produce an [i] sound with a fundamental frequency (f_o) of 150 Hz, followed by another [i] sound with a f_o of 300 Hz, the harmonics which would pass through the vocal tract would differ, but the resonant frequencies of the tract would remain constant. Vocal tract output reflects the source function in the presence of the actual harmonics and in the decrease in intensity of the higher frequencies, but primarily it reflects the transfer function of the cavities, because no matter what the vocal source, the pattern of resonances remains similar for a particular vowel. Notice that the center frequency of a vocal tract resonance (2500 Hz as an instance) does not necessarily correspond with an actual harmonic component of the sound (2250 and 2400 Hz in these instances). The harmonics closest to the resonances of the tract are amplified and those furthest from the resonances lose energy in transmission. A *sound spectrogram* of [i] (Fig. 4.66) depicts the resonances of the vocal tract as broad bands of energy known as *formants*. Formants are traditionally numbered from low to high frequency. The formant centered around 300 Hz is F_1, at 2500 Hz is F_2, and at 3000 Hz is F_3. Looking at a spectrogram is as if one were looking down upon the peaks of a continuous line of spectra. Each band of acoustic energy becomes a formant, with intensity indicated by relative darkness. A description of the sound spectrograph is given in Chapter 6.

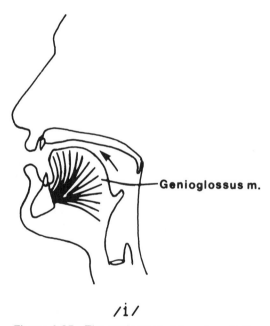

/i/

Figure 4.65. The genioglossus muscle pulls the tongue up and forward for the vowel [i].

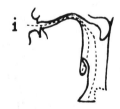

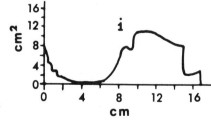

Figure 4.64. On the *left* is shown a lateral view of the tongue for the vowel [i]. The *right panel* shows the cross-sectional area of the vocal tract for [i]. The *abscissa* indicates distance from the lips. (Adapted from G. Fant: *Acoustic Theory of Speech Production,* Mouton, The Hague © 1970.)

Low, Back Vowel. For the vowel /ɑ/, the configuration of the vocal tract is the reverse of that for /i/. The oral cavity widens, and the pharyngeal cavity narrows (Fig. 4.67). The tongue is lowered in the oral cavity by jaw opening or by active tongue depression, presumably effected by the hyoglossus muscle (Fig. 4.68). The lower and farther back the tongue, the larger the space which it occupies in the pharyngeal cavity. The vocal tract configuration for /ɑ/, then, is small at the pharynx and large in the oral cavity. This type of tract elevates the lowest resonant frequency, which in this case is largely a reflection of the resonant response of the back cavity. The F_2 is much lower than that for /i/, due largely to the increased volume of the oral cavity.

High, Back, Rounded Vowel. For /u/, the distinctive acoustic characteristic is the lowering of the resonant frequencies by an elongated vocal tract. To lengthen the tract, speakers usually protrude the lips by contracting the orbicularis oris muscles while elevating the back of the tongue toward the palate, by contracting the styloglossus muscles (Fig. 4.69), to effect a double resonator (Fig. 4.70). If the speaker should try to continue to smile for a photographer while saying something like 'Take two,' it would be necessary to lengthen the tract for the [u] by lowering the larynx instead of protruding the lips; but the acoustic effect would be similar. The resonances for an adult male vocal tract might approximate 300, 900, and 2500 Hz. Absolute frequencies cannot be given,

SPECTRUM   SPECTROGRAM

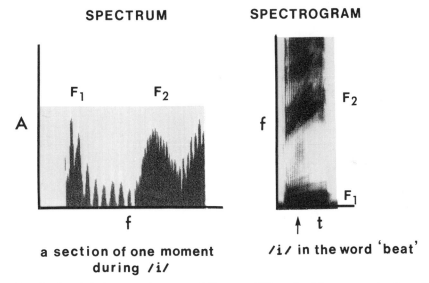

a section of one moment during /i/   /i/ in the word 'beat'

Figure 4.66. On the *right* is a spectrogram of the vowel [i] excised from a production of the word "beat." On the *left* is shown a section of the same sound. The *arrow* indicates the location of the section in time. F_1 and F_2 represent the vocal tract resonances. The spectrogram shows frequency (*f*) changes in time (*t*). The spectrum shows the amplitude (*A*) of the component frequencies (*f*).

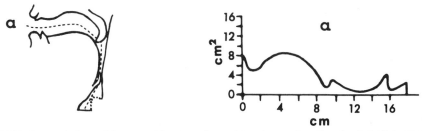

Figure 4.67. Lateral view of the vocal tract and vocal tract area function for [ɑ]. (Adapted from G. Fant: *Acoustic Theory of Speech Production,* Mouton, The Hague © 1970.)

for the frequency response of every vocal tract is slightly different, which partially explains why we can recognize one another as well as we can by voice alone.

The Vowel Triangle

It can be seen that the determinant of vowel quality is vocal tract resonance. Each vowel has a slightly different pattern of resonances than the others (Fig. 4.71). It is convenient to view the tract as a single tube transmission line, although in reality, the tract is more complex. For vowel production, however, it is a good first approximation. Changes in the shape of the vocal tract alter the resonances. As we saw, when the vocal tract is shaped like a tube of uniform cross-section, in a shape similar to that for the neutral vowel [ʌ], its resonances are odd multiples of the lowest resonance. When the shape is changed to that for /i/, /ɑ/, or /u/, parts of the tract are constricted, the resonances change frequency, and they lose their simple relationship to each other. The frequencies of the formants cannot be attributed solely to

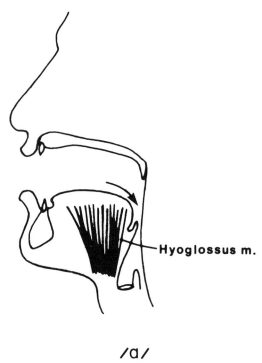

/ɑ/

Figure 4.68. The jaw opens and/or the hyoglossus muscle depresses the tongue for /ɑ/.

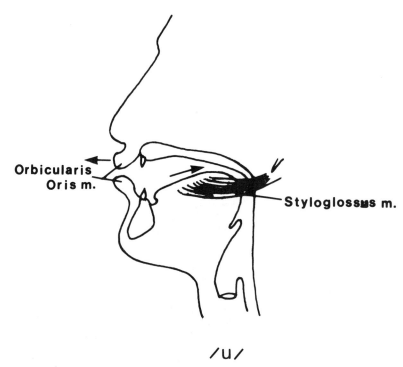

/u/

Figure 4.69. The activity of the orbicularis oris muscle protrudes the lips, while the styloglossus muscle elevates the back of the tongue for /u/.

a particular part of the tract. In general, the formants should be viewed as the response of the tract as a whole, although a case may be made that F_2 is often closely associated with the front cavity. Two-formant vowels schematized from spectrograms (Fig. 4.72) serve to demonstrate the relative formant patterns for some of the vowels of American English. In general, the first formant (F_1) decreases in frequency as pharyngeal enlargement accompanies tongue elevation, and it increases in frequency when the constriction moves back in the vocal tract. F_2 is high in frequency when the oral cavity is constricted and low in frequency when it is more open or elongated.

Effect of Vocal Tract Size. Relative formant positions for a particular vowel are similar for men, women, and children, but the actual resonant frequencies are higher for smaller vocal tracts. The difference in the frequencies of formants is not simply related to change in length, however, because the larger vocal tracts of men have a relatively larger ratio of pharyngeal area to oral cavity area compared to women or children. Peterson and Barney averaged the formant frequencies for men, women, and children from the spectrograms of 76 speakers producing English vowels. Table 4.5 shows the frequency shift with change in vocal tract size. For ease in remembering the acoustic distribution of vocal tract

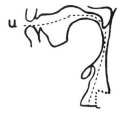
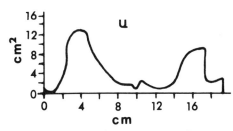

Figure 4.70. Lateral view of the vocal tract and vocal tract area function for /u/. Note that there are two distinct cavities for this vowel. (Adapted from G. Fant: *Acoustic Theory of Speech Production,* Mouton, The Hague © 1970.)

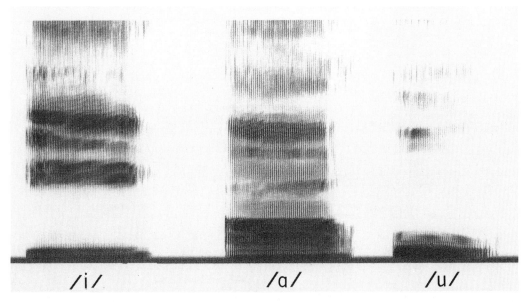

Figure 4.71. Spectrogram of steady state productions of the vowels [i], [ɑ], and [u].

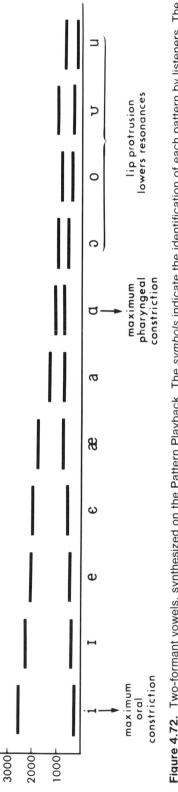

Figure 4.72. Two-formant vowels, synthesized on the Pattern Playback. The *symbols* indicate the identification of each pattern by listeners. The vocal tract characteristics of the corresponding vowels are indicated.

resonances for the extreme vowels in American English, pick round numbers which uphold the general formant pattern across speakers (Fig. 4.73).

Relationship between Acoustics and Physiology

The vowel triangle or quadrilateral, traditional in phonetic literature, represents tongue height on the ordinate and tongue backing on the abscissa (Fig. 4.74). The front of the tongue is high for /i/ and the back of the tongue is high for /u/. For front vowels, the lips remain unrounded in English, but are rounded for most of the back vowels. Observe yourself in a mirror as you say the front vowels in 'eat' [i], 'it' [ɪ], 'ate' [eɪ], 'Ed' [ɛ], 'at' [æ], and you will notice little lip movement. Tongue height seems important in determining the distinguishing resonances for the front vowels. Watch the back series from high to low: 'Sue' [u], 'soot' [ʊ], 'sew' [oʊ], 'saw' [ɔ], 'sock' [ɑ], and you will notice lip rounding in addition to cavity changes for the first four and maximum mouth opening for the low back vowel [ɑ]. Figure 4.75 shows the relative tongue positions for the vowels and indicates the lip adjustments for rounded back vowels and the mouth opening which usually accompanies the low back vowel. These relationships are approximate and simply indicate the most common but not the only method of altering cavity shapes to produce the acoustic requirements for each vowel. X-ray studies of tongue position during the production of the vowel series reveal that the highest point of the tongue for each vowel does not chart as the quadrilateral or triangle traditional in books on phonetics. Phoneticians as a group are probably endowed with 'good ears,' the ability to make fine distinctions in the perception of speech sounds. The traditional vowel charts may only grossly reflect tongue position but quite accurately reflect the relative frequencies of vocal tract resonances when the formants are plotted.

In the Peterson and Barney study, the men, women, and children were recorded as they produced English vowels in a /hVd/ context. The utterances were 'heed, hid, head, had, hod, hawed, hood, who'd,

Table 4.5
Averages of Fundamental and Formant Frequencies of Vowels by 76 Speakers*

		i	ɪ	ε	æ	ɑ	ɔ	ʊ	u	ʌ	ɝ
Fundamental frequencies (cps)	M	136	135	130	127	124	129	137	141	130	133
	W	235	232	223	210	212	216	232	231	221	218
	Ch	272	269	260	251	256	263	276	274	261	261
Formant frequencies (cps)											
F_1	M	270	390	530	660	730	570	440	300	640	490
	W	310	430	610	860	850	590	470	370	760	500
	Ch	370	530	690	1010	1030	680	560	430	850	560
F_2	M	2290	1990	1840	1720	1090	840	1020	870	1190	1350
	W	2790	2480	2330	2050	1220	920	1160	950	1400	1640
	Ch	3200	2730	2610	2320	1370	1060	1410	1170	1590	1820
F_3	M	3010	2550	2480	2410	2440	2410	2240	2240	2390	1690
	W	3310	3070	2990	2850	2810	2710	2680	2670	2780	1960
	Ch	3730	3600	3570	3320	3170	3180	3310	3260	3360	2160

* Taken from G. E. Peterson and H. L. Barney, Control methods used in a study of the identification of vowels. Journal of the Acoustical Society of America 24, 1954, 183.

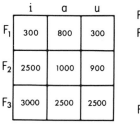
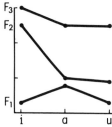

Figure 4.73. Relationships among F_1, F_2, and F_3 for /i/, /ɑ/, and /u/.

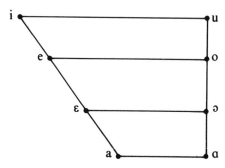

Figure 4.74. The cardinal vowels, represented as a vowel quadrilateral. The cardinal vowels are extremely placed reference points for vowel articulation. Vowels on the same horizontal line were believed to have an equally high tongue height, while vowels in the left-right position were assumed to be equally backed or fronted. (Adapted from *A Course in Phonetics* by Peter Ladefoged, © 1975 by Harcourt Brace Jovanovich, Inc. By permission of the publisher.)

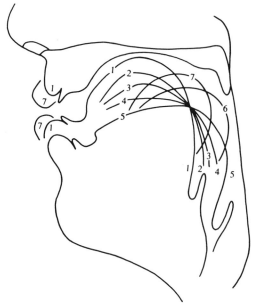

Figure 4.75. The vocal tract shape, for the vowels in the words (*1*) 'heed,' (*2*) 'hid,' (*3*) 'head,' (*4*) 'had,' (*5*) 'father,' (*6*) 'good,' (*7*) 'food.' (Reprinted from *A Course in Phonetics* by Peter Ladefoged, © 1975 by Harcourt Brace Jovanovich, Inc. By permission of the publisher.)

hud, and heard.' The formant frequencies were measured and plotted by relating the first formant (F_1) to the second (F_2). This method, first presented by Joos (1948), shows the relationship between acoustics and physiology of vowels. Figure 4.76 shows F_1 on the abscissa and F_2 on the ordinate. If F_2 frequency is plotted on a Koenig scale, which is linear to 1000 Hz and logarithmic above, a scale designed to approximate the sensitivity of the human auditory mechanism, it is clear that a mirror image of the traditional vowel triangle emerges. The acoustic plot more nearly replicates the traditional phonetic chart than do X-ray plots of tongue position. Ladefoged achieves a closer match by plotting the formant frequencies on a chart with zero frequencies in the upper left corner and by plotting F_1 against the dif-

ference between F_2 and F_1, instead of the usual F_1 by F_2 plot. This results in a more physiologically accurate placement of the back vowels (Fig. 4.77), by showing [ɔ] and [ɑ] to be further back than [u] and [ʊ].

Apparently, phoneticians have been unconsciously charting the vowels according to their acoustic reality, thinking that they were charting physiological reality. It is clear, however, that the acoustic data are a direct reflection of the physiological adjustments. As Ladefoged points out, "vowel 'height' is more closely determined by the first formant frequency than by the height of the tongue, and the so-called front-back dimension is obviously more simply expressed by reference to the difference between the first and second formant frequencies than to any measure of the actual position of the tongue." Fant has also observed that the highest point of the tongue is not as important as the point of maximum constriction and the length of the tract from the glottis to this point. For example, the highest point of the tongue for /ɑ/ is in the oral cavity, but the point

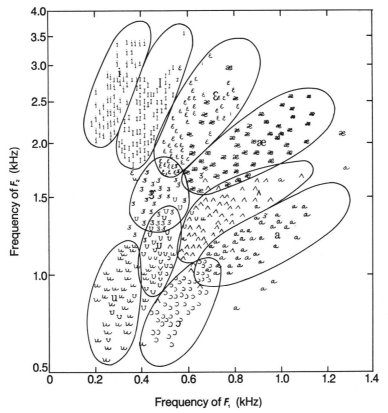

Figure 4.76. Frequency of the second formant *versus* frequency of the first, for 10 vowels spoken by 76 speakers. (Adapted from G. E. Peterson and H. L. Barney, *Journal Acoustics Society of America. 24,* 1952, 182. Reprinted with permission from P. Lieberman: *Speech Physiology and Acoustic Phonetics: An Introduction,* Macmillan © 1977.)

of maximum constriction is in the pharyngeal cavity, closer to the glottis.

Tense-Lax Vowels

Some of the vowels (and diphthongs) in English are intrinsically longer than others and are made by the tongue reaching a more extreme position. The vowels with more extreme tongue adjustments and longer duration are termed *tense* vowels, more for their function in the language than for their method of production. Tense vowels can appear in open syllables, such as 'see, say, lah, sew, Sue, saw, sigh, sow, soy, and cue.' Shorter vowels which can appear in closed syllables (syllables ending with consonants), but not in open syllables, are called *lax* vowels because they are produced with less extreme movements. In English, examples are the vowels in 'sing, strength, sang, song, and sung.' The longer tense vowels can be further divided according to whether the vocal tract is held fairly constant throughout the vowel, or whether there is a distinct change in vocal tract shape during production. Prolong each of the tense vowels given as examples and determine which of them involves changing vocal tract shape in midstream.

Diphthong Production

A diphthong is a vowel of changing resonance. Common diphthongs are the vocalic portions of the words in the following sentences:

> How Joe likes toy trains!
> /aʊ/ /oʊ/ /aɪ/ /ɔɪ/ /eɪ/
> I don't play cowboy.
> /aɪ/ /oʊ/ /eɪ/ /aʊ/ /ɔɪ/

Those 'tense' vowels which you found upon prolongation to require a changing

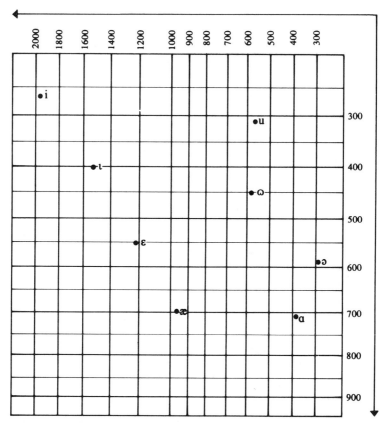

Figure 4.77. A formant chart showing the frequency of the first formant on the *ordinate* (the vertical axis) plotted against the difference in frequency of the first and second formants on the *abscissa* (the horizontal axis) for eight American English vowels. The symbol "ω" indicates "u" (Reprinted from *A Course in Phonetics* by Peter Ladefoged, © 1975 by Harcourt Brace Jovanovich, Inc. By permission of the publisher.)

vocal tract are considered to be diphthongs. Notice that the diphthongs ending with vocal tract cavities appropriate for [ɪ] ([eɪ], [aɪ], and [ɔɪ]) entail tongue movement forward up from the [e], [a], and [ɔ] positions, and the diphthongs ending with vocal tract cavities appropriate for [ʊ] ([oʊ] and [aʊ]) entail tongue movement back and up, concurrent with lip protrusion. The sounds [ɪi] and [ʊu] as in 'see' and 'Sue' are often diphthongized also, but the vocal tract and resonance changes are less extensive than in the others. Acoustic studies of formant changes in diphthongs have shown F_1 and F_2 formant shifts characteristic of each diphthong. Holbrook and Fairbanks measured formant frequencies of diphthongs from spectrograms of 20 male speakers saying 'My name is John __.' with Hay, High, Hoy, Hoe, Howe, and

Hugh as last names. F_1 by F_2 plots show acoustic overlaps, but when the samples are limited to those closest to the median, patterns are more discrete. Figure 4.78 shows that the longer diphthongs with more extensive changes ([aɪ], [aʊ], and [ɔɪ]) undershoot the final goals [ɪ] and [ʊ] more than the shorter diphthongs ([eɪ], [oʊ], and [ju]). The authors noted that [eɪ] extends from [aɪ] in an almost continuous fashion, as does [oʊ] from [aʊ]. Together, they form the trough of an inverted triangle. Muscle use for diphthongs is similar to that for vowels except contractions sometimes gradually shift to another muscle group. For example, to produce [aɪ], the tongue lowering muscles would gradually be replaced by tongue fronting and elevating muscles, such as the genioglossus and geniohyoid muscles. Peterson and Lehiste

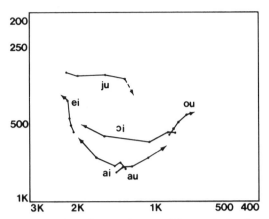

Figure 4.78. First and second formants for the diphthongs. The first formant frequencies are plotted on the ordinate and the second formant frequencies on the abscissa. The direction of formant movement is shown by the *arrows*. (Replotted with permission from data in A. Holbrook and G. Fairbanks: *Journal of Speech and Hearing Research. 5,* 1962.)

measured durations of diphthongs, along with other *syllabic nuclei*, and found the shorter diphthongs (which they called tense monophthongs) [eI], [oU], and [ɝ] to change slowly and continuously, whereas the longer diphthongs [aI], [aU], and [ɔI] evidenced a steady state at the beginning, followed by a longer transition, and ended with a shorter off glide near the terminal target. Vowels and diphthongs, at the heart of each syllable, are difficult for deaf speakers. The relatively open vocal tract changes are subtle and are difficult to specify without hearing the differences. Typically, deaf speakers tend to neutralize the formant contrasts among vowels.

Semivowel Production

The sounds /w/, /j/, /r/, and /l/ as in 'we,' 'you,' 'right,' and 'light' are often called semivowels because, like vowels, they are highly resonant. The /r/ and /l/ sounds, when produced in syllable final position, can be prolonged as in 'car' or 'full' and sound much like vowels. If you pronounce /w/ or /j/ slowly enough, new diphthongs [uʌ] and [iʌ] are formed. The vocal tract is relatively open as for vowels and diphthongs, yet the semivowels are considered to be consonants, not vowels. Why? More than a matter of acoustic dif-

ferentiation, the reason semivowels are classified as consonants is that they function in the language to release the vowel or diphthong. For example, 'win' /wIn/ is possible in English but /twn/ is not, because the syllable lacks a nucleus. Only the open tract, highly resonant vowels and diphthongs are commonly used as nuclei. The semivowels, being nearly as open and resonant, are always positioned next to the nucleus in contexts having consonant clusters. In 'spring,' 'splash,' 'twin,' and 'cute,' the semivowels are all adjacent to the vowels or diphthongs: /sprIŋ/, /splaeʃ/, /twIn/, and /kjut/. Occasionally, though, some of the semivowels serve as nuclei of syllables. They share this opportunity with their highly resonant neighbors, the nasals. For example, the word 'table' has two nuclei, the diphthong [eI] of the first syllable and the [l̩] of the second syllable. When a consonant pinchhits as a vowel, a dot is put under the phonetic transcription to indicate a *syllabic consonant*. Examples are 'bottle' [badl̩], 'chasm' [kaezm̩], and 'up or down' [ʌpr̩daUn] as may be heard in reference to the cooking of fried eggs.

Semivowels can be divided into the *glides* /j/ and /w/ and the *liquids* /l/ and /r/. Glides are well named, for spectrograms of them, like those of diphthongs, show the formants gliding up or down depending upon context (Fig. 4.79). The /j/ is a palatal glide. The tongue blade approximates the palate, at a more forward position for 'ye' than for 'ya,' but the position is not far from that for a front high vowel, thus involving genioglossus muscle action. During [ɑjɑ], the high first formant frequency for [ɑ] swings down as the mouth constricts, while the second formant swings up, reflecting the resonance of the narrowed front cavity. Production of glides requires movement of the tongue and lips to change vocal tract shape from the starting position (high front tongue at start of /j/, high back tongue and protruded lips at start of /w/) to the next vowel position. It is the sound of getting there that is the sound of the glide. Glides are similar to diphthongs but with faster transitions. Notice that the /w/ has two places of articulation: the bilabial protrusion effected by the orbicularis oris and

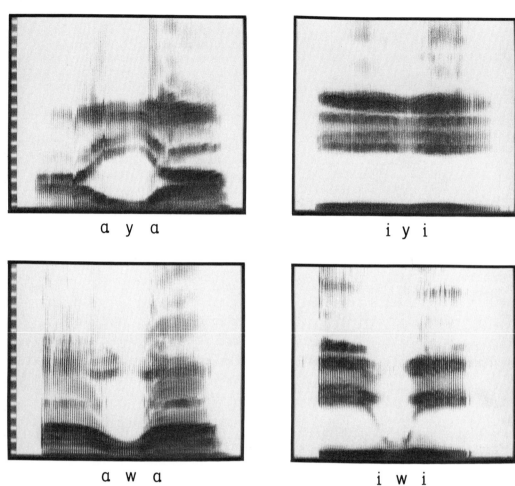

Figure 4.79. Spectrograms of /ɑjɑ/, /iji/, /ɑwɑ/, and /iwi/. Notice that F_2 movement is larger for /ɑjɑ/ than for /iji/, while F_2 movement is smaller for /ɑwɑ/ than for /iwi/.

other lip muscles and the lingua-palatal approximation effected by such muscles as the styloglossus to elevate and back the tongue when needed.

The liquids, /r/ and /l/ are produced in syllable initial position by raising the tongue toward the alveolar ridge, while voicing. Differences in tongue tip configuration and position create the distinctions between the two sounds. For /l/, the tip is resting lightly against the alveolar ridge dividing the pressure waves into two streams which emerge at each side (hence it is often termed a *lateral*). For /r/, the tongue is grooved and does not contact the alveolar ridge, so the acoustic energy emerges centrally. Lips are often rounded. Many speakers *retroflex* the /r/, which means the tongue tip is pulled back further

and tensed. Since tongue tip movement is crucial for the liquids, one would expect the superior longitudinal muscle to be particularly active. The antagonist muscle, the inferior longitudinal muscle, may act more for /r/ than for /l/, especially if the /r/ is retroflexed, whereas the shaping of the dorsum is probably achieved by vertical muscle and transverse muscle interaction. The acoustic results of these tongue tip adjustments (Fig. 4.80) are reflected somewhat in the second formant but are particularly obvious in third formant changes. For /r/, F_3 plunges below the F_3 frequencies typical for vowels, while for /l/, it does not depart from them significantly. Final position /r/ and /l/ differ from initial position. Initial /l/ is produced as the speaker releases the tongue-alveolar con-

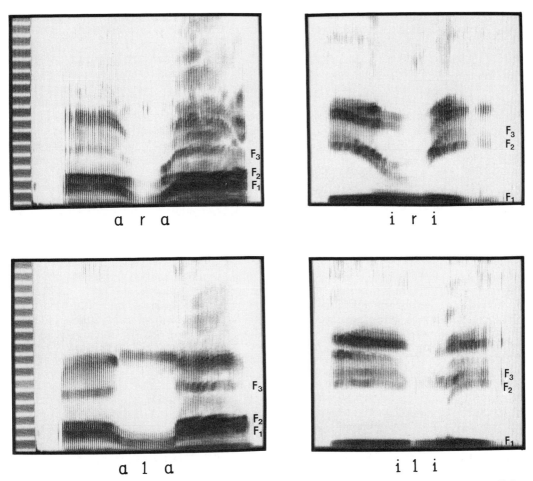

Figure 4.80. Spectrograms of /ɑrɑ/, /iri/, /ɑlɑ/, and /ili/. Notice that F_3 lowers close to F_2 for /r/, while it remains high for /l/.

tact; it cannot be held or it becomes a 'dark' [ł], the sound in 'full.' The /l/ in 'li-li-li' is a releasing lateral sound, but in 'full,' the contact is held during voicing and when finished, the speaker could continue to maintain lingua-alveolar contact and it would not matter beyond tiring the tongue. No wonder the two sounds differ, when one releases the vowel and the other arrests it. Final /r/ differs from its counterpart in initial position also. It loses its consonantal quality and simply colors whatever vowel it follows. Some speakers omit the [r] at the end of 'car,' 'hear,' or 'sure' and substitute vowel lengthening or movement to a neutral tract for the absent [r]; 'hear' becomes /hɪə/ or [hɪː]. Speakers who do produce 'r' coloring to indicate syllable final /r/ elevate the grooved

tongue dorsum toward the palate, which produces a lowered F_3 of the vowel, characteristic of /r/. The fact that /r/ and /l/ are so consistently confused by Oriental speakers for whom English is a second language demonstrates their acoustic similarity. Children with developmental speech substitutions often produce the easier /w/ for the liquids, or sometimes /j/ for /l/, and /w/ for /r/. 'The little rabbit likes carrots' might be rendered [dəjɪtəwæbəjaɪkskæwəts].

Velopharyngeal Port: Vocal Tract Modifier

Most of the speech sounds in the English language are resonated in a two-part tract consisting of the pharyngeal and oral cavities, extending from the vocal folds to the lips. There are three exceptions, sounds which require added resonance in the nasal cavities: the /m/, /n/, and /ŋ/ as in 'mining.' During continuous speech, the chambers of the nose must be closed off most of the time for the *oral sounds*, yet the entrance must be open for the three *nasal sounds*. The entrance to the large nasal chambers from the pharyngeal and oral cavities is called the *velopharyngeal port*, because the entrance lies between the velum and the walls of the pharynx. It can be closed by elevating and backing the velum until it approximates the posterior pharyngeal wall.

The chief muscle used to close the velopharyngeal port is the levator palatini muscle. This paired muscle arises from the petrous portion of the temporal bone and from the lower part of the eustachian tube cartilage. It courses down and forward, curving medially from each side to enter

the soft palate, anterior to the uvula. The fibers from each side intermingle and form the middle of the soft palate (Fig. 4.81). The muscle fibers are positioned like a sling coming from the upper back part of the nasopharynx down and forward to make up the soft palate. The angle of insertion of the levator palatini muscle results in soft palate elevation and backing when the muscle is contracted. This action closes the entrance to the nasal cavities. Innervation of the levator palatini muscles is by the *pharyngeal plexus*, a group of neurons formed from the accessory nerve XI, the vagus nerve X, and sensory fibers from the glossopharyngeal nerve IX. The motor innervation is primarily XIth nerve responsibility.

The uvula, although possessing its own musculature (the *uvular* muscle) adds little or nothing to velar elevation and backing necessary for oral speech sounds. Neither does the *tensor palatini* muscle, which is

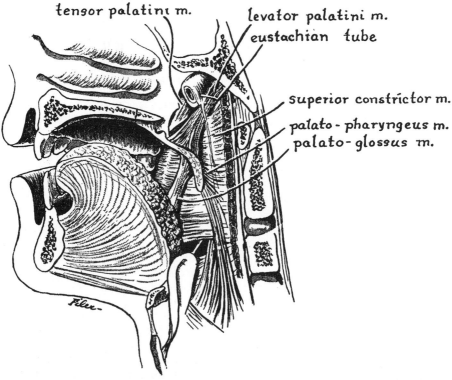

Figure 4.81. Mid-sagittal section of the head, showing the muscles of the pharyngeal part. The palatopharyngeus muscle is not discussed in the text, but it forms the bulk of the posterior faucial pillar. (Reprinted with permission from D. R. Dickson and W. M. Maue: *Human Vocal Anatomy*, Charles C Thomas © 1970.)

active in opening the eustachian tube leading to the middle ear. Electromyographic investigations conducted by Lubker, by Fritzell, and by Bell-Berti have demonstrated the importance of levator palatini activity as the prime agent for velopharyngeal closure. Cinefluorographic studies by Moll and others, along with fiberoptic studies by Bell-Berti and her colleagues, have provided movement information to relate to the information on muscle activity. See Chapter 6 for descriptions of research techniques involved in electromyography, cinefluorography, and fiberoptic viewing.

Speakers elevate and back the velum to achieve the tightest seal for consonants, especially fricatives such as /s/, because these sounds require large *intraoral pressure* (air pressure inside the oral cavity). Any leakage into the nasal cavities would decrease the needed pressure. In general, then, the levator palatini muscle is more active for consonants than for vowels, nasal consonants excepted. Pharyngeal wall movement normally accompanies velopharyngeal closure, but it is not clear whether the movement is a consequence of levator activity or contraction of the constrictor muscles.

The velum or soft palate is coupled to the tongue by a muscle confusingly termed the *palatoglossus* muscle in some references and the glossopalatus. muscle in others. The *anterior faucial pillars* which one can observe in an open mouth (see Fig. 4.82) are made up of the palatoglossus muscles. Since the palatoglossus muscle arises from the transverse muscle fibers within the back of the tongue, ascending to the soft palate on each side to form the anterior faucial pillar, contraction can either lower the palate or elevate the sides and back of the tongue. It is active for some speakers for tongue elevation involved in the production of velar consonants /k,g/ and possibly for lowering of the soft palate for /m,n,ŋ/. Speakers may produce nasal resonance by simply relaxing the levator palatini muscles or in the case of initial nasal consonants, by not contracting the levator until just before the following vowel. Therefore, during most of the time that one is speaking, the velum is actively elevated. When nasal resonance

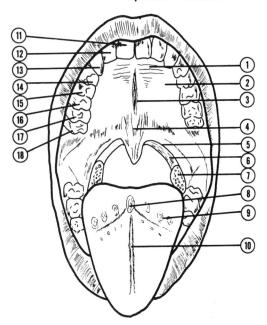

Figure 4.82. Schematic diagram of the structures of the oral cavity. The uvula can be seen at the rear of the soft palate. (*1*) Alveolar ridge; (*2*) hard palate; (*3*) midline of the palate; (*4*) soft palate; (*5*) anterior faucial pillar; (*6*) posterior faucial pillar; (*7*) tonsil; (*8*) sulcus terminalis of the tongue (this V-shaped furrow serves as a boundary between the oral and pharyngeal parts of the tongue); (*9*) vallate papillae (a specialized modification of the tongue surface); (*10*) tongue midline; (*11* and *12*) incisor teeth; (*13*) cuspid teeth; (*14* and *15*) *bicuspid teeth;* (*16, 17* and *18*) molar teeth. (Reprinted with permission from W. R. Zemlin: *Speech and Hearing Sciences: Anatomy and Physiology*, Prentice-Hall, Inc. © 1968.)

is required for /m/, /n/, and /ŋ/, the velum lowers.

The degree of constriction or closure of the velopharyngeal mechanism varies according to phonetic context, from the open position typical for nasals, the intermediate positions typical for low vowels, the more nearly closed positions typical for high vowels, to the closed positions typical for oral consonants. The high vowels, /i/ and /u/, as in 'see' and 'Sue,' are accompanied by a higher velum than are the low vowels, /ɑ/ and /æ/ as in 'hot' and 'hat.' The levator palatini is least active for nasal consonants and most active when going from a nasal consonant to an oral consonant demanding high intraoral pressure. A general rule is that when the velum comes within 2 mm of the pharynx (producing an open area of about 20 mm^2) there is no apparent nasality. A wider opening produces nasal resonance, and speech is definitely perceived as nasal by 5 mm (50 mm^2 in area).

Velar height also plays an important role in adjusting the volume, and thereby the pressure, within the cavities above the larynx. This adjustment aids the voiced-voiceless distinction in consonant production. You recall that in order to maintain vocal fold vibration, pressure below the vocal folds (subglottal pressure) must exceed pressure above the vocal folds (supraglottal pressure). This pressure drop across the glottis is difficult to maintain during voiced stops, for the very act of stopping the airstream creates a sudden build up of supraglottal air pressure, thus destroying the pressure difference across the vocal folds. A brief enlargement of the supraglottal volume during the stop reduces the pressure in order to maintain voicing. Bell-Berti reports electromyographic findings which indicate that speakers vary in their method of enlarging the supraglottal space, some by elevating the velum more, others by relaxing the constrictor muscles more or by lowering the larynx. This function of the velum will be discussed further, when we consider the production of stop consonants later in this chapter.

Failure to make perceptually acceptable adjustments of the velopharyngeal mechanism can be divided into two disorders: *hypernasality* and *hyponasality*, with too much nasal resonance in the first instance and too little nasal resonance on /m,n,ŋ/ in the second instance. The problem of hypernasality is most apparent in speakers who are born with a *cleft palate*, a condition in which part or all of the palate has failed to fuse. Even after surgery to close the palate, the velum may be too small or lack muscle force to adequately close off the nasal cavities. This condition not only results in too much nasal resonance for the vowels but also prevents the speaker from building up sufficient pressure in the oral cavity for stops and fricatives. The air escapes through the nose. Deaf speakers also produce inappropriate degrees of nasal resonance for a different reason; they cannot hear the oral-nasal distinctions made by hearing speakers.

Too little nasal resonance often occurs when speakers suffer from nasal congestion due to colds. In some cases, hypernasality and hyponasality occur in the same speaker because both velar contraction and relaxation are mistimed. People with cerebral palsy sometimes evidence this disorder.

Nasal Production

For vowels and diphthongs, we had only to consider the source of the sound and the resonances of the vocal tract. For consonants, however, the vocal tract becomes sufficiently constricted that not only does it vibrate with greater amplitude at certain frequencies (resonances), but the constrictions and occlusions necessary to produce the consonants create decreased energy in certain frequency ranges (antiresonances). These antiresonances and resonances affect each other. A resonance and antiresonance cancel one another if close in frequency. Sometimes a narrow antiresonance occurring in the midst of a broad resonance will have the effect of making one resonance appear to be two resonances.

Nasal resonance is mandatory for the production of /m,n,ŋ/ in English, so the velum is low, leaving the entrance to the nasal cavaties open. Simultaneously, the oral cavity is occluded in one of three ways. For /m/, the lips are closed by facial nerve (VIIth cranial nerve) innervation of the orbicularis oris muscles. The sound from the vocal folds is thus resonated not only in the pharyngeal cavity and in the cul-de-sac created by the closed oral cavity, but in the spacious chambers of the nasal cavities as well. The alveolar nasal /n/ and the palatal nasal /ŋ/ are produced in much the same way as the bilabial nasal /m/, except the place of oral cavity occlusion differs. For /n/, the blade or tip of the tongue touches the upper alveolar ridge of the hard palate, with the back sides of the tongue touching the upper molars. For /ŋ/, the tongue dorsum touches the posterior part of the hard palate or the soft palate, allowing much less of the oral cavity to resonate as a side branch of the vocal tract. Produce the nasal consonants /m/, /n/, and /ŋ/, one after another to feel the place of occlusion move back in the mouth. You can verify the presence of nasal resonance by placing your fingers lightly against the side of your nose as the sounds are produced.

The addition of the nasal branches to the vocal tract creates a larger, longer resonator. We know that the longer the resonator, the lower the frequencies to which it naturally responds. Fujimura describes the acoustic results of closing the oral cavity while keeping the velum low to give nasal resonance to the voiced sounds /m,n,ŋ/ as the addition of a characteristic nasal 'murmur,' within the 200–300 Hz range for a male tract. This resonance, or formant as it is seen on a sound spectrogram, is a bit lower for [m] than for [n], and lower for [n] than for [ŋ], because of the progressively decreased volume of the oral cavity as the closure moves back in the mouth. Equally characteristic of nasals is an attenuation of upper formants relative to those of neighboring vowels. The damping of the resonances is partly a result of the broader band frequency response set up in the elongated tract. It is a fact of acoustics that a broadly tuned resonator is damped more quickly than a narrowly tuned resonator (Fig. 4.83).

Another reason that nasals suffer a loss in intensity is that sound is absorbed by the soft walls and convolutions within the nasal cavities. The mucous membrane-covered conchae soak in sound energy like acoustic tiles in a sound-treated room. Also, the mouth is not coupled in line with the vocal tract and the energy is diffused at the nostrils to a great extent. In addition to the general decrease in formant intensities and the prominent low frequency nasal resonance, there are *antiresonances* which are frequency bands of conspicuously low energy. The engineering terms used to describe resonances and antiresonances are *poles* and *zeros*, respectively. The frequency ranges for the antiresonances associated with [m], [n], and [ŋ] vary with place of articulation (and thus with the size of the oral cavity, which acts like an acoustic cul-de-sac). The labial nasal consonant [m] is characterized by an antiresonance which is lower (in the 500–1500 Hz range) than that for [n] (around 2,000–3,000 Hz) or for [ŋ] (above 3,000 Hz). A second antiresonance in the area of 600 Hz for a male tract seems to be consistent regardless of place of articulation. Figure 4.84 shows the usual formants for [i] which fade for the nasals. Note the added nasal murmur for [m] and [n].

Vocal Tract as Sound Source

We have seen how vowels, diphthongs, semivowels, and nasals are typically produced by creating a periodic sound in the

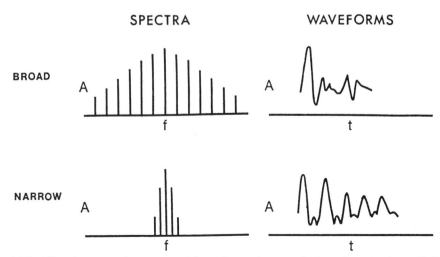

Figure 4.83. Waveforms and spectra of broadly and narrowly tuned resonators. Notice that damping occurs more rapidly for a broadly than for a narrowly tuned resonator.

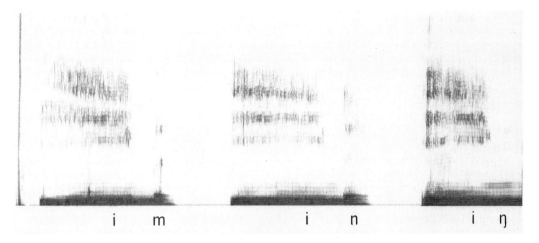

Figure 4.84. Spectrograms of [im], [in], and [iŋ]. Note that formants lose intensity during the nasal.

larynx (the source function) which is resonated in the vocal tract (the transfer function). A contrasting strategy for making speech sounds is to create an aperiodic sound in the vocal tract, usually in the oral cavity. These noises will also be resonated in the vocal tract, most effectively in that part of the tract anterior to the source of the sound. Three *manners* of consonant production that set up noisy pressure waves in the vocal tract are stops, fricatives, and affricates.

Stops or Plosives

Similar to the nasal consonants in *place of articulation* (bilabial, alveolar, and palatal) are the six stop consonants or plosives in English: /p,b,t,d,k,g/, as in 'pie,' 'buy,' 'two,' 'do,' 'cow,'' and 'go.' In each example, like the nasals, the oral cavity is closed at some point. Unlike the nasal closure, which can be prolonged so the sounds are called continuants, the closure for stops creates a rapid growth of air pressure within the oral cavity, which is suddenly released by relaxing the occlusion. The audible burst of air which results is impossible to prolong. It is a transient. A second difference between stops and nasals is that the stops are emitted from the mouth rather than via the nasal cavities. A third difference is that the nasals do not require the high intraoral pressure of the stops, so that there is more freedom to change oral cavity shape during nasal production, a point we shall delineate further when we discuss coarticulation. Finally, nasals are voiced, whereas stops can be either voiced or voiceless. Contrast /p/ and /m/ to demonstrate for yourself the basic differences in duration, resonance, and intraoral air pressure between stops and nasals.

Each voiceless stop in English has a voiced cognate or counterpart. To the voiceless stops /p,t,k/ (an aperiodic sound source), add voice (a periodic sound source) and you get /b,d,g/, a combination of two sound sources. Let us consider syllables made up of an initial [p] or [b] and a vowel. For each, we form an occlusion at the lips, which is released sometime later. The two sounds differ, however, in what is happening at the larynx. For [b], the vocal folds are vibrating when the lips part, while for [p], the folds come together sometime after the occlusion in the upper vocal tract is broken. It is the relative timing of glottal and supraglottal events that identifies the sounds as 'voiced' or 'voiceless.' This relative timing of stop release and onset of voicing has been termed by Lisker and Abramson *voice onset time* (*VOT*). In English, initial voiceless stops have a long delay between releases and voicing onset. However, when a 'voiceless' stop is preceded by a fricative, as in 'pin' *versus* 'spin,' the VOT shortens and becomes more like that for [b].

It is common to describe American English stops like [p] in 'pin' as *aspirated* and those in 'spin' as *unaspirated*. These words describe the difference in air emitted. You can feel this difference by putting your finger in front of your lips while you say [pɪn] and [spɪn]. It is not clear whether the difference between these productions is because of the changes in timing, however.

Muscle activity in the orbicularis oris and other facial muscles contributes to labial closure for /p/ and /b/. The alveolar stop /t/ and its voiced cognate /d/ are produced by moving the tip or blade of the tongue forward and up to contact the alveolar ridge of the hard palate. The superior longitudinal muscle, fibers of which course along the dorsum of the tongue from front to back, aids in producing this closure of the oral cavity. It, like the other tongue muscles, is innervated by the hypoglossal nerve (XII n.). Closure for /k/ and /g/, like /ŋ/, results from elevation of the back of the tongue, along the dorsum, to contact the hard or soft palate. The place of articulation often depends upon the context. For example, the place of articulation for 'key' is further forward than for 'caught.' Thus, although /k,g,ŋ/ are often classified as velar consonants, palatal-velar is more correct. Styloglossus and palatoglossus muscles are in positions to be instrumental in the tongue backing and elevation necessary for this closure. The mylohyoid muscle (Fig. 4.85), a flat trough-like muscle which is attached to each inner

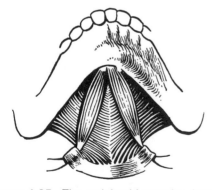

Figure 4.85. The mylohyoid muscles form the floor of the mouth. (The paired muscles lying below the mylohyoids are the anterior bellies of the digastric muscle, which act in lowering the jaw. They are not discussed further in this text.) (Reprinted with permission from J. V. Basmajian: *Primary Anatomy*, 7th Ed., The Williams & Wilkins Co. © 1976.)

side of the mandible, serves as the floor of the oral cavity. This muscle, like the anterior belly of the digastric muscles below it, is innervated by the mylohyoid branch of the trigeminal nerve (V n.), normally considered to be a sensory nerve serving the facial area, but having this motor component. Contraction of the mylohyoid fibers elevates the floor of the oral cavity, assisting in raising the heavy back of the tongue for /k,g,ŋ/. Figure 4.86 contrasts the places of articulation for the labial, alveolar, and palatal-velar stops.

When intraoral pressure has grown sufficiently to produce the stop, the muscles responsible for the closure relax, letting the air escape. In addition, there may be muscles involved in the release. Final stops are often unexploded. The closure is made, but the speaker can simply maintain the articulatory closure made by the lips or tongue. It would seem artificial to release the stops everytime we said words like 'tap,' or 'hat,' although we are more apt to release the [k] in 'sack.' In a successful effort to minimize work for ourselves, we say words with two stops together, such as 'apt' [æpt] or 'kicked' [kɪkt] with only one aspirated release. We simply close for the first stop and during closure shift to the second place of articulation and produce the release for that one.

There is a seventh stop, the glottal stop, which we often hear although it does not enjoy full recognition in English. (We discussed the glottal stop in the section on phonation.) The place of vocal tract closure is the glottis. It is the sound Jimmy Conners makes on each tennis serve. It is the sound some New Yorkers have been heard to substitute for the /t/ in 'bottle,' [baʔl], and many people say in 'rotten' [raʔn̩]. The dots under the /l/ and /n/ indicate that they are serving as syllabic consonants; their high degree of resonance enables them to stand in for a vowel as the nucleus of a syllable.

Acoustically, stops consist of three events: the closure, the opening, and sometimes aspiration (the noise of air emission). During closure, there is silence for the voiceless stops and sometimes the low sound of voicing for the voiced stops, but in both voiced and voiceless cases, there is a noticeable acoustic gap in the formant

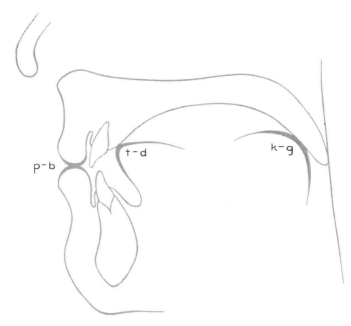

Figure 4.86. The place of articulation for bilabial, alveolar, and palatal-velar stops. (From Arthur J. Bronstein: *The Pronunciation of American English: An Introduction to Phonetics,* p. 68, © 1960. Reprinted by permission of Prentice-Hall, Inc., Englewood Cliffs, N. J.)

pattern. Figure 4.87 contrasts the spectrograms of voiced and voiceless stops. Notice the gaps, periods of silence occurring during the occlusion of the oral cavity. When the air pressure, which has built up behind the closure, is released, there is a burst which often looks like a spike on the spectrogram, as it takes extremely little time but covers a broad range of frequencies. The emphasis is in the high frequencies for /t/ and /d/, the low frequencies for /p/ and /b/, and varies for /k/ and /g/. The burst is often followed by some noise, especially when the plosives are voiceless. The noise looks like random markings on the spectrograms. In general, the bursts of voiceless stops are of greater intensity than are their voiced counterparts.

When initial stops are adjacent to vowels, the difference in timing between /p,t,k/ and /b,d,g/, which Lisker and Abramson called voice onset time (VOT), can be seen on a sound spectrogram. The time between the spike, which represents the burst of air, and the onset of voiced formants, which represent the following vowel is negligible or even negative for the voiced stops.

Negative values of VOT mean that the voicing begins before the burst. In English, voiceless stops in initial position have positive values of voice onset time. There is a relatively long delay between the release-spike and the onset of voiced formants. The voiced-voiceless distinction in initial stops, then, can be understood as a contrast in timing between the opening of the articulatory occlusion and the start of voicing. Other languages employ different timing contrasts. Spanish, for example, is characterized by smaller VOT values than English. The voiceless stops /p,t,k/ are less aspirated and the voiced stops /b,d,g/ often have negative VOTs with voicing occurring during closure and, therefore, before the burst.

A final acoustic effect of stops is a rapid formant *transition* to the relatively steady state of a neighboring vowel. These formant transitions reflect the changes in resonance as the vocal tract changes shape from the stop closure to the more open vowel. The possible acoustic characteristics of stops are many: silence, voice bar, burst, aspiration, VOT, and formant transitions. We shall consider later, in the chapter on speech perception, the importance of this redundancy.

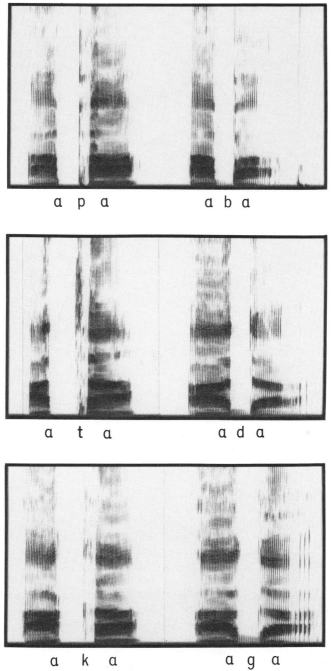

Figure 4.87. Spectrograms of the voiceless and voiced stops, with [ɑ]. They are [ɑpɑ], [ɑbɑ], [ɑtɑ], [ɑdɑ], [ɑkɑ], and [ɑgɑ]. Notice the silence, or gap, during closure. The bursts indicating release of the occlusion are more conspicuous for voiceless than for voiced stops.

Fricatives

A variety of noises can be created in the vocal tract by sending the breath stream through constrictions formed in the tract. The airflow must be strong enough and the constriction must be narrow enough to create friction (noisy random vibrations in the airstream). Similar to the hiss of steam escaping from a radiator, the fricative sounds of speech depend upon compressing a continuous airflow through a narrow passage. In English, there are four primary places of articulation used to produce the constrictions: labiodental, linguadental, alveolar, and palatal. Figure 4.88 schematizes the four constriction sites. If the glottis is open, the airstream is made audible at the point of constriction, but if the glottis is closed with the vocal folds vibrating, the result is two sound sources, the periodic sound of voicing and the aperiodic sound of the fricative. To develop enough air pressure in the oral cavity to produce a noise, the levator palatini muscle must contract, closing the velopharyngeal port sufficiently to avoid leakage. This is particularly important for stops, fricatives, and affricates. Fricatives, like the stops, come in voiced-voiceless pairs.

Labiodental fricatives, /f/ and /v/, as in 'fan' and 'van,' require facial nerve (VIIth cranial nerve) innervation of the appropriate muscles in the lower part of the face (including the inferior orbicularis oris m.) to bring the lower lip close to the inferior edges of the upper central incisors. The linguadental fricatives /θ/ and /ð/, as in 'thigh' and 'thy' are formed by approximation of the tip of the tongue with the upper incisors. This strategy is not very different from that used for the labiodentals, but the motor activity is centered in the tongue muscle group, with the superior longitudinal muscle, (XIIth nerve innervation), playing a primary role. The /f,v,θ,ð/ fricatives are not only similar in production but are also similar, as a result, in their acoustic properties, as we shall discuss shortly.

The alveolar /s,z/ and palatal /ʃ,ʒ/ fricatives are produced a bit differently, and their distinctive, hissing, shushing quality has earned them a subtitle among fricatives, the *sibilants*. Let us first analyze the production of [s] and [z] as in 'Sue' and 'zoo.' The constriction is between the alveolar ridge and the tongue, but speakers vary in which part of the tongue is ele-

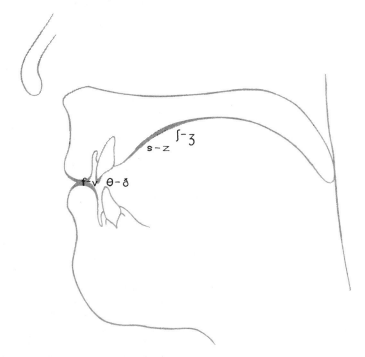

Figure 4.88. Place of articulation for the fricatives of American English; labiodental; linguadental, alveolar, and palatal. (Adapted from Arthur J. Bronstein: *The Pronunciation of American English: An Introduction to Phonetics,* p. 84, © 1960. Reprinted by permission of Prentice-Hall, Inc., Englewood Cliffs, N. J.)

vated. Many speakers form the constriction between the tip of the tongue and the ridge, while others tuck the tip down behind the lower incisors humping the dorsum of the tongue up, so the constriction is formed between the blade of the tongue and the alveolar ridge. Pinch the tip of your tongue so you can sense where it is, and try to locate it relative to your teeth as you prolong an [s]. Is it up behind the upper incisors, down behind the lower incisors, or somewhere in between?

For [s] and [z], a groove is often formed along the tongue midline to channel the airstream. This is accomplished by touching the sides of the tongue to the side teeth. A second constriction is important to the production of the alveolar fricatives; the opening between the upper and lower incisors must be narrow. The difficulties in producing /s/ and /z/ for someone with an open bite or missing front teeth demonstrate the importance of this second constriction.

The muscle groups implicated in these maneuvers are those of the jaw and of the tongue. Depending, of course, upon the jaw and tongue positions at the onset of motor activity for /s/ or /z/, the jaw closers (principally the *medial pterygoid* m. Fig. 4.89), innervated by the mandibular branch of the trigeminal nerve (Vth cranial nerve) and tongue elevators (genioglossus m. and geniohyoid m.), are more or less active. The pattern of muscle activity within the intrinsic muscles of the tongue varies too with the individual methods of forming the alveolar constriction. 'Tongue-tip-up' speakers evidence more activity in the superior longitudinal muscle, while 'tongue-tip-down' speakers show active contraction of the inferior longitudinal muscle.

The palatal / ʃ / and /ʒ/, as in 'shoe' and 'azure' are quite similar to /s/ and /z/. The constriction is made a bit further back and the opening is slightly wider. Also, the lips may be rounded a little. Since the shape of the lips is less critical for /s/ (they are sometimes spread, but need not be), try a lip-rounded /s/, and moving your tongue back slowly, widening the constriction, produce / ʃ /. These fricatives are often confused in production. The alveolar constriction for /s/ averages about 1 mm and

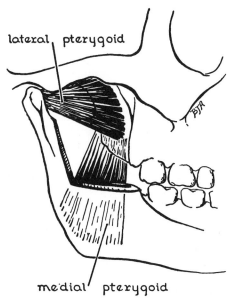

Figure 4.89. The lateral and medial pterygoid muscles in lateral view. The medial pterygoid acts to raise the jaw in speech. (The lateral pterygoid muscle is a complex muscle which acts to pull the jaw forward. Its functions in speech are poorly understood. It will not be discussed in the text.) (Reprinted with permission from J. V. Basmajian: *Primary Anatomy*, 7th Ed., The Williams & Wilkins Co. © 1976.)

the incisor constriction about 2–3 mm, according to X-ray studies by Subtelny. The length of the alveolar constriction (~2.5 cm) may be more important than the width. A wide range of openings beyond those for /s/ result in / ʃ /-type sounds; therefore, it is not surprising that the prevailing misarticulation is / ʃ / in place of /s/ and not the other way around.

There is another fricative which fits less neatly into the scheme of articulatory phonetics. The *aspirate*, /h/, is a fricative with the constriction located in the larynx, typically at the glottis. It is usually voiceless as in 'hat' but can be voiced when embedded between voiced segments, as in 'ahead.' The only required movement is the approximation of the folds, controlled by the laryngeal adductors and abductors. The vocal tract takes the shape of whatever vowel is to follow. During the production of [h] for 'heat' and for 'hot,' the vocal tract takes the shape of [i] and [ɑ], respectively.

Fricatives are *continuants*. Unlike stops,

they can be prolonged. In common with all speech sounds, fricatives are the product of a sound source (sometimes two sources) modified by transfer through a resonator and further modified by the effect of the sound radiating at the output. The source of the fricative noise is at the constriction. Heinz and Stevens have shown that the spectrum of the sound at the lips is determined largely by the resonant characteristics of the constriction and the vocal tract anterior to the noise source. Figure 4.90 shows sound spectrograms of the fricatives. At first glance, it can be seen that fricative energy is very low for /f/, /v/, /θ/, and /ð/. Despite the low energy, the frequency band is broad. A narrower band of high frequency, high energy noise characterizes the sibilants. The intensity difference between the labio- and linguadentals and the alveolar and palatal fricatives, is represented in spectrograms by the darkness of the friction. Most of the sound energy for /s/ is above 4 kHz, while for /ʃ/ it is around 2500 Hz and above. The effective resonator for /ʃ/ is longer than that for /s/, hence its lower frequencies, due not only to the more posteriorly placed constriction but also to the lengthening which may be provided by lip rounding.

As an example of the source-filter account of consonant production, let us detail the acoustic production of /s/, much as we did with /i/, /ɑ/, and /u/ for the vowels. The poles, or resonances, for /s/ are derived from the natural resonant frequency of the constriction and the natural resonant frequency of the cavity in front of the constriction. Figure 4.91 shows a vocal tract configuration appropriate for /s/ production. The narrow constriction can be considered to resonate like any tube open at both ends; the lowest resonant frequency has a wavelength (λ) 2 times the length of the tube. To use Subtelny's measurements, this would be 2 × 2.5 cm. or 5 cm. The natural resonant frequency for such a tube is thus about 6880 Hz.

$$f = \frac{\text{velocity of sound}}{\lambda \text{ (wavelength)}} = \frac{34,400 \text{ cm}}{5 \text{ cm}} = 6,880 \text{ Hz}$$

The source of the fricative noise is at the anterior edge of the constriction. The air-filled cavity in front of the noise source can be likened to a tube closed at one end, because the constriction is extremely narrow at the source. Tubes closed at one end and open at the other are ¼ wave resonators rather than ½ wave resonators, as you may recall from the earlier discussion on vocal production, so that the resonance for the anterior cavity approximates 8600 Hz.

$$f = \frac{\text{Velocity}}{\lambda} = \frac{34,400 \text{ cm}}{4 \ (1 \text{ cm})}$$
$$= \frac{34,400 \text{ cm}}{4 \text{ cm}} = 8,600 \text{ Hz}$$

Because of the narrowness of the constriction, the back cavity resonances are not heard. Thus, there is little energy below 4000 Hz. The resonances that would have been produced below 4 kHz are cancelled by the back cavity antiresonances. We have seen that most of the energy for /s/ lies above 4000 Hz. For /ʃ/ the energy is above 2500 Hz.

Uldall reported that when /s/ is next to a stop, the lower border of the fricative noise changes, reflecting vocal tract adjustments being made during the fricative. The border lowers in frequency as the tract approaches labial closure, increases in frequency during the approach to alveolar stops, and remains stable for the palatal-velar stops.

Affricates

There are only two affricates in English, [tʃ] and [dʒ], as in 'chair' and 'jar.' An affricate is simply a stop with a fricative release. The alveolar closure is made for the [t] or [d], but when the speaker releases the closure, constriction noise is produced. The lips are rounded slightly and the tongue is retracted slightly for the constriction, producing [ʃ] noise. Figure 4.92 shows the expected acoustic results of the closure (with its voicing striations for /dʒ/ and silence for the /tʃ/ closure), the burst or sudden onset of noise, and the duration of frication.

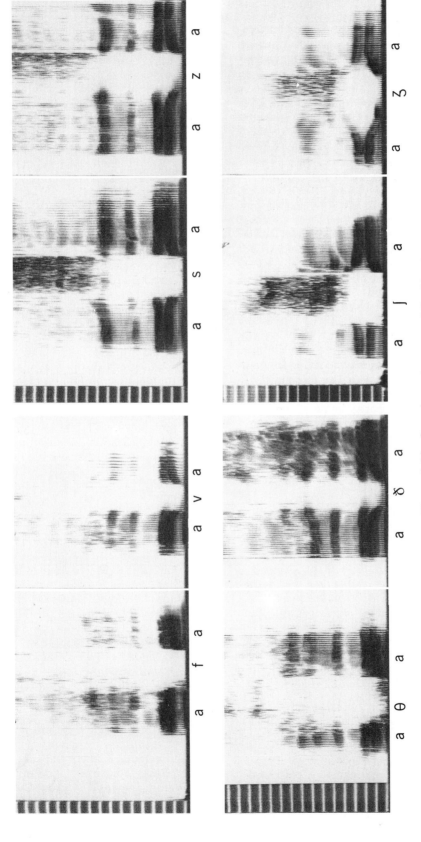

Figure 4.90. Sound spectrograms of the fricatives.

ENGLISH SPEECH SOUNDS

Having surveyed the sounds of our language, it may be helpful to relate them to one another in two ways: first, by manner and place of articulation in the vocal tract and second, by considering some of the ways they affect one another in context. Place of articulation for vowels and consonants are traditionally charted separately. The vowel triangle or quadrilateral was shown in Figure 4.74. Consonants are charted by manner of articulation on the vertical axis and place of articulation on the horizontal axis as shown in Figure 4.93. As part of an effort to systematize the terminology used in acoustic and articulatory phonetics, Peterson and Shoup arranged the speech sounds according to place of articulation in an interesting way. Figure 4.94 is an adaptation of their figure, in which all but the English sounds have been omitted. The vertical axis represents complete vocal tract closure at the top and proceeds to an open tract at the bottom, with sounds having a common manner of articulation connected. For example, following the level for stops across the chart and around the corner, one ends at the glottal stop. Place of articulation is repre-

sented horizontally by the front-back dimension. 'Vertical Place of Articulation' unites the tongue height and consonant manner of articulation descriptions.

Sound Influence

Adaptation

Speech is a continuously changing acoustic stream produced by dynamic articulatory processes. The sounds of speech in context are influenced and altered by their neighboring sounds. Central to a better understanding of speech production is the study of these influences which speech sounds have upon one another, as evidenced in acoustic, movement, and muscle activity information. There are three primary aspects of sound influence which can be studied: adaptation, assimilation, and coarticulation, as we shall define them. One kind of influence we have chosen to call *adaptation*. Phonetic adaptations are variations in the ways in which articulators move and the extent to which cavities change shape, according to what phonemes are neighbors.

Articulator positions and cavity shapes for one phone determine the movements necessary to produce nearby phones. The results of adaptation are evident in acoustic, movement, and EMG data. Figure 4.95 offers acoustic evidence of adaptation. To produce the [t] closure at the end of 'eat,' a relatively small change in oral cavity shape is made, resulting in a small F_2 transition, while the same closure after [ɔ] requires a shortening of the vocal tract (which had been lengthened for [ɔ]) and a more extensive tongue elevation, reflected in a large positive F_2 transition. Thus, the method of producing each /t/ has been adapted to its vowel environment. X-ray studies have also shown influences of position upon movement. Tongue-palate contact for the [k] in 'key' is often less back than for the [k] in 'caught,' as the consonant is again adapted to the vowel. MacNeilage has given a different sort of example: speaking with a pipe clenched between the teeth. Tongue elevation for an alveolar stop would have to adapt to this high mandible position compared with the

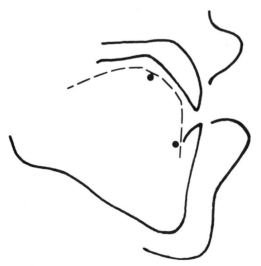

Figure 4.91. Tracing made from a lateral view X-ray film of the vocal tract in position for [s] production. The *black dots* represent lead pellets. Movements of the tongue were analyzed by following the movements of the pellets from frame to frame.

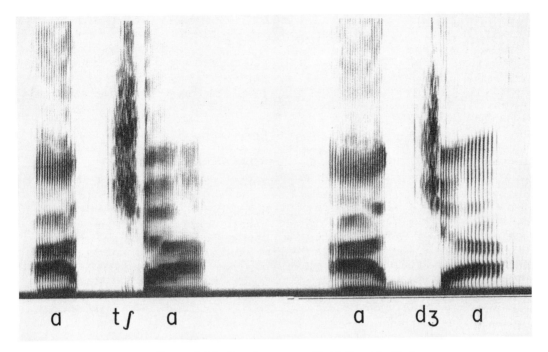

a   tʃ   a   a   dʒ   a

Figure 4.92. Spectrograms of [atʃa] and [adʒa].

	Both Lips (bilabial)	Lip—Teeth (labio-dental)	Tongue—Teeth (lingua-dental	Tongue—Ridge (alveolar)	Tongue—Hard Palate (post-alveolar)	Tongue Blade—Palate (palatal)	Tongue—Velum (velar)	Glottis (glottal)
Stops	p b			t d			k g	?
Continuants Fricatives Frictionless Sounds	ʍ	f v	θ ð	s z	ʃ ʒ		(ʍ)	h
Nasals	m			n			ŋ	
Laterals				l				
Glide-semivowels	w			r		j	(w, r)	
Affricates					tʃ dʒ			

Figure 4.93. Classification of the American English consonants. Voiceless consonants appear to the *left* in each column, voiced consonants to the *right*. Secondary forms of the same sound are shown in *parentheses.* From Arthur J. Bronstein: *The Pronunciation of American English: An Introduction to Phonetics,* p. 66, © 1960. Reprinted by permission of Prentice-Hall, Inc., Englewood Cliffs, N. J.)

movement required were the mouth open and the jaw lowered for /ɑ/.

On the level of muscle activity, electromyographic recordings associated with a given speech sound vary with phonetic context. MacNeilage and De Clerk found pervasive influences of adjacent vowels or consonants upon the EMG signal associated with a particular phone. An example of adaptation, drawn from the work of

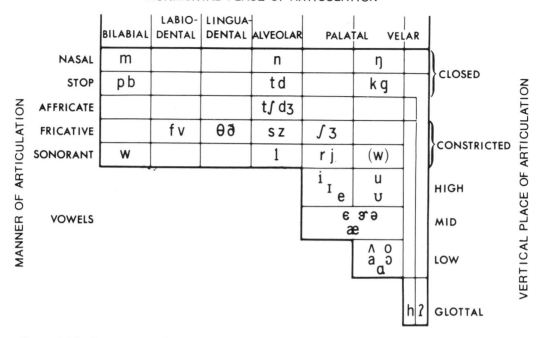

Figure 4.94. Peterson and Shoup's chart for the sounds of American English. (See text for further discussion.) (Adapted from G. E. Peterson and J. E. Shoup: *Journal of Speech and Hearing Research. 9,* 1966.)

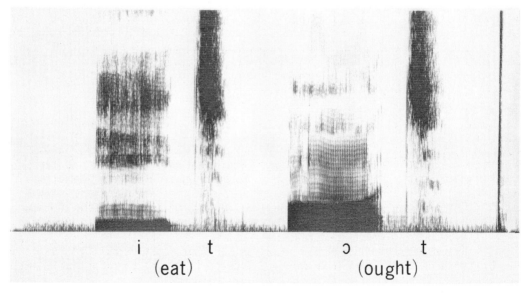

Figure 4.95. Acoustic adaptation. The F_2 transition for [t] in 'eat' is very small relative to the F_2 transition for [t] in 'ought.'

Bell-Berti and Harris, is the activity of the genioglossus muscle, which you recall fronts and elevates the mass of the tongue. Genioglossus muscle activity (see Fig. 4.96) was found to be larger for [u] after the low vowel [ɑ] plus consonant than it was after an already elevated vowel, [i] plus the same consonant. The tongue had farther

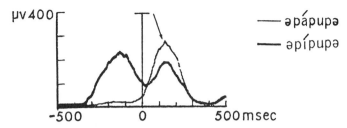

Figure 4.96. Genioglossus muscle activity for [u] after [ɑ] and [i]. The amount of activity is greater after [ɑ] because the tongue must move a greater distance. *Arrow* indicates peak activity for [u]. (From F. Bell-Berti and K. S. Harris: *Some Aspects of Coarticulation,* 8th International Congress of Phonetic Sciences, Leeds, England, Aug. 1975).

to go in its travels from the low, back [ɑ] position to the high [u] position. In contrast, when the tongue was already high, for [i], it had less of a journey to the [u] position. Thus, articulatory positions at a given time affect the muscle activity necessary to produce forthcoming movements. The resulting adaptations are apparent at all levels of physiological and acoustic investigation.

A special case of adaptation is the result of a change in rate of speaking. Faster speaking rates result in the tongue falling short of its target positions. Lindblom has shown by spectrographic analysis of vowels that increasing rate neutralizes the formant patterns toward the unstressed schwa /ə/, which can thus be considered an allophone of all vowels. Usually, the neutralization is more subtle, but you can hear the sound change if you compare the /æ/ in the protest 'But you have!' with a quickly delivered 'You have seen it,' with primary stress on 'seen.'

An extreme form of adaptation is called assimilation.

Assimilation

We have viewed adaptation as meaning that production of a given speech sound varies according to its neighboring vocal tract shapes. If these accommodations go far enough, a phone may actually change to be more like its neighbors. This change in speech sound is called *assimilation.* Phoneticians have carefully described the process of assimilation in speech. A feature of one sound is extended to another. The voicing feature, for example, is extended to the /s/ in 'husband' because of the influence of its voiced surroundings.

The feature of velar-palatal placement is extended to the normally alveolar /n/ in 'think,' producing [θɪŋk], thus assimilating the nasal to the more posterior /k/ place of articulation.

The influence can be either in anticipation of the next sound, anticipatory (also called right-to-left) assimilation, or it can be carryover (left-to-right) assimilation in which an ongoing feature is continued to the next sound. The example 'think' [θɪŋk] is an anticipatory assimilation, for the [n] is changed to [ŋ] in anticipation of the [k]. Carryover assimilation is exemplified by the plural ending after voiced consonants: the /s/ in 'cats' remains an [s], but the /s/ in 'dogs' has become [z]. The voicing in the /g/ is carried over to the /s/, producing [z].

Coarticulation

Another kind of phonetic influence evident in speech production is called coarticulation. A strict definition of *coarticulation* is that two articulators are moving at the same time for different phonemes. This differs from adaptation (one articulator modifying its movements due to context) and from assimilation (actual sound change), although they are obviously related. Coarticulation may result in the smear of features found in assimilation, yet coarticulation may also exist without a sound change. An example of coarticulation is when a speaker, saying 'two' [tu], rounds the lips for [u] while the tongue is active for [t]. A simple trial will verify that it is possible to say 'two' with a large lip-rounding lead, and it is equally possible to say 'two' with little or no lip rounding during the [t]. Coarticulation has been reported from acoustic, movement, and EMG studies. Kozhevnikov and Chistovich of the Soviet Union found that lip rounding for [u] can start at the beginning of a CCV (consonant-consonant-vowel) syllable, if there is no movement competitive to it. Öhman, of Sweden, postulated, from spectrographic evidence, that the tongue moves from vowel shape to vowel shape with the consonantal gestures superimposed, overlapping in time with the articulatory gestures for the vowels, hence coarticulation. X-ray investigations also present evidence of coarticulation. Perkell cites examples, one of which is the coarticulation of the mandible and the tongue for nasal plus vowel utterances, as in 'not' [nɑt]. If the nasal involves tongue movement, as it does for /n/, the mandible is free to move for the /ɑ/ at the same time, whereas if it were a stop, /t/, the mandible would have to wait until the alveolar closure to start toward the vowel opening. Stops require high pressure behind the closure which nasals, as you know, do not. Premature jaw lowering would threaten the loss of that pressure. If an articulator is free to move, it often does. Daniloff and Moll found the lips to move for /u/-rounding several phones before the vowel. Bell-Berti and Harris, who reported orbicularis oris muscle activity for the /u/, found it to occur at a relatively fixed time before the vowel sound, coarticulating with the activity for the consonant or consonant cluster preceding it, but unaffected by the number of consonants there. Öhman noted from his observations of spectrograms that the tongue might act as three somewhat independent articulators with the tip, blade, and dorsum coarticulating. Borden and Gay, in a cinefluorographic study, verified this theory with movement data. That part of the tongue free to lower for /ɑ/ during stop production, proceeded to lower. If the tip of the tongue were elevated for /t/, the back of the tongue lowered simultaneously for the /ɑ/. If the dorsum were involved with /k/ closure, the front of the tongue got a head start in lowering. The tongue can coarticulate with itself. There are individual differences in the pattern of coarticulation, however.

Coarticulation and adaptation of one articulatory movement to another is pervasive in running speech. It is what Liberman has called, in both perception and production of speech, *parallel processing*. It is the combination of adaptation and coarticulation which makes speech transmission rapid and efficient as a code. The segmental modifications necessary for rapid transmission should not be confused with a different, but interesting, kind of sound change, stemming from speaker variations, as in dialects. Thus, there may be deletions [laɪbɛrɪ] for [laɪbrɛrɪ] in 'library,' additions [aɪdiɜ:v] for [aɪdiə:v] in 'idea of,' and *metathesis* or sound exchange, as [æks] for 'ask' or [larnɪks] for 'larynx.' All sound influences, however, demonstrate that speech is not produced as beads are put on a string, one phone after another. The sounds overlap and flow into one continuously changing stream of sound, further bonded by slowly changing modifications overlaid upon it. These overlaid changes are the *prosody*, the rhythm and music of speech.

Suprasegmentals

The *suprasegmental*, or prosodic, features of a language are variations larger than individual segments. They are overlaid upon a word, phrase, or sentence. The suprasegmental features which we shall consider are stress, intonation, duration, and juncture. We have treated phonemes as the segments of speech. Yet we know that phonemes exist as independent units only in our minds. Since we know the language, we know which families of sounds act contrastively, as the family of /p/ sounds contrasts with the family of /t/ sounds, in utterances such as 'pie' and 'tie.' In running speech, however, these segments rarely exist independently. Sometimes, we use a speech sound alone, as when we exclaim 'Oh!' or when we quiet someone with 'sh.' In utterances such as 'pie,' however, the production is never accomplished by saying [p] and then quickly saying [aɪ]. No matter how quickly the [aɪ] follows upon the [p], it does not become [paɪ]. Because we understand the contrastive function of phonemes in the language, we use separate symbols for them in writing even though they merge in speech. Occasionally, a child who suffers from difficulties in learning to read (dyslexia) will be aided by a well-meaning teacher who mistakenly views speech as a succession of independent sounds, like the separate letters on the page, and accordingly asks the child to sound the [p], then the [aɪ]. The child obediently and predictably repeats [pəʔaɪ], and the teacher wonders why speeding it up fails to produce [paɪ]. The answer, of course, is that speakers produce more than one phoneme at the same time: while the lips are closed for the [p], the tongue is lowering for the beginning of the [aɪ], and while the lips are opening to release the burst, the tongue is fronting and elevating for the off-glide of the diphthong. This coarticulation produces a unit well known as the *syllable*. Utterances are organized as monosyllables, such as 'bat,' 'eat,' and 'tea,' as disyllables, such as 'beyond,' 'hidden,' and 'table,' and as polysyllables, such as 'unicorn,' 'immediate,' and 'unsophisticated,' which consist of more than two syllables. People can usually tell you how many syllables there are in a sentence, even though they do not always know the source of their information. We know the number of syllables by counting the highly resonant centers of each syllable, the syllabic nuclei. We count each nucleus as a syllable, whether it is stressed or unstressed. In the following translation, there are only 4 syllables with primary stress, but there are 13 syllables.

"What 'wisdom can you 'find that is 'greater than 'kindness?"

Jean Jacques Rousseau
Emile; On Education (1762)

Stress

Linguistic stress is one of the suprasegmental features of English. English uses stress contrastively: 'permit, with the first syllable stressed is a noun meaning 'a document of authorization,' but per'mit, with the second syllable stressed, is a verb meaning 'to allow.' Stress is signaled by increased effort, intensity, pitch, duration, and a change in formant pattern. It is a complex signal. More articulatory effort is involved in producing the stressed syllable than the unstressed syllable. Fundamental frequency usually increases for the

stressed syllable, and the formants for the stressed vowels reflect articulatory achievement of target positions, along with the necessarily higher muscle activity. For de-stressed samples of the same vowels, however, the formants are neutralized, reflecting articulatory undershoot. Vowels are longer in duration in the stressed condition and tend to be of higher intensity, primarily due to greater subglottal air pressure. Stress can be indicated with various combinations of these cues. It can be shifted for emphasis, as in the sentence: 'It's not her 'mother; it's her mother-in-'law.' (Usually the primary stress is on the first syllable of 'mother' rather than on 'law.') Stress changes can make differences in meaning. In some disyllables, moving the stress to the second syllable changes nouns into verbs, as in 'extract,' 'digest,' 'contract,' 'increase,' and the previously cited 'permit.' In polysyllables, there is a tendency to retain the second stress for verbs ['ɛstə'meɪt] as 'to estimate,' but to lose the secondary stress for the noun, ['ɛstəmət] as 'an estimate.' There is also a tendency toward alternating stressed and unstressed syllables in English with stressed syllables occurring at fairly regular intervals.

Intonation

The suprasegmental features are a direct bridge to meaning, revealing as they do the attitudes and feelings of the speaker in ways the segmental information alone can never do. Stress, for example, when used for emphasis, can express disdain for children in general, 'not that 'child!' or dislike of a particular child, 'not 'that child!' The use of changing f_o, perceived as the pitch pattern or intonation contour of a phrase or sentence is particularly effective in expressing differences in attitude (f_o would increase for the stressed words in the example above) and also differences in meaning. 'Today is Tuesday' said with rising intonation, the pitch increasing during 'Tuesday,' turns a declaration into a question. Prosodic information is transmitted along with the segmental information in the sentence 'That's a pretty picture!', but the prosodic features alone can signal opposite meanings, since they can convey genuine admiration of the picture or sarcasm. This intonation pattern (perceived changes in fundamental frequency) can be imposed on a sentence, a phrase, or even a word. American English sentences are often characterized by a rise-fall intonation curve. The pitch rises during the first part of an utterance and falls at the end. This is generally true of declarative sentences and of questions which are impossible to answer with yes or no.

Declarative sentence:

He left an hour ago.

[hilɛftən ʔaʊə əgoʊ]

Question impossible to answer with yes/no:

How do you like it here?

[haʊdəju laɪk ɪthɪɚ]

Special emphasis:

Wow!

[wa ʊ]

Another intonation curve common in English is the end-of-utterance pitch rise. Pitch rise indicates a question to be answered with yes or no. It may also indicate that a sentence is incomplete.

Yes/no question:

Is it ready?

[ɪzɪt rɛdi]

Incomplete sentence:

As I think about it . . .

[æzaɪθ ɪŋk əbaʊt ɪt]

Pitch rise can be used by speakers to 'hold the floor' during a discussion. If a speaker pauses to think in the midst of a phrase, with the pitch rising, a polite discussant will be less likely to interrupt than if the pause occurred at a fall in intonation. Rising intonation results chiefly from increased cricothyroid muscle activity, lengthening the vocal folds for faster vibration. Falling intonation accompanies the decrease in intensity at the end of what Lieberman calls the breath group. The decrease in subglottal pressure is accompanied by both intensity and f_o declines. This pattern Lieberman called an unmarked breath group. There is disagreement about the relative contributions of subglottal air

pressure and decrease in cricothyroid muscle activity to the f_o decline. When pitch rises at the end of a phrase it is a marked breath group. Review the section on phonation of this chapter for more information on frequency-intensity relationships.

Intonation marks syntactic contrasts (phrase endings, interrogation *versus* declaration), changes meaning, and signals attitudes and feelings. Excitement, including some kinds of anger and states of enthusiasm, is often accompanied by large shifts in intonation, while calm, subdued states, including some forms of grief, anger, peacefulness, and boredom are characterized by a narrow range of intonation variation. We know how a person feels as often by how he says his message as by the message itself.

Duration and Juncture

Segmental duration has been mentioned, in the discussion of vowels. Speech sounds vary in intrinsic duration, with diphthongs and 'long' vowels being longer than the 'short' and the unstressed vowels. Continuous consonants, the fricatives, nasals, and semivowels are, of course, longer than the bursts of stops. There are durational relationships which extend over units larger than segments, however. Vowels are longer before voiced consonants, as in 'leave,' than before voiceless consonants, as in 'leaf.' They are also longer before continuants as in 'leave,' than before stops, as in 'leap.' It is a question for further research whether this relationship is learned in English or is physiologically expedient.

A final suprasegmental feature, related to duration, is *juncture*. Differences in juncture result from changes in duration combined with other sound changes. An example of a change in juncture is the contrast between 'an aim' [ən'eɪm] and 'a name' [ə'neɪm]. There is a small lengthening of the alveolar nasal in the first case and perhaps the intrusion of a glottal stop, [ən:ʔeɪm], while in the second case, there may be increased adaptation of the [n] to the following diphthong. Junctural distinctions are being studied in an effort to produce more natural synthetic speech and to better understand speech production rules.

FEEDBACK MECHANISMS IN SPEECH

Speech scientists are interested in how a speaker controls the production of speech. To what degree does the speaker monitor his actions, and to what degree and under what situations might he produce speech with little or no information on how he is proceeding? The 20th century is an age of *cybernetics*, the science of self-regulating machines. The term, coined by Norbert Weiner, from the Greek word meaning "steersman," refers to the study of systems which are controlled on the basis of their actual performance rather than the performance expected of them. A thermostat which turns off the furnace when the temperature actually reaches the set temperature is an example of a *servomechanism*, the engineering term for a self-regulating machine. During the Second World War, the United States government was interested in developing antiaircraft artillery which could track airplanes by predicting their future position based upon information on changes in position fed back to the machine. The computers of today are programmed to perform certain computations based upon the results of previous computations.

In servomechanisms, the output of the machine is fed back to some point in the assembly, where the feedback information controls the ensuing output. When errors are fed back to keep an activity within certain limits, it is *negative feedback.* When the information fed back serves to promote more of the same activity, it is *positive feedback.* Systems operating under feedback control are described as *closed loop* systems. Figure 4.97 contrasts *open loop* and closed loop systems in machines and in biological organisms. The difference between them is that in open loop systems, the output is preprogrammed, while in closed loop systems, the performance of the system is fed back to be matched with the program. If there is a discrepancy between the program and the performance, adjustments are made to correct the error.

The production of speech requires the simultaneous and coordinated use of respiratory, phonatory, and articulatory mechanisms, an activity which is so complex that some method of feedback control seems likely. There are at least four kinds of information available to a speaker which could be used in feedback control: auditory, tactile, proprioceptive, and central neural feedback.

Auditory Feedback

Interest in the role of feedback mechanisms in the control of speech was aroused by an accidental discovery made by a New Jersey engineer, Bernard Lee, in 1950. While he was recording himself on a tape recorder, he noticed that under some circumstances, the auditory feedback from his own speech could make him dysfluent. In a tape recorder, the record head ordinarily precedes the playback head, as diagrammed in Figure 4.98. If a speaker listens to his own previously recorded speech through a headset plugged into the playback head, which provides a slight time delay, fluent speech often becomes dysfluent, syllables are repeated, and voicing is prolonged. This *delayed auditory feedback (DAF)* effect provoked much excitement and a flurry of studies in the 1950s. The DAF effect was interpreted by many as proof that speech acts like a servomechanism, with auditory feedback as the chief control channel. This theory has been challenged by some, who note that some speakers can continue to speak fluently under DAF by attending to the printed page and ignoring the acoustic signal, that the duration of the error corrections, when they occur, in the form of stalls, are not linearly related to the amount of delay time, and that DAF is disruptive only at high intensity. An alternate interpretation of the DAF effect, is that it is a result of forcing attention upon auditory feedback information which conflicts with information received from articulatory movements. It is a case of your muscles telling you 'Yes,' you have said something, but your ears telling you 'No.'

There are ways of interfering with auditory feedback other than delaying it. In general, the speaker will normalize any distortion. If the air-conducted sound is amplified, speakers decrease vocal inten-

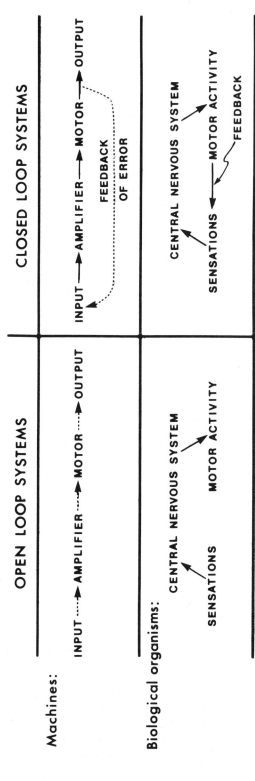

Figure 4.97. Schematic diagram comparing open and closed loop control, for machines and biological systems.

DELAYED AUDITORY FEEDBACK

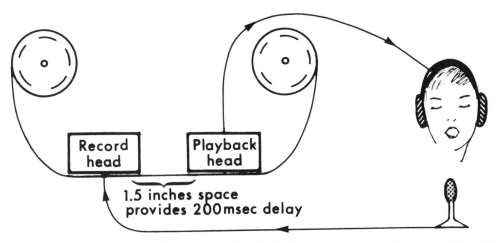

Figure 4.98. The delayed auditory feedback effect. A speaker records his own voice, while listening to the recording at a time delay, by monitoring the playback head of the tape recorder. A 1.5-inch space provides a 200-msec delay at a tape speed of 7.5 inches per sec. This delay leads to maximum speech interference in adults.

sity; if it is attenuated, they increase vocal intensity. If they cannot hear themselves at all, they increase intensity (the *Lombard effect*) and prolong voicing, as you know if you have ever tried to talk to someone sitting under a hairdryer. Even filtering out frequency regions of the speech has some effect upon the resonance characteristics of the speech produced. Garber has found that if speakers hear their own speech through a low pass filter, they will respond by decreasing the low frequency nasal resonance, raising fundamental frequency and increasing intelligibility. The explanation is that speakers are presumably attempting to restore the missing high frequency information.

These effects demonstrate that audition does operate as a feedback system for speech control, but they fail to settle the question of whether auditory feedback is essential for a skilled speaker. If so, is it used continuously or only in difficult speaking conditions? Adventitiously deafened speakers suffer little immediate effect upon the intelligibility of their speech; after a period of deafness, certain sounds deteriorate, notably /s/. Despite evidence that speakers attempt to compensate for distortions in auditory feedback, audition

may not serve effectively as a feedback mechanism to monitor ongoing, skilled articulation, because for many transient sounds it provides information to the speaker too late; he has already spoken and can only make corrections after the fact. Speakers do use audition, however, to sharpen their speech sound targets, and if they are listening to themselves, to catch errors.

Tactile Feedback

In producing speech, the lower lip touches the upper lip, the tip of the tongue or the blade touches the alveolar ridge of the hard palate, the lateral edges of the tongue touch the molars, the velum touches the pharyngeal walls, air pressure differences impinge on the walls of the vocal tract, and many other possibilities for touch sensations occur. Tactile sensations include the feeling of light touch, mediated by free nerve endings of sensory fibers lying near the surface of articulators, and of deeper pressure, mediated by more complex nerve bodies further from the surface. When touch receptors are stimulated, the surrounding cells are inhibited, which aids in localizing and sharpening the sensation. The lips, alveolar ridge, and anterior tongue are highly endowed with surface receptors responsive to light touch. The tongue dorsum contains more sensory fibers than any other part of the human body. In addition to touch, some of these receptors are responsive to taste, temperature, and pain.

A method of measuring tactile sensation is to explore *two-point discrimination* with an instrument called an esthesiometer. A subject can feel two separate points on the tip of the tongue when the points are only 1–2 mm apart, but further back on the tongue or on its lateral margins, the points must be nearly 1 cm apart to be differentiated. There are more touch receptors on the superior surface of the tongue than on the inferior surface and more in the alveolar ridge area of the hard palate than on the posterior part of the palate. Tactile sensation from the anterior ⅔ of the tongue is transmitted by sensory fibers in the lingual branch of the trigeminal nerve (V n.). The trigeminal nerve also transmits impulses from touch receptors of the lips and palate. The glossopharyngeal nerve (IX n.) carries sensory information from the posterior ⅓ of the tongue. It is thought that some of the sensory fibers of the lingual nerve may course with the motor nerve to the tongue, the hypoglossal nerve (XII n.).

A second method of evaluating tactile sensation in the mouth is by testing *oral stereognosis*, by putting shapes in the mouth of subjects for either identification or discrimination. The ability to identify the shapes by feeling them with the tongue and palate and then pointing to the appropriate pictures was found to have little or no relationship to speech proficiency, although Ringel at Purdue University found some relationship between form discrimination (i.e., judging whether two forms were the same or different) and the ability to articulate speech sounds with normal proficiency.

There have been attempts to determine the importance of taction to speech by interfering with normal tactile feedback and looking for the effects of the interference upon speech. Using the same techniques which dentists use to block the conduction of nerve impulses from the oral area, speech scientists have anesthetized various branches of the trigeminal nerve, thus depriving the speaker of tactile feedback. Such nerve block conditions often result in distorted articulation of speech, especially the consonant /s/, but in general, speech remains highly intelligible. Oral stereognosis and two-point discrimination are markedly reduced or absent, yet subjects can move the tongue in all directions and feel its position. When auditory masking is added to the nerve block, no significant increase in articulation errors occurs. Several theories have been advanced to account for the speech distortions, ranging from the peripheral sensory theory (sensory feedback is needed for accuracy of articulation), the central sensory theory (a more general reorganization of motor activity occurs as a result of sensory loss), a peripheral motor theory (based upon evidence of effects upon motor as well as sensory neurons), and the central motor theory (the anesthesia having entered the blood stream produces a small motor effect rather like drunk speech). Due to problems in controlling variables inherent in the nerve block technique, these theories have not been adequately tested.

Audition and taction can be considered as *external feedback* systems, because the signals arise as consequences of motor events. The muscle contractions necessary for speech result in movements of air and of articulators which stimulate the tactile receptors of the oral area. They also result in sound waves that can be heard by the speaker. This information arises as a result of muscle activity, but does not contain direct feedback from the muscle activity itself. Direct feedback from the muscles is faster than external feedback, and is part of the sense of movement and position called proprioception.

Proprioceptive Feedback

In the early part of the 19th century, Charles Bell differentiated touch from the muscle sense which he called *kinesthesis*. Later in the same century, Bastian enlarged the definition of kinesthesis to include a complex sense of movement derived from receptors in the joints, tendons, and muscles. In 1900, Sherrington proposed the term exteroceptors for the receptors of taction and proprioceptors for the receptors stimulated by the action of the body itself, giving the sense of movement and position. Sensors in joints transmit information about bone angles. Receptors along tendons respond to any contractions in the muscle to which they are attached and thereby transmit information about both muscle stretching and shortening.

Of special interest to speech physiologists are the receptors embedded in striated muscles. These receptors are called *muscle spindles* because they are often shaped like the slender fiber holders from which thread is twisted in spinning. Muscle spindles are more complex in their innervation than tendon and joint receptors. They have efferent as well as afferent neurons. The spindles (Fig. 4.99) are encapsulated muscle fibers (intrafusal fibers) lying in parallel with the main muscle fibers (extrafusal fibers). When the efferent neurons stimulate the main muscle, the smaller efferent neurons which supply the muscle spindles are activated simultaneously. The motoneurons to the main muscle are larger (8–20 μm in diameter) and are therefore called *alpha* (α) *motoneurons*, in contrast to the smaller motoneurons (2–8 μm in diameter), called *gamma* (γ) *motoneurons*, which innervate the spindle fibers at each end. Primary (Ia) and secondary (IIa) afferents are stimulated by lengthening of intrafusal fibers and by rate of change in length. As the spindle fibers are stretched in response to muscle contraction, the spindle afferent conveys information about the contraction back to the central nervous system. The primary afferents from spindles are among the largest of human neurons, ranging from 12 to 20 μm in diameter, conducting impulses up to 120 meters/sec. The velocity with which the spindles convey the feedback information makes them attractive as possible mechanisms for ongoing control of rapid motor activities including speech. Muscle spindles are found in the intercostal muscles, all of the laryngeal muscles, the genioglossus muscle, the intrinsic muscles of the tongue and, sparsely, in the facial muscles. Thus, muscles involved in speech production seem well supplied with spindles which can be tuned to feed back information on muscle length changes.

While the neural pathways for spindle information from some muscle systems are known, the route is not clear for the tongue. Spindle afferents from the tongue are currently believed to course along the otherwise motor hypoglossal nerve (XII n.) and to enter the brain stem by way of the dorsal cervical nerves C_1–C_3.

The proprioceptive feedback system may operate on both reflex and voluntary levels. Some pathways go to the spinal

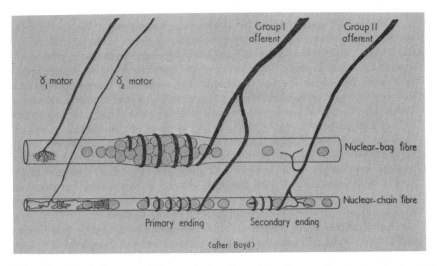

Figure 4.99. Simplified diagram of the central region of two types of muscle spindles. (Reprinted with permission from P. B. C. Matthews: *Physiological Review. 44*, 1964.)

cord, but some also go to the cerebral cortex and the cerebellum. Although the sensation of muscle activity is usually unconscious, it can be made conscious. Goodwin, McCloskey, and Matthews stimulated the spindles of a man's arm with a vibrator. The blindfolded man was instructed to flex his other arm to match the position of the arm under stimulation. The subject misjudged the position, thinking the muscles in his vibrated arm were more extended than they actually were. The investigators then paralyzed the joint and cutaneous afferents in the index finger of a subject to see if spindles alone were consciously perceived without information from joint receptors. As one of the investigators manipulated the finger, the subject could sense the movement and the direction of the movement; hence, the spindle output could be consciously perceived.

Proprioception for speech is difficult to investigate directly. Indirectly, proprioceptive feedback has been investigated by mechanically interfering with normal positional relationships to study compensatory adaptations. Subjects try to speak with bite blocks interfering with normal jaw raising; with metal plates unexpectedly opening between the lips, interfering with labial closure; or with palatal prostheses placed in the mouth, altering the width of the alveolar ridge. There is much to be learned about the nature of speaker compensations made in response to these mechanical alterations. At this time, it is not clear what feedback information, auditory, tactile, proprioceptive, or some combination of these, is instrumental in directing the compensations observed.

Two interesting attempts have been made to block γ motoneurons from speech muscles directly. Critchlow and von Euler paralyzed the γ fibers to the external intercostal muscles. The Ia fibers stopped firing during inspiration, firing during expiration only because of passive stretch of the inspiratory muscles. This had no effect upon speech but indicated that the γ and α motoneurons are activated together, since the spindle afferents are normally active from the inspiratory muscles during inspiration. Had the experiment involved paralysis of the less accessible expiratory intercostals, any effect there might have been upon speech would have become apparent.

In another study, Abbs attempted to selectively block the γ motoneurons to the mandibular muscles by blocking the mandibular branch of the trigeminal nerve bilaterally, thus blocking both the large fibers (α motoneurons to main muscle fibers and afferents from tactile and proprioceptive receptors) and small fibers (γ motoneurons and afferents for pain and temperature). Since large fibers recover before smaller fibers, it was assumed that when muscle force and touch returned to normal but pain and temperature senses were still blocked, the motor supply to the spindles would be blocked. Under this condition, subjects moved the jaw with less velocity and acceleration when jaw lowering was required. There were no perceptually obvious effects on speech, however.

Direct studies of proprioception are possible on animals. Recent investigations on monkeys deafferented bilaterally from muscles of the limbs or from jaw muscles, suggest that purposeful movements can be performed without either vision or somatic sensation from the muscles involved. Further study is needed to establish whether control of fine motor adjustments is perfect despite the deafferentation. Well-learned motor patterns are maintained, at least grossly, but ability to adjust to unexpected change needs further exploration, as does the ability to learn new motor patterns.

Internal Feedback

In light of the many neural connections among the motor areas of the cerebral cortex, the cerebellum, and the thalamus, neurophysiologists have suggested that the control of skilled patterns of movement, as found in piano-playing or speech, may operate under a feedback system housed in the central nervous system. Learned patterns under cerebellar control might be activated by the midbrain in association with the motor strip of the cerebrum. *Internal feedback* is the conveyance of information on motor commands prior to the motor response itself. Accordingly, information might return to the cerebellum from the motor cortex about whether the motoneurons were dispatched as intended, well before the muscle response. There is as yet no direct evidence for internal feedback. Although it is known that the cerebellum and thalamus are active about 100 msec prior to movement, this discharge cannot be related directly to a specific feedback loop with present techniques.

In summary, there are several kinds of feedback available to the speaker (Fig. 4.100): the theoretically rapid, central internal feedback systems in the central nervous system, capable of feedforward (prediction) and high-level feedback of initiated motor commands; the fairly fast, proprioceptive response feedback systems of the peripheral nervous system, capable of movement and positional feedback for fine control needed in skilled motor acts; and the slower, external feedback of the results of motor acts, including for speech, the acoustic signal, the air pressure variations, and the articulators touching one another.

The more central the system, the earlier it can feed back information and the more effective it can be for ongoing control of rapid and complex motor patterns. The more peripheral systems, operating after the motor response, can be effective for comparing result with intention and may, therefore, be important for learning a new motor pattern.

Developmental Research on Feedback Mechanisms

The degree of dependence upon control systems used by adolescents and adults may be quite different from the degree to which infants and young children use these feedback systems when they are learning to speak. No one who knows the difficulty encountered by the deaf in learning speech can doubt the importance to the developing speaker of comparing his own auditory output to the speech of the

MOTOR CONTROL SYSTEMS IN SPEECH

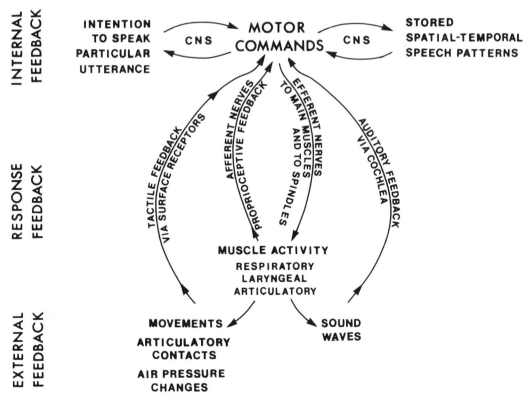

Figure 4.100. A conceptualization of the feedback systems available to a speaker.

community in which he lives. Many studies of delayed auditory feedback with children, however, found them to be less affected by time-distorted feedback than were older children and adults. Investigation by MacKay showed younger children are maximally affected by a different delay than adults—500 msec for the 4–6-year-olds and 375 msec for the 7–9-year-olds, rather than the adult 200 msec. Very young infants, furthermore, show a different type of speech disturbance from adults. DAF makes infants shorten rather than prolong their phonation time, and when their own productions are amplified but played back simultaneously, they reduce intensity less than older children. Experiments on interference with taction by the nerve block technique in children show the same limited effects upon speech as in the adult studies.

The essential combination for learning coordinated speech gestures is perhaps proprioception and audition. Proprioceptive information is available during muscle length changes and the child need not wait for the result of the movement to get the feel of the gestural pattern. Also, the primary afferents from the spindles, being larger than the afferents from the tactile receptors, feed back the information more quickly. The sense of movement can then be associated with its acoustic and tactile results, and the whole sensation can be compared to the intended sound pattern. Thus, a child trying to perfect his production of the word 'ball,' makes a stab at it based on what he has learned from previous trials, senses the movement and positions of his vocal tract which he quickly associates with their tactile and acoustic results, and compares his sound with the adult sound of 'ball,' a sound pattern he has stored. It is difficult to test the importance of proprioception. Auditory or tactile masking alone are insufficient to disrupt speech when testing linguistic items that the child already knows. Future studies should focus on the effects of interference with feedback channels while subjects, both children and adults, are learning new speech patterns.

MODELS OF SPEECH PRODUCTION

When we partially understand something, we sometimes make a model of it. A model is a simplification of the system for which it stands. It is usually built to test a certain aspect of that system. By testing the model under various conditions, to see if it behaves like the system that we seek to understand, we may learn something about the system. People fashion mechanical models, mathematical models, natural language models, and computer models. In his efforts to better understand the auditory mechanism, von Békésy constructed a mechanical model of the cochlea, with a basilar membrane made of rubber of varrying thickness. The model looked like a tank of water with a flexible shelf in it. No attempt was made to have it look like the cochlea. Yet it served as the model of von Békésy's traveling wave theory of hearing. At high frequencies of vibration, the waves set up in the tank produced maximum vibrations of the thin part of the flexible shelf, and at low frequencies of vibration, the displacement of the membrane was greatest for the thicker portion at the far end of the tank.

Computer models can be mathematically based or mechanically based. Information describing the system is fed into a computer along with the rules by which the system is presumed to operate. The fast calculating abilities of the computer can then be used to determine the outcome for such a system under various conditions. With the graphic capabilities of computers, the model can be drawn as it will change under different circumstances. Flanagan, at Bell Telephone Laboratories, has developed a two-mass model of the vocal folds (upper and lower parts to reflect the vertical phase difference described under "Framework of the Larynx") which has been computerized to test its efficiency in predicting the workings of a real human larynx.

Most speech production models are expressed in natural rather than mathematical language, consisting of verbal descriptions, with charts, definitions, and rules.

Three models with a strong linguistic emphasis will be briefly described here: Peterson and Shoup's model of the physiology and acoustics of phonetics, Chomsky and Halle's theory of binary distinctive features, and Liberman's model of encoding rules for phoneme to acoustic transformation. Several models with a strong biologic emphasis will follow the linguistic models, some of them addressed to the goal of speech production, some to the timing, and some to the use of feedback.

Peterson and Shoup: Physiological and Acoustic Phonetics

In 1966, Gordon Peterson and June Shoup, taking the International Phonetic Alphabet as a starting point, attempted to describe all the sounds of spoken language, using information from experimental phonetics, both physiological and acoustic, as the foundation for the description. The physiological model is built from 19 preliminary definitions, 22 axioms, and 77 definitions, followed by 2 phonetic charts, the first representing 8 manners of articulation according to 13 horizontal places of articulation and 13 vertical places of articulation, and the second chart representing 12 secondary phonetic parameters. Finally, the 3 prosodic parameters of phonetics are detailed. The acoustic model is constructed of verbal and mathematical descriptions of 6 types of speech waves, 6 types of acoustic phonetic parameters, and 3 acoustic parameters of prosody. Finally, the authors relate acoustic phonetics to physiological phonetics by discussing the transformation possible from acoustic to physiological characteristics of speech.

Chomsky and Halle: Distinctive Features

Roman Jakobson, Gunnar Fant, and Morris Halle presented a model to account for the phonetic features of all known languages. An account of the model, "Preliminaries to Speech Analysis," appeared in a Massachusetts Institute of Technology Acoustics Laboratory Report in 1952 and was later published by the M. I. T. Press. The model is based upon a binary system, each feature contrasted with an opposing one. The features are largely based on observations of sound spectrograms, which were then being systematically explored for the first time. The model posits fundamental and secondary acoustic source features and resonance features, 12 sets of features in all.

In 1968, with the publication of *The Sound Pattern of English,* Noam Chomsky and Morris Halle redesigned the distinctive feature system. The features are stated in articulatory rather than acoustic terms and are again binary. For example, instead of the Jakobson, Fant, and Halle distinction of 'grave' *versus* 'acute,' in which the 'grave' feature applies to sounds which occupy the lower frequency regions of the spectrum, and the 'acute' feature to the high frequency regions of the spectrum, Chomsky and Halle reformulated the distinctions in more articulatory terms such as the cavity features of ± 'rounded,' ± 'high tongue body,' and ± 'back tongue body.' Divided into major class features, cavity features, manner of articulation features, and source features, there are 27 feature pairs in all. The features marked with an asterisk (*) are not important in English.

I. Major class features
    Sonorant (voicing with adducted folds)
    Vocalic (openness of oral cavity)
    Consonantal (obstruction of vocal tract)
II. Cavity features
    Coronal (tongue blade up)
    Anterior (palatoalveolar obstruction)
    Tongue body
      High (above neutral)
      Low (below neutral)
      Back (retracted)
    Rounded (lips narrow)
    Distributed (extended constriction)
    Covered (narrow tense pharynx)*
    Glottal constrictions
    Nasal
    Lateral
III. Manner of articulation features
    Continuant
    Instantaneous release (/t/ is +,
      /tʃ/ is −)
    Suction*
      Velaric suction (clicks)
      Implosion
    Pressure*
      Velaric pressure
      Ejectives
    Tense (muscular effort)

IV. Source features
     Heightened subglottal pressure
     Voice
     Strident
     Prosodic features
         Stress
         Pitch
         Length

By the nature of the description, this model is necessarily static and does not account for the dynamic nature of speech. The authors are less interested in the realization of speech, however, than in the phonological competence of man. Even so, the Chomsky and Halle features are more applicable to a speech production model than a purely acoustic set of features would be. The authors suggested them as descriptions of the phonetic capabilities of man, with examples from many different languages in the world. A complete model might incorporate the acoustic results of the physiological features with articulatory rules for the derivation of the acoustic output.

Liberman: The Speech Code

Although a paper by Liberman, Cooper, Shankweiler, and Studdert-Kennedy written in 1967 is on the subject of speech perception, it does contain a model of speech production which presents the transformations thought necessary in the encoding rules speakers use. The model depicts phonemes, or the sets of features which comprise them, as a high-level derivation of the syntactic-semantic formulations within the central nervous system. The model rejects the notion that speech sounds are a direct phoneme to sound conversion, but holds that there is acoustic smearing of the phonemes, resulting from parallel processing of more than one phoneme simultaneously (Fig. 4.101). According to the appropriate neuromotor rules, neural signals are simultaneously sent to many muscles. The gestures produced by these muscle contractions form variations in vocal tract shapes according to a set of articulatory rules, and the time varying cavity changes are converted into what we hear as speech by acoustic rules. The point is, that in these multiple conversions, the phoneme as a static entity is modified by its context. Since more than one phoneme is often being transmitted by the motor system of the speaker at one time, the muscle activity, movements, and acoustic signals may all reflect this overlay. We will describe this model further in the context of speech perception in the next chapter. The models discussed above are strongly influenced by linguistic considerations. Other models of speech production emphasize neurophysiological considerations more strongly.

Speech Goals: Target Theory and Auditory Theory

Peter MacNeilage, in a 1970 paper "Motor Control of Serial Ordering of Speech," has presented a speech production model compatible with Hebb's idea of motor equivalence and the then current work on γ loop control in motor systems. An example of motor equivalence is the fact that you can write the letter B with your right hand, left hand, or by holding the pencil between your toes, although the muscles used differ in each case. The example of motor equivalence in speech given by MacNeilage is the ability of any speaker to produce 'pipe speech,' even though the jaw, tongue, and lip movements and underlying muscle activity must be altered. You can sense the difference by saying 'hot' with your mouth open and then with teeth immobilized as if you were holding a pencil or pipe between your teeth. MacNeilage argues that speakers do not issue a set of motor commands for each speech segment, because speakers approach the vocal tract shapes for a particular segment from many different positions. Rather, the goal of the speaker is a spatial target. In the brain, there is an internalized spatial representation of the oral area. To reach a desired target, the speaker can adjust from any of various positions to the target position. The theory posits speech production to be an open loop system, with a series of targets specified in advance, but with the possible aid of the γ loop feedback mechanism in predicting muscle behavior under some circumstances.

The concept of targets is also implicit in Björn Lindblom's observations on vowel

SCHEMA FOR PRODUCTION

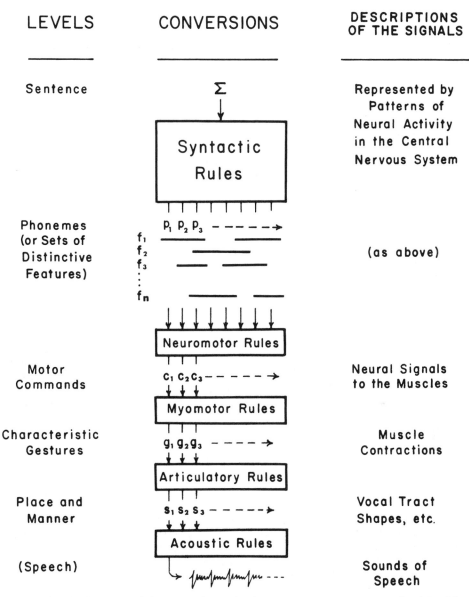

LEVELS	CONVERSIONS	DESCRIPTIONS OF THE SIGNALS

Figure 4.101. A diagram of the speech production process, as conceptualized by Liberman. Perception is conceived as the reverse of the process diagrammed here. (Reprinted with permission from A. M. Liberman *et al.: Psychological Review. 74,* © 1967, American Psychological Association.)

reduction, mentioned earlier, but these targets are in terms of vowel formant frequencies. The speaker aims for invariant acoustic targets, though they may be reduced during rapid and unstressed delivery. The listener is able to correct for the reductions perceptually and thus restore the vowel targets. Hence, the target is a psychological idealization of the actual vowel production.

Sibout Nooteboom, of Holland, concurs with MacNeilage's target theory, finding an internalized spatial coordinate system more efficient than stored motor patterns for each possible action, but he proposes that MacNeilage did not go far enough in his model. MacNeilage proposes spatial targets as the goals with γ loop control of context changes. Nooteboom, referring to the work of Lindblom, cautions that the goal of the speaker is to be understood, and is, therefore, primarily a perceptual one. Even spatial targets sometimes vary. Nooteboom offers the example of speakers producing [u] with and without lip rounding. If lip protrusion is not used to lengthen the tract for the lowering of formants, then depressing the larynx may be substituted to achieve the same acoustic result. The spatial targets differ, but both are perceived as the same phoneme, /u/. Nooteboom's speech production model would include an internal representation of an auditory perceptual space. Using both the auditory and the spatial representations, the brain of the speaker uses rules relating these representations to calculate the motor commands necessary to achieve the targets from the current articulatory state.

Peter Ladefoged has also suggested an auditory theory of speech production, at least for vowels. He implies that there may be a difference in production control for consonants and for vowels.

Timing Models

The search for the invariant correlate of the phoneme is not the only concern of the experimental phonetician. The fact that speech is ordered in time has led to several speech production models which emphasize timing. Karl Lashley's classic paper published in 1951 succeeded in discrediting associate chain theories of speech production in the minds of most theorists who have followed him. An associate chain theory holds that the stimulus of one movement is required to trigger the next movement. Lashley theorized, by contrast, that speech production incorporates several interacting but independent systems corresponding to the speaker's intention, which he called the 'determining tendency,' the store of images and words, the motor organization, and a temporal ordering mechanism. The important point here is that the

temporal ordering, as viewed by Lashley, is not inherent in the idea, the word, or the motor organization, but it can control the ordering of them. The temporal ordering device is a syntax, an integrating schema. He presents it as ordering the words and also ordering the motor actions. Lashley's is an open loop model, with constantly interactive systems.

Sven Öhman, of Sweden, has constructed a mathematical model of the production of VCV (vowel-consonant-vowel) utterances. An articulatory model with 50 lines sectioning the vocal tract, with the highest point of the palate and the beginning of the curved oral cavity as coordinates, it is used to mathematically summarize the coarticulation which Öhman described from spectrograms. The model includes static properties of phonemes and dynamic rules which blend the phonemes into running speech. Öhman views the temporal ordering as the result of the speaker moving from vowel to vowel, with the releasing and arresting consonants superimposed upon the vocalic stream. This accounts for the observed coarticulatory effects and also implies separate control mechanisms for vowels and consonants.

William Henke has developed a computer model based on articulatory data. The model supports a scan ahead mechanism for motor control. Motor commands are initiated for as many segments as are not contradictory. The model generates a string of phonemes with coarticulation resulting in the spread of features from a particular phone to adjacent ones.

Related to temporal ordering is another dimension of timing, the pattern of relative timing of the segments in a phrase. James Martin has proposed a model of speech rhythm in which the timing of stressed items is planned first and given primary articulatory emphasis by the speaker, with the timing and articulation of the less accented parts of the phrase receiving secondary consideration. The production mechanism is under central control. Although some languages (English is one) are more obviously stress-timed than others, Martin considers such relative timing patterns, or rhythms, to be universal. Stress timing is the tendency for stress to occur at equal intervals. Listeners seem to sense the rhythm of speech and use it to help predict the rest of the message.

However when one sets out to measure the rhythm of speech in the laboratory, it is as elusive as the phoneme. It may be that the rhythm exists in the mind of the speaker but is temporally blurred as it is transformed into the acoustic stream of speech. The listener, however, as Martin suggests, enters into the rhythm of the speaker and follows it, despite speaker rate changes and other factors that make the rhythm difficult to specify objectively.

Feedback Models

A book written in 1965 by the husband and wife research team of Kozhevnikov and Chistovich of the Pavlov Institute in Leningrad stimulated thought on speech organization by presenting a model of speech timing and of syllable control. By measuring the duration of phrases (syntagma) separated by pauses (the syntagma is sometimes one syllable, but averages seven), the investigators showed the pauses to be much more variable than the intervals within the syntagma. They concluded that time can only be measured meaningfully within a syntagma. When the rate of speech is changed within a syntagma, they found that the relative durations of the syllables and words remained constant; only by measuring the changes in consonants and vowels within each syllable did they find a significant difference in relative time. The consonant

of the syllable changes little with faster or slower rate, but the vowel changes considerably. Kozhevnikov and Chistovich concluded that the articulatory organization of timing was in syllable commands. The commands for syllable 'a' (Fig. 4.102) include instructions for both the consonant 'a_1' and the vowel 'a_2.' Further, movements required by the syllable may be initiated simultaneously unless they are contradictory.

The control of the syllable commands was hypothesized to be open loop on the basis of a comparison of predictions from an open loop and a closed loop model. Figures 4.103 and 4.104 contrast the alternate hypotheses. In the first hypothesis, the command to begin each syllable awaits afferent feedback indicating that the preceding syllable command was issued. This is a form of closed loop control. The second hypothesis is that syllable commands are issued without afferent return from the muscle response. Testing these two hypotheses by measuring the inevitable durational changes obtained when a phrase is repeated about 150–200 times, Kozhevnikov and Chistovich tentatively concluded the first hypothesis of closed loop control to be less probable. The phrase was 'Tonya topila banyu' which means 'Tonya heated the bath.' The investigators reasoned that if syllable duration varied more than the variability for the whole phrase, and if adjacent syllables were negatively correlated, it would support an open loop model. Finding the variance of

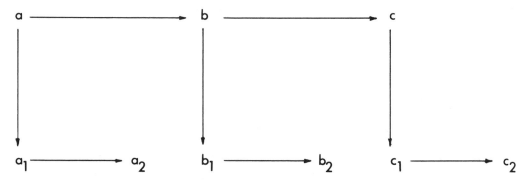

Figure 4.102. Commands for syllables *a*, *b*, and *c*. The syllable commands include consonant commands (*a_1*, *b_1* and *c_1*) and vowel commands (*a_2*, *b_2*, and *c_2*). Commands for consonants and vowels may be issued simultaneously through they are realized sequentially. (Adapted from V. A. Kozhevnikov and L. A. Chistovich: *Speech: Articulation and Perception,* United States Department of Commerce © 1966.)

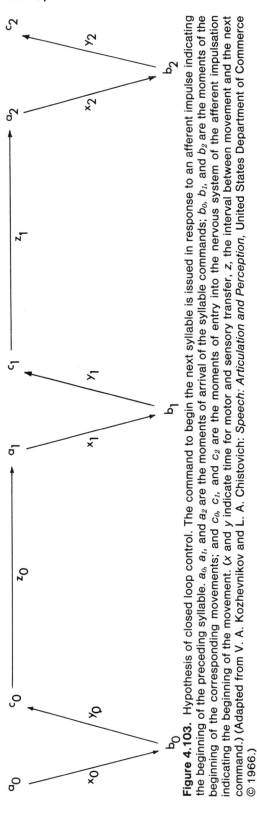

Figure 4.103. Hypothesis of closed loop control. The command to begin the next syllable is issued in response to an afferent impulse indicating the beginning of the preceding syllable. a_0, a_1, and a_2 are the moments of the beginning of the corresponding movements; b_0, b_1, and b_2 are the moments of the beginning of the movement indicating the beginning of the afferent impulsation indicating the beginning of the movement. (x and y indicate time for motor and sensory transfer, z, the interval between movement and the next command.) (Adapted from V. A. Kozhevnikov and L. A. Chistovich: *Speech: Articulation and Perception*, United States Department of Commerce © 1966.)

the syllables to be considerably greater than the variance of the whole phrase, and a negative correlation between adjacent syllables, they concluded that syllables are articulatory events independent of adjacent syllables, in the sense that each syllable command is automatically initiated under the guidance of an unspecified rhythm generator in the nervous system.

Although taction and audition were deemed by Kozhevnikov and Chistovich to be unnecessary to the control of skilled speech, Grant Fairbanks had stressed their importance, along with proprioception, in his model of the speech mechanism as a servomechanism. The model was published in 1954 during the wave of interest in the relatively new field of cybernetics (Norbert Weiner's *The Human Use of Human Beings* was published the same year). Fairbanks was the first to model speech as a closed loop system in any detail. In Figure 4.105, the motor, generator, and modulator parts of the effector unit represent respiration, phonation, and articulation, respectively. *Sensors 1, 2,* and *3* represent audition, taction, and proprioception, with audition divided into bone and air conduction channels. The storage component serves as a buffer for the batch of speech to be effected. The comparator not only relates the intended signal to the feedback of the actual output for correction, but it includes a predicting device so that the process need not be delayed until the error signal disappears. When a discrepancy between the intended and the obtained signal appears in the comparator, it is sent to the mixer, so that the motor or effector unit can be adjusted.

Questions of the role of closed and open loop control systems for speech remain unresolved today. So, too, do the fundamental principles governing motor programming, as they are revealed in speech rhythm and coarticulation. As our sophistication increases, the models, the feature systems, and even the definitions will continue to be modified. There is no better way to realize how little we know and how complex speech production must be, than to take a short utterance and try to detail just the peripheral events involved in its production. The last section of this chapter is such an attempt.

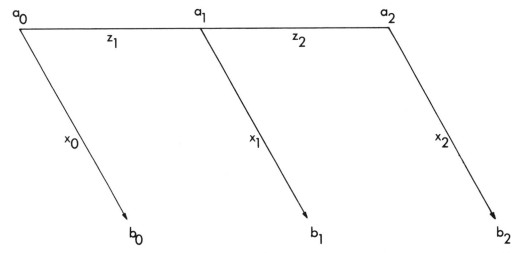

Figure 4.104. Hypothesis of open loop control. Commands for successive syllables are centrally issued. Afferent impulses do not affect the onset of successive syllables. *Symbols* as in Figure 4.103. (Adapted from V. A. Kozhevnikov and L. A. Chistovich, *Speech: Articulation and Perception,* United States Department of Commerce © 1966.)

PRODUCTION OF A SENTENCE

We beat you in soccer:

    [ˌwi'biˌtjuən'sakɚ] or [ˌwi'biˌtʃuṇ'sakɚ]

Having been soundly defeated by a rival college football team, a member of the defeated team retorted to a comment by one of the victors with 'We may have lost in football, but we beat you in soccer.' If we were inside the brain of that speaker pushing buttons to produce 'we beat you in soccer,' what might be the order and integration of commands? The phrase is appealing because it contains stops, fricatives, a nasal, semivowels, and our favorite vowels [i], [a], and [u]. Also, when said with the [ju] unassimilated with the [t] as in the first alternative pronunciation, there is a pleasing symmetry in having [wi] and [ju], which are not only opposites in allegiance to the rival teams but are spectrographic mirror images of one another, with [wi] starting at an acoustic [u] and gliding to [i], while [ju] starts at an acoustic [i] and glides to [u] (Fig. 4.106).

Whatever intentions the speaker may have had of retribution, of a desire to inform, or merely of offering a friendly but slightly barbed joke, we shall not attempt to determine. Nor shall we trace the interactions of syntactic and semantic recall and decision. Presuming that 'we beat you in soccer' was put momentarily in a buffer for output, and that the timing and prosodic control was imposed upon it as it was fed out into motor commands, we shall indicate some of the motor events peripheral to the more general motor goals, whatever they may have been. The logical way to indicate the motor events is in terms of nerves, muscles, movements and resulting cavity changes, air pressure changes, and acoustic results. Omissions outweigh inclusions. Not included are all the constantly effective passive forces of elasticity, gravity, mass, and inertia. Only some of the obvious active muscle forces are included. Auxiliary muscle activity and agonist-antagonist relationships are not detailed. Also omitted are the many possible afferent transmissions of changes in muscle length, touch, and auditory signals, supplying the speaker with information about his progress. We have made some specific assumptions, however, about a particular one of the many ways of articulating the sentence, to make the description concrete. Despite these shortcomings, the exercise is worth doing, if only to interrelate the processes of respiration, laryngeal activity, and articulation which are usually kept pristinely apart and to remind ourselves of the complexity of speech.

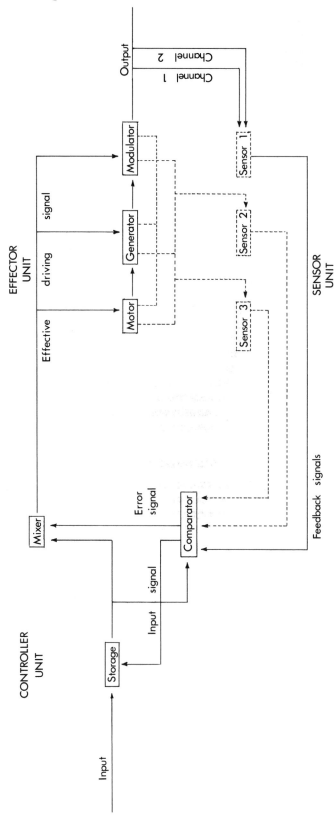

Figure 4.105. Fairbanks' model of the speech production process. (See text for explanation.) (Adapted from G. Fairbanks: *Journal of Speech and Hearing Disorders. 19*, 1954.)

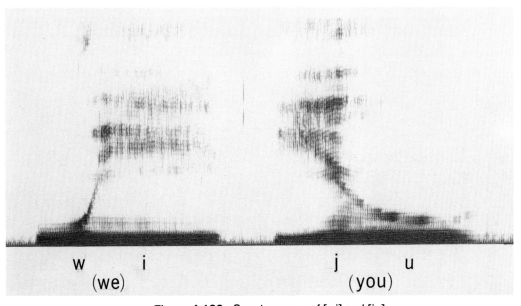

Figure 4.106. Spectrograms of [wi] and [ju].

The speaker, let us say, needs a quick inhalation for the phrase to begin.

Innervation	Muscles	Movements	Pressure changes	Result
Phrenic n.	Diaphragm	Lowering thoracic floor	Thoracic vertical volume increase, pressure decrease	Inhalation
Thoracic n. (T₁–T₁₁)	EIm and interchondral IIm	Ribs elevated and expanded	Lateral and anterior-posterior thoracic volume increase, pressure decrease	Inhalation (~65% VC)
XII n.	GGm	Tongue elevated to 'ready' position		
VII n.	OOm	Lip protrusion for [w]		
XI n.	LPm	Velum raised and backed to block nasal resonance during [wibitju]		
XII n.	SGm	Tongue dorsum elevated to [u] position for [w]	Lower the resonance characteristics by elongated vocal tract	
X n.	IAm	Adduction of vocal folds for [wibi]		
X n.	LCAm	Aids in adduction of vocal folds		

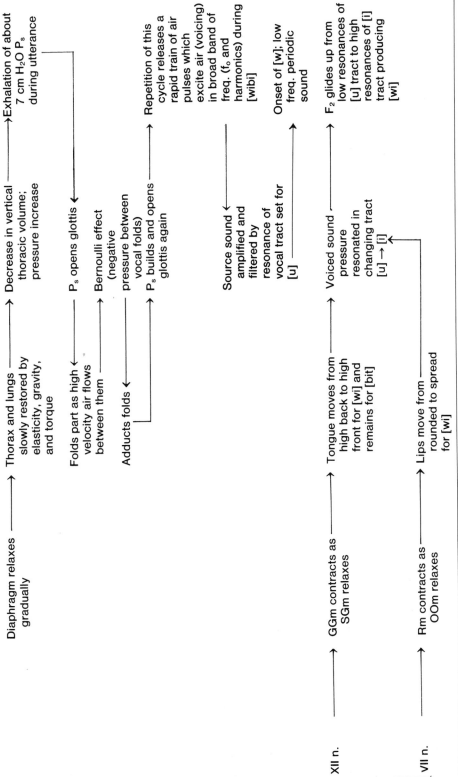

Chart—*Continued*

Innervation	Muscles	Movements	Pressure changes	Result
X n.	IAm continues to contract but LCAm relaxes	Glottis more open; continues to vibrate	More 'P$_s$ air released into tract for stop	
VII n.	OOm	Lips close	Pressure builds behind closure	Vocal tract resonances damped
	OOm relaxes	Lips forced open for [b]	Sharp air pulse released without aspiration	Transient aperiodic burst added to voicing [b]
T$_1$–T$_{11}$	IIm	Depresses ribs	Adds pressure to P$_s$	Increases intensity for stressed [i]
XII n.	GGm remains contracted	Tongue blade high in oral cavity; pharyngeal cavity larger, oral smaller than neutral	Pressure wave from glottis amplified by resonances of vocal tract	Low F$_1$; high F$_2$ and F$_3$ due to small oral cavity [i]
X n.	PCAm	Abduct vocal folds; vibration stops	Increased airflow into oral cavity for stop/affricate	
XII n.	SLm added to GGm	Tongue tip and blade up for alveolar contact	Intraoral pressure builds behind occlusion	Silence during closure

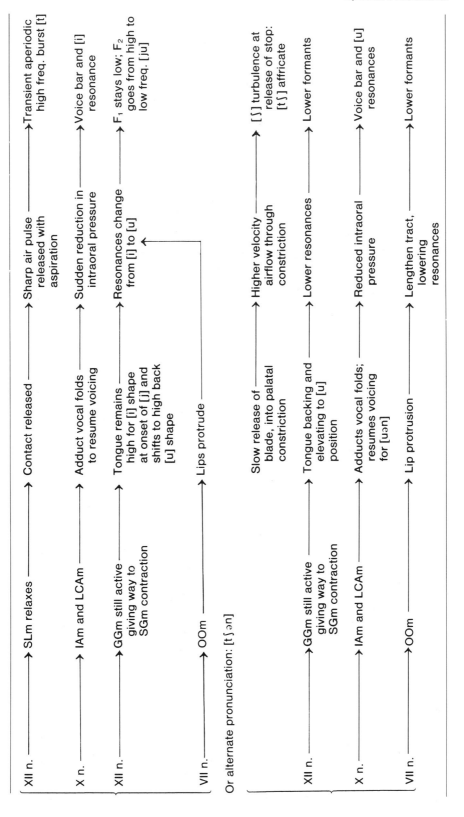

XII n. ———→ SLm relaxes ———→ Contact released ———→ Transient aperiodic high freq. burst [t]

X n. ———→ IAm and LCAm ———→ Adduct vocal folds to resume voicing ———→ Voice bar and [i] resonance

XII n. ———→ GGm still active giving way to SGm contraction ———→ Tongue remains high for [i] shape at onset of [j] and shifts to high back [u] shape ———→ Resonances change from [i] to [u] ———→ F_1 stays low; F_2 goes from high to low freq. [ju]

VII n. ———→ OOm ———→ Lips protrude

Or alternate pronunciation: [tʃən]

Slow release of blade, into palatal constriction ———→ Higher velocity airflow through constriction ———→ [ʃ] turbulence at release of stop: [tʃ] affricate

XII n. ———→ GGm still active giving way to SGm contraction ———→ Tongue backing and elevating to [u] position ———→ Lower resonances ———→ Lower formants

X n. ———→ IAm and LCAm ———→ Adducts vocal folds; resumes voicing for [uən] ———→ Reduced intraoral pressure ———→ Voice bar and [u] resonances

VII n. ———→ OOm ———→ Lip protrusion ———→ Lengthen tract, lowering resonances ———→ Lower formants

Chart—*Continued*

Innervation	Muscles	Movements	Pressure changes	Result
XII n. inactive		→ Tongue returns to neutral	→ Neutral resonances of [ə]	→ Evenly spaced formants
XII n. active	→ SLm	→ Blade raised to alveolar ridge	→ Small pressure increase within oral cavity	→ F_2 rising
XI n. decreases activity	→ LPm relaxes	→ Velum lowers; opening to nasal cavities	→ Pressure drop as tract volume increases	→ Low freq. nasal resonance added; also antiresonances [n]

Or alternate: /n̩/

(Same as above but timing is different, with first alternative [ən] having oral to nasal resonance transition and second alternative [n̩] having faster velar lowering.

Innervation	Muscles	Movements	Pressure changes	Result
XII n.	→ SLm	→ Blade up to alveolar ridge	→ Intraoral pressure increase	→ F_2 rising
XI n.	→ PGm	→ Lowers velum	→ Sudden pressure drop; nasal resonance	→ Low freq. nasal resonance; upper formant antiresonances

Nerve	Muscle	Articulation	Aerodynamics	Acoustics
XI n.	LPm	Abrupt high elevation and backing of velum, especially for [s] but maintained for rest of utterance		
X n.	PCAm	Abduction of vocal folds to stop voicing	Airflow increased for high pressure fricative	
XII n.	GGm with SLm (or ILm if tip down)	Blade to palate constriction	High pressure flow through constriction; turbulence	Aperiodic noise 4 kHz and higher [s]
XII n.	SLm (or ILm) remains active / HGm contracts	Blade remains high for [s] as / Dorsum starts to lower for [ɑ]	Pressure reduced as oral cavity enlarges	
V n.	ABDm	Opens jaw		
X n.	IAm and LCAm	Adducts vocal folds resume voicing	Sound pressure from glottis	
T_1–T_{11}	IIm	Ribs depressed	P_s increased; vocal fold increases opening amplitude	Increased intensity for stressed [ɑ]
X n.	CTm	Lengthens vocal folds	Increased tension of folds; faster vibration	Raise f_o for [sɑ] prominence
XII n.	Maintains HGm activity, as GGm and tip muscles relax	Ant. tongue lowers, occupying space in pharyngeal cavity	Increased volume in oral cavity; open tract increases SPL at output	High F_1; low F_2 for [ɑ] resonance

Chart—Continued

Innervation	Muscles	Movements	Pressure changes	Result
X n.	PCAm	Opens vocal folds	P_s decreases; voicing stops; air released to tract	
V n.	MHm	Raises floor of oral cavity and tongue mass		
XI n.	PGm	Raises back of tongue		
XII n.	SGm	Raises and backs tongue dorsum	Pressure builds behind occlusion, (in oropharynx)	Silence during occlusion
XII n.	SGm relaxes	Occlusion opens by air pressure as dorsum lowers		Aperiodic transient burst with aspiration [k]
X n.	IAm	Adduction of vocal folds	Voicing resumes	Voice bar
XII n. lessens activity	Tongue muscles except for SLm and intrinsics relax	Tongue goes to neutral position except for retroflexed anterior	Oral cavity increased	Decrease in F_2 and F_3 at end of [ɚ]

The abbreviations used in the chart are: Elm, external intercostal muscle; Ilm, internal intercostal muscle; VC, vital capacity; GGm, genioglossus muscle; OOm, orbicularis oris muscle; LPm, levator palatini muscle; SGm, styloglossus muscle; IAm, interarytenoid muscle; LCAm, lateral cricoarytenoid muscle; P_s, subglottal pressure; f_o, fundamental frequency; F_1, F_2, F_3, first, second, and third formants; freq., frequency; Rm, risorius muscle; LCAm, lateral cricoarytenoid muscle; PCAm, posterior cricoarytenoid muscle; SLm, superior longitudinal muscle; PGm, palatoglossus muscle; ILm, inferior longitudinal muscle; HGm, hyoglossus muscle; ABDm, anterior belly of digastric muscle; CTm, cricothyroid muscle; SPL, sound pressure level; MHm, mylohyoid muscle.

Model of Speech Production

Perceptual Target /wibitʃuənsɑkɜ˞ /
An abstract auditory perceptual representation of the sound stream to be produced that relates to an abstract spatial representation of the speech mechanism.

Internal Feedback
Interactions among the cerebrum, basal ganglia, and cerebellum to ready the system to produce the phrase in the form of a motor schema leading to activation of muscle groups.

Motor Schema
A rough plan of speech production based upon the abstract representation of the mechanism. General instructions are fed forward in syllable chunks. Instructions are flexible enough to allow for variations.

/wi/   /bi/   /tʃu/   /ən/   /sɑ/   / kɜ˞/

Muscle Group Cooperatives
Respiratory P_s adjusters
Laryngeal position adjusters
f_o adjusters
Velopharyngeal adjusters
Back cavity adjusters
Front cavity adjusters
Mouth position adjusters

Response Feedback
Accounts for self-regulation of muscle groups and also reports to schema centers for feedforward predictive control of general instructions.

Articulator Movements and Cavity Changes
Both phoneme and syllable disappear in the quasi-continuous movements involved in producing the phrase. Coarticulatory variations are accounted for by self-regulation within muscle groups.

External Feedback
Sensations of touch, air pressure, and audition relay information to the speaker about his own speech for self-correction.

Air Pressure and Acoustic Output
Air pressure variations within the vocal tract set up audible pressure waves heard as [wibitʃuənsɑkɜ˞].

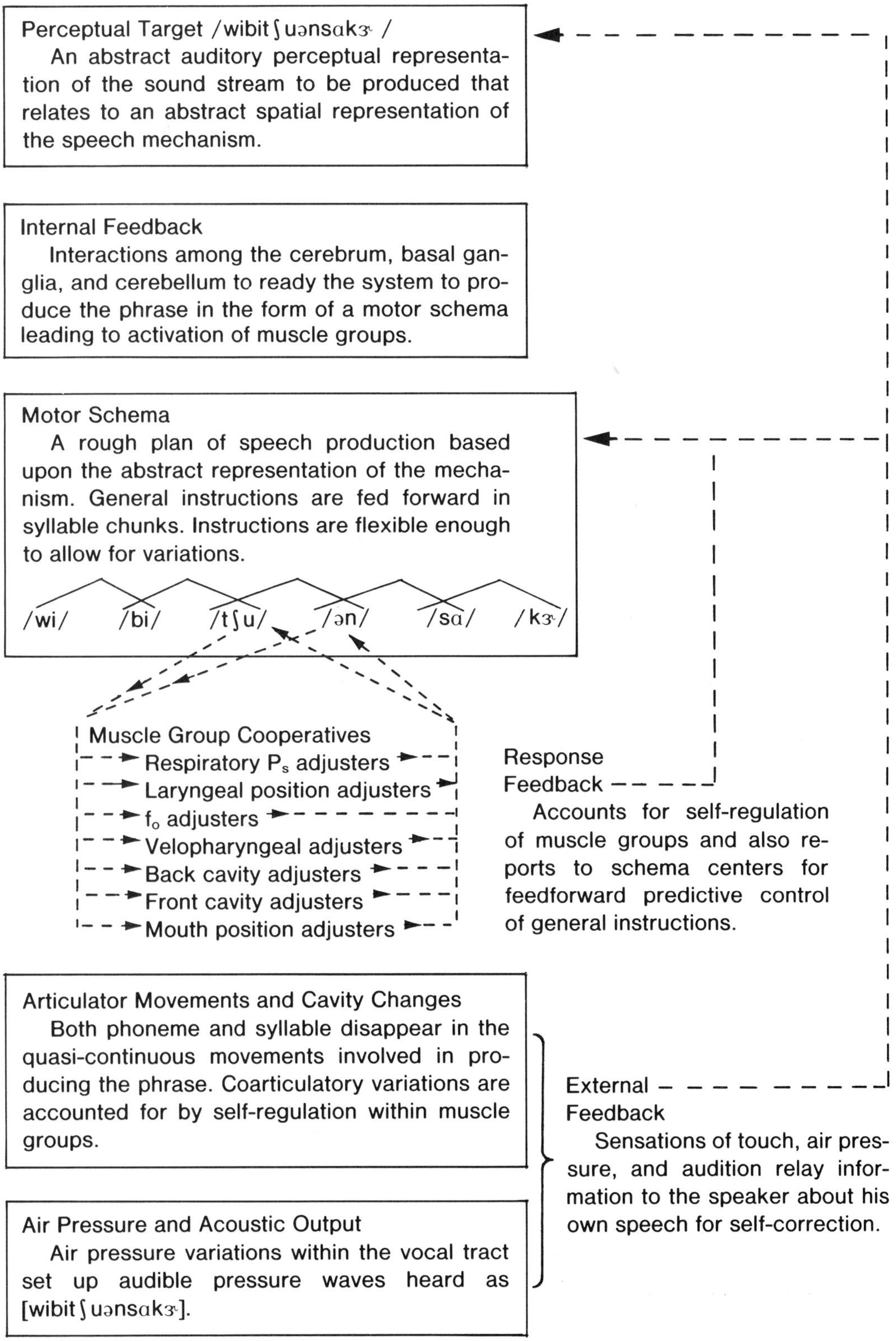

Figure 4.107. Model of speech production. (See text for discussion.)

Lest this attempt to interweave the respiratory, phonatory, and articulatory events of speech give anyone the mistaken notions that speech is the result of parallel but separate nerve to air pressure transformations or that there are direct phoneme to sound conversions, permit us to frame the process another way with a model that may better represent the coordination among muscle groups involved in speech. Figure 4.107 shows the initial speech goal to be an auditory perceptual representation of 'we beat you in soccer.' We know the general sound of the phrase that we plan to say. At this prespeech stage, there may be an internal loop of neural activity among the basal ganglia, cerebrum, and cerebellum of the brain, readying the system for speech output. The motor schema for producing the phrase may be in a rather abstract and flexible state, allowing for variations in the actual production. Rough specifications for changes in the speech mechanisms might form the schema. The general changes of the vocal tract for the utterance may be elicited from storage through cerebellar control of the motor areas of the cerebrum, and this representation may be fed forward in chunks of at least syllable size. The organization of particular muscle groups, such as the muscles that cooperate to regulate f_o, may be self-regulating via the response feedback of muscle spindles. We indicate how two chunks might overlap as the schema for [tʃuən] activates the muscle groups.

The muscle groups organized for a particular function not only are coordinated among themselves but also are coordinated with other muscle groups organized for a different function. This larger coordination may be made possible largely by feeding forward well-practiced interactions of specifications. The movements of articulators and the changes in cavity shapes are continuous, blurring phoneme and syllable boundaries as we define them. Variations in movement due to context or due to differences in initial position are the rule and are automatically produced as a result of the intimate coordination within each muscle group. Air pressure variations and the resultant acoustic stream are likewise dynamic in the ways they change across time. External feedback of the tactile and auditory feedback sensations may be too late to influence the peripheral motor patterns of muscle group activity, but they do influence the more general schema so that any mistake may be corrected on the next attempt.

The goal of the speaker, then, is to produce sounds that fit an auditory perceptual target, in order to be understood by the perceptual system of a listener. Let us turn in the next chapter to a consideration of that perceptual system and of the processes that may be involved in listening.

BIBLIOGRAPHY

General Works on Speech Production

Dickson, D. R., and Maue, W. M., *Human Vocal Anatomy*. Springfield, Ill.: Charles C Thomas, 1970.

Harris, K. S., Physiological Aspects of Articulatory Behavior. In *Current Trends in Linguistics*, Vol. 12, No. 4, T. A. Sebeok (Ed.) The Hague: Mouton, 1974, pp. 2281–2302.

Lieberman, P., *Speech Physiology and Acoustic Phonetics: An Introduction*. New York: Macmillan, 1977.

MacNeilage, P., Speech Physiology. In *Speech and Cortical Functioning*. J. H. Gilbert (Ed.) New York: Academic Press, 1972, pp. 1–72.

Minifie, F., Hixon, T. J., and Williams, F. (Eds.), *Normal Aspects of Speech, Hearing, and Language*. Englewood Cliffs, N. J.: Prentice-Hall, Inc., 1973.

Perkell, J. S., *Physiology of Speech Production: Results and Implications of a Quantitative Cineradiographic Study*. Cambridge, Mass.: M. I. T. Press, 1969.

Van Riper, C., and Irwin, J. V., *Voice and Articulation*. Englewood Cliffs, N. J.: Prentice-Hall Inc., 1958.

Zemlin, W. R., *Speech and Hearing Sciences: Anatomy and Physiology*. Englewood Cliffs, N. J.: Prentice-Hall Inc., 1968.

Neurophysiology References

Broca, P., Remarques sur la siege de la faculté du langage articule, suivies d'une observation d'aphémie (perte de la parole). *Bull. Soc. Anatom. Paris. VI: 36*, 1861, 330–357.

Eccles, J. C., *The Understanding of the Brain*. New York: McGraw-Hill, 1973.

Fromkin, V. A., Slips of the Tongue. *Sci. Am. 229*, 1973, 110–116.

MacKay, D. G., Spoonerisms: The Structure of Errors in the Serial Order of Speech. *Neuropsychologia 8,* 1970, 323–350.

Milner, B., Branch, C., and Rasmussen, T., Observations on Cerebral Dominance. In *Psychology Readings: Language.* R. C. Oldfield and J. C. Marshall (Eds.) Baltimore: Penguin Books, 1968. (Later figures given in present text from oral presentation by Milner at ASHA meeting, Las Vegas, 1974.)

Penfield, W., and Roberts, L., *Speech and Brain-Mechanisms.* Princeton, N. J.: Princeton University Press, 1959.

Pribram, K. H., *Languages of the Brain.* Englewood Cliffs, N. J.: Prentice-Hall, Inc., 1971.

Wada, J., and Rasmussen, T., Intracarotid Injection of Sodium Amytal for the Lateralization of Cerebral Speech Dominance: Experiments and Clinical Observations. *J. Neurosurg. 17,* 1960, 266–282.

Wernicke, C., *Der Aphasische Symptomencomplex.* Breslau: Max Cohn and Weigert, 1874.

Acoustiques Fondamentaux de la Voix Chantée. Thesis, University of Paris, 1950.

Müller, J., *The Physiology of the Senses, Voice, and Muscular Motion with the Mental Faculties.* Translated by W. Baly. London: Walton and Maberly, 1848.

Negus, V. E., *The Comparative Anatomy and Physiology of the Larynx.* New York: Hafner Publishing Co., 1962. (A rewriting of V. E. Negus, *The Mechanism of the Larynx.* London: William Heinemann Medical Books, Ltd., 1928.)

Shipp, T., Vertical Laryngeal Position during Continuous and Discrete Vocal Frequency Change. *J. Speech Hear. Res. 18,* 1975, 707–718.

Van den Berg, J., Myoelastic-Aerodynamic Theory of Voice Production. *J. Speech Hear. Res. 1,* 1958, 227–244.

Von Helmholtz, H., *Die Lehre der Tonempfindungen als physiologische Grundlage für die Theorie der Musik.* Braunschweig: F. Vieweg und sohn, 1863.

Respiration References

Campbell, E., The Respiratory Muscles. *Ann. N. Y. Acad. Sci. 155,* 1968, 135–140.

Draper, M. H., Ladefoged, P., and Whitteridge, D., Respiratory Muscles in Speech. *J. Speech Hear. Res. 2,* 1959, 16–27.

Fenn, W. O., Mechanics of Respiration. *Am. J. Med. 10,* 1951, 77–91.

Hixon, T., Respiratory Function in Speech. In *Normal Aspects of Speech, Hearing, and Language.* F. D. Minifie, T. J. Hixon, and F. Williams (Eds.) Englewood Cliffs, N. J.: Prentice-Hall, Inc., 1973.

Mead, J., Bouhuys, A., and Proctor, D. F., Mechanisms Generating Subglottic Pressure. *Ann. N. Y. Acad. Sci. 155,* 1968, 177–181.

Netsell, R., Subglottal and Intraoral Air Pressures during the Intervocalic Contrast of /t/ and /d/. *Phonetica. 20,* 1969, 68–73.

Rahn, H., Otis, A. B., Chadwick, L. E., and Fenn, W. O., The Pressure-Volume Diagram of the Thorax and Lung. *Am. J. Physiol. 146,* 1946, 161–178.

Stetson, R., *Motor Phonetics.* Amsterdam: North-Holland, 1951.

Van den Berg, J., Direct and Indirect Determination of the Mean Subglottic Pressure. *Folia Phoniatr. (Basel). 8,* 1956, 1–24.

Phonation References

Atkinson, J. E., Correlation Analysis of the Physiological Factors Controlling Fundamental Voice Frequency. *J. Acoust. Soc. Am. 63,* 1978, 211–222.

Faaborg-Andersen, K., Electromyographic Investigation of Intrinsic Laryngeal Muscles in Humans. *Acta Physiol. Scand 41,* Suppl. 140, 1957, 1–148.

Hirose, H., and Gay, T., The Activity of the Intrinsic Laryngeal Muscles in Voicing Control. *Phonetica. 25,* 1972, 140–164.

Husson, R., Étude des Phénomènes Physiologiques et

General References in Acoustics of Speech

Denes, P. B., and Pinson, E. N., *The Speech Chain.* New York: Doubleday, 1973.

Fant, G., *Acoustic Theory of Speech Production.* The Hague: Mouton, 1970.

Flanagan, J. L., *Speech Analysis, Synthesis, and Perception.* Berlin: Springer-Verlag, 1965.

Fry, D. B. (Ed.), *Acoustic Phonetics: A Course of Basic Readings.* New York: Cambridge University, 1976.

Lehiste, I. (Ed.), *Readings in Acoustic Phonetics.* Cambridge, Mass.: M. I. T. Press, 1967.

Potter, R. K., Kopp, G. A., and Green, H. C., *Visible Speech.* New York: D. Van Nostrand Co., Inc., 1947.

Articulation and Resonance References

Bell-Berti, F., The Velopharyngeal Mechanism: An Electromyographic Study. *Haskins Laboratories Status Report (Suppl.).* New Haven, Conn.: Haskins Laboratories, 1973.

Bell-Berti, F., Control of Pharyngeal Cavity Size for English Voiced and Voiceless Stops. *J. Acoust. Soc. Am. 57,* 1975, 456–461.

Berti, F., and Hirose, H., Palatal Activity in Voicing Distinctions: A Simultaneous Fiberoptic and Electromyographic Study. *J. Phonetics. 3,* 1975, 69–74.

Chiba, T., and Kajiyama, M., *The Vowel: Its Nature and Structure.* Tokyo: Kaiseikan, 1941.

Crandall, I. B., Sounds of Speech. *Bell Syst. Tech. J. 4,* 1925, 586–626.

Fritzell, B., The Velopharyngeal Muscles in Speech: An Electromyographic and Cinefluorographic Study. *Acta Otolaryngolog. (Stockh.) Suppl. 250,* 1969.

Fujimura, O., Analysis of Nasal Consonants. *J. Acoust. Soc. Am. 34,* 1962, 1865–1875.

Heinz, J. M., and Stevens, K. N., On the Properties of Voiceless Fricative Consonants. *J. Acoust. Soc. Am. 33*, 1961, 589–596.

Holbrook, A., and Fairbanks, G., Diphthong Formants and their Movements. *J. Speech Hear. Res. 5*, 1962, 38–58.

Joos, M., Acoustic Phonetics. *Language.* Monograph 23 (Suppl. to *Vol. 24*), 1948.

Kuhn, G. M., On the Front Cavity Resonance and its Possible Role in Speech Perception. *J. Acoust. Soc. Am. 58*, 1975, 428–433.

Ladefoged, P., *A Course in Phonetics.* New York: Harcourt Brace Jovanovich, Inc., 1975.

Lisker, L., and Abramson, A. D., A Cross-Language Study of Voicing in Initial Stops: Acoustical Measurements. *Word 20*, 1964, 384–422.

Lubker, J. F., An Electromyographic-Cinefluorographic Investigation of Velar Function during Normal Speech Production. *Cleft Palate J. 5*, 1968, 1–18.

Moll, K., and Daniloff, R. G., Investigation of the Timing of Velar Movements during Speech. *J. Acoust. Soc. Am. 50*, 1971, 678–684.

Peterson, G. E., and Barney, H. L., Control Methods Used in a Study of the Identification of Vowels. *J. Acoust. Soc. Am. 24*, 1952, 175–184.

Peterson, G. E., and Lehiste, I., Duration of Syllable Nuclei in English. *J. Acoust. Soc. Am. 32*, 1960, 693–703.

Peterson, G. E., and Lehiste, I., Transitions, Glides, and Diphthongs. *J. Acoust. Soc. Am. 33*, 1961, 268–277.

Rayleigh, J. W. S., *Theory of Sound.* London: Macmillan, 1878.

Stevens, K. N., and House, A. S., An Acoustical Theory of Vowel Production and Some of its Implications. *J. Speech Hear. Res. 4*, 1961, 303–320.

Stevens, K. N., and House, A. S., Development of a Quantitative Description of Vowel Articulation. *J. Acoust. Soc. Am. 27*, 1955, 484–493.

Subtelny, J. D., Oya, N., and Subtelny, J. D., Cineradiographic Study of Sibilants. *Folia Phoniatr. (Basel) 24*, 1972, 30–50.

Uldall, E., Transitions in Fricative Noise. *Lang. Speech. 7*, 1964, 13–15.

English Speech Sounds

Sound Influence References

Bell-Berti, F., and Harris, K. S., Some Aspects of Coarticulation. Paper presented at the International Congress of Phonetic Sciences, Leeds, England, Aug. 1975.

Borden, G. J., and Gay, T., Temporal Aspects of Articulatory Movements for /s/-Stop Clusters. *Phonetica. 36*, 1979, 21–31.

Daniloff, R. G., and Hammarberg, R. E., On Defining Coarticulation. *J. Phonetics. 1*, 1973, 239–248.

Daniloff, R. G., and Moll, K., Coarticulation of Liprounding. *J. Speech Hear. Res. 11*, 1968, 707–721.

Kent, R. D., and Minifie, F. D., Coarticulation in Recent Speech Production Models. *J. Phonetics. 5*, 1977, 115–135.

Kozhevnikov, V. A., and Chistovich, L. A., Rech artikulyatsya i vospriyatie. Moscow-Leningrad, 1965. Translated as *Speech: Articulation and Perception.* Springfield, Va.: Joint Publications Research Service, United States Department of Commerce, 1966.

Liberman, A. M., Cooper, F. S., Shankweiler, D. P., and Studdert-Kennedy, M., Perception of the Speech Code. *Psychol. Rev. 74*, 1967, 431–461.

Lindblom, B. E. F., Spectrographic Study of Vowel Reduction. *J. Acoust. Soc. Am. 35*, 1963, 1773–1781.

MacNeilage, P. F., Motor Control of Serial Ordering of Speech. *Psychol. Rev. 77*, 1970, 182–196.

MacNeilage, P. F., and De Clerk, J. L., On the Motor Control of Coarticulation in CVC Monosyllables. *J. Acoust. Soc. Am. 45*, 1969, 1217–1233.

Öhman, S. E. G., Coarticulation in VCV Utterances: Spectrographic Measurements. *J. Acoust. Soc. Am. 39*, 1966, 151–168.

Perkell, J. S., *Physiology of Speech Production: Results and Implications of a Quantitative Cineradiographic Study.* Cambridge, Mass.: M. I. T. Press, 1969.

Peterson, G. E., and Shoup, J. E., A Physiological Theory of Phonetics. *J. Speech Hear. Res. 9*, 1966; 5–67.

Suprasegmentals References

Fry, D. B., Prosodic Phenomena. In *Manual of Phonetics.* B. Malmberg (Ed.) Amsterdam: North-Holland, 1970.

Lehiste, I. *Suprasegmentals.* Cambridge, Mass.: M. I. T. Press, 1970.

Lieberman, P., *Intonation, Perception and Language.* Cambridge, Mass.: M. I. T. Press, 1967.

Feedback References

General

Borden, G. J., An Interpretation of Research on Feedback Interruption. *Brain Lang. 7*, 1979, 307–319.

Ringel, R. L., Oral Sensation and Perception: A Selective Review. *ASHA Rep. 5*, 1970, 188–206.

Wiener, N., Cybernetics, *Sci. Am. 179*, 1948, 14–19.

Weiner, N., *The Human Use of Human Beings.* 2nd Ed. Rev. Garden City, N. Y.: Doubleday, 1954.

Auditory Feedback

Black, J. W., The Effect of Delayed Side-Tone upon Vocal Rate and Intensity. *J. Speech Hear. Disord. 16*, 1951, 56–60.

Borden, G. J., Dorman, M. F., Freeman, F. J., and Raphael, L. J., Electromyographic Changes with Delayed Auditory Feedback of Speech. *J. Phonetics. 5*, 1977, 1–8.

Fairbanks, G., and Guttman, N., Effects of Delayed Auditory Feedback upon Articulation. *J. Speech Hear. Res. 1*, 1958, 12–22.

Fairbanks, G., Selective Vocal Effects of Delayed Auditory Feedback. *J. Speech Hear. Disord. 20,* 1955, 333–346.

Garber, S. F., The Effects of Feedback Filtering on Nasality. Paper presented at ASHA convention, Houston, Nov., 1976.

Lane, H. L., Catania, A. C., and Stevens, S. S., Voice Level: Autophonic Scale, Perceived Loudness, and Effects of Side Tone. *J. Acoust. Soc. Am. 33,* 1961, 160–167.

Lane, H. L., and Tranel, B., The Lombard Sign and the Role of Hearing in Speech. *J. Speech Hear. Res. 14,* 1971, 677–709.

Lee, B. S., Effects of Delayed Speech Feedback. *J. Acoust. Soc. Am. 22,* 1950, 824–826.

Peters, R. W., The Effect of Changes in Side-Tone Delay and Level upon Rate of Oral Reading of Normal Speakers. *J. Speech Hear. Disord. 19,* 1954, 483–490.

Siegel, G. M., and Pick, H. L., Jr., Auditory Feedback in the Regulation of Voice. *J. Acoust. Soc. Am. 56,* 1974, 1618–1624.

Stromsta, C., Delays Associated with Certain Side-tone Pathways. *J. Acoust. Soc. Am. 34,* 1962, 392–396.

Von Békésy, G., The Structure of the Middle Ear and the Hearing of One's Own Voice by Bone Conduction. *J. Acoust. Soc. Am. 21,* 1949, 217–232.

Webster, R. L., and Dorman, M. F., Changes in Reliance on Auditory Feedback Cues as a Function of Oral Practice. *J. Speech Hear. Res. 14,* 1971, 307–311.

Yates, A. J., Delayed Auditory Feedback. *Psychol. Bull. 60,* 1963, 213–232.

Tactile Feedback

Borden, G. J., Harris, K. S., and Catena, L., Oral Feedback II. An Electromyographic Study of Speech under Nerve-Block Anesthesia. *J. Phonetics. 1,* 1973, 297–308.

Borden, G. J., Harris, K. S., and Oliver, W., Oral Feedback I. Variability of the Effect of Nerve-Block Anesthesia upon Speech. *J. Phonetics. 1,* 1973, 289–295.

Gammon, S. A., Smith, P. J., Daniloff, R. G., and Kim, C. W., Articulation and Stress/Juncture Production under Oral Anesthetization and Masking. *J. Speech Hear. Res. 14,* 1971, 271–282.

Hardcastle, W. J., Some Aspects of Speech Production under Controlled Conditions of Oral Anesthesia and Auditory Masking. *J. Phonetics. 3,* 1975, 197–214.

Horii, Y., House, A. S., Li, K.-P, and Ringel, R. L., Acoustic Characteristics of Speech Produced without Oral Sensation. *J. Speech Hear. Res. 16,* 1973, 67–77.

Hutchinson, J. M., and Putnam, A. H. B., Aerodynamic Aspects of Sensory Deprived Speech. *J. Acoust. Soc. Am. 56,* 1974, 1612–1617.

Leanderson, R., and Persson, A., The Effect of Trigeminal Nerve Block on the Articulatory EMG Activity of Facial Muscles. *Acta Otolaryngol. (Stockh.) 74,* 1972, 271–278.

Locke, J. L., A Methodological Consideration in Kinesthetic Feedback Research. *J. Speech Hear. Res. 11,* 1968, 668–669.

Prosek, R. A., and House, A. S., Intraoral Air Pressure as a Feedback Cue in Consonant Production. *J. Speech Hear. Res. 18,* 1975, 133–147.

Putnam, A. H. B., and Ringel, R., A Cineradiographic Study of Articulation in Two Talkers with Temporarily Induced Oral Sensory Deprivation. *J. Speech Hear. Res. 19,* 1976, 247–266.

Putnam, A. H. B., and Ringel, R., Some Observations of Articulation during Labial Sensory Deprivation. *J. Speech Hear. Res. 15,* 1972, 529–542.

Scott, C. M., and Ringel, R. L., Articulation without Oral Sensory Control. *J. Speech Hear. Res. 14,* 1971, 804–818.

Proprioceptive Feedback References

Abbs, J., The Influence of the Gamma Motor System on Jaw Movements during Speech: A Theoretical Framework and Some Preliminary Observations. *J. Speech and Hear. Res. 16,* 1973, 175–200.

Bowman, J. P., *Muscle Spindles and Neural Control of the Tongue: Implications for Speech.* Springfield, Ill.: Charles C Thomas, 1971.

Cooper, S., Muscle Spindles and Other Muscle Receptors. In *The Structure and Function of Muscle,* Vol. I. G. H. Bourne (Ed.) New York: Academic Press, 1960, pp. 381–420.

Critchlow, V., and von Euler, C., Intercostal Muscle Spindle Activity and its Motor Control. *J. Physiol. 168,* 1963, 820–847.

Fitzgerald, M. J. T., and Law, M. E., The Peripheral Connexions between the Lingual and Hypoglossal Nerves. *J. Anat. 92,* 1958, 178–188.

Folkins, J. W., and Abbs, J. H., Lip and Jaw Motor Control during Speech: Responses to Resistive Loading of the Jaw. *J. Speech Hear. Res. 18,* 1975, 207–220.

Goodwin, G. M., and Luschei, E. S., Effects of Destroying the Spindle Afferents from the Jaw Muscles upon Mastication in Monkeys. *J. Neurophysiol. 37,* 1974, 967–981.

Goodwin, G. M., McCloskey, D. I., and Matthews, P. B. C., The Contribution of Muscle Afferents to Kinaesthesia Shown by Vibration Induced Illusions of Movement and by the Effects of Paralyzing Joint Afferents. *Brain 95,* 1972, 705–748.

Hamlet, S. L., Speech Adaptation to Dental Appliances: Theoretical Considerations. *J. Baltimore Coll. Dent. Surg. 28,* 1973, 52–63.

Higgins, J. R., and Angel, R. W., Correction of Tracking Errors without Sensory Feedback. *J. Exper. Psychol. 84,* 1970, 412–416.

Ladefoged, P., and Fromkin, V. A., Experiments on Competence and Performance. *IEEE Trans. Audio Electroacoust.* March 1968, 130–136.

Matthews, P. B. C., Muscle Spindles and their Motor Control. *Physiol. Rev. 44*, 1964, 219–288.

Mott, F. M., and Sherrington, C. S., Experiments upon the Influence of Sensory Nerves upon Movement and Nutrition of the Limbs. *Proc. Roy. Soc. Lond. Biol. 57*, 1875, 481–488.

Smith, T. S., and Lee, C. Y., Peripheral Feedback Mechanisms in Speech Production Models? In *Proceedings of 7th International Congress of Phonetic Sciences*. A. Rigault and R. Charbonneau (Eds.) The Hague: Mouton, 1972, 1199–1202.

Taub, E., Ellman, S. J., and Berman, A. J., Deafferentation in Monkeys: Effect on Conditioned Grasp Response. *Science. 151*, 1966, 593–594.

Vallbo, Å. B., Muscle Spindle Response at the Onset of Isometric Voluntary Contractions in Man: Time Difference between Fusimotor and Skeletomotor Effects. *J. Physiol. (Lond.) 218*, 1971, 405–431.

Internal Feedback

Eccles, J. C., *The Understanding of the Brain*. New York: McGraw-Hill, 1973.

Evarts, E. V., Central Control of Movement. *Neurosci. Res. Program Bull. 9*, 1971.

Stelmach, G. E. (Ed.), *Motor Control*. The Hague: Mouton, 1976.

Models of Speech Production

Chomsky, N., and Halle, M., *The Sound Pattern of English*. New York: Harper & Row, 1968.

Fairbanks, G., A Theory of the Speech Mechanism as a Servosystem. *J. Speech Hear. Disord. 19*, 1954, 133–139.

Fant, G., Auditory Patterns of Speech. In *Models for the Perception of Speech and Visual Form*. W. Wathen-Dunn (Ed.) Cambridge, Mass.: M. I. T. Press, 1967.

Hebb, D. O., *The Organization of Behavior*. New York: Wiley, 1949.

Henke, W., Dynamic Articulatory Model of Speech Production Using Computer Simulation. Ph.D. thesis, Massachusetts Institute of Technology, Cambridge, Mass., 1966.

Jakobson, R., Fant, C. G. M., and Halle, M., Preliminaries to Speech Analysis. Cambridge Mass.: M. I. T., Press, 1963. (Originally published in 1952 as *Technical Report No. 13*, Acoustics Laboratory, Massachusetts Institute of Technology).

Kozhevnikov, V. A., and Chistovich, L. A., *Rech: Artikulyatisiya i Vospriyatiye*, Moscow-Leningrad, 1965. Translated as *Speech: Articulation and Perception*. Springfield, Va.: United States Department of Commerce, Joint Publications Research Service Vol. 30, 1966.

Ladefoged, P., De Clerk, J., Lindau, M., and Papçun, G., An Auditory-Motor Theory of Speech Production. *UCLA Working Papers in Phonetics* Vol. 22, Los Angeles: UCLA, 1972, pp. 48–75.

Lashley, K. S., The Problem of Serial Order in Behavior. In *Cerebral Mechanisms in Behavior*. L. A. Jeffress (Ed.) New York: Wiley, 1951.

Liberman, A. M., Cooper, F. S., Shankweiler, D. P., and Studdert-Kennedy, M., Perception of the Speech Code. *Psychol. Rev. 74*, 1967, 431–461.

MacNeilage, P., Motor Control of Serial Ordering of Speech. *Psychol. Rev. 77*, 1970, 182–196.

Martin, J. G., Rhythmic (hierarchical) versus Serial Structure in Speech and Other Behavior. *Psychol. Rev. 79*, 1972, 487–509.

Nooteboom, S. G., The Target Theory of Speech Production. *IPO Annual Progress Report*. Vol. 5, Eindhoven, Netherlands: Institute for Perception Research, 1970, pp. 51–55.

Peterson, G. E., and Shoup, J. E., A Physiological Theory of Phonetics. *J. Speech Hear. Res. 9*, 1966, 5–67.

Peterson, G. E., and Shoup, J. E., The Elements of an Acoustic Phonetic Theory. *J. Speech Hear. Res. 9*, 1966, 68–99.

Stevens, K. N., The Quantal Nature of Speech: Evidence from Articulatory-Acoustic Data. *In Human Communication: A Unified View*. E. E. David and P. B. Denes (Eds.) New York: McGraw-Hill, 1972.

Stevens, K. N., and House, A. S., Speech Perception. In *Foundations of Modern Auditory Theory*. Vol. 2., J. V. Tobias (Ed.) New York: Academic Press, 1972.

Wathen-Dunn, W. (Ed.), *Models for the Perception of Speech and Visual Form*. Cambridge, Mass.: M. I. T. Press, 1967.

CHAPTER 5

Speech Perception

> The intellect pierces the form, overleaps the wall, detects intrinsic likeness between remote things and reduces all things into a few principles.
>
> Ralph Waldo Emerson, *Intellect* 1841

The only reason that we understand one another at all, and there are those who may argue that we do a poor job of it, is that the human mind has developed into a remarkable seeker of patterns. It receives the seemingly chaotic variety of sights, sounds, and textures, searches for common properties among them, makes associations, and sorts them into groups. In this sense, then, we all perceive in the same way. In speaking to one another, we seem to extract the essences of sound and meaning from utterances diverse in dialect, vocabulary, and voice quality.

There is a duality, however, in our perception of other speakers; although we seek common denominators, we also impose ourselves upon what we perceive. Like the legend of the blind men describing an elephant, each having touched a different part of the animal, each person perceives the world a bit differently, depending upon individual experiences and expectations. In perceiving the speech communications of others, we tend to impose our own points of view upon the messages. We often think we hear what we expect to hear. If part of a word is missing, our minds supply it and we fail to notice its absence. Even the sounds of speech are heard within the framework of our particular language, so that if we hear a less

familiar language being spoken, we try to fit the less familiar sounds into the categories of speech sounds we have in our own language. Adults trying to imitate a new language, for this reason, speak with an obvious 'accent,' retaining the sound categories of their first language. In trying to say 'tu' in French, an English speaker might say /tu/ instead of /ty/ and not even perceive the difference in the vowels of a French person saying 'tu' /ty/ and 'vous' /vu/.

Yet, we normally do perceive an elephant with enough of a common ground of shared experiences that we agree that it is an elephant. In speech communication, despite the fact that we retain our individual and language-based perspectives, we receive the same acoustic signal, and our ears act upon this signal in similar ways. Thus, we have learned the acoustic patterns that correspond to the distinctive speech sounds in our language. We seem to learn these despite the fact that the acoustic cues for individual speech sounds overlap in time. In this chapter, we shall discuss speech perception in terms of how we English speaking listeners act in common upon the sounds of English, bearing in mind that we differ from speakers of other languages, and to some extent, from one another.

THE LISTENER

Communication by speech is the transmission of thoughts or feelings from the mind of a speaker to the mind of a listener. The concepts and attitudes that the

speaker intends to express are embodied in a linguistic frame and rendered audible by the physiological processes that we considered in the last chapter. This chapter continues the discussion of what Denes and Pinson have called the 'speech chain,' the chain of events from speaker to listener. The listener hears the speech signal and interprets its meaning. These events are obviously interrelated, but we shall consider them separately. *Audition,* the process of registering the sounds in the brain of the hearer, will be considered first, and *speech perception,* the process of decoding a message from the stream of sounds coming from the speaker, will form the main consideration of the chapter.

We can appreciate the difference between speech audition and speech perception when we compare the effects of deafness with those of developmental aphasia. When a child is born deaf or hard-of-hearing, the difficulty in learning language is based on dysfunction of the peripheral hearing mechanism. If the child could hear speech, he or she could learn to interpret it. When a child is born with brain damage that specifically interferes with speech perception, the child has normal hearing but is unable to interpret the sounds in any linguistically useful way. Although there are several different syndromes called by such terms as developmental aphasia or *auditory agnosia,* a common difficulty seems to lie in the processes leading to the discrimination and identification of speech sounds rather than in the auditory processes themselves.

Listeners use more than acoustic information when they receive a spoken message. They use their knowledge of the speaking situation, their knowledge of the speaker, as well as visual cues obtained by watching the face and gestures of the speaker. These non-acoustic cues used in speech perception are important, but they fall outside the range of study usually ascribed to speech science as we have defined it. In this chapter, we shall limit ourselves to a discussion of what is known and conjectured about the perception of speech as it involves extracting the sounds of speech from acoustic information. This limitation means that we shall largely ignore other important areas of investiga-

tion: the processes by which listeners arrive at meaning through semantic and syntactic analyses of the message.

Usually, listeners are only aware of the meaning of speech and remain quite unconscious of the components of the message. As a person who sees a dog run by is conscious of perceiving a dog, not a changing pattern of light, so a person perceiving speech is aware of the meaning of the message, not the individual sounds or sound patterns that form it. Linguistic information seems to be stored by meaning or by imagery. For example, Bartlett found that people tested repeatedly on folk stories that they had read, often used entirely different words to relate the tale than the words used in the original, but the story outline and prominent images were remembered.

As strongly as listeners seem to seek meanings, they must be extracting these meanings from the sound patterns of speech. We shall focus upon the acoustic, phonetic, and phonemic analyses that presumably form the basis for further linguistic decisions. It does seem unlikely, however, that a listener would take the auditory information and proceed 'up the ladder' to make phonetic, then phonemic, then morphemic, and finally syntactic decisions, to arrive at the meaning of the message. More likely, operating on certain expectations of what the speaker may be saying, the listener hears some of the message, makes a rough analysis, and leaps to synthesize it into something meaningful, simultaneously verifying it at all the levels mentioned.

No matter how the listeners analyze a message, the data upon which they operate are the acoustic patterns of speech. The first thing that listeners do, then, is hear the speech. Since the nature of the hearing mechanism per se is somewhat outside the mainstream of this book, we will merely say a few words about the peripheral reception of speech, as the auditory system itself imposes certain changes upon speech sounds.

HEARING

The human auditory mechanism analyzes sound according to changes in frequency and intensity across time. As a receptor, the ear falls short of the eye in sensitivity, but seems to be remarkably responsive to sounds that humans produce, the sounds of speech. These sounds change not only in amplitude but in their mode of transmission as they travel through the outer ear, middle ear, cochlea, and auditory nerve to the brain. Figure 5.1 differentiates these parts of the mechanism. As we know from Chapter 3, the pressure waves of speech are usually disturbances in air and thus they continue in the outer ear. In the middle ear, however, they are converted from pressure waves to mechanical vibrations by a series of small bones leading to the cochlea of the inner ear. In the *cochlea,* a snail-shaped cavity within the temporal bone of the skull, the vibrations are again transformed. This time the transformation is from mechanical vibrations to vibrations in fluid, since the cochlea is filled with fluid. Finally, the

nerve endings in the cochlea act to transform the hydraulic vibrations into electrochemical changes that are sent to the brain in the form of nerve impulses.

The Outer Ear

The outer ear is composed of two parts: the external part you can readily see, called the *auricle* or *pinna,* and the ear canal, named the *external auditory meatus,* leading from the pinna to the eardrum. Meatus means 'channel,' and the channel of the outer ear is specified by the term 'external,' distinguishing it from the internal auditory meatus that runs from the inner ear out of the temporal bone to the brain. The pinna funnels the sound somewhat, being a little more receptive to sounds in front of the head than behind. The pinna also serves to protect the en-

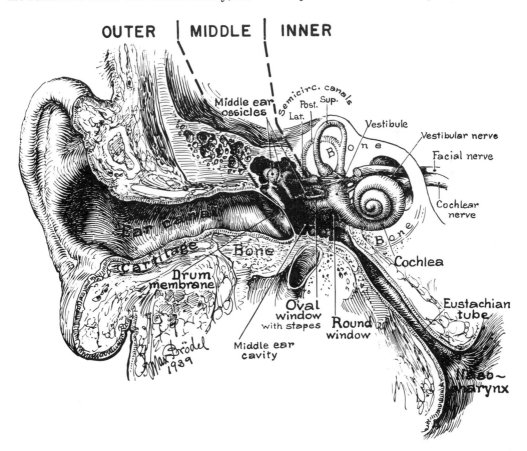

Figure 5.1. Drawing of the outer, middle, and inner ear based on a frontal section of the head. (Reprinted from J. D. Durrant and J. H. Lovrinic: *Bases of Hearing Science,* The Williams and Wilkins Co. © 1977. Adapted from M. Brodel: *Three Unpublished Drawings of the Anatomy of the Human Ear,* W. B. Saunders Co. © 1946.)

trance to the canal, especially the small projection of the pinna, situated over the opening to the canal, called the *tragus*. One way to reduce the intensity of a loud sound is to press the tragus into the entrance to the auditory meatus with your finger.

The external auditory meatus protects the more delicate parts of the ear from trauma and from the intrusion of foreign objects. A waxy substance called *cerumen* is secreted into the canal and aided by the hairs lining the canal, *cilia*, filters out dust and any flying insects that may have intruded into the canal. Some people constantly clean out the cerumen, but they are depriving themselves of their natural protection. If the cerumen should harden or an object become lodged in the meatus, it should be removed by an otolaryngologist.

In addition to offering protection to the more critical parts of the ear, the external auditory meatus functions to boost the high frequencies of the sounds it receives. The canal is an air-filled cavity, open at one end, and therefore acts as a quarter wave resonator. The lowest resonance has a wavelength 4 times the length of the tube, and the higher resonances are its odd multiples. Thus, the first resonance of a canal 2.5 cm long is about 3440 Hz.

$$f = \frac{\text{velocity of sound}}{4 \text{ (length)}} = \frac{34,400}{10} = 3,440 \text{ Hz}$$

A female or child's ear canal would probably be shorter than 2.5 cm and would resonate at even higher frequencies. High frequency emphasis provided by the outer ear is important for speech perception, because much of the sound energy helpful in distinguishing fricatives are in the frequency range above 2000 Hz.

Before leaving the outer ear, consider why we have ears on both sides of our heads. To reverse the question, what happens when there is a loss of hearing in one ear because of something like a case of mumps in adulthood? The good ear hears perfectly well, so there is little loss of acuity in a quiet environment, but large group conversations become difficult for the person to follow. Localization of the sound is impaired. Normally, having an ear on each side of the head aids in localizing the source of the sound. In a meeting

room with voices coming from all directions, the unilaterally deaf person may look in the wrong direction, seeking to locate the speaker.

The Middle Ear

The outer ear is separated from the air-filled *middle ear* cavity by the eardrum, properly called the *tympanic membrane* (Fig. 5.2). The tympanic membrane is slightly concave as seen from the outer ear and is responsive to small pressure variations across a wide range of frequencies. The tension of the eardrum can be altered by a muscle, the *tensor tympani,* which pulls on the *manubrium* or handle of a small bone attached to the inside of the drum. The bone is called the *malleus.* At low frequencies, the tympanic membrane vibrates as a whole, but at high frequencies, different areas of the membrane are responsive to different frequency ranges. On the internal side of the tympanic membrane is the *ossicular chain,* three tiny bones connected to one another, called the *ossicles.* The aforementioned malleus (hammer) is attached to the tympanic membrane, the *incus* (anvil) acts as a fulcrum between the other two bones, and the *stapes* (stirrup) inserts into the membranous *oval window* leading to the inner ear. Thus, the ossicular chain bridges the space between the tympanic membrane

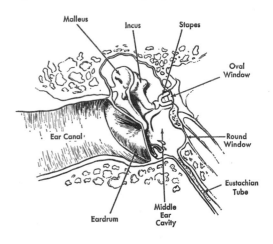

Figure 5.2. Cross-sectional diagram of the middle ear and ossicles. (Reprinted with permission of Doubleday & Co., Inc. from P. B. Denes and E. N. Pinson: *The Speech Chain,* Bell Telephone Laboratories, Inc. © 1963.)

and the cochlea. The chain is suspended in the air-filled cavity of the middle ear by ligaments and is held in such a delicate balance that no matter what position the body takes, the tiny bones are held in suspension, free to vibrate in response to sound. The vibrations in the outer ear take the form of disturbances of air molecules, but in the middle ear, take the form of mechanical vibrations of the bony ossicles. The tympanic membrane and the ossicular chain taken together are especially responsive to the frequencies of the acoustic signal that are important for speech.

Why have a middle ear at all? Why not have the fluid-filled cochlea on the other side of the tympanic membrane? The problem is a mismatch in *impedance*. Impedance is a force determined by the characteristics of the medium itself (gas, liquid, or solid) and is a measure of the resistance to transmission of signals. Liquid offers a higher impedance or resistance to the sound pressure, than does gas. When sound pressure waves traveling through air (a gas) suddenly come to a fluid, most of the sound energy is reflected back, with very little admitted into the liquid. The cochlea is filled with fluid. In order to overcome the difference in impedance between air and fluid, a transformer is needed to increase the sound pressure so that more of it will be admitted into the liquid. The transformer function is performed by the middle ear.

The middle ear increases sound pressure by approximately 30 dB. The ossicles by themselves are not able to effect such a large amplification of the signal, although they do act like a lever to increase the sound pressure by about 5 dB (Fig. 5.3). Leverage is the force long used by farmers to remove a heavy rock from a field. If the rock is too heavy for the farmer to lift, leverage can be used by placing a pole over a fulcrum, with the shorter part of the pole under the heavy object, and the longer part on the other side of the fulcrum. The farmer puts pressure on the long end of the pole. The fulcrum works with the farmer, resulting in an increased pressure under the rock to be moved. Thus, a given pressure applied by the farmer results in a much larger pressure under the rock. In somewhat the same way, the pressures

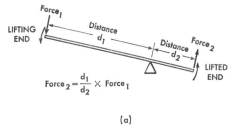

(a)

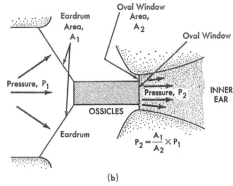

(b)

Figure 5.3. The *a* portion shows the lever principle of the ossicles. The *b* portion shows the effect of the area difference between the tympanic membrane and the oval window. (Reprinted with permission of Doubleday & Co., Inc. from P. B. Denes and E. N. Pinson: *The Speech Chain,* Bell Telephone Laboratories, Inc. © 1963.)

applied to the relatively long malleus are transmitted by the incus acting something like a fulcrum to the much smaller stapes, with the result that the pressure has increased a few decibels in transmission.

The leverage applied along the ossicles adds some pressure to overcome the impedance mismatch, but the larger part of the increase in pressure comes from the design of the tympanic membrane relative to the oval window. The area of the tympanic membrane is about 0.85 cm^2, although only about 0.55 cm^2 of that area is active in vibration. When the same force applied to a large area is focused on a smaller area, the pressure is increased. Pressure is force over area (p = F/A). If a force has to be spread across a large area, the pressure at any point will be less than if the same force is spread across a small area. As an analogy, if your friend were to fall through the ice, you would be well advised to spread your weight over a large area in attempting to reach the victim. By lying flat, or better, by distributing your weight over an even larger area, by crawling along on a ladder, you are in much less danger of falling through the ice yourself. The pressure on any point is much less than if you were to attempt to walk to your friend on the ice. So it is that sound vibrations occurring over the effective vibrating area of the tympanic membrane, estimated at about 0.55 cm^2, when applied from the stapes into the 0.03 cm^2 area of the oval window, result in an increase in pressure of approximately 25 dB. The area of the tympanic membrane vibrating at any one time is approximately 18 times the area of the oval window. Thus, the impedance matching function of the middle ear is accomplished by the area difference between the tympanic membrane and the oval window, which boosts the signal about 25 dB, and by the leverage afforded by the ossicular design, which adds a few more decibels, overcoming the loss caused by differences in impedance.

Besides the important function of impedance matching between the air and the cochlear fluid, the middle ear mechanism serves two other functions. First, it attenuates loud sounds, by action of the *acoustic reflex*. Second, by the action of the eustachian tube, it works to maintain relatively equal air pressure on either side of the eardrum despite any changes in atmospheric pressure.

The acoustic reflex is elicited when a sound having a pressure level of 85 or 90 dB reaches the middle ear. This results in contraction of the smallest muscle in the body, the *stapedius muscle* attached to the neck of the smallest bone in the body, the stapes. There are two theories to account for the function of this acoustic reflex. The first theory, that it is to protect the inner ear from loud sounds, posits that the contraction of the stapedius muscle pulls the stapes to one side, changing the angle of its vibration in the oval window and thereby deflecting some of the pressure. The second theory is that the stapedius along with the tensor tympani muscle acts to stiffen the ossicular chain, thereby regulating intensity changes, much as the eye adjusts to changes in light. In either case, the stapedius muscle takes a few milliseconds to act, allowing sounds with sudden onset to penetrate the inner ear before the reflex has occurred. Also, like any muscle, it eventually fatigues, so that in a noisy environment, the reflexive attenuation of the sound will gradually lessen, allowing the full impact of the sound pressure to impinge again upon the inner ear. The stapedius muscle is innervated by the facial nerve (VIIth cranial nerve) but is somehow associated with the innervation of the larynx (vagus; Xth cranial nerve) because voicing activates the acoustic reflex. It is interesting that the acoustic reflex attenuates by about 10-dB frequencies below 1 kHz; the spectral energy of the human voice is also largely below 1 kHz. The acoustic reflex may keep us from hearing ourselves too loudly, for we hear our own voices not only by the air-conducted sound coming through our outer ears, but by bone-conducted sound, as our facial and skull bones vibrate in response to our own voices.

Another function of the middle ear is to equalize the pressure within and outside the middle ear. This is accomplished by the *eustachian tube*, leading from the middle ear to the nasopharynx. The eardrum does not vibrate properly if the air within the middle ear is different in pressure from the air in the external meatus. Relatively high pressure within the middle ear pushes out on the tympanic membrane, causes discomfort, and attenuates outside sounds. A sudden change in pressure, as when one drives up into the mountains or ascends in an airplane, can create this pressure difference if the eustachian tube, normally closed, fails to open. The outside air is suddenly lower in pressure, while the air in the middle ear cavity (containing the same air as when one was at sea level) is relatively higher in pressure. Swallowing, yawning, and chewing facilitate the opening of the tube, which is why airline attendants sometimes offer chewing gum to passengers on takeoff.

The Inner Ear

Within the temporal bone of the skull, there are several coil-shaped tunnels filled with fluid called *perilymph*. The fluid is like seawater in many of its properties. Floating in the fluid are coiled tubes made of membrane and filled with a more viscous fluid called *endolymph*. Figure 5.4 depicts the membranous labyrinth. The snail-shaped coil is the *cochlear duct*, containing the sensory receptor for hearing, and the system of three coils is the *vestibular system*, consisting of the *semicircular canals*, which, along with the *vestibule* (utricle and saccule) connecting them, contain organs that sense changes in body position and movement.

We shall limit our description to the cochlea, for audition is the first step in speech perception. As the footplate of the stapes vibrates in the oval window, the vibrations set up disturbances in the perilymph of the cochlea. These pressure waves in the perilymph surrounding the snail-shaped cochlear duct, set up vibrations in the duct itself. Especially important are the resulting vibrations of the

'floor' of the duct, called the *basilar membrane*.

The cochlea in humans is a cavity within bone which coils around a bony core almost three times. The membranous duct (or cochlear duct) within is attached to the bony core on the inside and by a ligament to the bony wall on the outside. It is perhaps easier to visualize if we imagine the cochlear chambers uncoiled as in Figure 5.5. Pressure variations applied by the stapes rocking in the oval window are translated into pressure variations within the fluids of the cochlea, which in turn lead to displacements of the basilar membrane. The beauty of the system is that different parts of the basilar membrane respond to different frequencies. The membrane is narrow and stiff at the base, gradually getting wider and less stiff at the apex (the opposite of what one might ex-

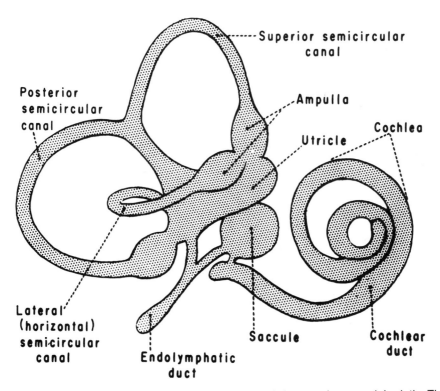

Figure 5.4. Schematic drawing representing the parts of the membranous labyrinth. The three semicircular canals, the ampulla, utricle, and saccule make up the vestibular organs which are responsible for sensing body position and movement. The cochlea contains the organ of hearing. (Reprinted from J. D. Durrant and J. H. Lovrinic: *Bases of Hearing Science,* The Williams and Wilkins Co. © 1977. From D. D. DeWeese and W. H. Saunders: *Textbook of Otolaryngology,* Ed. 3, C. V. Mosby Co., St. Louis © 1968.)

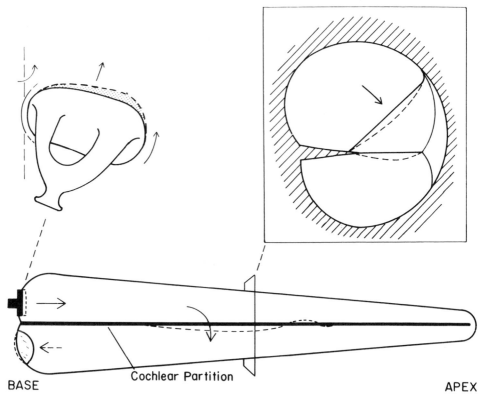

BASE   Cochlear Partition   APEX

Figure 5.5. The *lower section* shows the uncoiled cochlea, while the *upper right section* shows a cross-section. The stapes, shown in the *upper left,* rocks in the oval window, leading to displacement of the cochlear partition, and the basilar membrane in particular. (Reprinted from J. D. Durrant and J. H. Lovrinic: *Bases of Hearing Science,* The Williams and Wilkins Co. © 1977. Adapted from G. von Békésy: *Experiments in Hearing,* translated and edited by E. G. Wever, McGraw-Hill © 1960.)

pect). As a result, low frequency sounds produce traveling waves in the fluid which stimulate the basilar membrane to vibrate with the largest amplitude of displacement at the wider, more flaccid tip. On the other hand, high frequency sounds create pressure waves with the largest displacement of the basilar membrane at the thinner, stiffer base (Fig. 5.6).

The basilar membrane is not the sense organ of hearing, however. It is the *Organ of Corti,* lying on the basilar membrane for the length of the cochlear duct, that is the auditory receptor. It consists of rows of hair cells, along with other cells for support. Above the rows of thousands of hair cells is a gelatinous mass called the *tectorial membrane.* The basilar membrane and the tectorial membrane are attached at different places in the cochlear duct and therefore move somewhat independently.

Figure 5.7 shows a cross-section of the cochlea. The scala vestibuli and scala tympani containing perilymph lie on either side of the cochlear duct. Pressure waves in the perilymph set up traveling waves within the cochlear duct. In some way imperfectly understood, the undulating motions of the basilar membrane cause the hair cells to be stimulated. The tectorial membrane above the hairs shears across the hairy endings of the cells, and the result is an electrochemical excitation of the nerve fibers serving the critical hair cells.

The cochlea performs a frequency analysis, a Fourier separation of complex sounds into their component frequencies. The sound of [i] as in 'see' would result in many traveling waves moving along the basilar membrane with at least two maxima of displacement: one near the apex for

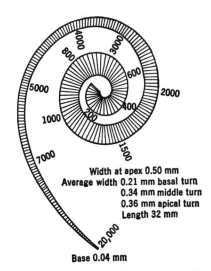

Width at apex 0.50 mm
Average width 0.21 mm basal turn
0.34 mm middle turn
0.36 mm apical turn
Length 32 mm

Base 0.04 mm

Figure 5.6. Schematic diagram showing the width of the basilar membrane (somewhat exaggerated) as it approaches the apex. The approximate positions of maximum amplitude of vibration in response to tones of different frequency are also indicated. (Reprinted with permission from O. Stuhlman, Jr.: *An Introduction to Biophysics,* Wiley & Sons © 1952.)

the lower resonance and one near the base of the cochlea for the higher resonance. If the speaker were to say [si], 'see,' the membrane displacement would initially be maximum even closer to the base of the cochlea for the high frequency [s]. Also, the traveling waves would be aperiodic during [s], becoming periodic during the vocalic part of the word. Both the *traveling wave theory* and the description of the stiffness gradient of the basilar membrane are the result of the work of the late Georg von Békésy.

Frequency information is extracted from the signal by the combined factors of place of stimulation activating the sensory nerve fibers at that place along the basilar membrane, the *place theory,* as we have just described, and also by timing of impulses along the nerve fibers. Ernest Glen Wever theorized that, at low frequencies, the displacement is not sharp enough to distinguish the frequencies by place; rather, they may be signaled by the number of cycles per second translated into a corresponding number of clusters of nerve impulses per second (Fig. 5.8). At high frequencies, place is probably important for

indicating frequency because neurons cannot fire at high frequencies. Another possibility is Wever's *volley theory,* by which several neurons would cooperate in the neural transmission of high frequencies (Fig. 5.9). The coding of intensity may well be as complicated as frequency coding. It is thought, though, that it is primarily transmitted by relative rate of nerve impulse spikes, as it is throughout the body.

The Auditory Nerve

The 30,000 nerve fibers serving the cochlea, each fiber coming from a few hair cells and each hair cell exciting several nerve fibers, form a bundle known as the *auditory nerve* or *VIIIth cranial nerve.* Another branch of the VIIIth nerve picks up information from the semicircular canals. When the nerve fibers are excited by the stimulation of the hair cells, the frequency analysis performed by the Organ of Corti

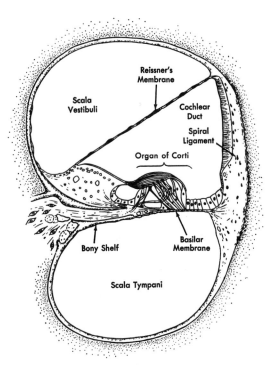

Figure 5.7. A cross-section through the cochlea, showing the scala vestibuli, the scala tympani, and the cochlear duct. The Organ of Corti lies within the cochlear duct. (Reprinted with permission of Doubleday & Co., Inc. from P. B. Denes and E. N. Pinson: *The Speech Chain,* Bell Telephone Laboratories, Inc. © 1963.)

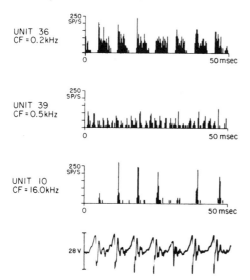

Figure 5.8. Responses of single neurons of the auditory nerve of a cat to a presentation of a segment of the vowel [æ]. The *bottom display* shows the acoustic signal. The three *upper displays* show the responses of three different neural units. Notice that although different units have different firing frequencies, they maintain a fixed relationship to the signal. (Reprinted with permission from N. Y. S. Kiang and E. C. Moxon: *Journal of the Acoustical Society of America.* 55, 1974.)

is further refined due to *lateral inhibition*: when a certain place along the basilar membrane is maximally stimulated, surrounding cells and nerve fibers are inhibited in their response, to sharpen the effect.

The VIIIth nerve does not have far to go between the cochlea and the temporal lobe of the brain. It exits the temporal bone by the *internal auditory meatus* and enters the brainstem where the medulla meets the pons. In the brainstem, most nerve fibers from each ear decussate (cross) to the contralateral pathway. At that point, comparisons can be made between signals from each ear to localize the sounds. It is thought that VIIIth nerve fibers in the brainstem may be specialized to detect certain auditory features. Such a specialization would be useful in detecting distinctions important to speech processing. From the brainstem, the VIIIth nerve courses to the midbrain and then to the temporal lobe. Along the way, fibers go off

to the cerebellum and to a network of the brainstem that acts to focus attention. Motor fibers of the auditory nerve also descend to control the sensitivity of the cochlea.

When signals arrive at the auditory cortex of the temporal lobe, the impulses have preserved the place-frequency arrangement of the basilar membrane. In a three-dimensional display along the superior part of the temporal lobe, low frequency stimulation near the apex of the cochlea excites the layers of cortical cells along the lateral part of the primary auditory area, while high frequency stimulation of the base of the cochlea is registered in columns of cells within the lateral fissure. This topographical representation is present in both temporal lobes. Most of the contribution to each lobe comes from the contralateral ear. Thus, hearing is accomplished, but the signals must be processed further in order to 'understand' what is heard.

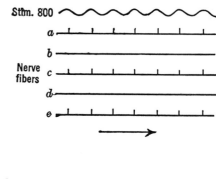

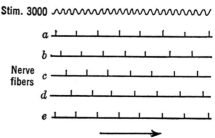

Figure 5.9. A diagram showing Wever's volley principle. Individual neurons can fire for each cycle of the stimulus, at low frequencies, but at high frequencies, frequency is indicated by the organized firing of groups of neurons. (Reprinted with permission from C. E. Osgood: *Method and Theory in Experimental Psychology,* Oxford University Press, Inc., © 1953.)

Cortical processing of speech sounds will be discussed further in this chapter when we consider the neurophysiology of speech perception.

PERCEPTION OF SPEECH

There is evidence that the auditory system is especially tuned for speech, or, to look at it in evolutionary terms, that our speaking mechanisms and auditory mechanisms have developed together, so that we are best at hearing speech sounds. Looking at it from the perspective of historical linguistics, we can consider that the languages of the Earth may have developed as they have by taking advantage of, and at the same time being constrained by, the speech mechanisms and auditory mechanisms of the human being. As we shall discover later in the chapter, infants, according to their powers of auditory discrimination, categorize sounds of speech into groups similar to those used in many languages as distinctive categories or phonemes.

Given that we are especially endowed to perceive the same sounds of speech that we are especially endowed to produce, the processes involved in speech perception remain far from clear. The evidence indicates that speech perception is a specialized aspect of a general human ability, the ability to seek and recognize patterns. In this case, the patterns are acoustic, and much of this chapter will describe acoustic patterns which listeners use as cues to the understanding of speech. The cues are often redundant, which permits speech perception to take place under difficult conditions. Speech sounds are rarely produced in isolation, as we have discussed in Chapter 4; they overlap and influence one another as a result of their production. For perception, this means that speech sounds often are not discrete and separable, as one can separate the letters in a written word. The listener, therefore, must use context to decode the message. A speech sound is often perceived by simultaneously perceiving neighboring acoustic information. In addition, there is evidence that speech perception is a somewhat specialized and lateralized function in the brain, a subject we shall consider further. Finally, in this chapter, we shall consider some of the current theories of speech perception.

Acoustic Cues in Speech Perception

We know from the study of spectrograms of speech that the acoustic patterns are complex and constantly changing. Does the listener use all of this information or are there parts of the acoustic patterns more important to speech perception than other parts? By synthesizing speech or by tape-splicing, speech scientists have altered various parameters of the acoustic signal and then tested listeners to discover the effects on perception.

In Chapter 4, we detailed the production of speech sounds in general classes according to manner of articulation, going from vowels, with the most open vocal tract, to the stops and fricatives, with a more constricted vocal tract. We attempted to explain the production of each class of speech sound in terms of its articulatory features as well as its acoustic features. Following the same order, we shall consider the perception of the sounds of speech.

Vowels

The acoustic cues to the perception of vowels lie in the patterns created by the vocal tract resonances (formants) of the speaker. The formant patterns by themselves, however, are not always sufficient for listener identification. In the early 1950s, Delattre, Liberman, Cooper, and Gerstman at Haskins Laboratories synthesized vowels by painting formants on the Pattern Playback (as described in Chapter 2), systematically varying the formant frequencies, in a search for the best patterns for listener identifications of each vowel (Fig. 5.10). They found that listeners required only two of the formants naturally produced, in order to identify the vowels. They also found that although two formants were required for front vowels, a single formant could be used to approxi-

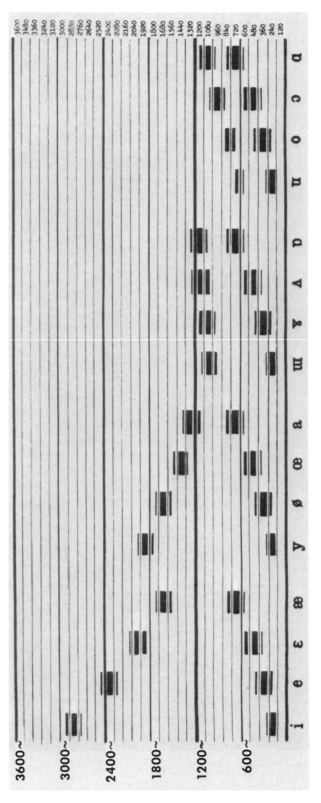

Figure 5.10. Two-formant synthetic vowels as patterns painted for the Haskins Pattern Playback. (Reprinted with permission from P. Delattre et al.: *Word 8*, 1952.)

mate the back vowels. In Gunnar Fant's laboratory in Sweden, it was found that the best two-formant synthetic vowels differ systematically from natural vowels. For /i/, the second formant must be very high, close to the natural third formant, while for the rest of the front vowels, the second formant was best placed between what would naturally be F_2 and F_3. Back vowels were best synthesized with the second formant close to a natural F_2. For speech perception, apparently F_3 is more important for front vowels than for back vowels.

Formant patterns alone do not insure listener recognition of vowels, however, because of two problems. The first problem is the variety of vocal tract sizes producing the formants. We know from the Peterson and Barney study cited in Chapter 4 that men, women, and children produce the same vowel with different formant frequencies. Individuals vary, too, within groups. To make matters more complicated, no simple formula works to allow the listener to normalize the frequencies. Not only do women have shorter vocal tracts than men, but they have a different shape vocal tract; a female vocal tract is shorter by about 2 cm in the pharynx, while only 1.25 cm shorter in the oral cavity. Thus, listeners must use general patterns for formant relationships rather than exact frequencies or even an exact ratio of frequencies.

The second problem that listeners will have in identifying vowels is that in the normal rate of speaking, vowels are often neutralized to some extent. Lindblom has shown that, when vowels are not stressed, they become more similar to each other and to schwa /ə/. For example, F_2 for /i/ would lower, while F_2 for /u/ would rise. The listener, then, must use contextual cues in addition to the formant patterns for vowel identification. Ladefoged and Broadbent demonstrated that other vowels of a given speaker could be used by listeners to normalize for different vocal tract lengths. In their study, the vowel in a word was heard as /bit/ or as /bet/, depending on which of two different voices was used to speak a carrier phrase. Lieberman has suggested that the 'point'

vowels /i/, /ɑ/, and /u/ might be used by listeners to calibrate a speaker's vocal tract, and Gerstman developed an algorithm which a computer can use to estimate formant frequencies for vowels, given the /i/, /ɑ/, and /u/ extremes. Nordström and Lindblom suggest that as a first approximation, listeners may estimate the total length of the vocal tract and use a simple scaling factor multiplication to adjust the formant pattern. This normalization procedure may be possible despite the non-linearity of the oral-pharyngeal size differences. It is not known, though, whether human listeners actually need to perform such a computation. Verbrugge, Strange, Shankweiler, and Edman have shown that listeners can perceive vowels more accurately when they have at least an adjacent consonant as context. It appears that listeners can fit the formant pattern to a certain vocal tract on the basis of evidence in a VC or CV syllable.

Perception of vowels is easy because they are voiced and thus relatively high in intensity; the vocal tract is relatively open for them, producing prominent resonances; and the formant frequencies are often held steady for a hundred milliseconds or so, allowing the listener to perceive the formant pattern. The listener makes use of other bits of speech to determine the approximate vocal tract size and thus to know what frequency range to expect for the formant patterns. Finally, he or she uses knowledge of the language, the vowel system, and the stress rules in particular, to track the vowel changes in running speech.

Diphthongs

Synthesized diphthongs used in listening tests reveal that gliding formants are sufficient acoustic cues for identification. Typically, there is, in addition to the glide, a brief steady-state formant pattern at the beginning and end of each glide. Gay systematically varied the duration of the F_2 glide and found the rate of frequency change to be a more important cue than the exact formant frequencies at the end of the diphthongs /ɔɪ/, /aɪ/, and /aʊ/.

Semivowels

The sounds /w/, /j/, /r/, and /l/, as in 'wet,' 'yet,' 'red,' and 'led,' like vowels and diphthongs, are voiced and are characterized by changes in formant frequencies, called transitions. Vowel formant transitions occur as the vowel precedes or follows a consonant, reflecting changes in resonance as the vocal tract moves to or from the more constricted consonant position. The formant transitions which form diphthongs and semivowels are the critical acoustic cues to the identification of the diphthongs and semivowels themselves. Especially important to the perception of semivowels are the glides in F_2 and, in some cases, F_3. Semivowels are distinguished from diphthongs in their more rapid formant transitions, which make them more consonant-like.

O'Connor, Gerstman, Liberman, Delattre, and Cooper found that they could synthesize perceptually acceptable /w/ and /j/ with only two formants. This finding is not surprising when we recall that /w/ begins with a formant pattern similar to /u/, and /j/ with one similar to /i/. Three formants are usually required, however, for perception of /r/ and /l/, and it is the third formant that distinguishes them. For /r/, F_3 is lower than for /l/; therefore, in the context of a vowel, the F_3 must rise from the /r/ formant to that of the vowel. For /l/, F_3 is higher, and in most vowel contexts does not vary in frequency. The second formant differentiates the semivowels. It is low for /w/, at a mid frequency for /l/ and /r/, and high for /j/. Although F_1 is not as important a cue as F_2 or F_3, it must be low for a good /w/ and /j/, and not be too low for /l/ or the lateral might sound more like /n/. The best /aja/, /ala/, /ara/, and /awa/, as painted on the Pattern Playback by Lisker and tested on naive listeners, are schematized in Figure 5.11. Note that the acoustic cues presented for /l/ are sufficient for only 74% identification compared to the 100% identification for the other semivowels. Further cues must be needed for an unambiguous lateral sound. The F_2 by F_3 chart (Fig. 5.12) summarizes the formant relationships used by listeners.

Nasal Consonants

Perception of nasals may be considered to involve two decisions: whether a segment is nasal or non-nasal, and if nasal, whether it is labial /m/, alveolar /n/, or palatal-velar /ŋ/ in place of articulation. By computer segmentation of natural speech for recognition tests, Mermelstein found the transition segments to and from the nasal murmur to be effective as cues for detecting the nasals as a class. The obvious change in spectrum from an orally produced vowel to a nasal includes, as was mentioned in Chapter 4, a weakening of the upper formants because of antiresonances and the addition of a resonance below 500 Hz, often centered around 250 Hz. The overall decrease in intensity from vowel to nasal consonant may be used as a cue by the listener. The low frequency murmur itself is a sufficient cue when upper formants are omitted in nasals synthesized on the Pattern Playback. In VC syllables in natural speech, a terminal nasal consonant can be cued by the vowel. In a tape-splicing study, Ali, Gallagher, Goldstein, and Daniloff found that listeners could perceive developing nasality in the vowel portion with the nasal consonants and their immediate transitions cut out. It is especially easy for listeners to perceive open vowels as being nasal. This is because open vowels lack a low frequency resonance unless produced with nasality. High vowels, such as /i/ and /u/, normally have a low frequency resonance and, therefore, are acoustically more like nasals.

Perception of the place of nasal articulation is cued mainly by the direction of the transition (of F_2 particularly) to an adjacent vowel. Cooper, Delattre, Liberman, Borst, and Gerstman found that the nasals /m,n,ŋ/ could be synthesized on the Pattern Playback with the same formant transitions used to synthesize /p,b/, /t,d/, and /k,g/, respectively. Malécot found by tape-splicing natural speech, that listeners used the murmur itself as a minor cue for place of articulation of the nasal, but the powerful cue for place was the transition. After removing the transition between the vowel steady states and the

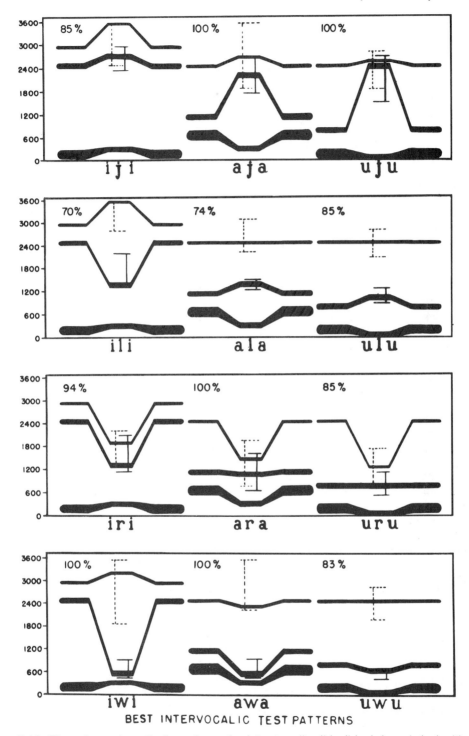

Figure 5.11. Three-formant synthetic patterns for inter-vocalic /j/, /l/, /r/, and /w/ with the vowels /i/, /a/, and /u/. Listeners were asked to identify each of a series of patterns as one of the four stimuli. The patterns shown here are those that were most consistently identified. (Reprinted with permission from L. Lisker: *Word. 13*, 1957.)

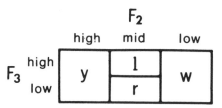

Figure 5.12. Schematic diagram describing the formant relationships for y, w, r, and I sounds. (Adapted from L. Lisker: *Word. 13,* 1957.)

nasal murmur, he found listeners much less able to report which nasal they were hearing. There are both frequency and durational cues in the transitions, with the transition from /m/ lowest in frequency and shorter in duration, /n/ higher in frequency and a bit longer in duration, and /ŋ/ highest and most variable in frequency and longest in duration. The transition duration difference between /n/ and/ŋ/ is probably because the back of the tongue is slower to move than the tongue tip. It is not known how well listeners are able to trade off transition and nasal murmur cues for one another. In analog studies of the nasals, House found the resonance and antiresonance configurations sufficient to distinguish the /m/ and /n/, but perception of /ŋ/ by listeners was less accurate; for /ŋ/, additional cues may be important. We shall find the same problem with /k/ and /g/ as we consider the perception of stop consonants.

Stops

The stop consonants /p,b,t,d,k,g/ have been studied more than have any other class of speech sounds. The stops are interesting because they clearly demonstrate the non-linearity of human perception when the stimuli are speech or speech-like synthesized sounds. This phenomenon of non-linear perception of speech will be discussed further in the section on categorical perception. Stops also demonstrate the redundancy of acoustic cues available to distinguish speech sounds. Finally, the nature of stop perception provides the best example of listener use of the acoustic overlapping of phonemes in the speech stream. The acoustic cues for the stops are to some degree overlaid upon the acoustic cues for neighboring vowels. Thus, the listener perceives the stop and its adjacent

vowel according to their acoustic relationship to one another.

The obvious differences between stops and the sounds we have thus far considered are, first, that there is an oral occlusion which is heard either as silence in the voiceless stops /p,t,k/, or as a brief attenuation of sound in the voiced stops /b,d,g/, and second, that the stopped air is often released in a burst, heard as a sharp transient. A difference between stops and semivowels is the duration of the change in formant frequencies between the burst and the steady state of the next vowel. This change in formant pattern is the acoustic result of moving from the vocal tract position for the stop or semivowel to the configuration required for the vowel. The Haskins group found that they could paint spectrograms on the Pattern Playback which were heard as /bɛ/ and /gɛ/ without including the burst cues and, further, that by varying the duration of the F₂ transitions (Fig. 5.13) they could produce stimuli which listeners perceived as the stops /b,g/ when the transitions were of short duration, as the semivowels /w,j/ when the transitions were of 40 or 50 msec duration, and as the vowels of changing color /uɛ/, /iɛ/ when the transitions were of 150 to 200 msec duration.

These acoustic cues to the manner of articulation for stops—the relative silence, the burst, and the short transitions to the next vowel—are apparently more resistant to the masking effects of noise than are the acoustic cues to place of articulation, which distinguish the labials /p,b/, from the alevolars /t,d/, from the palatal-velars /k,g/. Miller and Nicely analyzed perceptual confusions of English consonants in the presence of noise and found that listeners can identify the manner of production even when place cues are masked.

There are several cues which serve to indicate the place of articulation of a stop to listeners. Early tests, using Pattern Playback stimuli based upon real spectrograms, isolated two place cues as separate but sufficient: the frequency position of the burst in relation to a vowel and the F₂ transition. High frequency bursts combined with formants for seven vowels were all perceived as /t/. Low frequency bursts were perceived as /p/, but bursts

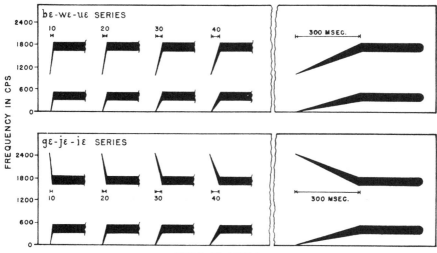

Figure 5.13. Spectrographic patterns with varying transition durations. The first four patterns in each row show how the tempo of the transitions was varied. At the *extreme right* of each row is a complete stimulus pattern, *i.e.,* transition plus steady-state vowel, for the longest duration of transition tested. The patterns at the *extreme left* and *right* of the *top row* are judged as /bε/ and /uε/ respectively. The corresponding patterns in the *bottom row* as /gε/ and /iε/. (Reprinted with permission from A. M. Liberman *et al.: Journal of Experimental Psychology,* 52, © 1956, American Psychological Association.)

perceived as /k/ were slightly above the F_2 of the particular two-formant synthesized vowel (Fig. 5.14), resulting in high burst /k/ percepts with front vowels and lower frequency burst /k/ percepts with back vowels.

Listeners could also use synthesized vowels and short F_2 transitions without bursts to identify stop consonants. The investigators held the vowel formants constant and changed the slope of the F_2 transition systematically from a negative or falling transition, to a flat F_2, to a sharply positive or rising transition (Fig. 5.15) in 10 steps. Listeners perceived all of the rising F_2 transitions as labial /p,b/, but divided the falling F_2 transitions into two groups; they were perceived as alveolar /t,d/ if the F_2 were slightly falling for front vowels or sharply falling for back vowels and were perceived as palatal-velar /k,g/ if the F_2 were sharply falling for front vowels or slightly falling for back vowels.

Further work on perception of F_2 transitions by Delattre, Liberman, and Cooper resulted in a theory that an acoustic locus existed for each place of articulation. In order to explain the concept, we must return to a consideration of stop consonant

production. When a stop consonant occlusion is released, the vocal tract shape will be associated with particular formant resonances which change as the vocal tract changes toward the following vowel. Since the occlusions for a given stop in various vowel contexts are roughly the same, there should be a systematic relationship between consonant-vowel combinations and the starting frequency of the F_2 transition. It is this articulatory relationship that underlies the findings of the locus experiment.

Two-formant patterns were synthesized, with some stop-like characteristics and a steady-state F_2. The best /g/ sound was perceived when the flat F_2 was at 3000 Hz, the best /d/ at 1800 Hz, and the best /b/ at 720 Hz. When stimuli were painted with constant F_1 transitions, but with F_2 transitions graded from sharply rising to sharply falling, it was found that if the transitions all pointed to the loci (the best frequencies listed above) and if the first half of the transitions were removed or silent (Fig. 5.16), listeners could distinguish the place of articulation on the basis of these acoustic loci. The locus was the place on the frequency scale to which the F_2

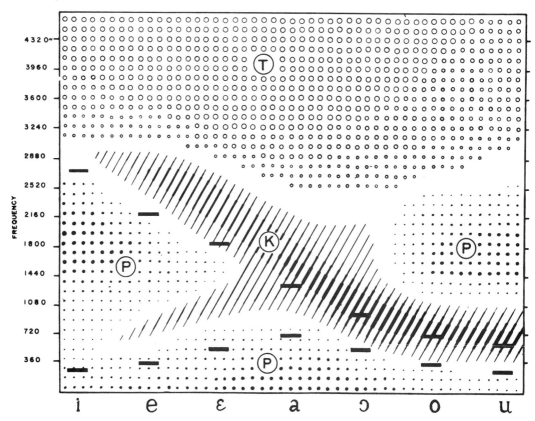

Figure 5.14. Center frequency of burst which will be perceived as a given voiceless stop, with various vowels. The *bolder face symbols* in the grid indicate greater listener agreement. The two-formant pattern with which each burst was paired is indicated for each vowel. (Reprinted with permission from A. M. Liberman *et al.: American Journal of Psychology. LXV,* 1952.)

transitions pointed. This method worked particularly well for /d/, the alveolar stop. The difficulty in identifying a particular F_2 transition or locus with /g,k,ŋ/ results partly from the articulatory fact that these consonants are not restricted to one place of articulation on the palate and partly from the acoustic fact, pointed out by Kuhn, that as the place of constriction moves back in the oral cavity, the consonant resonance may change its allegiance from one formant to another.

Stops differ in voicing as well as place of articulation. For each place of articulation, there is a voiced and a voiceless stop. Cues for voicing are the presence or absence of a low frequency voice bar, the presence or absence of noise indicating aspiration, and a change in F_1 onset time. The Haskins group studied the effects on perception of progressively 'cutting back'

the first formant transition in a series of stimuli. The first stimulus had a voice bar and transition rising from the baseline. In successive stimuli, 10 msec were removed from F_1 (Fig. 5.17). The resulting delay of F_1 relative to F_2 onset is referred to as F_1 cutback. Listeners required more cutback of F_1 to hear /t/ instead of /d/, than they required to hear /p/ instead of /b/. The investigators were then interested in whether the 'voiceless' response of listeners were cued by the delay alone or by the fact that for the voiceless response, F_1 started at a higher frequency. Keeping other things constant, they fashioned a listening tape with changes only in the delay of F_1 and found that the delay was sufficient for the perception of the voiced-voiceless distinction, with the boundary between /d/ and /t/ at a 20 to 30 msec delay of F_1.

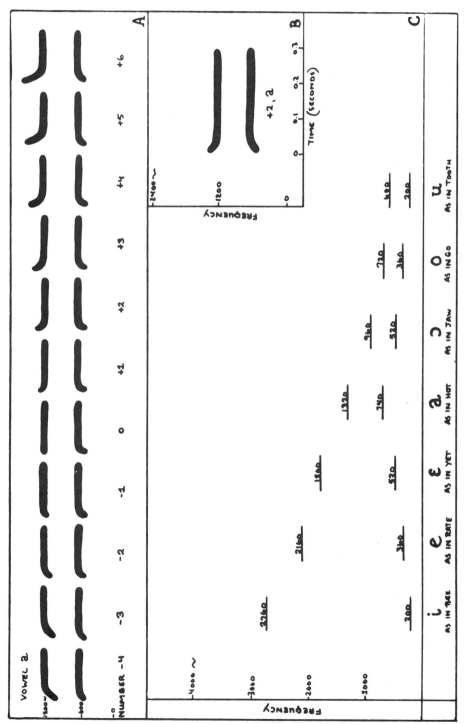

Figure 5.15. Two-formant synthetic pattern for the voiced stops. *Part A* shows the vowel /a/ with a full range of transitions. *Part B* shows a single pattern. *Part C* shows the two-formant synthetic patterns for various vowels, which were combined with the range of transitions shown in *Part A*. (Reprinted with permission from A. M. Liberman et al.: *Psychological Monographs: General and Applied*. 68, © 1954, American Psychological Association.)

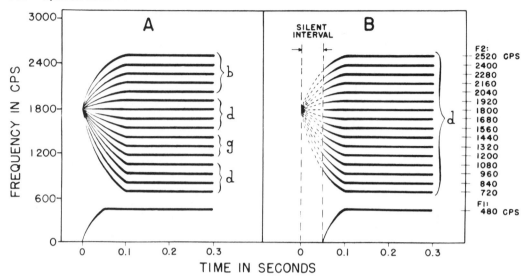

Figure 5.16. The locus principle. *Part A* shows the varying perceived identity of two-formant patterns with a rising first formant, and a second formant with the origin at 1800 Hz. If the first 50 msec of the pattern is erased, as in *Part B*, the patterns will all be heard as /d/, with a varying vowel. (Reprinted with permission from P. Delattre *et al.: Journal of the Acoustical Society of America., 27,* 1955.)

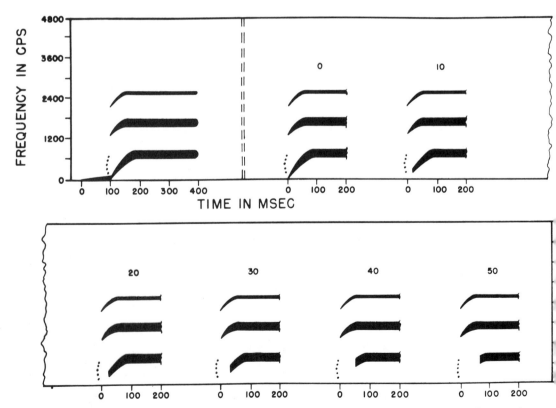

Figure 5.17. Synthetic patterns varying in F₁ cutback. The pattern at the *top left corner* has a voice bar. In the "*0*" pattern, F₁, F₂, and F₃ begin simultaneously. In successive patterns, F₁ onset is delayed, in milliseconds, by the time indicated above the pattern. (Reprinted with permission from A. M. Liberman *et al.: Language and Speech. 1,* 1958.)

The noise of aspiration did not serve as a sufficient cue to voiceless stops by itself, but when noise was added to the upper formants of stimuli with an F_1 cutback, listeners got a stronger impression of voicelessness than they did with the F_1 cutback alone. Figure 5.18 summarizes the Pattern Playback spectrograms which resulted in perceptual distinctions in place, manner, and voicing for stops and nasals.

Lisker and Abramson point out that the acoustic consequences of timing differences between laryngeal and supralaryngeal events serve as a complex of cues for voicing for stops in initial position in many languages. English speakers hear stops as voiced if the voice onset time (VOT) is small and as voiceless if it is over 25 msec for labials, 35 msec for alveolars, and 40 msec for velars. Notice that the further back the stop place of articulation is in the oral cavity, the longer the VOT needed for listeners to hear it as a voiceless stop.

The presence of silence has been mentioned as an acoustic cue for stops. Silence inserted between the /s/ and /l/ of 'slit' will cause the word to be heard as 'split.' Differences in the duration of silence sometimes serve to cue the voiced-voiceless distinction. The word 'rabid' can be synthesized with a short silence. When the duration of the silence is increased to over 70 msec, listeners hear 'rapid.'

Finally, listeners use vowel duration relative to final consonant duration to make judgments about the voicing of the final consonant. Raphael used the Pattern Playback technique to test listeners' perception of voicing distinctions in a variety of final consonants and consonant clusters including stops. He found that vowels of shorter duration were more often perceived as followed by a voiceless consonant ('Burke'), while vowels of longer duration provoked the perception of voiced final consonants ('Berg'). Raphael points out that speakers of American English do not always release final stops, making preceding vowel duration potentially important as a cue.

In summary, there are acoustic cues which listeners use to determine the manner, place, and voicing for stops. Silence,

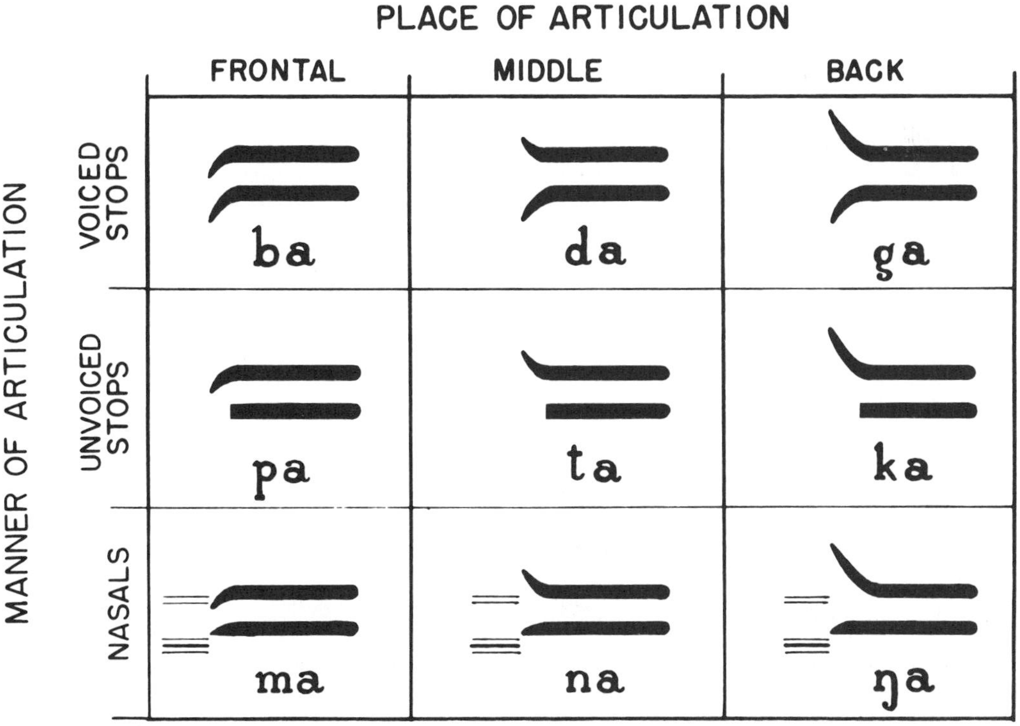

Figure 5.18. Summary figure showing synthetic patterns for consonants varying in place and manner of articulation. (Reprinted with permission from A. M. Liberman *et al.: Journal of Experimental Psychology. 52,* © 1956, American Psychological Association.)

burst, and relatively rapid formant transitions serve as cues to the plosive manner of articulation. The acoustic cues for place of articulation are the frequency of the burst relative to the vowel and the formant transitions, especially F_2. For the voiced-voiceless contrast, listeners use several cues: voice bar, aspiration, F_1 delay, duration of silence, and duration of preceding vowel. Obviously, some of these acoustic cues arise from the same articulatory event, that is, VOT. Increased aspiration and F_1 cutback, for example, are acoustic correlates of increased VOT. Listeners seem to be making decisions about place on the basis of frequency patterns and decisions about voicing on the basis of timing patterns.

Fricatives and Affricates

The acoustic nature of fricatives was discussed at some length in Chapter 4. When fricatives occur in natural speech, they consist of the friction or noise portion and adjacent portions that are transitions from and to neighboring vowels. To assess the relative importance of the noise and transition cues in perception of fricatives, Harris cut the friction segments away from the vocalic segments of fricative-vowel syllables and by tape-splicing, recombined segments for listening tests. The syllables used in the first part of the experiment were /fi/, /θi/, /si/, and /ʃi/. The friction part of each syllable was combined with each of the vocalic parts. An oscilloscope was used to locate the division, in addition to listening for the change from the high frequency noise part to the high intensity, low frequency vocalic part. The same procedures were used for each of the fricatives before the vowels /e/, /o/, and /u/. A second listening test was constructed for the four voiced fricatives /v/, /ð/, /z/, and /ʒ/.

Results were the same regardless of the particular vowel used. Whenever the noise segment for /s/ or /ʃ/ was paired with any vocalic portion, listeners reported that they heard /s/ or /ʃ/, respectively. Listener judgments of /f/ or /θ/, however, depended upon the vocalic segment. The voiced fricatives /z/ and /ʒ/ were perceived almost entirely by their friction

cues like their voiceless cognates. Voiced /v/ and /ð/ were perceived with less consistency and with more dependency upon the vocalic portions.

Miller and Nicely found /v/ and /ð/ to be among the most confusable of speech sounds to listeners when noise is added to the stimuli. The low intensity of the /θ/, /ð/, /f/, /v/ friction accounts for the difficulties that listeners have in identifying them out of context.

Fricatives as a group, then, are distinguished by the fact that they have a continuant noisy, aperiodic component. Listeners seem to divide them on the basis of relative intensity into two groups: the sibilants of higher intensity, /s,z,ʃ,ʒ/, and the low intensity fricatives /θ,ð,f,v/. The sibilants can be further distinguished according to place of articulation on the basis of relative frequency, with alveolar fricatives /s/ and /z/ generally high frequency, having a first spectral peak at about 4000 Hz, and the palatal fricatives /ʃ/ and /ʒ/ having a first spectral peak at about 2500 Hz. The study by Harris indicates that listeners need both the friction cues and the transitions into neighboring vowels to determine the place of articulation of the linguadental /θ/ and /ð/ and labiodental /f/ and /v/ fricatives.

To detect voicing of fricatives, the presence of a voice bar, the low frequency sound of glottal pulsing, remains a salient cue, but even without it, listeners can make judgments about the voicing of a syllable-final fricative based upon its duration relative to the duration of the preceding vowel. Denes used tape-splicing techniques to interchange the final fricatives in 'use' /jus/ and 'to use' /juz/. In making the change, he shortened the normally longer /s/ and lengthened the /z/. The /s/ from /jus/ was heard as /z/ when spliced on the end of the /ju/ of /juz/, because of the longer /u/ before voiced consonants than before voiceless consonants. Conversely, the /z/ from /juz/ was heard as /s/ when spliced after the shorter /u/. Denes showed that it is not the vowel duration alone that listeners take as their cue to final fricative voicing, but the relative durations of the vowel and the fricative.

Affricates, being stops with a fricative

release, contain the acoustic cues inherent in both stops and fricatives. The silence, the burst, the friction, are all presumably used by listeners. Raphael and Dorman altered friction duration, closure duration, and rise time of the noise in utterances such as 'ditch' /dɪtʃ/ and 'dish' /dɪʃ/, and found that the cues trade off for one another. For example, longer /ʃ/ duration will be heard as /dɪʃ/ despite an increase in the silent interval (closure duration) which would ordinarily cue /dɪtʃ/. Again, the cues are relative, one to another.

Cues for Manner, Place, and Voicing

To summarize the wealth of information on acoustic cues important to the perception of speech segments, it may be helpful to recapitulate, by dividing the cues into those important to the perception of manner, place, and voicing distinctions. To identify the manner of a speech sound, listeners determine whether the sound is harmonically structured with no noise (which signals vowels, semivowels, or nasals) or whether the sound contains a nonperiodic component (which signals stops, fricatives, or affricates). The periodic, harmonically structured classes present acoustic cues in energy regions that are relatively low in frequency. In contrast, the aperiodic, noisy classes of speech sounds are cued by energy that is relatively high in frequency.

How do listeners further separate the harmonically structured vowels, nasals, and semivowels? The main manner cues available are relative intensity of formants and formant frequency changes. The nasal consonants have formants of abruptly lower intensity than semivowels and vowels. In addition, there is the distinctive low frequency resonance, the nasal murmur. Semivowels have formants which in context glide from one frequency to another compared to the relatively steady state of the vowels and nasals. Some diphthongs glide as much as any semivowel, but the glides are generally more rapidly changing for semivowels.

Manner cues for the group of sounds having an aperiodic component, the stops, fricatives, and affricates, are the duration of the noise, which is transient for stops, but lasts longer for affricates and lasts the longest for fricatives. Our summary figure showing the acoustic cues for manner of articulation (Fig. 5.19) shows all of the parameters of sound to be important; manner contrasts rest on relative frequency, intensity, and timing.

The acoustic cues for place of articulation depend more upon a single parameter of sound—frequency. For vowels and semivowels, the formant relationships, as we have seen, serve to indicate tongue placement, mouth-opening, and vocal tract length. Vowel placement is reflected in the F_1-F_2 acoustic space, with F_1 frequency indicating tongue height or mouth-opening and F_2 frequency indicating place of maximum approximation of the tongue with the walls of the vocal tract. Semivowel production is mainly reflected in the frequency changes in F_2. The semivowel /j/ begins with the highest F_2, with /r/ and /l/ in the middle frequencies, and /w/ relatively low. F_3 serves to contrast the acoustic results of tongue tip placement for /r/ and /l/.

For stops, fricatives, and affricates, two prominent acoustic cues to place of articulation are the F_2 transitions into neighboring vowels and the frequency of the noise components (Fig. 5.20). In general, a transition of the second formant with a low locus is perceived as labial; with a higher locus, it is alveolar; and with a varied, vowel-dependent locus, it is palatal or velar. The F_2 transition is used to cue the difference between the labiodental and linguadental fricatives also.

The frequency of the noise itself indicates place of production. The low frequency cut off of noise for /s/ friction is often above 4000 Hz, while for the more retracted /ʃ/, it is more often 2500 Hz. If the friction covers a wide band of frequencies, it is more likely to be /f/, /θ/, or /h/. Frequency of the noise indicates place of articulation even when extremely brief as in stops or affricates, with frequency loci similar to those reflected in the F_2 transitions.

Finally, the acoustic cues for consonant voicing depend more upon relative durations and timing of events than upon frequency or intensity differences. There is an exception, the cue of the presence or

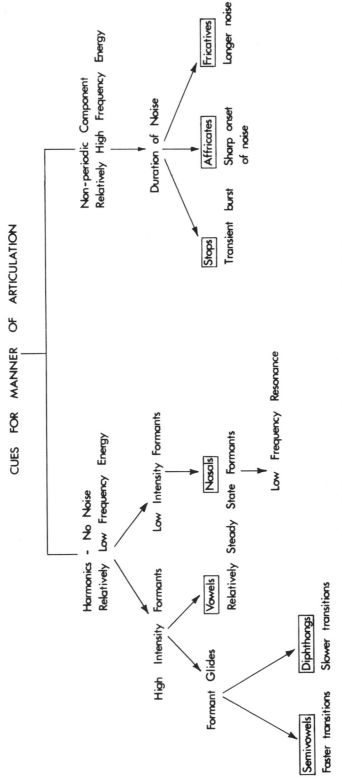

Figure 5.19. Summary of the cues for manner of articulation.

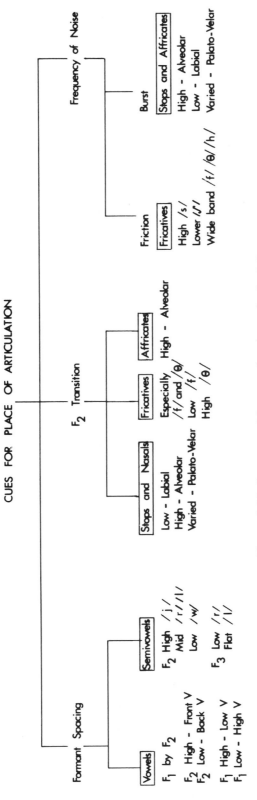

Figure 5.20. Summary of the cues for place of articulation.

absence of a voice bar. The periodic sound of voicing itself, reflected in the voice bar, is important, but the fact that you can whisper 'The tie is blue' and 'The dye is blue' and perceive a 'voicing' distinction despite the absence of vocal fold vibration, indicates that timing is a critical cue to the perception of the voiced-voiceless distinction in consonants. The timing differences in the voiced-voiceless contrast have been measured in different ways (see summary Fig. 5.21). Listeners perceive relatively long duration of the closure period (the silence before the burst), of aspiration (the noise following the burst), or of the time between the burst and the beginning of voicing for the following vowel as cues for the voiceless cognates /p/, /t/, or /k/. The voiced /b/, /d/, and /g/ are perceived when the stimuli have a relatively short closure period, aspiration, and delay between burst and voicing onset. Other things being equal, cutting back the first formant in synthesized speech, to mimic the aspiration and voicing onset delays, results in the perception of voiceless stops.

Thus, a stop-vowel syllable synthesized with F_1 rising from the baseline is perceived as voiced.

Fricatives and affricates are perceived as voiceless when the friction is relatively long, and in the case of affricates, when the closure duration is also relatively long. Finally, duration of the vowel before a final consonant can cue the perception of differences in voicing, with vowels of longer duration perceived to be followed by a voiced consonant and vowels of shorter duration perceived to be followed by a voiceless consonant.

Suprasegmentals

No one knows about the mechanism that listeners use to track fundamental frequency and thereby perceive significant changes in f_o that we call intonation. Do they keep a running average of zero crossings per unit of time? Do they 'hear' the common denominator of a set of harmonics? They must do something of the sort, since listeners perceive the proper fundamental frequency even when it is absent,

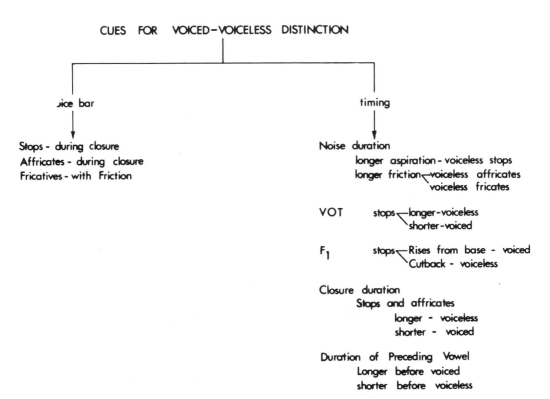

CUES   FOR   VOICED-VOICELESS   DISTINCTION

voice bar

Stops - during closure
Affricates - during closure
Fricatives - with Friction

timing

Noise duration
   longer aspiration - voiceless stops
   longer friction — voiceless affricates
              voiceless fricates

VOT   stops — longer - voiceless
                shorter - voiced

F_1 stops — Rises from base - voiced
             Cutback - voiceless

Closure duration
   Stops and affricates
      longer - voiceless
      shorter - voiced

Duration of Preceding Vowel
   Longer before voiced
   shorter before voiceless

Figure 5.21. Summary of the cues for the voiced-voiceless distinction.

as long as they can hear the harmonic structure, formed by multiples of the f_o. It is known that given ambiguous speech material, a rising intonation pattern is perceived by English (and Swedish) listeners as a question, and a falling intonation pattern as a statement.

To perceive the prosodic feature of stress (`permit versus per`mit), listeners apparently use frequency, intensity, and duration, as perceptual cues, any one of them significant by itself. Fry has shown fundamental frequency to be the most powerful cue to stress.

The prosodic feature of juncture (marking the difference between 'a name' and 'an aim') can be cued by silence, vowel-lengthening, or by features such as presence of voicing or aspiration. We like an example that Darwin cited from Shakespeare's *Troilus and Cressida*. The crowd shouts "the Troyans' trumpet!" which, if given improper juncture by lengthening the friction of the /s/ in 'Troyans' and decreasing the aspiration of the initial /t/ of 'trumpet,' would sound as if the crowd were announcing a prominent prostitute (Fig. 5.22).

Context Dependence

The importance of context to speech perception is apparent in the recovery of both segmental information and suprasegmental information. One word which we find ourselves writing repeatedly in this chapter is 'relative.' The importance of f_o to the perception of stress is that it tends to be higher on the stressed syllable or word relative to surrounding syllables or words. Similarly, formants need not be of particular frequencies to be recognized as vowels, but they must bear a certain general relationship to one another, and further, to be identified with certainty, must often be perceived in relation to the frequencies of some other bit of speech uttered from the same vocal tract.

Machines can be made to read print much more easily than they can be made to recognize speech, because the letters in printing or writing are discrete items that can be identified individually and then identified as a word. The letters, T, A, P, are segments and do not vary. T may appear as t or change size, but it is always a nearly vertical line with a nearly horizontal line crossing it near the top. It is difficult to make a machine that can recognize speech, because the sound [tæp] changes continuously so that it is not as segmentable as is the written TAP. One of the important acoustic cues to the /t/ is in the initial transition part of the vowel /æ/. The final transition in /æ/ supplies the listener with information for the /p/ to follow. Thus, humans behave very differently in perceiving speech than many speech-recognizing machines which act on a segment by segment basis.

A question often asked by Liberman in connection with his work in speech perception is: why do people understand speech so much more easily than they can read? People find speech easy and natural, yet it is easier to design a machine to read print than to recognize speech. It may be that when we learn to speak and understand speech, it is naturally coarticulated, producing a constantly changing pattern that is not easily segmentable, and we perceive it, too, as a dynamic assimilated event. The imposition of the idea of 'phonemes' is a linguistic device, useful in constructing an alphabet or in describing a language, but artificial and one step removed from the flow of speech itself. The more abstract phoneme has to be learned as part of a system imposed on speech and is hence inherently more difficult.

Invariant segments are suited for machines, however. Computers deal with continuous information by digitizing it, segmenting, and assigning numbers to it. An alphabet is thus easier for such a machine to cope with than speech with its overlapping phones. The human brain is adept at seeing and hearing relationships, at finding patterns, at adapting to change, and at what we shall consider next, placing items into categories.

Categorical Perception

In searching for the acoustic events in speech which are particularly important to listeners, investigators found that a graded change in F_2 transition, including 13 or more different transitions, resulted in the perception of only three different speech sounds. Subjects heard /ba/, for example, for those stimuli having the most

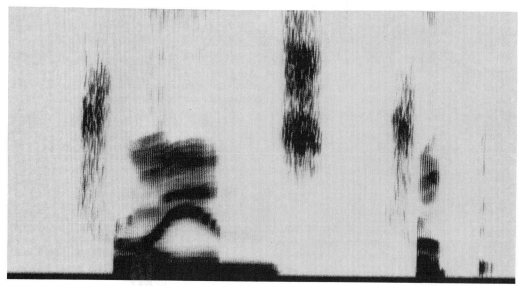

t r o y a   n   's ——— t r u m p e t

t r o y a n — s   t r u m p e t

Figure 5.22. Spectrograms of "Troyans' trumpet!" and "Troyan strumpet!"

sharply rising transitions. Then, as the transitions became less sharp or even began to fall, they quite abruptly began to hear /dɑ/, finally shifting to /gɑ/ at the falling transition end of the continuum. When listeners were asked to discriminate between items along the continuum, they were able to do so only if they labeled them differently. This phenomenon, the ability to discriminate only as well as one can identify, is called *categorical perception*. We shall present the details of one study of categorical perception as an example of how such studies are usually conducted.

There are two necessary components to

studies of categorical perception in speech. People group speech sounds according to the ways they choose to identify or label them and also the ways they discriminate between them. The study published in 1957 by Liberman, Harris, Hoffman, and Griffith has served as the model for many studies of categorical perception conducted since then. The stimuli were produced originally on the Pattern Playback speech synthesizer for precise control of frequency, intensity, and duration. Fourteen two-formant vowel patterns were produced differing only in the direction and extent of the F_2 transition. The rapidly rising F_2 transition necessary for perception of a good /b/ formed the first of the stimuli, the rapidly falling F_2 transition necessary for perception of a good /g/ formed the last, and the stimuli in between were constructed by increasing the starting frequency for the F_2 transition in equal steps of 120 Hz as illustrated in Figure 5.23. After recording the stimuli on magnetic tape, the investigators copied, cut, and spliced the tape, producing several ran-

domizations of two kinds of listening tests. One test is an *identification test* in which the items are presented one at a time for labeling. The other kind of test is a *discrimination test*, in this case arranged in *ABX* design, so that subjects hear one of the 14 stimuli (A), then a different one (B), followed by the third (X) which is the same as one of the first two. The task of the subject after hearing each triad is to determine whether X is like A or like B. The percentage of correct matching of X with its identical member of the AB pair was the measure of discrimination in this test. The non-identical stimulus was sometimes 1 step away from X, sometimes 2 steps removed, or 3 steps or items away on the continuum of 14 steps.

The discrimination test was administered first, to subjects uninformed about the nature of the study and the fact that the stimuli were synthetic speech sounds. After many testing sessions, they were told the nature of the stimuli and were given the identification test for labeling. No response choices were provided by the

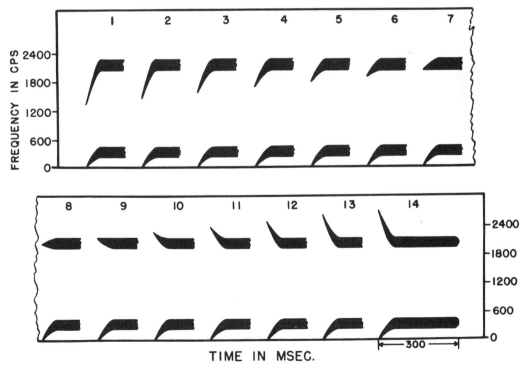

Figure 5.23. Two-formant synthetic CV pattern series: the stimuli for /ba/, /da/, and /ga/. (Reprinted with permission from A. M. Liberman *et al.*: *Journal of Experimental Psychology. 54,* © 1957, American Psychological Association.)

experimenters. After several more sessions, the subjects were told to identify the stimuli as /b/, /d/, or /g/, forcing the choice. Thereafter, the identification test was given first, followed by the discrimination test. Since there was no obvious difference between the discrimination tests given before and after the instructions to label the identification test stimuli as /b/, /d/, or /g/, the results of these tests were combined. Also, since most subjects reported speech responses of /b/, /d/, or /g/ on the identification test from the beginning, even before they were told it was synthetic speech and instructed to choose one of the above consonants, the forced choice has been generally used in subsequent research on categorical perception of speech.

Figure 5.24 shows the results of the identification test and a two-step discrimination test for one subject. The subject identified 100% of a total of 32 presentations of the first stimulus as /b/. Stimulus 3 was judged more often as a /b/, but Stimulus 4 was judged more often as a /d/. Stimuli 5 through 8 were unambiguously perceived as /d/. The last stimuli were judged to be /g/. The identification function as plotted in this figure indicates a sharp perceptual boundary between /b/ and /d/ occurring between Stimuli 3 and 4 and another sharp boundary between /d/ and /g/ perception occurring between Stimuli 9 and 10.

The discrimination function for the same subject, also shown in Figure 5.24, represents the percentage of correct responses to the 42 ABX triads for which the A and B were two steps apart in the stimulus series. Points at the 50% correct level, of course, represent guesses. Notice the two 100% peaks in the discrimination function. The first peak, plotted at Stimulus 3, represents responses by this subject to ABX triads of 3-5-3 stimuli. Recall that this subject's phoneme boundary between the perception of /b/ and /d/ was between the synthetic Stimuli 3 and 4. That is just the part of the series which this subject discriminates most accurately. The identification boundary between /d/ and /g/ perception was between 9 and 10 in the series for this subject. Again, discrimination was perfect between Steps 8 and 10. Thus, this subject discriminates best at phoneme boundaries and reports fewer discriminations within the series of stimuli identified as a certain phoneme.

The investigators computed the predicted discrimination function for each subject based on the subject's identification test. They tested the significance of the correlations between the predicted and obtained discrimination tests for all sub-

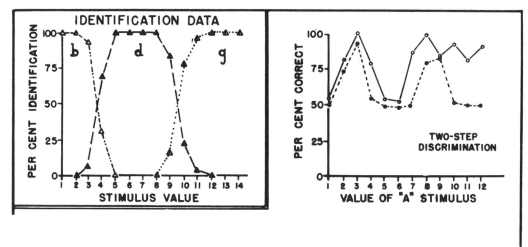

Figure 5.24. Result of identification and discrimination tests. The *left panel* shows the percentage of the time each stimulus was identified as /b/, /d/, or /g/. The *right panel* shows the result of the two-step discrimination test, compared to predictions derived from the identification test, using the technique described in the text of the article. (Reprinted with permission from A. M. Liberman *et al.: Journal of Experimental Psychology. 54,* © 1957, American Psychological Association.)

jects and found them to be significantly correlated ($p = < 0.001$) for the two- and three-step ABX tests. Actual discrimination, although strongly correlated with that predicted by the identification tests, was better than the prediction. This indicates that the subjects might have been using some acoustic, as well as phonetic, information in forming their discrimination judgments.

It was surprising to find that people, listening to speech-like sounds that change in equal steps in some acoustic dimension, discriminate among them little better than they can identify them. It is a well-known fact of psychoacoustics that in judging the relative pitch of pure tones, people can discriminate as many as 3500 different frequency steps, but they can only label a few pitches. Pitch perception is not linear with frequency change, because listeners can discriminate between low (50–500 Hz) frequency tones having only a fraction of a Hertz difference, while at 4000 Hz, about 4 Hz difference is needed for discrimination. Although not linear, pitch perception is a continuous function. There are no sudden changes in one's ability to detect differences with frequency change. In light of these facts, the categorical discontinuity of the discrimination function found in speech perception is extremely interesting and has given rise to several questions addressed in speech perception research.

Do people perceive speech quite differently from the way they perceive nonspeech? Does the learning of a language sharpen some perceptions and dull others? Is categorical perception innate or learned? The first study reporting the categorical perception of speech did not answer these questions. It did make explicit the phenomenon, however, and sparked interest in looking further for the relative auditory and linguistic contributions to the effect.

Within-language and Cross-language Studies in Adults

There are many acoustic dimensions distinctive in speech that can be systematically varied by speech synthesis in the construction of tests for the identification and discrimination of speech sounds.

Acoustic cues important to manner of articulation, such as duration of F_2 transitions or intensity rise time of noise have been varied along a continuum. When transition durations are increased in equal steps, listeners categorically report /bɑ/, then /wɑ/, and finally /uɑ/, and the discrimination peaks correspond to the boundaries between the different manners of speech sounds. Noise patches representing friction can be arranged to continuously vary from sudden rise time to gradual rise time, with listeners reporting a sudden perceptual shift from /tʃ/ as in 'chop' to /ʃ/ as in 'shop.'

Acoustic cues important to place perception have also been systematically varied. We have explained how changes in the direction of F_2 transition reveal the categorical perception of /b/, /d/, and /g/. If F_3 transition changes are varied appropriately, a continuum of acoustic steps from /rɑ/ to /lɑ/ can be synthesized. One example of typical test results will suffice to illustrate the categorical way in which such continua are perceived. A 10-step /rɑ/ to /lɑ/ continuum was synthesized on the OVE synthesizer. The third formant transition was graded from a relatively low to a relatively high starting frequency and the second formant transition was similarly varied, but to a lesser extent (Fig. 5.25). Subjects were asked to identify two randomized lists of 50 items (each of the 10 steps was presented adjacent to each of the others, reversing orders). In this identification test, each stimulus followed a precursor phrase in natural speech: 'Does this sound more like rock or lock?' Typical identification functions are presented in Figure 5.26. This graph represents the pooled responses of one of our undergraduate speech science classes. The first five stimuli were perceived almost unanimously as /rɑ/, for Stimulus 7, the listeners were guessing, and none of the listeners heard Stimuli 8 through 10 as /rɑ/. The mirror image of the graph for /rɑ/ represents the /lɑ/ identification function. The boundary between /rɑ/ and /lɑ/ percepts for these listeners occurred, then, between Stimuli 6 and 7.

Stimuli from the same continuum were paired in an AX discrimination test, using one-step, two-step, and three-step differ-

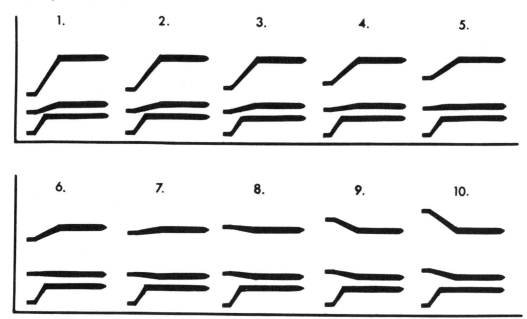

Figure 5.25. A continuum of synthetic stimuli perceived as /rɑ/ or /lɑ/. Frequency is represented on the ordinate and time on the abscissa.

IDENTIFICATION TEST

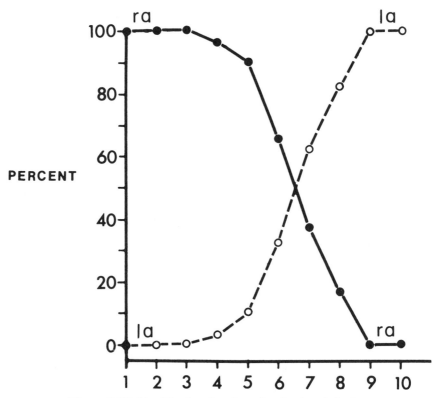

Figure 5.26. Identification functions for /rɑ/ and /lɑ/.

ences. Paired in every order, the test consists of 48 stimuli randomized four times. Each pair of items follows the question in natural speech 'Do these sound the same or different?' Subjects respond by checking either the column marked SAME or the column marked DIFFERENT. The one-step discrimination function for the speech science class plotted in Figure 5.27 shows a peak in discrimination occurring as expected between Stimuli 6 and 7. Thus, discrimination is sharper at the phoneme boundary indicated by the identification test than it is within phoneme categories. For contrasts not phonemically different (those lying within a group of stimuli identified as one phoneme), subjects do not discriminate between them.

Like categorical perception of changes in manner and place, responses to continua of smooth variations in voice onset time demonstrate categorical perception of voicing. By increasing VOT in equal steps, continua can be synthesized which are perceived as going from /bɑ/ to /pɑ/, from /dɑ/ to /tɑ/, or from /gɑ/ to /kɑ/. Again, listeners group the stimuli into voiced and voiceless categories and perceive and are sensitive to differences between stimuli at the voiced-voiceless boundary, while they are relatively insensitive to equal VOT differences within categories.

The phenomenon of categorical perception for consonants has been demonstrated for manner, place, and voicing contrasts. For vowels, results are a bit different. Fry, Abramson, Eimas, and Liberman showed that changing continua from /ɪ/ to /ɛ/ to /æ/ do not show the same close relationship between identification and discrimination functions. When the vowels are shorter and embedded in CVC contexts, however, as reported by Stevens, the discrimination-identification relationship is more like that for consonants.

Since steady-state vowels and non-speech tones are not perceived categorically, while embedded vowels and consonants are perceived categorically, it seems that listeners perceive rapidly changing

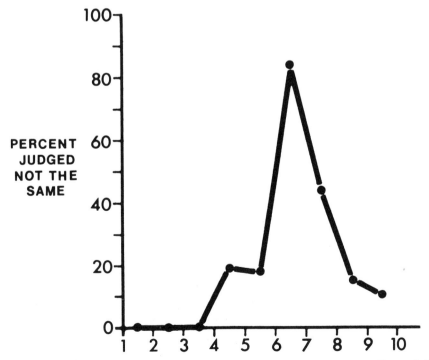

Figure 5.27. Discrimination function for adjacent pairs of stimuli shown in Figure 5.25.

stimuli differently than they do constant stimuli.

An important aspect of categorical perception is the influence that linguistic knowledge can have on the categories perceived. The reason we prefaced our /rɑ/-/lɑ/ stimuli with questions spoken in English is that Elman, Diehl, and Buchwald found the language 'set' that listeners have when making decisions about speech sound identity may change the boundary between categories. Bilingual subjects divide such stimuli according to the phonemic contrasts of the particular language they are using immediately before each stimulus.

Strange and Jenkins have reviewed many studies of both monolingual and bilingual speakers. These studies offer evidence that the language experience of adults can influence their perception. For example, Spanish, French, and Thai speakers use different VOT criteria for voicing contrasts than do English speakers. Japanese speakers, who do not contrast /r/ and /l/, perceive equal changes in F_3 in a /rɑ/ to /lɑ/ continuum differently than the two-category manner in which it is perceived by speakers of English.

Since categorical perception seems to be language-specific and strongly related to the phonemic contrasts made by the listener, investigators were surprised to find that creatures with little or no use of language (animals and infants) discriminate speech-like stimuli in a way that seemed to be related to the categorical perception of adults.

Infant Studies

The classic report on infant perception of speech-like stimuli was published in *Science* in 1971, by Eimas, Siqueland, Jusczyk, and Vigorito of Brown University. They monitored infants sucking a pacifier wired to a transducer which recorded infant responses to synthetic speech sounds differing by 20-msec increments of VOT. Infants as young as 1 month of age react to any new stimulus with a change in sucking. The investigators recorded the baseline rate of sucks per minute for each baby and then presented each auditory stimulus at an intensity which depended upon the rate of sucking. As long as the baby maintained a high rate of sucking responses, the sound continued at high intensity. As the rate of sucking decreased so did the loudness of the sound. Typically, the babies responded by increasing their rate of sucking. After a few minutes, as the novelty of the stimulus wore off, the sucking responses gradually decreased. This decrease in response rate, known as habituation, was allowed to proceed for 2 minutes and then a different VOT stimulus was presented for several minutes. Figure 5.28 schematizes the mean responses of the 4-month-old infant group. The *dots* at the *left* of the three graphs represent the baseline rate of sucking. With auditory reinforcement for sucking, the rate of responses increased, as can be seen by the sucking rates plotted to the *left* of the *dashed vertical line*, those representing 5, 4, and 3 minutes before the shift in stimulus. Then, the infants started to habituate to the stimulus, and sucking rate decreased. The graph at the *left* represents what happened when the first stimulus was a /ba/-like sound with +20 VOT and then changed without any hesitation to a /pa/-like sound with +40 VOT. The sucking rate increased dramatically, indicating that the infants heard this shift as something new. The middle graph in Figure 5.30 reveals no such jump in sucking responses, even though the stimuli also differed by 20 msec VOT. In this condition, the first stimulus was +60 VOT changing to +80 VOT (both perceived by adults as /pa/) or −20 VOT changing to 0 VOT (both perceived by adults as /ba/). The infants did not respond to these changes with a significant increase in sucking rate. The authors infer from these two functions that the infants are perceiving the first two stimuli as different but not perceiving the middle two stimuli as different. The control condition is represented by the graph on the *right* of the figure. When the 'shift' is made to the same sound as the initial stimulus, resulting in the control condition of no shift, habituation continues. There is no abrupt change in sucking behavior to indicate perception of a change. Eimas and his colleagues concluded that infants as young as 1 month old seem to perceive acoustic

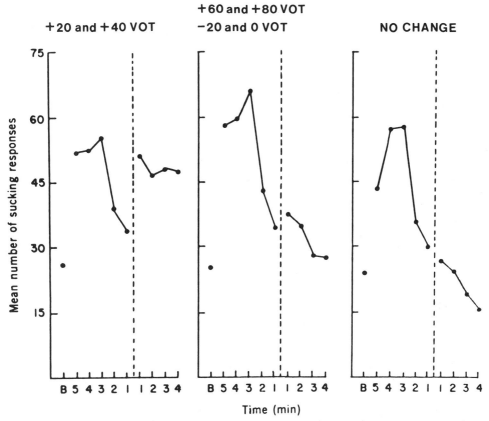

Figure 5.28. Mean number of sucking responses for 4-month-oid infants in three experimental conditions. *B* represents the baseline before presentation of a stimulus. Each panel shows sucking as a function of time with a change of stimulus at the point shown by the *dotted line,* or, in the *right-most panel,* at the time the change would have occurred. In the *left-most panel,* the stimuli straddle the /b/-/p/ category boundary for adults, while in the *middle panel,* contrasting stimuli are within one category. (Adapted with permission from P. Eimas *et al.: Science. 171,* 304, © 1971, American Association for the Advancement of Science.)

changes in speech continua within the same general categories as do adults.

There have been scores of studies in infant perception since this original study. Techniques have changed. Researchers find they may get more reliable results by conditioning infants to turn and look at a dancing bear or some such moving toy as a reinforcer. (Infants younger than 6 months, however, are generally too immature motorically for head-turning.) The infant is conditioned to look at the toy only in response to a certain sound. Then sounds that are acoustically similar or different can be delivered to see if the infant perceives them as the same or different than the conditioned stimulus. Kuhl at the University of Washington, has reported

that 6-month-old babies tested with this technique indicate perception of vowel contrasts and consonant contrasts even when variations are made in pitch, talker, and phonetic context. Jusczyk finds that infants can perceive consonant contrasts in word-initial, -medial, or -final position, and the sounds can be in multisyllablic stimuli as well as in single syllablic stimuli. More research is needed to determine infant perception of suprasegmental contrasts, but there is some evidence that stimuli with contrastive stress are discriminated.

The question that results from the increasing evidence of infant perceptual abilities is whether infants are innately tuned to detect linguistically significant contrasts, or whether the distinctions they perceive are a result of characteristics of the auditory system without reference to language. The infants are obviously making auditory distinctions, and at this point, we cannot determine if they are also making phonetic distinctions. More information is needed on what distinctions infants universally make despite language environment and, further, how language learning affects the perceptual abilities of infants. Which distinctions become sharper? Which distinctions disappear?

Animal Studies

Some light is shed on this question by the finding that non-humans perceive acoustic changes in speech-like continua in what may be described as a categorical manner. Morse and Snowden monitored heart rate of rhesus monkeys in response to changes in F_2 and F_3 which mark place of articulation distinctions for humans. Waters and Wilson trained rhesus monkeys to avoid shock associated with a particular synthetic speech sound and thus measured the monkeys' perception of VOT changes. Kuhl and Miller used shock avoidance to study VOT contrast in the chinchilla. Results show that these non-human listeners display enhanced discrimination at adult category boundaries. The responses of chinchillas resemble those of people more than those of rhesus monkeys, perhaps because the auditory systems of humans and chinchillas are so similar.

It may be that the categorical perception of speech continua that we find for adult speakers and that we know to be highly influenced by linguistic experience, is based upon general auditory system characteristics found also in human infants and in some other mammals. Languages may make optimal use of those auditory properties in developing the contrastive patterns that signify differences in meaning. There are theories of how these auditory and phonetic levels of processing complex acoustic stimuli may interact in speech perception.

Auditory and Phonetic Analysis

We know that a specified complex acoustic event can result in a person reporting that he or she heard /ba/. Furthermore, such a person can report that the initial consonant was /b/. Since we know that the acoustic cues for /b/ are overlaid on those for /a/, listeners must be analyzing the event on an auditory level to identify the /ba/ (they have to hear it) and on a phonetic level to extract the /b/ (they have to segment it). The question that remains is how the transform from auditory to phonetic percept is made. How are phonemes individually recovered? Are features detected, and if so, are the features acoustic or phonetic? Is the syllable or some larger unit processed as a whole?

We have seen that categorical perception can be influenced by phonetic processing, in that boundaries between phonemes are different for different languages. On the other hand, the results with infants and animals seem more likely to be determined by auditory than by phonetic factors. Another approach to the attempt to separate auditory and phonetic factors in speech perception is to examine acoustically complex non-speech continua. Some non-speech continua have been shown to be perceived categorically. Cutting and Rosner constructed a continuum of non-speech, music-like stimuli varying in rise-time. They found subjects categorically differentiated the set of stimuli into a fast rise-time group, which sounded like 'plucked' violin strings, and a slow rise-time group of stimuli which sounded like 'bowed' violin strings. This finding was comparable to the same subjects' categorization of /tʃ/ to /ʃ/ gradations which similarly varied in rise-time. In both series, discrimination peaked at the identification boundary, with discrimination remaining poor among stimuli within each category. They also studied an acoustically simpler continuum and found that pure tones graded in rise-time were inconsistently identified, but were similar in discrimination peak value to the musical stimuli. Thus, gradations in rise-time seem to be categorically perceived whether speech or non-speech.

Pisoni has proposed that the procedures used in testing listeners can themselves favor either phonetic or auditory processing of the stimuli due to the fact that some methods put a greater load on memory than others. The usual method used to test discrimination in these studies is the ABX procedure, in which the listener hears A then B (always different) followed by X, and must report whether X is more like A or B. Another procedure is the 'oddball' method, in which subjects hear a triad of stimuli in which one stimulus differs from the other two. The task is to pick out the 'different' stimulus. A study by Pisoni and Lazarus showed the 4IAX (four-interval forced choice procedure), in which the subject is asked 'Which pair is more alike?' and the test items are AA AB or AB AA, to result in better discrimination—that is, auditory processing. The authors suggested that the difference in results is accounted for by the different loads on short-term memory of the different tasks. The AX paradigm puts less of a load on memory than the other techniques.

Another group of experiments that bears upon the distinction between auditory and phonetic levels of speech processing is based upon *adaptation*.

Adaptation Studies

If a listener hears one end of a speech-like continuum repeatedly, /dɑ/ for example, and is then presented with the usual randomized /dɑ/ to /tɑ/ continuum for identification, the boundary between phonemes that would normally result is shifted toward the /dɑ/ end of the continuum. That is, after exposure to so many strongly /dɑ/-like sounds, the listener identifies more of the stimuli as /tɑ/. Thus, VOT perception is adapted; the listener, having heard many tokens of the 'voiced' end of the continuum, will perceive a smaller increase in VOT as a change to the voiceless category.

These results might be explained by a theory positing phonetic feature detectors. If, in the nervous system, there are neurons especially tuned to detect contrastive linguistic features, then the particular detectors responsive to small VOT values corresponding to 'voiced' stops, for example, might be fatigued by multiple presentations of /dɑ/. With the detector for 'voicing' fatigued, subjects would identify more 'voiceless' items in the continuum.

Many studies on adaptation followed the original report by Eimas and Corbit in

1973. The studies are reviewed in detail by Darwin. As the data accumulate, it is becoming clear that many interpretations of these studies are possible. Adaptation studies do show, however, that auditory factors can have a great effect upon categorical perception, just as cross-language studies show the importance of phonetic factors.

Categorical Perception and Learning

We have mentioned cross-language studies which show the influence of a particular language upon perception of phoneme boundaries. We can infer from these that learning contributes to categorical perception. In addition, there are several more direct ways in which researchers have studied the effects of learning upon categorical perception: by direct training in the laboratory, by studying perception in children receiving speech therapy for an articulation disorder, and by testing second language learners. Reports are few, however, and conclusions are tentative. Strange succeeded in training English speakers to improve intraphonemic discrimination in VOT continua, but found that the training did not generalize to VOT continua of speech sounds at other places of articulation. Training on labial VOT stimuli had no effect on discrimination of apical VOT stimuli. Carney and Widin found considerable improvement in subjects' ability to discriminate after training. Several different labial VOT stimuli were used as standards. Subjects were trained to hear differences between each standard and the other stimuli in AX pairs, with immediate feedback. Listeners can be trained, then, to make auditory rather than phonetic distinctions in such continua.

Developmental studies are difficult to compare, because few have used stimuli that have been precisely specified and few have tested intraphonemic discrimination. The research on infant perception shows that babies discriminate in a similar fashion, no matter what language community they have been born into. For example, they can hear differences between +20 VOT and +60 VOT and between −20 VOT and −60 VOT. Babies do not discriminate between −20 VOT and +20 VOT. The reason may be that ±20 VOT sounds like a single event, while a large time gap between a burst and voicing onset sounds like two events. Perception of speech seems to begin with an innate ability to make certain auditory distinctions. Stevens and Klatt point to the fact that adults divide a non-speech continuum that is analogous to the VOT series with a boundary at approximately +20 VOT as further indication that some distinctions may be natural to the auditory system.

By 2 years of age, children identify categorically, and their phoneme boundaries are similar to those of adults. Zlatin and Koenigsknecht used continua varying from 'bees' to 'peas,' from 'dime' to 'time' as examples, and found that although 2-year-olds identified the stimuli with the same boundary between categories as identified by the 6-year-olds and adults, the younger childrens' boundary areas were wider, indicating that they needed larger acoustic differences to mark the distinction. The longitudinal development of this perceptual ability has never been studied; the difficulties in testing very young children in both identification and discrimination are considerable. There are hints, however, that identification and discrimination may not develop at the same rate.

It is easier to study changes in perception in people learning a second language, since they are typically older and easier to test, but we are not sure that the processes for learning the phonemes of a second language are the same as those for learning a first language. Williams found a slightly faster shift of phoneme boundaries toward the English boundary among younger (8–10 years) Spanish-speaking children learning English than among older children (14–16 years) (Fig. 5.29). She found indications that discrimination may be ahead of labeling as learning takes place. Again, longitudinal studies are needed to determine the progression. Particularly interesting would be more research in which production and perception are analyzed simultaneously.

Production and Perception

Williams did analyze both production (by measuring spectrograms of the sub-

Age	Crossover Values by Exposure		
---	One	Two	Three
14–16	+2.0	+5.7	+8.7
8–10	+4.7	+7.5	+12.0
Difference	2.7	1.8	3.3

Figure 5.29. Differences (VOT in milliseconds) in labeling crossover values for native Spanish-speaking children of two age groups. The children were also divided on the basis of exposure to English, as measured by time in the United States: Exposure one (0–6 months), Exposure two (1½–2 years), and Exposure three (3–3½ years). (From L. Williams: unpublished doctoral dissertation, Harvard, 1974.)

jects' speech samples) and perception (by identification and discrimination tests) of the phoneme contrasts important in the second language being learned. Establishing the monolingual identification boundaries for /b/ and /p/ and the discrimination peaks for both English and Spanish adult speakers, she found that their production of /b/ and /p/ in word-initial position corresponded to their perception. English speakers separated the phonemes at about +25 VOT, while Spanish speakers put the boundary at about −4 VOT. Spanish speakers learning English varied more than monolinguals in the crossover points of their identification functions, and the discrimination peaks spanned both the monolingual English and Spanish boundaries. Thus, perception of the /b/-/p/ series for adult bilinguals represented a compromise. For production, spectrograms showed that the bilinguals prevoice /b/ in accordance with the Spanish system, even in English words.

In a second study, Williams tracked changes in production and perception in young Puerto Rican Spanish-speaking children who were learning English. She found the labeling crossover point gradually shifting toward the English boundary as exposure to English increased. In production, the children were using VOT patterns closer to English, both in their English and Spanish words. Greater sensitivity to the phonological contrasts important in the language being learned may be a hallmark of young language learners and provide an explanation of how they manage to learn to speak a new language with so little interference from their first language.

Turning again to adult learners, a study by Goto indicates that adult bilinguals are often quite insensitive to perceptual distinctions in their non-native language, even if they can produce them. Japanese speakers judged by Americans to be making the English /r/-/l/ distinction appropriately as they produced words such as 'lead,' 'read,' 'pray,' and 'play,' nevertheless found difficulty in perceiving the distinctions either in recordings of their own speech or of other speakers. Have they lost the perceptual flexibility of the young? How can they produce distinctions which they fail to perceive? More information is needed, but this brings us to the interesting question of how perception of one's own speech may relate to perception of the speech of others.

The anecdotal observation that some children may perceive distinctions in their own speech that adults fail to distinguish, rests on experiences such as the following: A child protests when others imitate his misarticulation, "I didn't say wabbit, I said wabbit." This phenomenon can be interpreted as evidence that perception is ahead of production. When the child hears the adult say 'wabbit,' he perceives the mistake but is unable to produce an /r/ and fails to detect the mistake in his own speech. An alternate explanation is that the child perceives distinctions in his own speech in a different way than do adults. The child may make a perceptual distinction between his two /w/ sounds, in the example above, that the adult cannot; that is, the phoneme category for the child's /r/ is wide enough to include some sounds that the adult would classify as /w/. A third interpretation might be that the child's perception is confused, because he does not yet make the distinction productively. Thus, perception not only aids production, but the mastery of the production of speech sounds is viewed as an aid to the child in his efforts to discriminate the sounds in the speech of others.

Aungst and Frick found there was a low correlation between self-judgments of the correctness of /r/ production and the ability to discriminate phonemes in others' speech. Children with /r/ misarticulations had no problem perceiving the misarticulations of others but failed to detect their own errors. Kornfeld showed that children may produce /w/ sounds in [gwæs] for 'glass' and [gwæs] for 'grass' which seem the same to adult listeners. There are spectrographic differences, however, which may reflect the basis on which the children make distinctions. Goehl and Golden suggest that the child in this case has a phoneme representation differing from that of the adult /r/. The child's phoneme /r^w/ is directly represented phonetically [r^w], while the adult phoneme /r/ does not include the [r^w] sound. They found that children tend to recognize their own [r^w] as /r/ and are better at detecting it than other people.

This phenomenon of children perceiving a difference between their misarticulation and the substitution as perceived by an adult may not be as common, however, as is supposed. Locke and Kutz found that of 75 children who said /wɪŋ/ in response to a picture of a ring, only about 20% of them pointed to the picture of a ring when they later heard their own misarticulation, while 80% pointed to a picture of a wing upon hearing their misarticulation. McReynolds, Kohn, and Williams found that children with misarticulations are worse at discriminating their own error sounds than their error-free sounds. By "discrimination" investigators of self-perception often mean phonemic identification, since allophonic discrimination tests as we have defined them, represented by continua of changes in synthetic speech, are seldom administered.

It may be that in learning phonemic contrasts, identification of phonemes in the speech of others develops before the ability to perceive one's own errors, with production and self-perception developing in parallel as motor maturity permits. The time course of perception-production interaction remains unclear, and children learning a first language or correcting misarticulations may evidence quite a different time course of perceptual and production interaction than do second language learners.

Neurophysiology of Speech Perception

Both sides of the brain are important for hearing. The auditory nerve reports to the temporal lobes of both cerebral hemispheres. Further analysis of the sound patterns, such as those involved in the perception of speech, however, are to some extent lateralized to one cerebral hemisphere.

Cerebral Lateralization

Evidence that one cerebral hemisphere, usually the left, is dominant over the other during perception of speech comes from anatomical analyses, split brain experiments, dichotic listening studies, and electroencephalographic (EEG) recordings. Wernicke, mentioned in Chapter 4, was the first to implicate the temporo-parietal area surrounding the posterior portion of the Rolandic fissure in speech recognition and in linguistic expression. Not only did Wernicke find damage in the temporal part of that area upon autopsy of aphasic individuals, but Penfield and Roberts found stimulation of that area to interfere most severely with language in their patients.

Wernicke's area, as this part of the left cerebral cortex has come to be called, is important for decoding speech messages of others and for eliciting the acoustic model of what one intends to say. People who suffer a cerebral vascular accident (CVA) to the left temporo-parietal area articulate distinctly despite some substitution of phonemes, and they speak fluently. Their conversation often makes little sense, however. Goodglass and Geschwind describe the tendency of such patients to substitute a general word, such as "it" for the elusive nouns and a general verb, such as "do," for the missing verbs, resulting in the following kind of response in attempting to name something: "I know what it is, I use it to do my . . . I have one right here. . . . " Another paragrammatical, fluent but meaningless example from Goodglass and Geschwind: "The things I want to say . . . ah . . . the way I say things, but I understand mostly things, most of them and what the things are."

Along with the inability to call up the words necessary to convey an idea, there is often a decreased ability to recognize the meaning of something said aloud. A person with Wernicke's aphasia may recognize the class of a word but not its specific meaning. Thus, for the word "lamp," the person with such a comprehension disorder might point to a piece of furniture, but the wrong one.

If Wernicke's area itself is intact, but the connections between the auditory centers of the temporal lobes and Wernicke's area are damaged or poorly functioning, a form of auditory agnosia results. The person may hear a word repeatedly with no comprehension at all and then suddenly understand it completely. This link between the centers for audition and the centers for comprehension may be what is manipulated and fatigued in people with normal perception who experience *verbal transformation*. When an utterance is repeated over and over, people report several changes in perception as they listen to the repetitions. For example, the non-word 'flime' might be heard as "flying" for awhile, then "climb," then "flank." Although we know nothing of the neural underpinnings of this phenomenon, it simulates a dysfunction in the link between hearing and perception.

Dramatic evidence of the role of the left hemisphere in language production and perception is in the test responses of patients who have undergone surgical separation of the cerebral hemispheres by section of the corpus callosum. This operation is done to control severe epilepsy. The patients do not seem impaired unless certain tests are conducted to present information to the hemispheres independently. Since the main connecting body between hemispheres is severed, the patient has functionally separated hemicerebrums. Sperry and Gazzaniga, by testing one cerebrum at a time, have demonstrated that in split brain patients, the left side does not know what the right side is doing and vice versa (Fig. 5.30). With a curtain in front of such a patient, visually masking objects such as a key, a fork, a letter, and a number, the patient can name an object touched with his right hand (referred to the left hemisphere) or flashed to his left visual field but cannot name it if the name of the object is flashed to his right visual

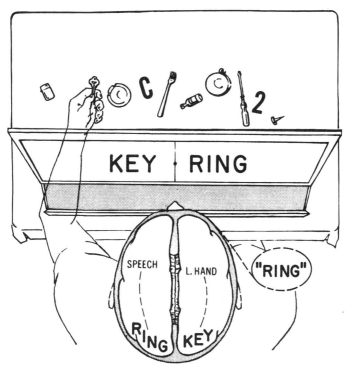

Figure 5.30. A Sperry experiment with a split-brain patient. A subject will report verbally on a visual stimulus (''ring'' in this case) presented to the left hemisphere. At the same time, the left hand correctly retrieves objects presented to right hemisphere although the subject verbally denies knowledge of it. When asked to name an object selected by the left hand, the subject names the stimulus presented to the left hemisphere. (Reprinted with permission from R. W. Sperry: In *Hemispheric Specialization and Interaction,* B. Milner (Ed.), M. I. T. Press © 1975.)

hemisphere, although he can point to its picture or select it with his left hand. Research by Sperry and others has shown the left hemisphere to be dominant in most people for both spoken and written language expression. For perception, however, the right hemisphere displays some understanding despite left side dominance.

Zaidel designed special contact lenses used with prisms and mirrors to separate the left and right visual fields in one eye. Visual images thus can be directed to only one cerebral hemisphere in people who have had their corpus callosum severed and are wearing a patch over one eye. By such methods, written sentences and phrases of various complexity have been presented to each side of the brain independently. Results show that the left side is clearly more linguistically sophisticated. Whole sentences can be read from this side, while only single words can be read from the right side.

Lateralization of speech perception has been studied in normal subjects as well. A classic study in the neurophysiology of speech perception was Kimura's study of cerebral dominance by use of dichotic stimuli. You recall that in dichotic listening, one sound goes to one ear and another sound to the opposite ear, both delivered through earphones. Kimura used spoken digits. When subjects were asked to report what they heard, they made mistakes because of the conflicting stimuli. Subjects make fewer mistakes in reporting stimuli fed to the right ear than to the left ear. This effect is known as the *right ear advantage (REA)*. Kimura's interpretation of this effect was based upon anatomical evidence that more neurons of the auditory nerve cross to the contralateral temporal lobe than course directly to the ipsilateral lobe. Thus, information sent along VIIIth nerve fibers from the right cochlea would be strongly represented in the left cerebral hemisphere. Since the right ear demonstrates an advantage over the left in speech perception accuracy, she concluded that the left hemisphere is specialized for speech perception.

Shankweiler and Studdert-Kennedy in a series of studies have found that CV nonsense syllables, such as /ba/, /ta/, or /ga/ presented dichotically to right-handed listeners, show the right ear to have a small but consistent advantage. The advantage for the right ear is obtained for stop-vowel syllables whether in synthetic or natural speech. Steady-state vowels, however, show no consistent ear advantage.

Listeners make fewer errors in perception when the conflicting syllables share a phonemic feature. For example, /da/ in one ear and /ta/ in the other are both apt to be reported correctly since they share place of articulation. Conflicting /da/ and /ka/ might be less accurately reported. When the conflicting pair share voicing, /da/ and /ba/ instead of /da/ and /pa/, accuracy is again enhanced. Shared place, however, yields greater accuracy than shared voicing. There is no difference in ear advantage, however. Both ears are better when the dichotic pairs share features. Cutting, and Day and Vigorito, have shown the right ear advantage to be strongest for contrastive stops, less advantageous for liquids, and least, if at all, for vowels.

If a dichotic test of vowel contrasts is made more difficult, however, a REA emerges. The consonant-vowel differences noted in categorical perception studies are found for dichotic studies as well. Vowels, being more accessible to auditory analysis by virtue of their longer duration and higher intensity, may be held longer in auditory memory, are less categorically perceived, and yield a weaker right ear advantage. Stop consonants, being less accessible to auditory analysis due to their brevity and relatively low intensity, may be held only briefly in auditory memory, are categorized immediately, and yield a stronger right ear advantage. These results have been explained by positing a special speech processor in the left hemisphere or, alternatively, by suggestions that the left hemisphere is especially equipped to analyze any fast-changing, difficult stimulus.

Dichotic listening tests have been constructed with words, syllables, and non-speech sounds. Subjects have been instructed to report both stimuli or the stronger stimulus, or to attend to one ear at a time. Dichotic tapes have been used to test people with normal and abnormal language development. Such tests show promise as a diagnostic tool for obtaining information on cerebral lateralization.

One finding of interest is that normal listeners presented with a pair of dichotic stimuli having a *stimulus onset asynchrony (SOA)* estimated to be about 100 msec can identify the second stimulus with more accuracy than the first. This is called the *lag effect*, because subjects are better at reporting the lagging syllable. It is an example of backward masking; the second syllable masks the first. Again, if the syllables share voicing or other features, there is little backward masking or lag effect. Yet, as one might expect, the more acoustically similar the vowels of the syllables are to one another, the more pronounced is the backward masking, as demonstrated by Pisoni and McNabb. So, vowel similarity seems to produce a backward masking effect that can be explained on an auditory level, whereas consonant feature sharing seems to facilitate perception and might be explained on either a phonetic or an auditory level.

The final bit of evidence for cerebral lateralization of speech perception comes from a study of electroencephalographic recordings made from the surface of the heads of subjects who are listening to speech. Wood, Goff, and Day recorded evoked auditory responses from 10 right-handed subjects as they performed two identification tasks on a series of synthesized speech stimuli differing in F_2 transition and in f_o. Task 1 was considered to be linguistic, as subjects identified syllables as either /ba/ or /da/ by pressing an appropriate response key. Task 2 was considered to be non-linguistic, as subjects identified /ba/ syllables to be either low in pitch or high in pitch. Recordings were made from both hemispheres at central locations and over the temporal areas during each task. Evoked potentials from the right hemisphere were identical for both the linguistic and non-linguistic tasks. The patterns from the left hemisphere for Task 1, however, were significantly different from those for Task 2. This result has been interpreted to mean that auditory processing occurs in both hemispheres but that phoneme identification is lateralized to the left hemisphere.

Something special is happening in the left hemisphere when we listen to speech, whether it is some kind of auditory analysis of transient, difficult stimuli, or whether it is some form of linguistic analysis, such as the extraction of features or phoneme categorization. Since any analysis presumes short-term memory, let us consider what is conjectured about the role of memory in speech perception.

Memory and Speech Perception

When one knows a particular language, it must mean that one has stored the rules and the lexicon of the language in long-term memory. The rules include the phonological rules and the articulatory rules for producing speech as well as the syntactic and semantic rules of the language. These rules are used as a reference not only for speech production but for speech perception. We hear speech patterns, analyze them, and refer to our stored knowledge of the speech patterns in that particular language for recognition of what was said.

It is assumed that there is also a short-term memory for auditory events. Recent work has presented the possibility of two forms of short-term auditory memory. The first is a brief echo of an auditory event, lasting only a few milliseconds. This auditory image may present itself in the form of a neural spectrogram, and is continuously being replaced by new information.

The second, a longer lasting auditory memory, called *precategorical acoustic storage (PAS)* by Crowder and Morton, is evidenced by the *recency effect*. When a list of items (syllables, digits) is presented to subjects for recall, performance declines from the first item to the next to last item progressively, but the decline is reversed for the last item. Subjects tend to recall the most recent item in the list most accurately. The recency effect is stronger for lists in which the vowel changes than for lists in which the consonant changes. Lists differing only in voiced consonants produce little or no recency effect. One interpretation of the effect is that the last item suffers no interference from a following item, so phonetic analysis can take place uninterrupted. Darwin suggests that since acoustically similar items, like consonants, are auditorally confusable, they show little recency effect, fading quickly in precategorical acoustic storage. Items that are acoustically distinct, however, such as vowels, are posited to remain longer in PAS and are available for finer auditory analysis, resulting in a recency effect.

In natural speech, a listener is likely to be perceiving a stream of acoustically more dissimilar sounds than the /ba/, /da/, /ga/ series often synthesized in the laboratory. If this is true, precategorical acoustic storage of speech material might operate on virtually all of the speech stream, allowing time for syllable and cross-syllable analysis. Studdert-Kennedy points out that a memory store for several seconds of auditory information is required for the recognition of prosodic patterns, intonation contours, and patterns of relative stress, since they may last for that period.

Neurophysiological Development and Perception

The auditory system of the human infant performs amazingly well, as we have only recently determined from studies of infants' sound discrimination. Infant auditory sensitivity seems to be especially tuned to the sounds distinctive in human speech.

The occurrence of babbling, although considered to be non-linguistic, does signify that sensory-motor neural associations are being formed. The infant, who has already demonstrated his auditory prowess, is slowly developing sound production abilities and so can make correlations between articulatory events and auditory results. During the babbling period, before speech has developed, the infant reveals his sensitivity to intonation patterns of other speakers by mimicking them.

Whitaker theorizes that the connections between Wernicke's area and Broca's area are activated during a time when babbling temporarily ceases. An auditory template of the language spoken in the infant's community may be registered at this stage. (See Chapter 7 for further discussion of auditory templates in connection with bird song.) Thus, as the child starts to speak at approximately 1 year, he has been sensitized to the particular language and the particular dialect of the community. If the connections are not properly activated between the child's perceptual and production centers for speech, a delay in language acquisition will result. The child can hear sound but fails to associate sound with speech, and therefore, has difficulty in learning to speak himself.

Important in the neurophysiology of speech perception is the concept of a *critical period* for learning speech. The critical period applies to both perception and production and especially to the ability to relate perception to production. Lenneberg and Penfield and Roberts have independently claimed that the critical period continues to puberty. It is easier to learn a language before puberty than after, especially to learn the sounds of the language. Cerebral lateralization, too, is generally thought to be complete by puberty, but there are some indications that the left hemisphere may be dominant for speech at an early age, perhaps at birth. Kimura found the REA for dichotically presented speech to be established in 4-year-olds. The critical period for language learning relates to a flexibility and plasticity of brain function that diminishes in adulthood. Puberty is set as an outer limit; the younger the child, the more malleable the neural correlates of language learning. Thus, an acquired aphasia in a child is soon remedied by the other side of the brain assuming the functions of the damaged hemisphere. The neural flexibility during the youthful critical period allows children to compensate by establishing a linguistic center in an undamaged area of the brain, while the adult has lost access to an already established linguistic store, and has little neural flexibility left to establish a new one.

Theories of Speech Perception

Someone says "We beat you in soccer." How does a listener begin to extract the information necessary to understand that message? Disregarding the semantic and syntactic operations which must occur, how are the phonetic events isolated from the stream of sound? There are two general groups of theories on how this is accomplished. One group of theories views the listener as relatively passive and the process of speech perception as primarily sensory. The message is sensed, filtered, and mapped directly onto the acoustic-phonetic features of the language. The other group of theories views the listener as more active and postulates that the process of speech perception involves some aspect of speech production; the sounds are sensed, analyzed for their phonetic properties by reference to how such speech sounds are produced, and thus, are recognized. We shall discuss some active theories first, then some sensory, passive theories, and finally, the quantal theory, an idea that relates production and perception from a slightly different perspective.

Active Theories

There are two main theories of speech perception that emphasize some reference to speech production: the *Motor Theory* of Liberman and some of his colleagues at Haskins Laboratories and the *Analysis-by-Synthesis Theory* of Stevens and Halle at Massachusetts Institute of Technology. Both theories were born from efforts to find a one-to-one correspondence between phonemes and the acoustic speech signal. It is hard to find stable acoustic cues for each phoneme. Often cited examples of the lack of invariance in the acoustic signal are the /di/-/du/ example (Fig. 5.31) in

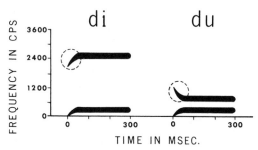

Figure 5.31. Synthetic patterns showing the syllables /di/ and /du/. Notice the difference in the direction of the F_2 transition. (Reprinted with permission from A. M. Liberman: *Cognitive Psychology. 1, 1970.)*

which a rising transition and a falling transition both serve as acoustic cues for /d/, and the /pi/-/ka/-/pu/ example in which the same burst at a constant frequency is perceived as a different phoneme before different vowel formants. The lack of correspondence between discrete acoustic events and separate phonemes, then, works both ways: different acoustic events can be perceived as the same phoneme, while the same acoustic event can be perceived as different phonemes in different contexts. Acoustic cues are conditioned by context and are transmitted in parallel. It would be inefficient for speech to be transmitted and received one phoneme at a time. Liberman calls the overlaid acoustic cues in speech *encoded*. A translation is necessary to decode the signal and arrive at the phonemes. The stop-vowel syllables are highly encoded and must be perceived as a whole syllable; the phonemes do not exist separately in the acoustic signal. The Motor Theory posits that the mechanism used by the listener to mediate between the acoustic signal and phonetic or phonemic information is the listener's articulatory knowledge. The fact that humans are inherently speakers aids them in their perception of speech even if some disability prevents them from speaking normally. Since coarticulation causes the acoustic encoding, subconscious knowledge of articulatory rules and vocal tract dynamics may aid in decoding the signal.

Another point made in the Motor Theory is that speech has special perceptual properties and is perceived differently from other acoustic signals. The categorical perception of some speech sound continua and the right ear advantage for some speech sounds suggested a special processor used to decode speech. This argument has been challenged by the results of animal and infant studies of categorical perception, and by the demonstration that some non-speech auditory signals seem to be analyzed categorically and in the left hemisphere. Also, the argument that there are few invariant acoustic cues corresponding to phonemes loses some of its strength when one considers relational cues to be critical rather than absolute cues and the syllable to be the smallest perceptual unit. Direct correspondence with phonemes has not been found in articulatory data any more than in acoustic data. The phoneme is hard to find in discrete muscle activity or discrete movements. Speech at all levels seems to be dynamic and context conditioned.

As we have seen, cross-language studies show linguistic expectations to be important in perception. Articulatory knowledge is important as well. Listeners fail to perceive sound combinations which a vocal tract could not make. Their perception is conditioned by their expectations, based upon knowledge of speech production possibilities. For example, Dorman, Raphael, and Liberman have found that if listeners hear /ɛbdɛ/, they normally hear the cues for closure for /b/ and the release for /d/, but if the /b/ and /d/ cues are synthesized and are moved closer together in time than would be humanly possible to produce, listeners report that they do not hear the first stop consonant at all, but only the release /ɛdɛ/. If one voice produces the [ɛb] and another voice the [dɛ], however, listeners report hearing [ɛbdɛ] at even the greatest temporal proximity.

The experimental work leading to the Motor Theory thus reveals the importance of relative cues, the importance of context, and the importance of linguistic and articulatory knowledge to perception.

The Analysis-by-Synthesis Theory, another attempt to explain perception in the face of so few invariant acoustic cues to phonemes, is similar to the Motor Theory in that the listener refers to production, but the reference is more acoustic, less articulatory, and it relies on a system of matching. The listener receives an auditory pattern and analyzes it by eliciting an auditory model of his own production of it. He hears [bitʃə], hypothesizes it to be "beat you," makes a quick neural synthesis of it himself, and, if the patterns match, accepts his perception as correct. An advantage of an active theory such as this, is that the listener can apply his knowledge of the phonological rules when performing the rudimentary synthesis and thereby can normalize variations caused by fast speaking rate and other distortions.

Work by Chistovich, Klass, and Kuzmin in Leningrad points to the importance of speech production knowledge in the perception of speech. Their shadowing experiments, in which a person says as quickly as possible an unexpected message heard through earphones, show that shadowers start to produce a consonant before they have heard all of the relevent cues. This finding indicates that cues at the beginning of the syllable signal what is to come, and listeners refer the incoming patterns immediately to motor articulatory patterns, before they "understand" the message.

Active theories of speech perception emphasize the role of linguistic knowledge, articulatory knowledge, knowledge of various vocal tract outputs, and knowledge of contextual influences in the decoding of speech.

Passive Theories

Passive theories of speech perception emphasize the sensory, filtering mechanisms of the listener, and relegate the role of speech production knowledge to a minor, secondary place, used only in difficult circumstances.

Fant in Stockholm models speech perception as primarily sensory. The perceptual mechanism shares with the speech production mechanism a common pool of distinctive features (see Fig. 5.32), but the listener need not refer to production for perception. Linguistic centers in the brain are common to both incoming and outgoing messages, but the centers responsible for subphonemic, more peripheral aspects of production and perception are viewed as independent. According to this passive model, as shown in Figure 5.32, speech

perception would proceed along the route ABCDE, while for an active model, the route would be ABCKFE. Fant's view is that listeners, having been exposed to language, are sensitive to the distinctive patterns of the speech wave and only need to refer to their own ability to speak when shadowing or listening under other unusual circumstances. A similar theory is held by Morton and Broadbent. They concur with Fant in the belief that listeners can decode directly, although reference to production may be made when the perceptual task is difficult, as in transcribing speech phonetically.

Two theoretical ideas related to speech perception that are essentially passive in their emphasis as described are the idea of *template* matching and the idea of *feature detectors*. The concept of an auditory template arises from experimental work in bird song. As discussed further in Chapter 7, some birds are born with a rudimentary version of the song characteristic of their species. This template is further refined as the young birds hear the song of mature birds in the environment. They later sing themselves, matching their efforts to their stored templates. Marler suggests that human infants may proceed somewhat similarly when learning speech. For adult speech perception, a similar concept is tenable. Adult speakers may have stored abstract patterns of speech (templates) which translate to phonemes or syllables, and when they listen to speech, they match

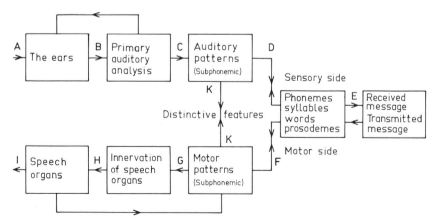

Figure 5.32. Fant's model of the brain mechanisms in speech perception and production. See text for explanation. (Reprinted with permission from G. Fant: *Models for the Perception of Speech and Visual Form*, W. Wathen-Dunn (Ed.), M. I. T. Press © 1967.)

incoming auditory patterns with the stored templates.

The feature detector concept was borrowed from research on vision. Specific cortical nerve cells are sensitive to a particular aspect of an image. For example, there are special detectors for horizontal lines. By analogy, a feature detector for speech is thought to be sensitive to specific complex stimuli, such as F_2 transitions. Initially, adaptation studies were interpreted in terms of Feature Detector Theory. If repetition of a particular stimulus resulted in a shift in phoneme identification, it was theorized that the shift was caused by the detector for that particular feature being fatigued by overstimulation. Infant studies were interpreted in these terms also. Infants were thought to be sensitive to certain features. The theory connotes a nativist approach; humans are viewed as possessing an innate linguistic capacity in the form of special neural receptors tuned to universal distinctive features of speech. Currently, some theorists are moving away from the idea of phonetic feature detectors and toward the idea of auditory feature detectors. An effort to incorporate the analysis of both acoustic and phonetic features into a speech recognition model has been made by Pisoni and Sawusch. This model also accounts for a short-term storage of information

elicited from the long-term store during the period of recognition. The recognized speech is then referred simultaneously for phonological, syntactic, and semantic analysis (Fig. 5.33). According to this theory, features detected by auditory property detectors are mapped onto a system of phonetic features as detected within a whole syllable and then combined into a rough feature matrix for further analysis. Feature Detector Theory does not address the relationship between production and perception. It is a theory about the sensory stage common to both active and passive theories and is included in this section merely because its emphasis is sensory.

Some writers combine the ideas of active and passive theorists. For example, Cole and Scott, although persuaded by the passive model, posit that perception of the syllable is accompanied by use of invariant cues and context-conditioned cues. For the [sɑ] of "soccer," the friction cue for [s] would be viewed as invariant, but there are context-conditioned cues for both the [s] and the [k] in [sɑkɚ] inherent in the transitions to and from the steady-state formants of [ɑ]. They agree with Liberman that transitions are important in providing the listener with the perception of the temporal order of sounds in a syllable. Cole and Scott suggest that the invariant and variant cues maintain their independence

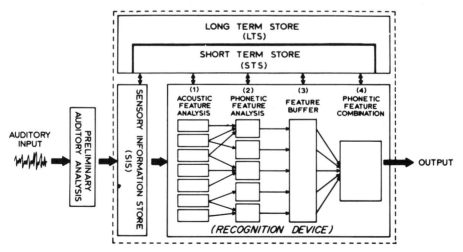

Figure 5.33. Pisoni and Sawusch's model of speech recognition. Phonetic and acoustic features are both analyzed, and short-term memory figures specifically in the model. (Reprinted with permission from D. B. Pisoni and J. R. Sawusch: In *Structure and Process in Speech Perception*, A. Cohen and S. G. Nooteboom (Eds.), Springer-Verlag © 1975.)

as cues, although listeners make use of both for syllable detection. Evidence of their separate nature is given by studies of the effects of repeated listening. For example, if a person hears the syllable [sɑ] repeatedly, the percept separates into a hiss in one stream, conditioned by the friction and [dɑ] in another stream, conditioned by the transition and steady state of the vocalic portion. In addition to the invariant cues and the context-conditioned cues, they propose a third cue, the waveform, which is perceived in a longer time frame for facts of relative intensity, duration, and pitch.

Quantal Theory

Not exclusively a theory of speech perception, the *Quantal Theory* of speech proposed by Stevens relates articulatory changes to acoustic results, but it has implications for speech perception theory. The thesis of the Quantal Theory is that there is a discontinuity between changes in articulatory positioning and the resultant changes in acoustic output. There are vocal tract regions in which small continuous differences in articulatory position cause little or no difference in the acoustic output, but there are other regions within which small articulatory differences result in large acoustic differences. In these critical regions, a slight adjustment of articulatory placement will cause a quantal leap in terms of sound change. An example of this discontinuity is apparent in making gradual articulatory changes from [ʃ] to [s]. Try to move the tongue-palate constriction from a posterior [ʃ] position forward in small equal steps to an alveolar [s]. You can hear very little difference in the sound as the constriction moves along the palate behind the alveolar ridge, but once it reaches the ridge, there is an immediate and substantial change in the frequency band of the friction noise. There is a quantal leap to [s]. Forward of the /s/-/ʃ/ boundary, there is another region of small acoustic effect for a relatively wide range of articulatory adjustments. The constriction can be moved forward along the alveolar ridge and behind the surface of the central incisors with little change in sound. Thus, there are articulatory regions in which large variations in production have

little effect upon acoustic output and other regions in which a small change in articulation may result acoustically in a different phoneme.

Stevens has shown acoustic discontinuity for the acoustic effects of pharyngeal and velar consonant constrictions. He suggests that the various languages of the world have taken advantage of these regions of little acoustic change for changes in place of constriction in developing consonant places of articulation.

It seems that the architecture of the vocal tract may partially account for the quantal principle. As a constriction moves from glottis to lips, there are regions of little topographical change: pharyngeal wall, palate, alveolar ridge, lips; but there are large structural discontinuities between these regions. The quantal principle applies to changes in front to back constriction location, but not to changes in tongue height. Although Stevens and Perkell have suggested a distinction between high and low vowels in general, according to acoustic differences and differences in tongue contact with other articulators, it may be true that changes in tongue position for vowels can be accomplished in a fairly continuous fashion. No quantal acoustic changes occur as a speaker continuously adjusts from /i/ to /a/ or from /u/ to /ɑ/, since the vocal tract may be made more open continuously.

All of this reminds us of the non-continuous fashion in which we perceive continuous changes in consonants and the more continuous way in which we perceive steady-state vowels of some duration. Stevens describes acoustic discontinuities, not perceptual ones; he finds them in actual formant changes. In the speech perception studies discussed earlier, the stimuli used in the perceptual tests were changed in equal acoustic steps (as a human never could because of the discontinuous architecture of the vocal tract), yet the listener perceives them according to the inherently quantal nature of articulatory place. If not some support for an active theory of speech perception, these conclusions indicate at least that the human auditory system is especially sensitive to those acoustic changes that the human articulatory system produces.

BIBLIOGRAPHY

General Readings

Bartlett, F. C., *Remembering*. Cambridge, England: University Press, 1932. Reprinted in 1950.

Darwin, C. J., The Perception of Speech. In *Handbook of Perception, Vol. 7: Language and Speech*. E. C. Carterette and M. P. Friedman (Eds.) New York: Academic Press, 1976, pp. 175–226.

Denes, P., and Pinson, E. N., *The Speech Chain*. New York: Bell Telephone Laboratories, Inc., 1963.

Fant, G., Descriptive Analysis of the Acoustic Aspects of Speech. *Logos. 5*, 1962, 3–17.

Studdert-Kennedy, M., Speech Perception. In *Contemporary Issues in Experimental Phonetics*. N. J. Lass (Ed.) Springfield, Ill.: Charles C Thomas, 1975, pp. 243–293.

Hearing

Durrant, J. D., and Lovrinic, J. H., *Bases of Hearing Science*. Baltimore: The Williams and Wilkins Co., 1977.

Fletcher, H., *Speech and Hearing in Communication*. Princeton, N. J.: Van Nostrand, 1953. First published as *Speech and Hearing* in 1929.

Geldard, F. A., *The Human Senses*. New York: Wiley & Sons, 1953.

Helmholtz, H. L. F., *On the Sensations of Tone*. New York: Dover, 1961. Reprint of translation by A. J. Ellis, London: Longmans, Green and Co., 1875.

Kiang, N. Y. S., and Moxon, E. C., Tails of Tuning Curves of Auditory-Nerve Fibers. *J. Acoust. Soc. Am. 55*, 1974, 620–630.

Stevens, S. S. (Ed.), *Handbook of Experimental Psychology*. New York: Wiley & Sons, 1951.

Stevens, S. S., and Davis, H., *Hearing*. New York: Wiley & Sons, 1938.

Van Bergeijk, W. A., Pierce, J. R., and David, E. E., Jr., *Waves and the Ear*. London: Heinemann, 1961.

Von Békésy, G., *Experiments in Hearing*. New York: McGraw-Hill, 1960.

Wever, E. G., and Lawrence, M., *Physiological Acoustics*. Princeton, N. J.: University Press, 1954.

Acoustic Cues

Vowels, Diphthongs, and Semivowels

Carlson, R., Fant, G., and Granstrom, B., Two-Formant Models, Pitch, and Vowel Perception. In *Auditory Analysis and Perception of Speech*. G. Fant and M. A. A. Tatham (Eds.) New York: Academic Press, 1975, pp. 55–82.

Delattre, P., Liberman, A. M., Cooper, F. S., and Gerstman, L. J., An Experimental Study of the Acoustic Determinants of Vowel Color: Observations on One- and Two-Formant Vowels Synthesized from Spectrographic Patterns. *Word. 8*, 1952, 195–210.

Fant, G., A Note on Vocal Tract Size Factors and Non-Uniform F-Pattern Scalings. *Q. Prog. Status Rep. Speech Transmission Lab. 4*, 1966, 22–30.

Fry, D. B., Abramson, A. S., Eimas, P. D., and Liberman, A. M., The Identification and Discrimination of Synthetic Vowels. *Lang. Speech. 5*, 1962, 171–189.

Gay, T., A Perceptual Study of American English Diphthongs. *Lang. Speech. 13*, 1970, 65–88.

Gerstman, L. J., Classification of Self-Normalized Vowels. *IEEE Trans. Aud. Electroacoust. AU. 16*, 1968, 78–80.

Joos, M. A., Acoustic Phonetics. *Language. Suppl. 24*, 1948, 1–136.

Ladefoged, P., and Broadbent, D. E., Information Conveyed by Vowels. *J. Acoust. Soc. Am. 39*, 1957, 98–104.

Lieberman, P., On the Evolution of Language: A Unified View. *Cognition. 2*, 1973, 59–94.

Lindblom, B. E. F., and Studdert-Kennedy, M., On the Role of Formant Transitions in Vowel Recognition. *J. Acoust. Soc. Am. 42*, 1967, 830–843.

Lisker, L., Minimal Cues for Separating /w,r,l,y/ in Intervocalic Position. *Word. 13*, 1957, 256–267.

Nordström, P.-E., and Lindblom, B., A Normalization Procedure for Vowel Formant Data. Paper Presented at 8th International Congress of Phonetic Sciences, Leeds, England, August, 1975.

O'Connor, J. D., Gerstman, L. J., Liberman, A. M., Delattre, P. C., and Cooper, F. S., Acoustic Cues for the Perception of Initial /w,j,r,l/ in English. *Word. 13*, 1957, 22–43.

Strange, W., Verbrugge, R. R., Shankweiler, D. P., and Edman, T. R., Consonant Environment Specifies Vowel Identity. *J. Acoust. Soc. Am. 60*, 1976, 213–221.

Verbrugge, R. R., Strange, W., Shankweiler, D. P., and Edman, T. R., What Information Enables a Listener to Map a Talker's Vowel Space? *J. Acoust. Soc. Am. 60*, 1976, 198–212.

Nasals, Stops, Fricatives, and Affricates

Ali, L., Gallagher, T., Goldstein, J., and Daniloff, R., Perception of Coarticulated Nasality. *J. Acoust. Soc. Am. 49*, 1971, 538–540.

Cooper, F. S., Delattre, P. C., Liberman, A. M., Borst, J. M., and Gerstman, L. J., Some Experiments on the Perception of Synthetic Speech Sounds. *J. Acoust. Soc. Am. 24*, 1952, 597–606.

Delattre, P. C., Liberman, A. M., and Cooper, F. S., Acoustic Loci and Transitional Cues for Consonants. *J. Acoust. Soc. Am. 27*, 1955, 769–773.

Denes, P., Effect of Duration on the Perception of Voicing. *J. Acoust. Soc. Am. 27*, 1955, 761–764.

Harris, K. S., Cues for the Discrimination of American English Fricatives in Spoken Syllables. *Lang. Speech. 1*, 1958, 1–7.

House, A. S., Analog Studies of Nasal Consonants. *J. Speech Hear. Disord. 22*, 1957, 190–204.

Kuhn, G. M., On the Front Cavity Resonance and its

Possible Role in Speech Perception. *J. Acoust. Soc. Am. 58*, 1975, 428–433.

Liberman, A. M., Delattre, P. C., and Cooper, F. S., The Role of Selected Stimulus-Variables in the Perception of the Unvoiced Stop Consonants. *Am. J. Psychol. LXV*, 1952, 497–516.

Liberman, A. M., Delattre, P. C., and Cooper, F. S., Some Rules for the Distinction between Voiced and Voiceless Stops in Initial Position. *Lang. Speech. 1*, 1958, 153–167.

Liberman, A. M., Delattre, P. C., Cooper, F. S., and Gerstman, L. J., The Role of Consonant-Vowel Transitions in the Perception of the Stop and Nasal Consonants. *Psychol. Monogr. (Gen. Appl.) 68*, 1954, 1–13.

Liberman, A. M., Delattre, P. C., Gerstman, L. J., and Cooper, F. S., Tempo of Frequency Change as a Cue for Distinguishing Classes of Speech Sounds. *J. Exp. Psychol. 52*, 1956, 127–137.

Liberman, A. M., Harris, K. S., Eimas, P., Lisker, L., and Bastian, J., An Effect of Learning on Speech Perception: The Discrimination of Durations of Silence with and without Phonemic Significance. *Lang. Speech. 4*, 1961, 175–195.

Lisker, L., and Abramson, A. S., A Cross-Language Study of Voicing in Initial Stops: Acoustical Measurements. *Word. 20*, 1964, 384–422.

Malécot, A., Acoustic Cues for Nasal Consonants. *Language. 32*, 1956, 274–278.

Mermelstein, P., On Detecting Nasals in Continuous Speech. *J. Acoust. Soc. Am. 61*, 1977, 581–587.

Miller, G. A., and Nicely, P. E., An Analysis of Perceptual Confusions among Some English Consonants. *J. Acoust. Soc. Am. 27*, 1955, 338–352.

Raphael, L. J., Preceding Vowel Duration as a Cue to the Perception of the Voicing Characteristic of Word-Final Consonants in American English. *J. Acoust. Soc. Am. 51*, 1972, 1296–1303.

Raphael, L. J., and Dorman, M. F., Perceptual Equivalence of Cues for the Fricative-Affricate Contrast. *J. Acoust. Soc. Am. 61*, 1977, S45 (A).

Suprasegmentals

Bolinger, D. W., and Gerstman, L. J., Disjuncture as a Cue to Constructs. *Word. 13*, 1957, 246–255.

Fry, D. B., Experiments in the Perception of Stress. *Lang. Speech. 1*, 1958, 126–152.

Fry, D. B., Prosodic Phenomena. In *Manual of Phonetics*. B. Malmberg (Ed.) Amsterdam: North-Holland Publication Co., 1968, pp. 365–410.

Hadding-Koch, K., and Studdert-Kennedy, M., An Experimental Study of Some Intonation Contours. *Phonetica. 11*, 1964, 175–185.

Lehiste, I., *Suprasegmentals*. Cambridge, Mass: M. I. T. Press, 1970.

Categorical Perception

Adults

Abramson, A. S., and Lisker, L., Voice-Timing Perception in Spanish Word-Initial Stops. *J. Phonetics. 1*, 1973, 1–8.

Elman, J. L., Diehl, R. L., and Buchwald, S. E., Perceptual Switching in Bilinguals. *J. Acoust. Soc. Am. 62*, 1977, 991–994.

Fry, D., Abramson, A., Eimas, P., and Liberman, A. M., The Identification and Discrimination of Synthetic Vowels. *Lang. Speech. 5*, 1962, 171–189.

Fujisaki, H., and Kawashima, T., Some Experiments on Speech Perception and a Model for the Perceptual Mechanism. *Annu. Rep. Res. Inst. (Tokyo Univ.) 29*, 1970, 207–214.

Liberman, A. M., Harris, K. S., Hoffman, H. S., and Griffith, B. C., The Discrimination of Speech Sounds within and across Phoneme Boundaries. *J. Exp. Psychol. 54*, 1957, 358–368.

Lisker, L., and Abramson, A. S., A Cross-Language Study of Voicing in Initial Stops: Acoustical Measurements. *Word. 20*, 1964, 384–422.

Miyawaki, K., Strange, W., Verbrugge, R. R., Liberman, A. M., Jenkins, J. J., and Fujimura, O., An Effect of Linguistic Experience: The Discrimination of [r] and [l] by Native Speakers of Japanese and English. *Percept. Psychophys. 18*, 1975, 331–340.

Stevens, K. N., Liberman, A. M., Studdert-Kennedy, M., and Öhman, S., Cross-language Study of Vowel Perception. *Lang. Speech. 12*, 1969, 1–23.

Strange, W., and Jenkins, J. J., The Role of Linguistic Experience in the Perception of Speech. In *Perception and Experience*. R. D. Walk and H. L. Pick (Eds.) New York: Plenum Press, 1978, pp. 125–169.

Infants and Animals

Eimas, P. D., Speech Perception in Early Infancy. In *Infant Perception*. L. B. Cohen and P. Salapatek (Eds.) New York: Academic Press, 1975, pp. 193–231.

Eimas, P. D., Siqueland, E. R., Jusczyk, P., and Vigorito, J., Speech Perception in Infants. *Science. 171*, 1971, 303–306.

Jusczyk, P. W., Perception of Syllable-Final Stop Consonants by Two-Month-Old Infants. *Percept. Psychophys. 21*, 1977, 450–454.

Kuhl, P. K., and Miller, J. D., Speech Perception by the Chinchilla: Voiced-Voiceless Distinction in Alveolar Plosive Consonants. *Science. 190*, 1975, 69–72.

Morse, P. A., Infant Speech Perception: A Preliminary Model and Review of the Literature. In *Language Perspectives: Acquisition, Retardation, and Intervention*. R. L. Schiefelbush and L. L. Lloyd (Eds.) Baltimore: University Park Press, 1974, pp. 19–53.

Morse, P. A., Speech Perception in the Human Infant and the Rhesus Monkey. Conference on Origins and Evolution of Language and Speech. *Ann. N. Y. Acad. Sci. 280*, 1976, 694–707.

Morse, P. A., and Snowdon, C. T., An Investigation of Categorical Speech Discrimination by Rhesus Monkeys. *Percept. Psychophys. 17*, 1975, 9–16.

Waters, R. S., and Wilson, W. A., Jr., Speech Perception by Rhesus Monkeys: The Voicing Distinction in Synthesized Labial and Velar Stop Consonants. *Percept. Psychophys. 19*, 1976, 285–289.

Auditory and Phonetic Analysis

Carney, A. E., and Widin, G. P., Acoustic Discrimination within Phonetic Categories. *J. Acoust. Soc. Am. 59*, 1976, S25 (A).

Cutting, J., and Rosner, B. S., Categories and Boundaries in Speech and Music. *Percept. Psychophys. 16*, 1974, 564–570.

Eimas, P. D., and Corbit, J. D., Selective Adaptation of Linguistic Feature Detectors. *Cognitive Psychol. 4*, 1973, 99–109.

Pisoni, D. B., and Lazarus, J. H., Categorical and Noncategorical Modes of Speech Perception along the Voicing Continuum. *J. Acoust. Soc. Am. 55*, 1974, 328–333.

Strange, W., The Effects of Training on the Perception of Synthetic Speech Sounds: Voice Onset Time. Unpublished doctoral dissertation, University of Minnesota, 1972.

Perception and Learning

Bremer, C. D., Discrimination and Identification of Synthetic Speech by a Child Exhibiting Voicing Confusions in Production. Paper presented at ASA meeting, Washington, D. C., 1976.

Simon, C., and Fourcin, A. J., Cross-language Study of Speech-pattern Learning. *J. Acoust. Soc. Am. 63*, 1978, 925–935.

Stevens, K. N., and Klatt, D. H., Role of Formant Transitions in the Voiced-Voiceless Distinction for Stops. *J. Acoust. Soc. Am. 55*, 1974, 653–659.

Williams, L., Speech Perception and Production as a Function of Exposure to a Second Language. Unpublished doctoral dissertation, Harvard University, 1974.

Zlatin, M. A., and Koenigsknecht, R. A., Development of the Voicing Contrast: Perception of Stop Consonants. *J. Speech Hear. Res. 18*, 1975, 541–553.

Production and Perception

Aungst, L. F., and Frick, J. V., Auditory Discriminability and Consistency of Articulation of /r/. *J. Speech Hear. Disord. 29*, 1964, 76–85.

Borden, G. J., Use of Feedback in Established and Developing Speech. In *Speech and Language: Advances in Basic Research and Practice*. Vol. IV, N. J. Lass (Ed.) New York: Academic Press (in press).

Goehl, H., and Golden, S., A Psycholinguistic Account of Why Children Do Not Detect their own Errors. Paper presented at ASHA meeting, Detroit, 1972.

Goto, H., Auditory Perception by Normal Japanese Adults of the Sounds 'L' and 'R.' *Neuropsychologia. 9*, 1971, 317–323.

Kornfeld, J. R., What Initial Clusters Tell Us About the Child's Speech Code. *Q. Prog. Rep. Res. Lab. Electron. M. I. T. 101*, 1971, 218–221.

Locke, J. L., and Kutz, K. J., Memory for Speech and Speech for Memory. *J. Speech Hear. Res. 18*, 1975, 176–191.

McReynolds, L. V., Kohn, J., and Williams, G. C., Articulatory-Defective Children's Discrimination of their Production Errors. *J. Speech Hear. Disord. 40*, 1975, 327–338.

Menyuk, P., and Anderson, S., Children's Identification and Reproduction of /w/, /r/ and /l/. *J. Speech Hear. Res. 12*, 1969, 39–52.

Neurophysiology of Speech Perception

Berlin, C., Hemispheric Asymmetry in Auditory Tasks. In *Contemporary Issues in Experimental Phonetics*. N. J. Lass (Ed.) New York: Academic Press, 1976.

Cutting, J. E., A Parallel between Encodedness and the Ear Advantage: Evidence from an Ear-Monitoring Task. *J. Acoust. Soc. Am. 53*, 1973, 358 (A).

Darwin, C. J., Ear Differences in the Recall of Fricatives and Vowels. *Q. J. Exp. Psychol. 23*, 1971, 46–62.

Darwin, C. J., Dichotic Backward Masking of Complex Sounds. *Q. J. Exp. Psychol. 23*, 1971, 386–392.

Day, R. S., and Vigorito, J. M., A Parallel between Encodedness and the Ear Advantage: Evidence from a Temporal-Order Judgment Task. *J. Acoust. Soc. Am. 53*, 1973, 358 (A).

Gardner, H., *The Shattered Mind.* Westminster, Md.: Knopf, 1975.

Gazzaniga, M. S., and Sperry, R. W., Language after Section of the Cerebral Commissures. *Brain. 90*, 1967, 131–148.

Godfrey, J. J., Perceptual Difficulty and the Right Ear Advantage for Vowels. *Brain Lang. 4*, 1974, 323–336.

Goodglass, H., and Geschwind, N., Language Disorders (Aphasia). In *Handbook of Perception, Vol. 7: Language and Speech.* E. C. Carterette and M. P. Friedman (Eds.) New York: Academic Press, 1976, pp. 389–428.

Kimura, D., Cerebral Dominance and the Perception of Verbal Stimuli. *Can. J. Psychol. 15*, 1961, 166–171.

Kimura, D., Functional Asymmetry of the Brain in Dichotic Listening. *Cortex. 3*, 1967, 163–178.

Lenneberg, E. H., *Biological Foundations of Language.* New York: Wiley & Sons, 1967.

Milner, B. (Ed.), *Hemisphere Specialization and Interaction.* Cambridge, Mass.: M. I. T. Press, 1975.

Penfield, W. L., and Roberts, L., *Speech and Brain Mechanisms.* Princeton, N. J.: Princeton University Press, 1959.

Pisoni, D. B., and McNabb, S. D., Dichotic Interactions of Speech Sounds and Phonetic Feature Processing. *Brain Lang. 4*, 1974, 351–362.

Shankweiler, D. P., and Studdert-Kennedy, M., Identification of Consonants and Vowels Presented to Left and Right Ears. *Q. J. Exp. Psychol. 19*, 1967, 59–63.

Sperry, R. W., and Gazzaniga, M. S., Language Following Surgical Disconnection of the Hemispheres. In *Brain Mechanisms Underlying Speech and Language.* C. H. Millikan and F. L. Darley (Eds.) 1967,

New York: Grune and Stratton, pp. 108–121.

Studdert-Kennedy, M., and Shankweiler, D. P., Hemispheric Specialization for Speech Perception. *J. Acoust. Soc. Am. 48*, 1970, 579–594.

Warren, R. M., Verbal Transformation Effect and Auditory Perceptual Mechanisms. *Psychol. Bull. 70*, 1968, 261–270.

Weiss, M., and House, A. S., Perception of Dichotically Presented Vowels. *J. Acoust. Soc. Am. 53*, 1973, 51–58.

Wernicke, C. *Der aphasische Symptomencomplex.* Breslau: Franck and Weigert, 1874.

Whitaker, H. A., Neurobiology of Language. In *Handbook of Speech Perception, Vol. 7: Language and Speech*. E. C. Carterette and M. P. Friedman (Eds.) New York: Academic Press, 1976, pp. 389–428.

Wood, C. C., Auditory and Phonetic Levels of Processing in Speech Perception: Neurophysiological and Information-Processing Analysis. *J. Exp. Psychol. (Hum. Percept.) 104*, 1975, 3–20.

Wood, C. C., Goff, W. R., and Day, R. S., Auditory Evoked Potentials during Speech Perception. *Science. 173*, 1971, 1248–1251.

Zaidel, E., Linguistic Competence and Related Functions in the Right Cerebral Hemisphere of Man. Unpublished doctoral dissertation, Calif. Institute of Technology, 1973.

Memory and Speech Perception

Cole, R. A., Different Memory Functions for Consonants and Vowels. *Cognitive Psychol. 4*, 1973, 39–54.

Crowder, R. G., Visual and Auditory Memory. In *Language by Ear and Eye; The Relationships between Speech and Reading*. J. F. Kavanagh and I. G. Mattingly (Eds.) Cambridge, Mass.: M. I. T. Press, 1972, pp. 251–275.

Crowder, R. G., and Morton, J., Precategorical Acoustic Storage (PAS). *Percept. Psychophys. 5*, 1969, 365–373.

Darwin, C. J., and Baddeley, A. D., Acoustic Memory and the Perception of Speech. *Cognitive Psychol. 6*, 1974, 41–60.

Massaro, D. W., Preperceptual Images, Processing Time, and Perceptual Units in Auditory Perception. *Psychol. Rev. 79*, 1972, 124–145.

Norman, D. A., *Memory and Attention.* New York: Wiley & Sons, 1969.

Studdert-Kennedy, M., Shankweiler, D. P., and Schulman, S., Opposed Effects of a Delayed Channel on Perception of Dichotically and Monotically Presented CV Syllables. *J. Acoust. Soc. Am. 48*, 1970, 599–602.

Theories of Speech Perception

Abbs, J. H., and Sussman, H. M., Neurophysiological Feature Detectors and Speech Perception: A Discussion of Theoretical Implications. *J. Speech Hear. Res. 14*, 1971, 23–36.

Ades, A. E., How Phonetic is Selective Adaptation?

Experiments on Syllable Position and Environment. *Percept. Psychophys. 16*, 1974, 61–66.

Bailey, P., Perceptual Adaptation for Acoustical Features in Speech. *Speech Perception Report on Speech Research in Progress.* Series 2, Belfast: Psychology Department, The Queens University, 1973, pp. 29–34.

Chistovich, L. A., Klass, V. A., and Kuzmin, Y. I., The Process of Speech Sound Discrimination. *Vopr. Psikhol. 8*, 1962, 26–39.

Cole, R. A., and Scott, B., Toward a Theory of Speech Perception. *Psychol. Rev. 81*, 1974, 348–374.

Cooper, W. E., Adaptation of Phonetic Feature Analyzers for Place of Articulation. *J. Acoust. Soc. Am. 56*, 1974, 617–627.

Cooper, W. E., and Blumstein, S., A 'Labial' Feature Analyzer in Speech Perception. *Percept. Psychophys. 15*, 1974, 591–600.

Dorman, M. F., Raphael, L. J., and Liberman, A. M., Some Experiments on the Sound of Silence in Phonetic Perception. *J. Acoust. Soc. Am. 65*, 1979, 1518–1532.

Fant, G., Auditory Patterns of Speech. *Models for the Perception of Speech and Visual Form.* W. Wathen-Dunn (Ed.) Cambridge, Mass.: M. I. T. Press, 1967, pp. 111–125.

Lane, H. L., The Motor Theory of Speech Perception: A Critical Review. *Psychol. Rev. 72*, 1965, 275–309.

Liberman, A. M., The Grammars of Speech and Language. *Cognitive Psychol. 1*, 1970, 301–323.

Liberman, A. M., Cooper, F. S., Shankweiler, D. S., and Studdert-Kennedy, M., Perception of the Speech Code. *Psychol. Rev. 74*, 1967, 431–461.

Marler, P., A Comparative Approach to Vocal Development: Song Learning in the White-crowned Sparrow. *J. Comp. Physiol. Psychol. 71*, 1970, 1–25.

Morton, J., and Broadbent, D. E., Passive *versus* Active Recognition Models or Is Your Homunculus Really Necessary? In *Models for the Perception of Speech and Visual Form.* W. Wathen-Dunn (Ed.) Cambridge, Mass.: M. I. T. Press, 1967, pp. 103–110.

Pisoni, D. B., and Sawusch, J. R. Some Stages of Processing in Speech Perception. In *Structure and Process in Speech Perception.* A. Cohen and S. G. Nooteboom (Eds.) Berlin: Springer-Verlag, 1975, pp. 16–34.

Stevens, K. N., The Quantal Nature of Speech: Evidence from Articulatory-Acoustic Data. In *Human Communication: A Unified View.* E. E. David, Jr. and P. B. Denes (Eds.) New York: McGraw-Hill, 1972, pp. 51–66.

Stevens, K. N., Further Theoretical and Experimental Bases for Quantal Places of Articulation for Consonants. *Q. Prog. Rep. Res. Lab. Electron. M. I. T. 108*, 1973, 248–252.

Stevens, K. N., and Halle, M., Remarks on Analysis by Synthesis and Distinctive Features. In *Models for the Perception of Speech and Visual Form.* W. Wathen-Dunn (Ed.) Cambridge, Mass.: M. I. T. Press, 1967, pp. 88–102.

Stevens, K. N., and House, A. S., Speech Perception. In *Foundations of Modern Auditory Theory. Vol. 2,* J. Tobias (Ed.) New York: Academic Press, 1972, pp. 3–57.

Stevens, K. N., and Perkell, J. S., Speech Physiology and Phonetic Features. In *Dynamic Aspects of Speech Production.* M. Sawashima and F. S. Cooper (Eds.) Tokyo: University of Tokyo Press, 1977, pp. 323–341.

Studdert-Kennedy, M., Liberman, A. M., Harris, K. S., and Cooper, F. S., Motor Theory of Speech Perception: A Reply to Lane's Critical Review. *Psychol. Rev. 77,* 1970, 234–249.

Whitfield, I. C., and Evans, E. F., Responses of Auditory Cortical Neurons to Stimuli of Changing Frequency. *J. Neurophysiol. 28,* 1965, 655–672.

CHAPTER 6

Research Tools in Speech Science

To know that we know what we know, and that we do not
know what we do not know, that is true knowledge.

Thoreau, *Walden* (quoting Confucius)

The purpose of research is to find answers to questions about ourselves and the world about us. This goal may never be perfectly attained, however, because the results of research must filter through our perceptions of them and are at best only abstractions of reality. Yet the process of research is the study of parts of complex phenomena with the aim of uniting the parts with better understanding. There are several ways of seeking answers to questions, two of which—observation and experimentation—are used in the study of phonetics.

OBSERVATIONAL AND EXPERIMENTAL RESEARCH

The observation method is based on the recording of events in order to systematize relationships. In the experimental method, relationships are observed under controlled conditions in which experimental variables are systematically changed by the experimenter.

An example of research based upon data collection by observation is the mapping of physiological functions by recording them. For example, the researcher who is interested in the factors controlling fundamental frequency in speech measures fundamental frequency, the output of a number of laryngeal muscles, and subglottal air pressure. The physiological parameters can then be correlated to the acoustic output. Relationships such as that of cricothyroid muscle activity to fundamental frequency of voicing can be observed. In another example, sound spectrograms can be examined to relate formant and noise patterns to contrasting phonetic features, such as the difference in high frequency ranges for /ʃ/ and /s/ friction in different vowel contexts.

The experimental method may be used in the study of physiological phonetics. A typical experiment might be the following: speech utterances produced normally (the *control* condition) are compared to the same utterances under an *experimental* condition, such as oral anesthetization, in order to observe the effects of the desensitization on speech. In this example, the *dependent variable* (the parameter observed for any changes) is the speech, and the *independent variable* (the parameter which the investigator manipulates) is the presence or absence of anesthetization.

The use of the experimental method is common in studies of speech perception. By controlling the frequency pattern, intensity, and timing of synthetic speech stimuli, changes can be introduced to find out what perceptual effects they may produce in listeners. Similarly, normal speech stimuli can be used in speech perception experiments. The independent variable might be the insertion of clicks into recorded speech, the deletion of parts of the message, or distortion of the signal. In such experimental designs, the way in which speech sounds are perceived after the manipulations would be the dependent variable.

When a research tool becomes available to researchers, as it did with the advent of the sound spectrograph and more recently with electromyography, there is a period of time in which research tends to be observational, for example, relating the acoustic patterns in spectrograms or the muscle activity patterns in EMG recordings to the features, phones, or syllables of speech. Usually, the period of mapping results in theories or models which are then tested by extracting from the more general theory a testable hypothesis and designing an experiment to test it. As more information becomes available, the model or theory is refined. Thus, observational and experimental research complement one another. Research in phonetics involves systematic study of the physiology of speech production, the acoustics of the speech signal, and the perception by listeners of the sounds of speech.

SOME INSTRUMENTS

Speech scientists must know how to take advantage of the many instruments appropriate for speech research. In general, the instrumental arrays can be divided into two set-ups: one for output analysis of the acoustics or physiology of speech, and the other for input analysis, for gathering responses of listeners in speech perception research. Figure 6.1 schematizes the basic instrumentation often used for speech output analysis. The speaker is recorded in various ways. The possibilities include recording the acoustic signal, articulator movement, or other physiological events such as air pressure or muscle activity. Recorded signals may be modified by amplifiers, attenuators, filters, and integrators, or can be digitized and averaged by computer before being displayed. Signal variations are sometimes displayed on meters or on oscilloscope monitors that are similar to television screens. More permanent is some form of "hard copy," a term for data on pieces of paper which can be analyzed after the experiment. Ink plotters, X-Y plotters, photography, either still or cinematic, and sound spectrographs produce hard copy. Cinefluorography of speech is a research method which depends upon a complex output array of instruments. The recorder is a motion picture camera, recording X-ray images of a speaker's vocal tract from an image intensifier which modifies the X-ray image by increasing the contrast between parts of it. The developed film is the display, which can be transformed to drawings via frame-by-frame analysis of the film. Alternatively, a single marked point on an articulator can be followed from frame to frame and graphed on a computer monitor, from which a hard copy can be made.

Acoustic Phonetics

Instruments used to analyze the sounds of speech are available in most college departments offering programs in speech and hearing studies, even those that have little equipment for studying the physiology of speech production. The use of tape recorders and oscilloscopes is almost universal and the sound spectrograph is increasingly familiar.

Recording Speech

Many of us are meticulous in our choice, calibration, and use of instruments for speech analysis, yet careless in the way we record the speech itself. The goal in tape recording is to capture a clear speech signal with little or no distortion and a low level of background noise. The location for making the recording is an extremely important consideration. An acoustically shielded booth with sound absorbent walls, (as pictured in Fig. 6.2) in which the speaker sits in front of the microphone with the door closed is ideal. If an acoustically shielded booth is not available, it is often sufficient to record speech in a quiet room, one with acoustic tiles, rugs, or other materials which absorb sound, and to record during the quietest time of day. A room in the core of a building is sometimes quieter than a room on a busy street, unless, of course, it is next to an elevator.

Microphones are responsive to pressure waves and convert the pressure variations

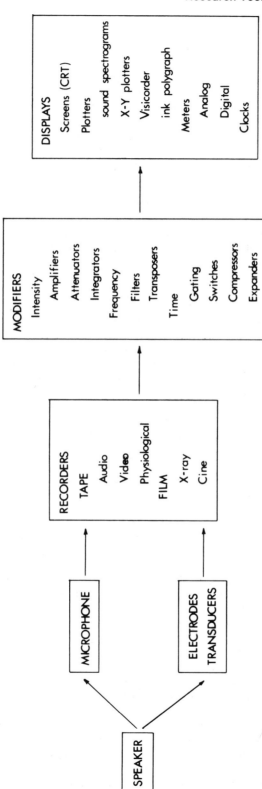

Figure 6.1. Instrumentation for speech production analysis.

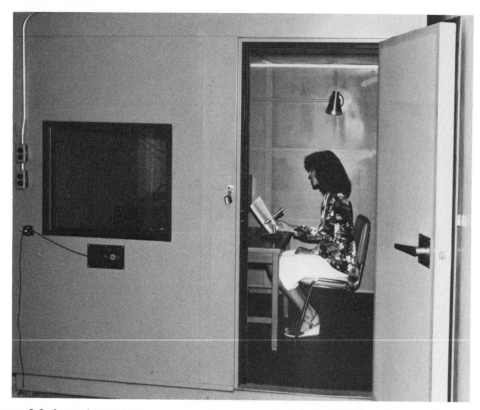

Figure 6.2. A speaker making a recording in an acoustically shielded booth (Temple University).

into time-varying electrical signals. The signals are fed to the recording head of a tape recorder, where the signal alters the magnetic field and thus lays down a pattern on the metallic oxide coating of plastic audio tape. The choice of microphone is also important. A unidirectional microphone placed several centimeters from the lips of the speaker transmits a higher signal-to-noise ratio than a multidirectional microphone that is responsive equally to the speaker and to sounds coming from other directions in the room. The tape recorder (Fig. 6.3) should transport the tape smoothly, have efficient and clean erase, record, and playback heads, and should incorporate an appropriate intensity meter.

The VU meter (volume unit) on many tape recorders is not ideal for measuring running speech because it does not respond rapidly enough to the wide intensity variation in such signals. Therefore, it is wise to keep the VU meter pointer a bit below the red area for the vowel peaks.

Too much amplification, or overloading, while recording exceeds the limitations of the recorder. The high amplitude peaks will be clipped off, resulting in a distorted signal.

There is usually a choice of tape speeds on a tape recorder. For example, the transport mechanism can pull 7.5 inches of the tape across the heads during 1 sec or only 3.75 inches per sec. The faster speed is preferred, because less tape noise is picked up when the tape passes the heads quickly.

Tape widths vary in different types of recorders. Tapes for cassette recorders are generally narrower and thinner than the tapes used in reel-to-reel recorders. The extent of the record on the tape depends upon the type of recording head on the recorder. A full-track recorder uses the whole width of the tape to lay down the signal; a half-track recorder uses one-half of the tape for each channel, or, if there is only one channel, for each direction (you can turn the tape over and record on the other half). A quarter-track recorder uses one-half of the tape for one channel (in both directions) and the other half for the other half for the other channel (in both directions). A brief inspection of Figure 6.4 will reveal the disastrous effects of making field recordings on a quarter-track tape recorder and trying later to dub the master tape or to analyze it by playing it back on a half- or full-track laboratory recorder.

If signals are recorded at high intensity and the tape is wound tightly on the reel, the signals on one section of tape can affect the magnetic field of a section of tape pressed against it, causing print-

Figure 6.3. A reel-to-reel tape recorder (Temple University).

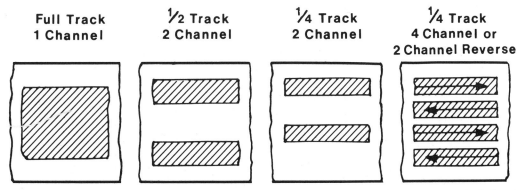

Figure 6.4. Some common tape arrangements. Each segment shows the arrangement of signal laid down on tape by the indicated head arrangement.

through. In playing back a tape which has printed through, the listener hears the original recording and, at one revolution of the reel, an echo of it. Using the "fast-forward" or "fast-rewind" options results in a tightly wound reel with greater chance for print-through. To avoid print-through, one can use thicker tape (1.5 mil should be adequate), record at lower intensity, and store the tape on the take-up reel after playback. (It is prudent to label stored tapes "rewind before using" to avoid frustration to other listeners.)

Waveform Analysis

One way to make sound waves visible for analysis is to use an instrument called an *oscilloscope* to display their wave-

forms. An oscilloscope (Fig. 6.5) can display any time-varying signal which has been converted into current or voltage variations. A narrow beam of electrons from a cathode ray tube (CRT) strikes against a screen. For displaying speech, the beam can be made to sweep across the screen and the speech signal—input either from a microphone or tape recorder—deflects the beam, to form an amplitude by time display. Figure 6.6 is a Polaroid picture taken from a *storage oscilloscope,* a special type of oscilloscope which will store and display a recorded waveform. If the investigator makes a permanent record of this sort from a storage oscilloscope, he can later make measurements of signal duration or amplitude. A storage oscilloscope

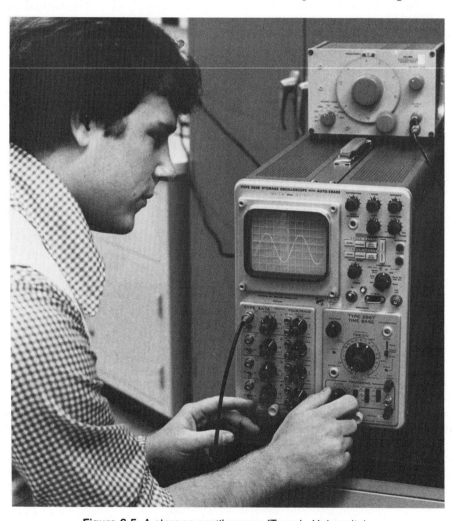

Figure 6.5. A storage oscilloscope (Temple University).

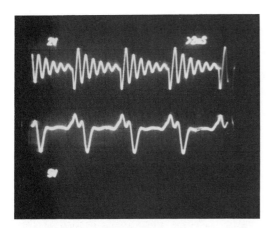

Figure 6.6. Hard copy from storage oscilloscope (Haskins Laboratories).

is not only appropriate for displaying the acoustic signal, but also for air pressure and flow, as recorded from the oral cavity, nasal cavity, or at the lips, transduced movement of articulators, electromyographic signals (EMG), brain waves (EEG), or any time-varying signal which has been transformed into electrical variation by microphones, transducers, or electrodes.

The frequency of periodic waveforms can be computed by measuring the period, the time in seconds taken for one cycle, and dividing 1 sec by the period. If, for example, the period of a signal is 5 msec (0.005 sec), its frequency would be 200 Hz.

$$f = \frac{1}{T} = \frac{1.000 \text{ sec}}{0.005 \text{ sec}} = 200 \text{ Hz}$$

Thus, the fundamental frequency of complex periodic waveforms typical of vowels can be established from an oscilloscope display. However, the other frequency components in complex periodic waves and the many frequency components in aperiodic speech signals are not easily measured from oscilloscope displays, because the waveform displayed is an *interference pattern*. An interference pattern is the sum of many different frequencies, having different amplitudes and phase relations. It would be difficult to quickly determine the component frequencies from this waveform alone. They can be determined however, by techniques to be described in the next section.

There are two other commonly used ways of displaying speech waveforms, both of which are essentially like oscilloscope displays. One way is to put the signals into a plotter, a device using pens or light beams to mark the waveform on paper moving at a constant speed. Figure 6.7 shows a Visicorder display of waveforms generated by transporting expensive light-sensitive paper under a vibrating light beam that is responsive to the electrical variations of the signal. Conventional pen writers use less expensive paper, but because of mechanical limitations, are apt to function poorly at the high speeds needed for speech analysis. The discussion above assumes that we are interested in the most rapid speech events, such as individual pitch periods. If we are interested in relatively slow events, for example, syllable to syllable changes in intensity, we can use a plotter called a *graphic level recorder* which will not respond to very rapid fluctuations in signal (Fig. 6.8). Of course, there are many more complex techniques for waveform analysis which require computer-processing.

Spectral Analysis

Most sounds, and certainly speech is among them, are complex, having more than a single frequency present in the signal. If an investigator wants information on the distribution of energy at various frequencies, the signal can be filtered to separate the component frequencies of complex signals into a spectral display. A spectrum, you recall, is a graphic display of the amplitude of each sine wave component. It is a frequency-by-amplitude display, with frequency represented along the abscissa and intensity on the ordinate axis. A *real time spectral analyzer* (Fig. 6.9) is an instrument which displays, on a CRT, the changing spectra of complex signals. Sound can be input from a microphone or a tape recorder. The investigator can set the spectral analyzer to display the frequencies of interest by specifying the center frequency and the range. A bank of filters separates the signal into components. A note played on a narrowly tuned musical instrument might result in a spectrum with energy at very few frequencies

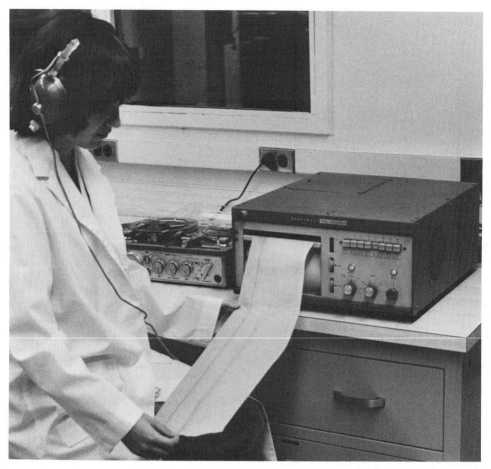

Figure 6.7. A Visicorder (Temple University).

(Fig. 6.10), while a broadly tuned instrument such as the human voice, generates a spectrum with energy at many frequencies between 100 and 4000 Hz. When the spectrum under study is fairly steady, as, for example, the sound inside a subway car, the spectrum can be photographed from the screen of the oscilloscope or averaged over a span of time with a computer. The broadly tuned speech resonators are quickly damped. Because it is difficult to follow the constantly changing spectrum of speech in real time with any precision, a spectral analyzer coupled to a storage oscilloscope is useful for stopping the action. Thus, the spectrum can be held for display for making measurements.

The development, in the 1940s, of an instrument designed especially to display the spectrum of speech, the *sound spectrograph* (Fig. 6.11), was revolutionary. Since spectra are constantly changing in running

speech, this instrument was designed to show energy peaks in the spectra as a function of time. The usual design of a sound spectrograph includes a system to record acoustic signals on a loop or on a drum, a system to play back the recorded signal over and over, and a filter system to scan the playback output in successive frequency bands. The energy in each frequency band is recorded on specially coated paper by a stylus which burns marks on the paper proportional to the signal intensity. High intensity sound produces a darker mark, lower intensity a lighter mark, and little or no intensity in a particular filter band results in an area of unmarked paper. The filter changes its center frequency, from low to high frequencies, scanning the recorded sample repeatedly. On the finished spectrogram, the output of the filter at the lowest frequencies is represented at the bottom of

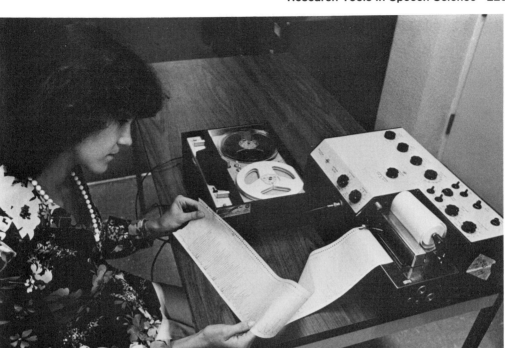

Figure 6.8. A graphic level recorder (Temple University).

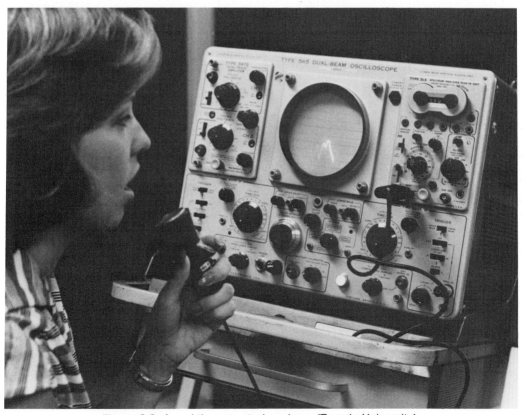

Figure 6.9. A real time spectral analyzer (Temple University).

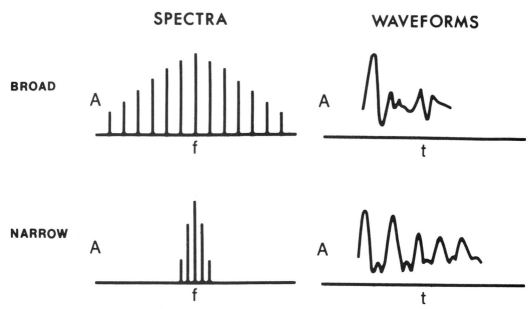

Figure 6.10. Broadly and narrowly tuned resonators produce spectra with different numbers of frequency components. The waveforms show that broadly tuned resonators are quickly damped compared to narrowly tuned resonators.

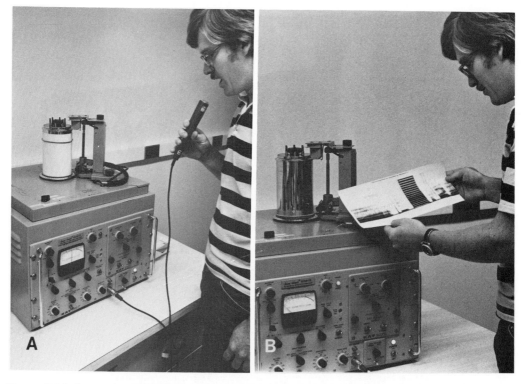

Figure 6.11. A sound spectrograph. (*A*) The speech is first recorded, then the recording is filtered to produce a spectrogram (*B*) (Temple University).

the y axis, while the highest frequency information appears at the top. Figure 6.12 shows a typical *spectrogram*. Since time is on the abscissa and frequency on the ordinate, looking at a spectrogram is somewhat like looking down upon a shoebox full of spectral cutouts. You only see the peaks 'closest' to you. The individual spectrum of [i] is represented in the figure as outside the 'box.' On many sound spectrographs, there is a device for sampling individual spectra from the spectrogram. These *sections* are conventional spectra, each representing one slice in time (Fig. 6.13).

The typical spectrograph permits the use of different filters with either of two bandwidth settings. If the filter is set to narrow (45 Hz is usual), it means that a bandwidth of only 45 Hz of the spectrum is sampled

at any one time, so that individual harmonics of voiced sounds are clearly shown (Fig. 6.14). Narrow band filtering produces better frequency resolution than wider band filtering; it is useful for tracking fundamental frequency of a voice. If you select a given harmonic, the frequency measured on the y axis of that harmonic divided by the harmonic number will be the f_o. For example, if the 10th harmonic is at 2000 Hz, f_o is at 200 Hz at that point. This method is particularly useful for women or children's recordings, because the harmonics of a high f_o are sufficiently widely spaced to be easily counted.

A wide band spectrogram (300-Hz bandwidth is usual) has better time resolution (Fig. 6.15). Since it passes any energy within a 300-Hz band, the individual harmonics are lost (unless they are extremely

w i   b i tʃ u ṇ s ɑ k ə   i

Figure 6.12. A spectrogram, on the *left*. The spectrum of the vowel [i] is shown at the *right*.

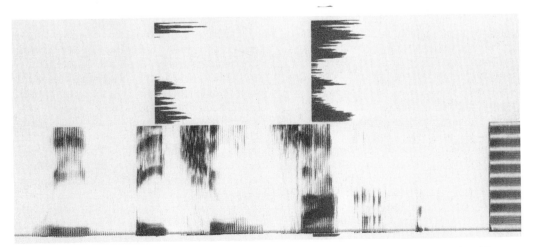

Figure 6.13. A spectrogram, with sections at selected points. A 500-Hz calibration signal is seen at the *far right*.

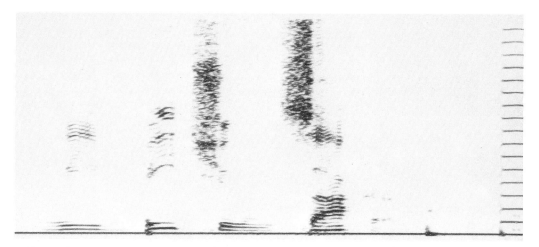

Figure 6.14. A narrow band spectrogram. A 500-Hz calibration signal is shown at the *right*.

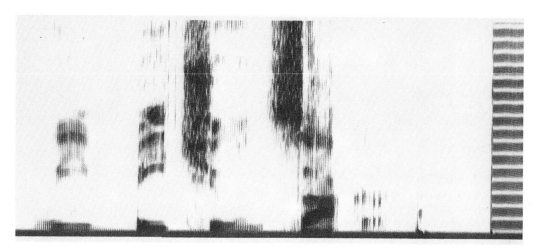

Figure 6.15. A wide band spectrogram. A 500-Hz calibration signal is shown at the *right*.

widely spaced as in a small child's voice), but the resonances of the vocal tract, the formants, are well defined. If f_o of the recorded voice is low enough, the glottal pulses can be seen as vertical stripes on the voiced parts of the spectrograms. Thus, f_o of a male voice can often be computed from wide band spectrograms by simply counting the number of pulses in 0.1 sec and multiplying by 10. Any other timing information such as vowel length, (which might be of interest in the study of, for example, pre-pausal lengthening, or stress effects), or VOT, can be measured from sound spectrograms by measuring distance along the horizontal axis which represents time. A useful measuring rule can be created by recording a 50-Hz calibration tone and making a wide band spectrogram

of it. The result is a series of vertical lines spaced 20 msec apart ($1,000/50 = 20$), with 50 spaces representing 1 sec (Fig. 6.16).

There are optional accessories for some sound spectrographs which extend their functions. One is a real time spectral analyzer for samples recorded on the spectrograph, which uses an oscilloscope for nearly immediate viewing. Another device provides an amplitude display, which marks the envelope of the overall intensities as a function of time on the top part of the spectrogram (Fig. 6.17). The amplitude display might be used, for example, in studies of the placement of stress in a recorded passage.

As investigators seek larger data bases, spectral analysis and waveform analysis are both increasingly performed by com-

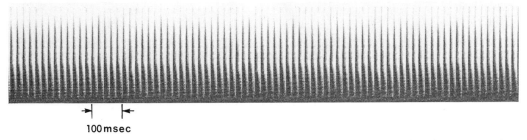

Figure 6.16. A spectrogram of a 50-Hz tone, used as a rule for measuring durations on spectrograms. Each striation marks 20 msec (Temple University).

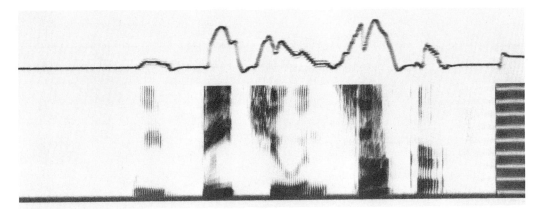

Figure 6.17. A spectrogram with the corresponding amplitude display shown above it.

puters. A digital spectrograph which can immediately store two spectrograms for comparison on a screen is commercially available. The fast filtering and comparison display features make this instrument especially useful for such clinical situations as feedback therapy. When coupled with a hard copy unit, this is also a useful research tool.

Physiological Phonetics

In studying speech physiology, scientists measure air pressure, volume, and flow, various facets of movement (extent, force, acceleration, and velocity), and, with recording electrodes, pick up muscle activity (EMG) and brain wave activity (EEG). Some experiments are designed to allow researchers to observe effects of perturbations of speech production, in an attempt to specify control mechanisms important in speech. For example, speakers may be asked to talk with bite blocks between their teeth, preventing normal jaw closure. Articulatory movements with and without bite block may be compared to see

how the production system adjusts to change. Other experiments are designed to test various models of speech organization or models of coarticulation.

Space prohibits us from considering all of the instruments used in physiological phonetics. We shall limit our descriptions to some instruments used in the study of air volume, pressure, and airflow, articulatory movements, and muscle activity. We can study air changes, movements, and muscles as they relate to respiration, laryngeal functioning, and articulation. Thus, the text below is divided into these general areas, and then subdivided by type of event measured. In contrast to the instruments discussed earlier, many of the more complex tools described below are more likely to be familiar to the student from reading than from hands-on experience.

Respiratory Analysis

In the study of respiration for speech, many instruments are available, each with its specific purpose. An investigator can

Figure 6.18. A manometer (Temple University).

record air pressure, airflow, air volume, thoracic and abdominal movements, and respiratory muscle activity. For example, air pressure is the force of the air on an area ($p = F/A$). It can be measured with an instrument called a *manometer* (Fig. 6.18). Pressure is indicated in units of cm of H_2O (centimeters of water). Air pressure can be converted into an electrical signal by a *pressure transducer* (Fig. 6.19). In this figure, a speaker with problems in the balance between nasal and oral resonance is aided by watching a signal displayed on an oscilloscope representing nasal air pressure as sensed by a nasal bulb placed in her nostril and transformed into a voltage for display. The speaker is trying to produce a large difference between 'bat' and 'mat.' Thus, the instrument is being used as a feedback device.

Nasal and oral air pressures can be sampled externally by using a face mask, with transducers built into it, or internally by insertion of a *catheter* into the supraglottal cavities. Subglottal air pressure can be measured directly via a tracheal puncture into the subglottal space. Subglottal air pressure has also been measured indirectly from measurements taken from the esophagus (the tube leading to the stomach behind the trachea) by having the subject swallow a small balloon attached by a long tube to a rubber drum. The excursions of the drum are amplified and displayed. Pressure readings taken directly from the subglottal area are more accurate than esophageal recording but involve puncturing the trachea.

Airflow is a measure of volume of moving air per unit of time and is often measured in milliliters per second. A face mask unit with individual flowmeters for nasal and oral chambers is called a *pneumotachograph* (Fig. 6.20). A speech sound produced with relatively high air pressure and flow, such as /s/, might show a value of 7 cm of H_2O oral air pressure and around 500 ml/sec airflow.

It is also possible to measure the dynamics of lung volume changes. The most com-

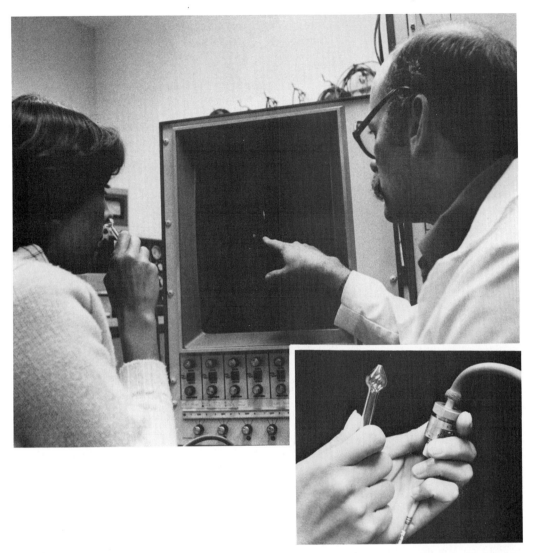

Figure 6.19. A nasal bulb and pressure transducer are shown in the *insert*. The bulb is placed at the nostril. Air pressure, from the bulb, is converted into a signal shown on the oscilloscope. Dr. Heuer uses visual feedback to decrease hypernasal production by the client (Temple University).

monly used instrument for recording from subglottal airways is the *spirometer* which measures air volume, such as the tidal volume or the vital capacity, and plots it on a revolving drum (Fig. 6.21). To record volume changes during speech, the air volume changes within a *body plethysmograph* (Fig. 6.22) can be recorded without the use of a face mask, which might interfere with speech. Instead the subject is seated in a sealed box so that any changes in thoracic or abdominal volume are reflected in the volume changes within the

plethysmograph, which can be attached to a spirometer for graphic output.

Laryngeal Function

It was in 1854 that Manuel Patricio Rodriquez Garcia, a Spanish singing teacher who had taught in Paris and in London, invented the *laryngoscope,* the first instrument for viewing vocal fold movements. He fashioned a mirror which could be inserted into the mouth and angled in such a way that sunlight shining on it reflected down upon the vocal folds, making them

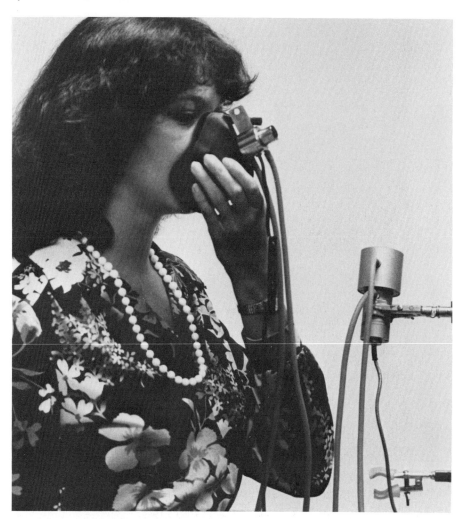

Figure 6.20. A pneumotachograph (Temple University).

visible in the mirror. Garcia's invention marked the beginning of modern laryngology, and his technique is still used today for laryngeal examinations. Garcia lived for over 100 years (1805–1906), and on the occasion of his 100th birthday, he was honored by a dinner and received many accolades. It is said that his modest response to it all was, "It was only a mirror!"

Laryngeal vibrations can be recorded by making very high speed motion pictures from the laryngoscope. The movies can then be replayed at speeds appropriate for frame-by-frame analysis. Alternatively, it is possible to observe the movements of the vocal folds by using a *stroboscope* (a light flashing at a fixed frequency). If the flash frequency is adjusted to be close to

the frequency of vocal fold vibration, the movements of the folds will appear to be slowed. A recent development in laryngeal endoscopes is the *fiberscope* (Fig. 6.23). Thin, flexible filaments of glass are assembled into bundles, conveying light from a strong white light source around the curves of the nasal cavity and vocal tract to illuminate the vocal folds. Other filaments within the bundle convey the image back to an eyepiece for viewing. The eyepiece can be attached to a motion picture camera for high speed photography. The advantage of fiberoptic viewing over traditional laryngoscopy is that the subject is free to speak, because the bundles are inserted through the nasal cavities, freeing the oral cavity for speech movements. The

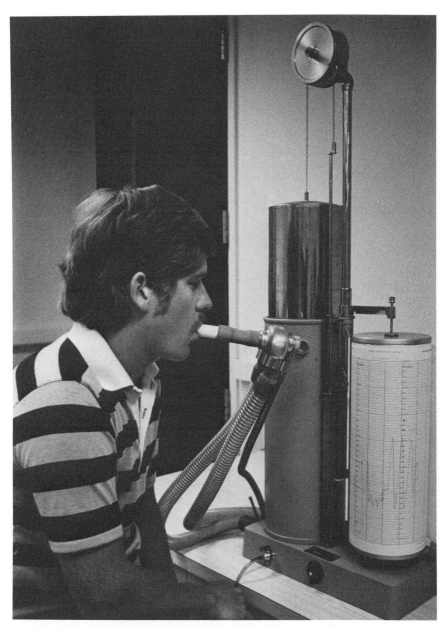

Figure 6.21. A spirometer (Temple University).

disadvantage of this technique is that the folds cannot be lighted brightly enough for observation of individual vibratory excursions. However, the technique is useful for direct observation of, slower laryngeal adjustments, for example, voicing adjustments.

There are also techniques for obtaining information on the area of glottal opening as an indirect measure of vocal fold ad-

justment. The photocell of a *glottograph* can be used to measure the amount of light shining through the glottis. This method is called *transillumination*, because a light source is placed either above or below the vocal folds and a light-sensing device is placed on the other side. Unlike endoscopic viewing, this technique gives no information on the shape of the glottis but only on the extent of the opening. Another

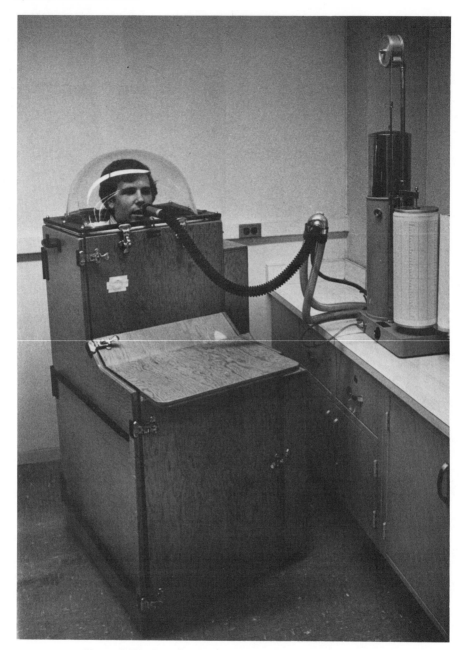

Figure 6.22. A body plethysmograph (Temple University).

instrument, which gives only information on laryngeal closure, is called the *laryngograph* which measures the relative conductance or impedance between two small electrodes placed on either side of the larynx. When the glottis is closed, and the current is easily conducted across the folds, the laryngograph signal peaks (Fig. 6.24), but as the folds separate, the signal decreases because of the impedance created by the open glottis; the signal must be transmitted along vocal fold tissue, then across the glottal airspace to the opposite fold, a journey which it fails to make efficiently due to the mismatch of impedances of muscle tissue and air. Hence, the laryngograph measures the duration of vocal fold closure in each vibratory cycle (Fig.

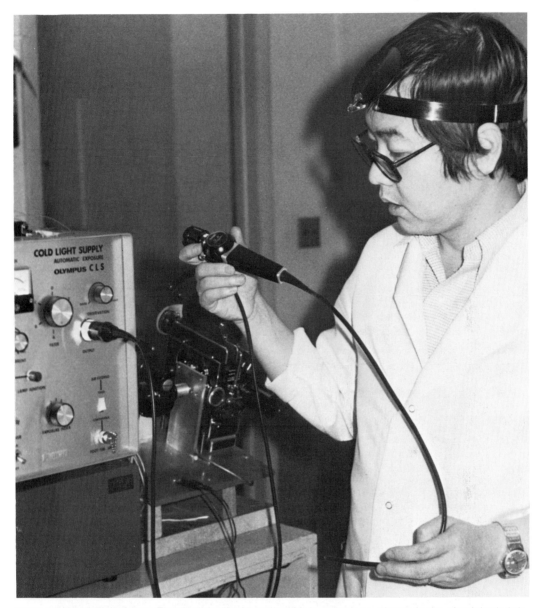

Figure 6.23. A fiberscope. The flexible fiber bundle with its eyepiece, shown in the physician's left hand, is inserted into the nasal cavity. The larynx can be viewed with the eyepiece, shown in the physician's right hand (Haskins Laboratories).

6.25), but tells us nothing about the width or shape of vocal fold opening. Since a laryngograph signal is free from the influence of the resonance frequencies of the upper tract, the device is used to record fundamental frequencies, by an added instrument that plots the frequency of the laryngograph peaks as a function of time. Laryngographs are thus useful for record-

ing f_o both for purposes of research and for voice therapy.

Electromyography of intrinsic and extrinsic laryngeal muscles is accomplished today with the use of fine wire electrodes, as fine as a human hair, which are inserted into the muscles to record the electrical potential produced upon muscle contraction. Once inserted, the fine wires are al-

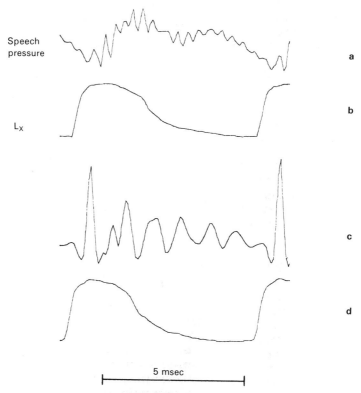

Speech pressure

L_x

a

b

c

d

5 msec

Figure 6.24. A comparison of the pressure waves at the lips for one cycle of the vowels /i/ (*a*) and /a/ (*c*) with the output of the laryngograph (*b* and *d*). Note the relative impedance across the folds (L_x) looks similar during the cycle of vibration for /i/ and /a/, although the pressure waves at the lips are quite different. (Reprinted with permission from A. J. Fourcin: Laryngographic Examination of Vocal Fold Vibration. In *Ventilatory and Phonatory Control Systems: An International Symposium*, B. Wyke (Ed.), Oxford University Press © 1974.)

most imperceptible to the subject. Most of the laryngeal muscles are accessible by transcutaneous insertions at the neck, using a hypodermic needle to guide the insertion. Some muscles, such as the posterior cricoarytenoid, are reached by insertion through the oral and pharyngeal cavities (Fig. 6.26). Bipolar recordings, that is, recordings of the difference in potential between two electrodes, are typically made to reduce ambient noise in the signal and to reduce field size. The EMG signals are amplified and recorded on magentic tape along with the acoustic signal (Fig. 6.27). Many laboratories *rectify* and smooth the signal for analysis. In full wave rectification, all the energy in the original signal is recorded as a positive signal (Fig 6.28). To smooth the signal, it is passed through an integrator which averages the voltage within a specified moving time frame: 25 msec, for example. There is some interest, too, in preserving the raw signal for studying individual motor units.

Movement of the larynx in the vertical plane has been studied by *cinefluorographic* methods. Motion pictures are taken from a *fluoroscope,* a screen displaying X-ray images. The image is derived from an X-ray pulse generator amplified by an image intensifier. Recently *laminographic* or *tomographic* techniques have been used to scan the body. These *tomographic* methods deliver the X-rays from more than one direction, focusing on a particular plane of the subject. Under these conditions, there is less exposure to radiation for the subject and better soft tissue definition. It would thus be an appropriate technique to use to study speech,

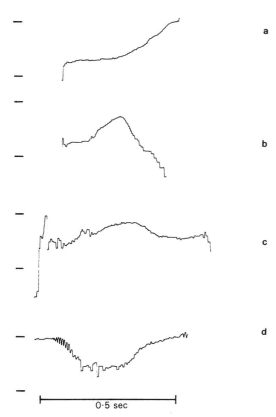

a

b

c

d

|← 0·5 sec →|

Figure 6.25. Waveforms of fundamental frequency as a function of time in a display derived from a laryngograph. *Waveforms a* and *b* show rising and rise-fall intonations from a normal adult saying "Do you." *Part c* shows a rise-fall pattern from the same speaker when she had laryngitis. The restricted range and irregular voicing onset are typical features of this condition. *Part d* was produced by a man with chronic laryngitis. In *a*, *b*, and *c*, the *upper* and *lower marks* to the *left* of each graph correspond to 800 and 200 Hz, respectively. The marks by *d* correspond to 200 and 50 Hz. (Reprinted with permission from A. J. Fourcin: Laryngographic Examination of Vocal Fold Vibration. In *Ventilatory and Phonatory Control Systems: An International Symposium*, B. Wyke (Ed.), Oxford University Press © 1974.)

but at present, this technique can only be used to examine structures which are not moving.

Supralaryngeal Movement

Cinefluorography is, of course, equally important in the study of articulatory movements above the larynx. The superior surface of the tongue can be identified on X-ray film if a contrast medium, a barium paste, is applied to the tongue dorsum. The tongue is an elastic mass of muscles, however, and it moves and stretches about in the oral cavity in such a complex fashion that it is often more useful to track the positions of specific points along the tongue body. Small lead pellets (such as BB shot) can be attached to the tongue with a cyanoacrylate adhesive (Fig. 6.29). The points are well defined on X-ray motion pictures and can be tracked during speech by measuring the distances between the pellets and stable reference points. Vertical and horizontal movements of the pellets can be determined by this method from lateral X-ray motion pictures. Hand measurements of each frame using a film analyzer are tedious and time consuming. Computer programs for measurement and display of the data can reduce the analysis time significantly. The experimenter can simply touch a light pen to each point to be measured in a given frame, using the computer to store x-y coordinates for each point and then compute distance between points.

Movements for speech can also be transduced by *strain gauges* (Fig. 6.30), thin plates which are bent by articulator movements. If the strain gauge is part of a circuit, any change in deformation due to movement creates a change in resistance, resulting in a signal which can be amplified, recorded, and plotted.

Movements can be inferred, too, from their effects upon light or sound. Just as transillumination of the glottis offers information about vocal fold opening, *photoelectric* methods can be applied to supraglottal areas. The amount of light shining through the velopharyngeal port can be sensed by a photocell on the other side and thus converted into an electric signal. Using *ultrasound,* the transmission of high frequency vibrations, the response of a crystal attached to the tongue or to the lateral walls of the pharynx can be measured as it varies according to its distance from the transmitter. Thus articulator movement, too, can be inferred.

Another method of determining tongue position is recording tongue contact with

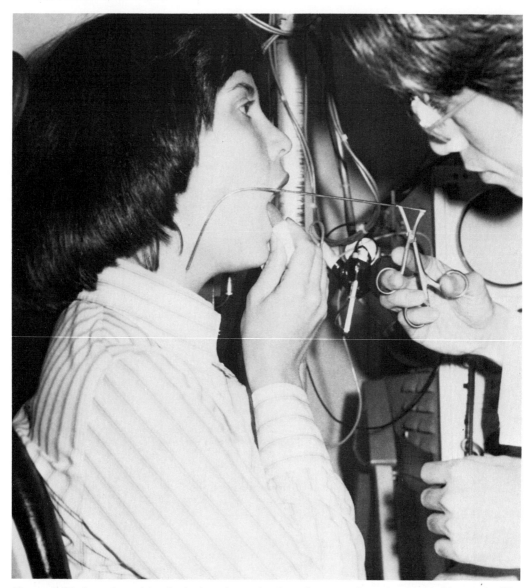

Figure 6.26. Insertion of hooked wire electrodes into the posterior cricoarytenoid muscle. The curved needle holder, shown in the physician's hand, is inserted perorally. When the wires have been inserted into the muscle, the needle and needle holder are withdrawn (Haskins Laboratories).

the palate, a method called *palatography*. In its simplest form, black powder is dusted on the palate, the tongue gesture is made, and a photograph taken of the palate, revealing the points of tongue-palate contact. The contact points are made obvious by the absence of black powder. Recently, several investigators have made palatal prostheses, often called artificial palates, with transducers embedded in them to record contact points. Prostheses have been developed having as many as 64 contact points. Transducer outputs can be displayed as lights on a monitor, or the pattern of contact points can be recorded on analog tape for data processing.

It is difficult to record the movement of supralaryngeal structures because their movements are extremely complex. Many of the available techniques cannot be used for tracking movement of many points simultaneously. Furthermore, the upper vo-

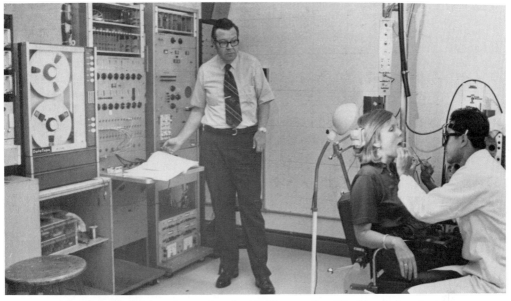

Figure 6.27. A laboratory set up for EMG recording (Haskins Laboratories).

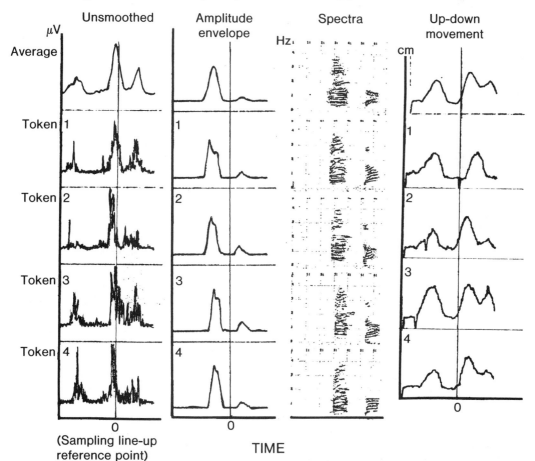

Figure 6.28. Results from an experiment on velopharyngeal closure. The movements of the velum, recorded by a fiberoptic endoscope, are shown in the *right-most* column. Spectrograms are also shown, as well as the audio envelope. The *left-most* column shows electromyographic signals from the levator palatini muscle, after rectification. Four individual samples of each token are shown. The *top* waveform shows an average of 16 tokens (Haskins Laboratories).

cal tract articulators vary in their accessiblity. For example, it is easier to follow the movements of the jaw than the tongue. The development of a more adequate technology for speech movement analysis is a widely recognized need. Recently, an X-ray microbeam system has been proposed which may fulfill this need, although it will be a one-of-a-kind installation, to be used by many research teams.

Muscle Activity

Movements within the oral and pharyngeal areas of speakers are the combined

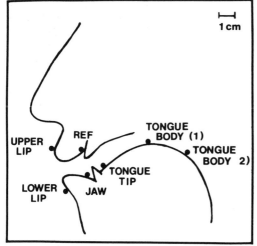

Figure 6.29. An outline of the upper vocal tract, derived from a projected film image. Position of pellets on various structures is shown. These points can be tracked in frame-by-frame analysis. (Reprinted with permission from T. Gay: *Journal of the Acoustical Society of America. 62,* 1977, 183–193.)

results of mass, muscle activity, elasticity, and air pressure forces. Muscle action potentials (the electrical activity accompanying muscle contraction) can be recorded from muscles which are accessible for electrode placement. Three types of bipolar electrodes are commonly used: 'paint-on' and preformed surface electrodes, and intramuscular hooked-wire electrodes. In addition, a grounding electrode is typically attached to the ear lobe. Paint-on electrodes are created by painting some silver-based paint onto the skin, placing a fine insulated wire, with the coating removed from the end, onto the dab of paint, and then painting another silver dot on top to hold the wire. Two electrodes are typically placed close together for bipolar recordings. Small preformed surface electrodes, such as Beckman electrodes, are about 10 mm in diameter and record from a larger area than the paint-on variety. They are easy to apply with tape. Adhesive collars are also available for attaching these electrodes. Finally, as mentioned previously, hooked-wire electrodes, made of very fine platinum-iridium alloy wire can be inserted directly into muscles using a hypodermic needle to implant the wires. Hooked wire electrode recordings are typically muscle-specific, whereas surface electrodes, recording from a larger area, may pick up action potentials from more than one muscle, especially if several muscles lie in close proximity or at different depths beneath the skin surface.

The EMG signal is an interference pattern, the sum of the action potentials of many motor units. A *motor unit* consists

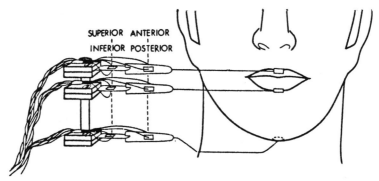

Figure 6.30. Two-dimensional lip and jaw strain gauge transducer. (Reprinted with permission from J. H. Abbs and B. N. Gilbert: *Journal of Speech and Hearing Research. 16,* 1973.)

of the muscle fibers innervated by a single motoneuron. A single electrode or pair of electrodes records the electrical activity (action potential) of motor units lying near it. Thus, the EMG signal from one placement does not necessarily represent the activity of the whole muscle, and the absolute amplitude of the EMG signal from one recording cannot be compared to that from another. Relative EMG signal amplitudes, firing rates of single motor units, and differences in timing and pattern, however, can be related to different phonetic events and to different conditions within the same experiment. For example, the activity of the orbicularis oris muscle for /p/ can be compared to that for /b/, or the activity for /p/ can be compared when it is produced under different conditions of stress or speaking rate.

Speech Perception

The instrumentation array required for studying the ways in which people perceive speech differs from that used in studying speech production (Fig. 6.31). Rather than analyze data produced by talkers, the investigator analyzes responses given by listeners to natural or synthetic speech.

Tape Splicing

The tape recorder is a useful tool in studying speech perception. Speech sounds may be shortened, exchanged, or otherwise altered by inserting noise or silence, all with tape-splicing techniques.

These same results can be accomplished with modern computer programs which digitize the waveform and provide more flexible and precise editing possibilities, including that of providing tapes arranged so that a listener hears a different stimulus in each ear. A tape recording can then be made from the edited signals to use for speech perception tests.

Listening Station

Several listeners can simultaneously take speech perception tests at a listening station. The stimuli are recorded on tape and played on a tape recorder having two amplifiers to provide maximum control over the output intensity of each channel, with a switch with several settings so that a two-channel recording can be presented dichotically (Channel A to one ear, Channel B to the other), binaurally (either channel split to go to both ears, or both channels to both ears), or monaurally (one channel to one ear). A *voltmeter* is used to calibrate the voltage going to each ear via the earphones. The listeners listen through headsets in a sound-treated room, making their responses by pushing response levers or marking answer sheets (Fig. 6.32), while the experimenter controls the test from the next room.

Use of Computers in Experimental Phonetics

The only functions computers have not yet undertaken in speech research are thinking of an experiment, designing it,

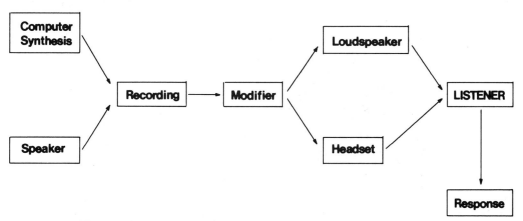

Figure 6.31. Instrumentation array used in speech perception studies.

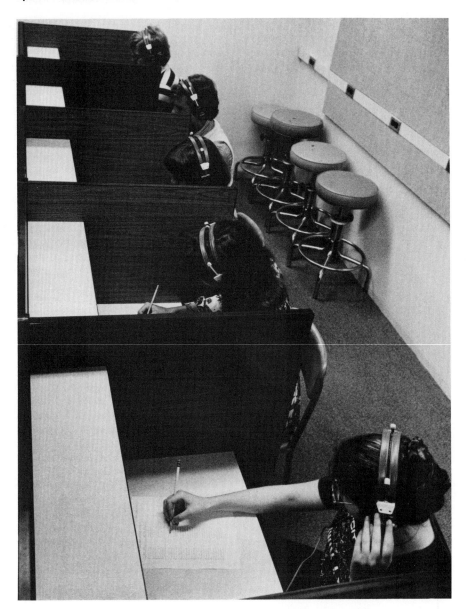

Figure 6.32. A listening station (Temple University).

and interpreting it. Admittedly, these are probably the most important steps in any experiment, but computers are used to do everything else: make the stimuli, control stimuli presentations, track responses, reduce the data, analyze its statistical significance, and graph the results.

In the study of acoustic phonetics, speech waveforms can be digitized for computer editing; the investigator can examine the details of the waveform by expanding and displaying it on a computer monitor, (frequently a CRT storage scope) or insert silence, lengthen parts of the waveform by concatenation, exchange parts as in tape splicing, or otherwise change the sound in amplitude, spectral, or temporal dimensions. The computer can also be programmed to extract and display signal parameters, for example the peak signal amplitude or the fundamental frequency. Thus, the acoustic phonetician can study duration, frequency, intensity, formant patterns, or transitions of speech signals with greater flexibility than was formerly possible.

In the study of physiological phonetics, any analog signal, for example, air pressure, transduced movement changes, EMG, or EEG, can be transformed into units by *analog to digital converters* for computer editing, averaging, and display. The computer can also be programmed to record subject responses, to measure reaction times, measure amplitude of signals or record frequency of occurrence. Graphical capabilities of computers enable the experimenter to take away hard copies of displays of all kinds.

In the study of speech perception, com-puter synthesis of speech enables the experimenter to create speech-like sounds with specified acoustic properties in order to discover what cues listeners use in perceiving speech and to derive rules for automatic speech devices which can read to the blind, answer the telephone, and give information. There are hardware synthesizers which can be controlled with or without a computer. Many such synthesizers generate speech on a formant principle. Some have the formants generated in series; in others, the formants are generated in parallel (Fig. 6.33). The parameters of synthetic speech are thus known and controlled, allowing the investigator to vary only the parameter under study. Obviously, such stimuli cannot be pro-

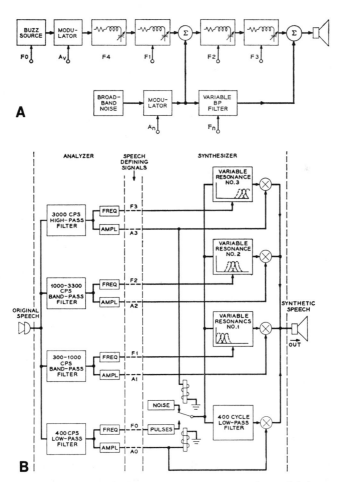

Figure 6.33. (*A*) Series (or cascade) and (*B*) parallel formant speech synthesizers. (Reprinted with permission from J. L. Flanagan: *Speech Analysis, Synthesis, and Perception*, Springer-Verlag © 1965.)

duced by human speakers. Recently, efforts have been made to synthesize speech according to articulatory rather than acoustic rules. Using X-ray data, vocal tract shapes and articulatory movements are organized into rules for generating changes in the speech waveform. Synthesis by articulatory rule should help us better understand speech production as well as speech perception.

BIBLIOGRAPHY

General Readings

Comprehensive

Flanagan, J. L., *Speech Analysis, Synthesis, and Perception.* New York: Springer-Verlag, 1965.

Acoustic Phonetics

Fant, G., Sound Spectrography. *Proceedings of the Fourth International Congress of Phonetic Sciences.* Helsinki Conference. A. Sovijarvi and P. Aalto (Eds.) New York: Humanities Press, 1961, pp. 14–33.

Koenig, W., Dunn, H. K., and Lacy, L. Y., The Sound Spectrograph. *J. Acoust. Soc. Am. 17,* 1946, 19–49. Reprinted in Lehiste, I. (Ed.), *Readings in Acoustic Phonetics.* Cambridge, Mass.: M. I. T. Press, 1969.

Wakita, H., Instrumentation for the Study of Speech Acoustics. In *Contemporary Issues in Experimental Phonetics.* N. J. Lass (Ed.) New York: Academic Press, 1976, pp. 3–40.

Physiological Phonetics

Abbs, J. H., and Watkin, K. L., Instrumentation for the Study of Speech Physiology. In *Contemporary Issues in Experimental Phonetics.* N. J. Lass (Ed.) New York: Academic Press, 1976, pp. 41–78.

Fujimura, O., Acoustics of Speech. In *Speech and Cortical Functioning.* J. H. Gilbert (Ed.) New York: Academic Press, 1972, pp. 107–165.

Harris, K. S., Physiological Aspects of Articulatory Behavior. In *Current Trends in Linguistics. Vol. 12, No. 4,* T. A. Sebeok (Ed.) The Hague: Mouton, 1974, pp. 2281–2302.

Perkell, J. S., *Physiology of Speech Production: Results and Implications of a Quantitative Cineradiographic Study.* Cambridge, Mass.: M. I. T. Press, 1969.

Sawashima, M., and Cooper, F. S. (Eds.), *Dynamic Aspects of Speech Production.* Tokyo: University of Tokyo Press, 1977.

Speech Perception

Cooper, F. S., Speech Synthesizers. *Proceedings of the Fourth International Congress of Phonetic Sciences.* Helsinki Conference. A. Sovijarvi and P. Aalto (Eds.) New York: Humanities Press, 1961, pp. 3–13.

Denes, P., The Use of Computers for Research in Phonetics. *Proceedings of the Fourth International Congress of Phonetic Sciences.* Helsinki Conference. A. Sovijarvi and P. Aalto (Eds.) New York: Humanities Press, 1961, pp. 149–154.

A Sample of Papers on Instrumentation

Allen, G. D., Lubker, J. F. and Harrison, E. Jr., New Paint-On Electrodes for Surface Electromyography. *J. Acoust. Soc. Am. 52,* 1972, 124 (A).

Baken, R. J., and Matz, B. J., A Portable Impedance Pneumograph. *Hum. Commun.* Autumn 1973, 28–35.

Cooper, F. S., and Mattingly, I. G., Computer-controlled PCM System for Investigation of Dichotic Speech Perception. *Haskins Laboratories Status Reports SR–17/18,* 1969, 17–21.

Fletcher, S. G., McCutcheon, M. J., and Wolf, M. B., Dynamic Palatometry *J. Speech Hear. Res. 18,* 1975, 812–819.

Fourcin, A. J., Laryngographic Examination of Vocal Fold Vibration. In *Ventilatory and Phonatory Control Systems: An International Symposium.* B. Wyke (Ed.) London: Oxford University Press, 1974, pp. 315–326.

Fujimura, O., Kiritani, S., and Oshida, H., Computer Controlled Radiography for Observation of Movements of Articulatory and Other Human Organs. *Comput. Biol. Med. 3,* 1973, 371–384.

Gay, T., and Harris, K. S., Some Recent Developments in the Use of Electromyography in Speech Research. *J. Speech Hear. Res. 14,* 1971, 241–246.

Hirano, M., and Ohala, J., Use of Hooked-wire Electrodes for Electromyography of the Intrinsic Laryngeal Muscles. *J. Speech Hear. Res. 12,* 1969, 362–373.

Hirose, H., Gay, T., and Strome, M., Electrode Insertion Techniques for Laryngeal Electromyography. *J. Acoust. Soc. Am. 50,* 1971, 1449–1450.

Huggins, A. W. F., A Facility for Studying Perception of Timing in Natural Speech. *Q. Prog. Rep. Res. Lab. Electron. M. I. T. 95,* 1969, 81–83.

Kent, R. D., Some Considerations in the Cineradiographic Analysis of Tongue Movements during Speech. *Phonetica. 26,* 1972, 293–306.

Lisker, L., Abramson, A. S., Cooper, F. S., and Schvey, M. H., Transillumination of the Larynx in Running Speech. *J. Acoust. Soc. Am. 45,* 1969, 1544–1546.

Moll, K. L., Cinefluorographic Techniques in Speech Research. *J. Speech Hear. Res. 3,* 1960, 227–241.

Moore, G. P., White, F. D., and von Leden, H., Ultra High Speech Photography in Laryngeal Physiology. *J. Speech Hear. Disord. 27,* 1962, 165–171.

Nakatani, L. H., Computer-aided Signal Handling for Speech Research. *J. Acoust. Soc. Am. 61,* 1977, 1056–1062.

Sawashima, M., Abramson, A. S., Cooper, F. S., and Lisker, L., Observing Laryngeal Adjustments during Running Speech by Use of a Fiberoptics System. *Phonetica. 22,* 1970, 193–201.

Subtelny, J. D., and Subtelny, J. D., Roentgenographic Techniques and Phonetic Research. *Proceedings of the Fourth International Congress of Phonetic Sciences.* Helsinki Conference. A. Sovijarvi and P. Aalto (Eds.) New York: Humanities Press, 1961, pp. 129–146.

Watkin, K. L., and Zagzebski, J. A., On-line Ultrasonic Technique for Monitoring Tongue Displacements. *J. Acoust. Soc. Am. 54,* 1973, 544–547.

CHAPTER 7

Evolution of Language and Speech

> . . . and out of the ground the Lord God formed every beast of the field and every fowl of the air; and brought them unto Adam to see what he would call them: and whatsoever Adam called every living creature, that was the name thereof.
>
> King James Version, *The Bible*, Genesis 2:19

Homo sapiens is a group of creatures who name the world about them. They attach verbal tags to almost every person, place, thing, event, circumstance, thought, and feeling within their experience. They use these tags to order the world for themselves, to transmit information, and to ask questions. Curious as creatures, they seem to be the only animals who constantly ask the questions: Who am I and how did I develop? Within this larger question is the query: how did language and speech originate and develop? In the 17th century, two philosophers wrote opposing theories of how human ideas develop, theories which continue to influence modern thought. Descartes (Fig. 7.1), the French philosopher and mathematician, was a *Rationalist,* holding that reason based on innate ideas was more important to human understanding than experiences with the physical world. He viewed the mind and the outside world as separate. A modern concept of human language which is consonant with Descartes' emphasis on innate ideas is that espoused by Chomsky of Massachusetts Institute of Technology. The concept holds that although a person learns whichever language is spoken in his particular community, competence for language is an innate characteristic of man, and that the general knowledge of language which he possesses at birth is fundamental to his learning of specific languages. The 17th century philosopher Locke (Fig. 7.2) was an *Empiricist,* holding that human beings understand through their experiences, especially those gained via the senses. The human mind was viewed as a blank slate, a *tabula rasa,* upon which all sensory experiences are registered, thereby leading to learning and understanding. Condillac, following soon after Locke, presented a theory of language and speech development as learned, not natural, in humans. Modern behaviorists who emphasize learning, as for example Skinner of Harvard, follow the empirical view of Locke.

The problem with theorizing about the origin and evolution of language and speech is that the evidence has been destroyed. We have no knowledge of how speech originated nor are we likely to obtain any. It is a mystery of lost sounds and disintegrated soft tissue. Stones and bones remain, offering only fragmentary clues. Speculation on the topic seemed so fruitless that in 1866, the Linguistic Society of Paris published an edict prohibiting discussion of the origin of language and speech in the papers of the society. The edict had little effect, however, and theories continued to proliferate. Even recently, when linguists, anthropologists, psychologists, neurologists, and speech scientists gathered in New York for a conference on the origin and evolution of language and speech at the New York Academy of Science, the theories expressed ranged widely from those which depict human speech as having evolved from animal vocalizations, to those which view it as having evolved from primate gestural

Figure 7.1. René Descartes, French philosopher and mathematician (1596–1650) (Culver Pictures).

communication, to those which view it as having occurred *de novo* in man. Some theorists suggest that speech developed as recently as 40,000 years ago, during the 4th glacial period, while others propose that it developed between 2 and 3 million years ago.

There is no single field of inquiry which can supply sufficient evidence by itself, but if we gather together the clues offered by fossil finds, by the study of vocal and gestural communication in living creatures, and by biological evidence to be found in the study of the brain and vocal tract, we can come closer to a likely theory of how the particular mode of expressing the language of man — speech — evolved and even a suggestion of how it originated.

SOCIAL FRAMEWORK

Fossil Hominids

If early *hominids* left the forest to wander in the savanna in search of food, it is conjectured by anthropologists that they needed to develop language to organize their kinship group for survival. The line of hominid evolution to modern man is unclear, however. Most texts on the subject view Australopithecus africanus, a

Figure 7.2. John Locke, English empirical philosopher (1632–1704) (Culver Pictures).

sil finds in Kenya and Ethiopia, however, have raised questions about the lineage of modern man. There is a possibility that the genus Homo was living as a contemporary of Australopithecus africanus, pushing man back to 3 or 4 million years ago. At Lake Turkana (formerly Lake Rudolph) in Kenya, Richard Leakey found a Homo erectus fossil in 1975 dated at about 1½ million years ago, and in 1972, a skull fragment of a Homo fossil dated 2 to 3 million years ago. This skull, called by its catalog number KNM-ER 1470 (Fig. 7.3), is important for its Homo erectus-like cranial capacity and shape. Holloway at Columbia University has reported that the Broca's region on the ER 1470 is larger than that on Australopithecus skulls. It seems likely, then, that modern man developed from the ER 1470 species of hominid rather than from Australopithecus africanus or from the more recent Neanderthal Man, fossils of which have been found in Europe and date from 100,000 to 70,000 years ago (Fig. 7.4). Further evidence of early man are the remains of a 'family' of adults and children found in Ethiopia by Johanson (an anthropologist from Case Western Reserve) and Taieb (a geologist at the Centre National de la Recherche Scientifique at Mendon-Bellevue outside Paris). The group of skeletons has been interpreted to be of the genus Homo and date from approximately 3 million years ago. Johanson and Leakey have suggested that the Homo skeletons are the remains of food-sharing cooperative groups and that, therefore, the possibility of their possessing some form of speech is strong. It may be that the complexity of life and the selective development of a problem-solving capacity to deal with this increasing complexity necessitated the parallel development of a complex and flexible communication code much earlier in history than has been assumed (Table 7.1).

Cognitive Prerequisites

In order for any language system to originate and be maintained, there must be a basic need for it by the species. Bees, dolphins, and many animals in the wild have developed sophisticated communication systems. The signals of the systems can be

small ape-like creature who lived from more than 4 million to about 1 million years ago to be an ancestor of Homo erectus, a larger brained hominid who lived from about 1 to ½ million years ago, who was in turn the ancestor of Homo sapiens, or modern man. Australopithecus africanus had a brain capacity of only around 400 cm^3 whereas Homo erectus had a capacity ranging from around 800 to 1300 cm^3, which overlaps with that of modern man. This represents a large change in brain size, and the classical view was that during the almost 4 million years which elapsed between Australopithecus and modern man, language, cognition, and brain size developed together. Recent fos-

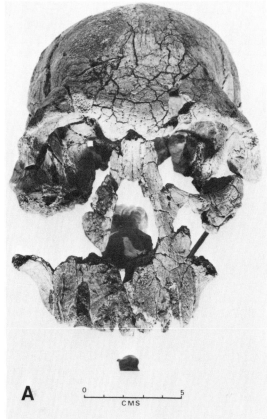

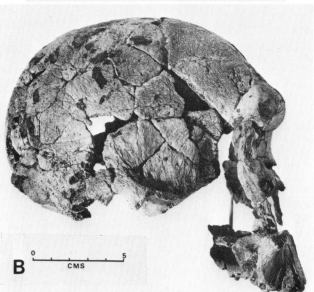

Figure 7.3. (*A* and *B*) Views of skull fragment KNM-ER 1470. (Reprinted with permission from M. H. Day, R. E. F. Leakey, A. C. Walker, and B. A. Wood: *American Journal of Physical Anthropology. 42,* 1975. Courtesy of the National Museums of Kenya.)

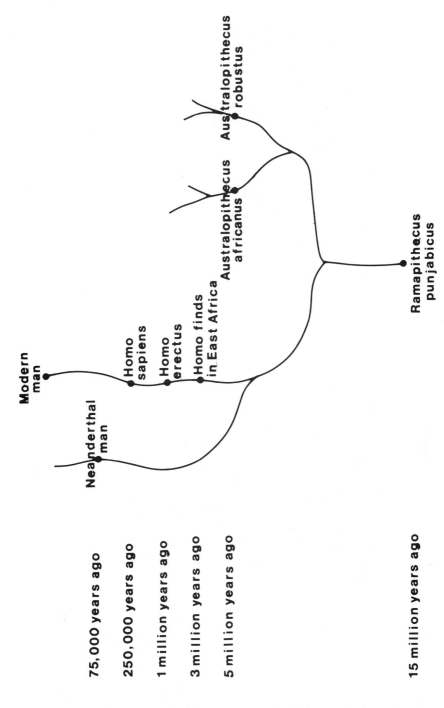

Figure 7.4. The evolution of man.

Table 7.1
Reconstructed Timetable Based on Recent Finds of Homo Fossils.

Years ago (approximate)		
4–5 million to 1 million	Australopithecus africanus	Became extinct
3 million	Homo finds in Ethiopia and Kenya	Ancestors of Homo sapiens?
2 million	First known tool	
1½ million to 500,000	Homo erectus	Ancestor of Homo sapiens
250,000	Homo sapiens	
100,000 to 70,000	Neanderthal finds in Europe	Became extinct
70,000 to 35,000	Evidence of religion and philosophy	
30,000	Evidence of art	
6,500	First known writing	

olfactory, tactile, auditory, or visual. In the case of water mammals, they are largely auditory. In the case of the greater apes, they appear to be a combination of visual and auditory. The most obvious need for a system of communication arises when creatures need to cooperate and share in order to survive. As living becomes more social, one creature depending upon another, and as that social existence grows in complexity, the communication system must also be extensive enough and flexible enough to convey the necessary information. For example, language may be a convenience in conveying information about making tools to use in hunting or gathering food. It is probably essential to convey information on how to fashion a tool to be used to make other tools. Planning, whether it be a strategy to be used by several creatures to catch an animal or to design tools to make other tools, involves postponement of impulses and thinking of the future. Normally, language assumes cognition and reflects its cognitive underpinnings. The more abstract the cognition, the more necessary is a complex language system. When early men moved about in tribes, hunting big game, sharing the conquests, and protecting one another from enemies, it became important to exchange information. Evidence of cognitive prerequisites to speech is scattered. The first known tool dates about 2 million years ago, and tools created as art objects date from 30,000 years ago. A skeleton found near La Chapelle-aux-Saints in southern France, dated to around 70,000 to 35,000 years ago, was found buried with tools, a tradition reported for many Neanderthal burials. This suggests the development of religion and philosophy, abstract concepts

which presumably require language for transmission of ideas.

According to van Lawick-Goodall, chimps use tools to obtain food, and they communicate with gesture, facial expressions, and over 20 calls. They lack language of the kind used by humans, however, in which the signals are segmented to be recombined for infinite numbers of messages. In a simple communication system, one gesture or one call, as the case may be, signifies something and forms a message. A certain bird cry can serve as a warning in danger, or a certain body posture in an animal can signify submission. In this kind of communication system, the numbers of distinct calls or gestures must be few enough to avoid overloading the memory. Furthermore, if they become too numerous they may lose their distinctiveness and become ambiguous. For both of these reasons, more complex communication systems are developed in which the calls or gestures become segmented and are used in combinations which generate multiple meanings without increasing the number of basic elements.

As an instance, Hockett and Ascher have made an analysis of the warning call. It could be modified one way to signal danger from above and another way to signal danger below. Further, parts of calls could be blended. They suggest that a new call meaning 'danger and food' could be made from segments from one call indicating 'food here' and another meaning 'danger coming.'

In a social situation in which there is much to think about, a language system helps pin the ideas down and hold them in memory. How often have we had a 'new' idea and raced to write it down in order to hold on to it? Naming something helps to fix attention on it, to remember it, and, in some minds, to overcome the fear of it. Early man may have needed to say the name of his prey as well as paint its picture in his cave in order to have power over it. It seems that not only was language needed to convey the increasingly complex concerns of early man, but that language in turn aided him in his cognition.

Why Speech?

If the social life of ape-men gave rise to the development of a complex communication system, why speech? The communication system might have been a complex gestural language such as the American Sign Language used by the deaf, or it might have been a vocal system such as that used by birds. Humans use gesture, facial expressions, and voice during speech, but the primacy of a vocal-auditory system allowed for nocturnal communication, for transmission over larger distances or in areas of poor visibility, and freed the hands to gather food or to use tools. Speech differs from other vocal call systems in the fact that it is encoded. It is composed of segments of silence and segments of sound. The sounds are often produced in parallel, thus blending the acoustic cues of one segment over another. This efficient system of signaling enables more information to be sent in a period of time than could be sent sequentially.

Liberman's example of the overlapping acoustic cues is the word 'bag.' Note in Figure 7.5 that the acoustic cues for the /b/ overlap those for the /æ/, which further overlap those for /g/. Thus, there is a shingling effect upon the acoustic output which the listener decodes. Not only does speech allow for extremely rapid transmission of acoustic information, much more rapid than the same sounds produced in sequence, but speech also offers such redundancy of information that communication is particulary effective. On the phonemic level, cues to the voicing of the phoneme /b/, for example, are given by the vocal pulsing of the sound itself, by the short time between the burst and voicing onset of the /æ/, and by the lack of aspiration of the burst. Intonation patterns, stress, and gesture are added to the syn-

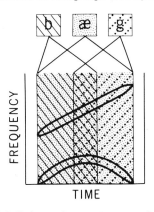

Figure 7.5. Schematic spectrogram showing the effects of coarticulation in the syllable [bæg]. (Reprinted with permission from A. M. Liberman: In *Coding Processes in Human Memory.* A. W. Melton and E. Martin (Eds.), Halsted Press © 1972.

tactic, semantic, and phonological information conveyed, so that the message must be massively distorted before intelligibility fails.

Mattingly has suggested that speech, with its semantic aspects appropriate for long-term storage in the human brain and its phonological aspects appropriate for on-line transmission by the human vocal tract, has not been selected by chance as a vehicle for human language. Rather, he posits it as a species-specific product of human intellect combined with a prelinguistic or innate 'social releaser,' similar in some ways to sign stimuli displayed by other creatures, such as the part of the song of the white-throated sparrow which signifies territory to other birds.

This innate propensity for speech sounds may have enabled man to plan hunting and gathering expeditions and to protect kinship groups. In other words, speech ability may have led to cooperative behavior. Equally valid in theory is the contrasting idea that the need to do these things for survival led to the development of a speech code adapted to handle the information needs: that is, behavior led to speech. It seems likely that it is not a question of which came first, speech or tribal behavior, but that rather the social needs, the cognitive abilities, and the language system developed together, each reinforcing and building upon the other.

PSYCHOLOGICAL FRAMEWORK

Chimpanzee Language

Some clues to the evolution of language and speech may be gleaned from observations of the communicative behavior of lower primates, birds, prelinguistic human infants, and the study of human and non-human auditory perception. Humans have long assumed that they alone had developed language, defined as a rule-governed symbolic communication system with which one can generate novel utterances. There has been a suspicion that dolphins might rival man in this ability, but the proof is not in, since humans have thus far failed to understand the system used by dolphins. Until the last two decades, however, humans felt no threat from their nearest living relatives, the greater apes, whose ability to learn human language was evidently poor.

Hayes tried to teach a chimpanzee named Vicki to speak and the only intelligible approximations to speech after years of effort were four words, 'mama,' 'papa,' 'up,' and 'cup.' During the '60s and '70s, however, humans have had to adjust their thinking about the linguistic abilities of chimps. Starting with the training of a chimp called Washoe by the Gardners from the University of Nevada, it was demonstrated that if the language is expressed in a gestural instead of vocal mode, chimps are capable of symbolic behavior which seems to be linguistic in that they learn the rules for the sequencing of symbols and offer evidence that they can use the system creatively by generating new utterances which they have never been taught. Washoe learned to communicate with humans by learning the American Sign Language for the Deaf (Fig. 7.6). At 15 months, she had learned her first word, by 2 years, the first sentence 'come-gimme sweet,' and by 5 years, had mastered over 130 signs. This was a huge step beyond Vicki's four words.

The work with signing is currently proceeding in many places with increasingly positive results; larger vocabularies and more evidence of novel utterances. Another system using a visual-manual mode was taught to a chimp named Sarah by

Premack at the University of California at Santa Barbara. A system of 125 words represented by 125 different plastic shapes was used to produce sentences such as 'Mary give apple.' This approach is being continued at several university centers by the use of typewriters with symbols displayed on keys which activate speech synthesizers. Another method, also visual-gestural, makes use of a computer-controlled teaching machine. Lana, a communicative chimp at the Yerkes Regional Primate Research Center in Atlanta, Ga. has been taught to push coded buttons on her side of a computer console to demand action or food and ask questions. She has thus learned the basic syntactic rules of English and has evidenced enough understanding of the rules to use them for new sentences (Fig. 7.7).

The surprise in these experiments was that chimps have at least some of the cognitive prerequisites for a simple language. They clearly have the concepts for hundreds of things, and if given gestural or visual symbols to associate with these concepts, they can learn the rules for generating sentences with them. They lack the creativity with language shown by human children, but are capable of some novel utterances. Lana, lacking the word for an orange, but having learned the word for the color orange, pushed buttons indicating the 'apple which-is orange,' and Washoe, not knowing the sign for 'ducks,'

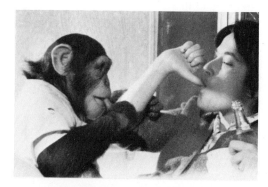

Figure 7.6. Washoe signing the word "drink" to Beatrice Gardner. (Photograph courtesy of R. Allen Gardner and Beatrice T. Gardner, University of Nevada.)

Figure 7.7. Lana at the keyboard of a computer. Each key has a distinctive symbol on its surface. (Photograph from Yerkes Regional Primate Research Center of Emory University, Atlanta, Ga.)

signed 'water birds.' Important, then, to a consideration of the evolution of language and speech in humans, is the knowledge that the living greater apes show some linguistic ability. The volitional control evidenced by chimps over the use of their hands in the visual-gestural mode is impressive. Their obvious limitations in the auditory-vocal mode are qualitatively different from the abilities of man and must be due to differences in neural control as well as other anatomical differences.

Some theorists take the gestural competence of contemporary chimps as evidence that early hominids may have evolved language and speech from a purely gestural language using vocal emotive suprasegmentals (intonation, stress) along with it. The vocal sounds, under this theory, gradually assumed more importance, with gesture gradually diminishing.

Other theorists suggest that the evidence from chimp language shows that man developed along a completely separate line from chimps. In any case, a certain level of cognitive ability is presumed for symbolic behavior; language is one form of symbolic behavior, and speech is but one form of language. Chimps can manage some form of gestural language but lack the auditory-vocal mechanisms for speech.

Bird Song

Since humans evolved a vocal language, with non-verbal communication having assumed an important but secondary role, what cues to its development can be discerned from studying birds, which also use a vocal communicative system? Marler of Rockefeller University in New York sees an analogy between much that linguists and psychologists have discovered about speech perception in humans and the studies which he and others have made on auditory perception and the development of bird song.

We have seen in the chapter on speech perception that humans perceive a continuum of speech-like sounds categorically, that is, they fail to distinguish acoustic differences within a phoneme, but make distinctions between similar acoustic changes at the boundary between phonemes. There has been some confusion about whether this perceptual categorization is done on a phonemic basis or whether it represents the discriminative function of the human auditory mechanism. The fact that rhesus monkeys and even chinchillas demonstrate similar categorical perception despite their obvious lack of phonemic information upon which to base categories, indicates that humans may build their language, especially their phonemic distinctions, upon the contrasts which the auditory system finds to be more distinctive, and that this auditory tuning may have developed phylogenetically to include man and other mammals. There is, then, an innate tuning of auditory perception toward certain acoustic contrasts which can become linguistically useful. Too, innate perceptual abilities evidently precede any corresponding production abilities. Eimas and others have demonstrated categorical perception in infants, long before the development of speech. Rhesus monkey and chinchilla perception may also be viewed as evidence that perception precedes production in phylogeny. Finally, there is the evidence of the critical period. Human beings are physiologically tuned to learning their first language during the first few years of life. When language learning is delayed, it becomes increasingly difficult. What seems to be learned almost effortlessly at 2 years of age is painfully difficult at 8, and at puberty, the plasticity of the brain for first language learning is almost lost. Hockett has pointed out that the longer period of childhood helplessness which evolved in man allows a longer time of plasticity for learning language.

The analogy between bird song and human speech is based on studies of the male white-crowned sparrow. As long as this sparrow hears the adult song during the critical period, when the bird is between 10 and 50 days old, and can hear himself singing, he will sing the full song, complete with local dialectal variations, when he is around 200 days old. If he is deafened during the critical period, however, the song will be abnormal (Fig. 7.8). If he is isolated so that he cannot hear the adult pattern but can hear himself, the song will be abnormal but will contain some normal characteristics. This indicates that a rudimentary trace of the song is innate, but, to sing the full song, the sparrow must hear the model which imprints itself in the brain and later sing it, modifying it to the imprinted model. Similarly, in human infants, innate perceptual and productive abilities are the foundation upon which the child learns a specific language to which he must be exposed during a critical period for language learning, and which he must hear himself use as he attempts to approximate the model in order to acquire normal speech.

The clues which vocalization theories offer to the evolution of language and speech are that, however it evolved, perceptual abilities probably preceded production abilities, in the sense that hominids may have chosen to contrast sounds, as they developed speech, which were already maximally differentiated by their auditory systems. Myers suggests that Homo erectus as a species had cortical control of vocalizations and of oral facial movements quite unlike other primates who used their hands for purposeful activities but had little cortical control over their calls. We know that the perceptual capabilities necessary for speech are widespread among animals, but there is no evidence of how production abilities developed. Chimps seem able to use language productively, meaning they can create new utterances, but lack the vocal-auditory capabilities for speech. Birds use the vocal-auditory mode, but seem set in their calls and lack a flexible production code with which to create new messages.

Child Language

It may be that the most persuasive clues to the evolution of speech may be found

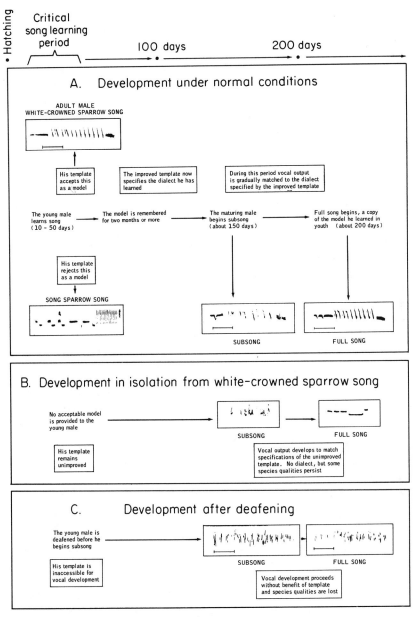

Figure 7.8. A representation of the "template" hypothesis for song learning in white-crowned sparrows, as applied to development (A) in a normal male, (B) in a social isolate, and (C) after early deafening. (Reprinted with permission from P. Marler: In *The Role of Speech in Language*, J. F. Kavanagh and J. E. Cutting (Eds.), M. I. T. Press, Cambridge, Mass, © 1975.)

by studying the development of speech in human infants. The prelinguistic vocalizations of an infant are involuntary cries of distress, when hungry or uncomfortable, and comfort sounds, when nursing or comfortable. The babbling stage may be similar to the innate rudiments of sparrow song evident in deafened song sparrows. Babbling seems to be innate; even deaf babies babble. However, the normal baby starts to evidence voluntary vocal play as he babbles, while babbling in the deaf infant gradually dies out. After the infant discovers that a sound means something, that he, like Adam, can name things, an event which has usually happened by 12 months of age, language development proceeds quickly. Only 6 months later, he is usually producing sentences. Infants use gesture with speech. As he is learning to name things, a child may point to something of interest, and through gesture and meaningless sounds, try to draw someone's attention to it. When gesture fails him, when it cannot signal all that he wants to express, he needs to name it. The development of syntax, too, is a direct reflection of the cognitive need underlying it. Relationships require the ordering of words into agent phrases and action phrases for full expression. Could it be

that *ontogeny* in some sense recapitulates *phylogeny?* Lamendella suggests that we may see modifications of our phylogentic history when we view the ontological development of a human being and that all of the seemingly disparate theories of speech evolution may be correct, as early man may have passed through successive stages similar to those experienced by a single infant. Figure 7.9 tracks the stages of communicative development during the first 2 years of a human child's life. Just as a child progresses from one type of communication system to another, man's ancestors may have gradually passed through similar stages.

BIOLOGICAL FRAMEWORK

Brain Organization

The final frame of reference for considering the nature of language and speech development in man, is from studies of the brain and the vocal tract. Mentioned previously was the large increase in brain size between Australopithecus africanus and Homo erectus, but if we interpret the finds during the 1970s in Ethiopia and Kenya of Homo skeletons, which were contemporary with Australopithecus, as ruling out Australopithecus africanus as a direct ancestor of modern man, then the difference in brain size becomes less significant. More important than size may be comparisons indicating brain reorganization. There is some evidence that the temporoparietal association cortex, critical to language, has increased in size as hominids evolved to the Homo genus. Also the earliest Homo skull fragments reflect a larger Broca's area, important to the motor control of speech, than that in primates outside the Homo genus. Holloway's study of hominid endocasts has led him to conclude that the human form of cortex emerged much earlier than is commonly thought. Fossil skulls are reconstructed from fragments, however, and it is hazardous to claim precision about the brains which once inhabited these skulls. Another way to approach the problem is to contrast and compare the intact brains of Homo sapiens and his non-speaking relatives. Geschwind of the Harvard Medical School in Boston

has demonstrated that the primary receptive areas in the brains of man and apes are similar; the difference between them lies in the development in man's brain of primary association areas, especially the temporoparietal area which conveniently lies in the midst of the auditory, visual, and motor-sensory areas (Fig. 7.10). The development of this association area presumably accounts for the naming behavior in man. He sees and senses something, hears its name, and learns to produce the name himself, after connecting the visual, auditory, and motor-sensory correlates of the object to be named. Naming triggers further linguistic development, and damage to the association area in the temporoparietal juncture interferes with the ability to name and with other linguistic abilities.

Those who support the gestural origin of speech find support in the proximity of the hand and vocal representation of motor and sensory functions in the brain. As we have seen in the chapter on speech production, motor control of the hand and of the vocal tract are close together in the frontal lobe of the brain, and the same is true of the sensory representation in the parietal lobe.

Lateralization

It is interesting to consider the possible importance to language of the lateralization of brain function evident in man. Hu-

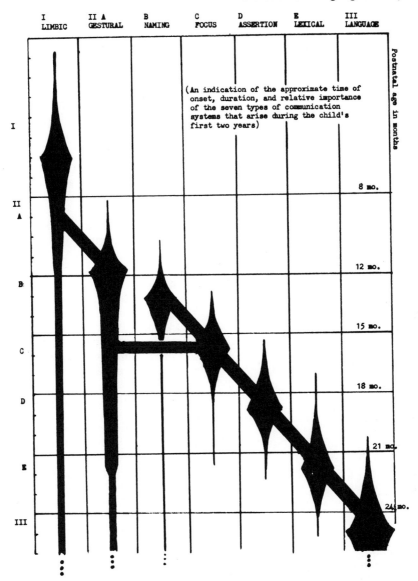

Figure 7.9. Outline of the maturational stages in the development of communication systems by the child. Starting with reflexive emotional messages governed by the limbic system, the child puts increasing emphasis upon conceptual messages through gesture, naming, focus of propositional messages into one-word sentences, two-word assertions, and lexical strings forming a telegraphic message. By 2 years, lateralized neocortical systems govern sentences that follow syntactic and morphophonological rules. (Reprinted with permission from J. T. Lamendella: *Annals of the New York Academy of Science. 280*, 1976, 408–409.)

mans use one cerebral hemisphere of the brain for some functions and the other hemisphere for other functions. Language is typically dominant in the left hemisphere, although there are individual variations. There is little evidence of lateralization of brain function in mammals lower than primates. The greater apes have shown hand preferences. (It has been reported, for instance, that gorillas show a right hand preference in starting chest beating.) However, most reports have shown hand preference randomly distributed, not predominantly to the right and preference to be switched easily by training. Control of dominant hand function

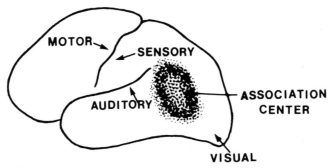

Figure 7.10. Illustration of the receptive and temporoparietal association areas in man. The latter area is well developed in Homo sapiens.

and of speech are not always housed in the same hemisphere in any case, since most left-handed people (right hemisphere control) use the left hemisphere to control speech and language processes. Asymmetries presumed to be related to the lateralization of language have been observed in human brains. The Sylvian fissure on the left hemisphere is longer posteriorly and is lower than on the right hemisphere. Yet, this same difference in the Sylvian fissure has been observed in the orangutan brain. Thus, hemispheric specialization may be a prerequisite to language development both phylogenetically and ontologically. It has been shown by Kimura that children 3 or 4 years old indicate lateralized speech perception when given dichotic tests. A dominant hemisphere for speech may be established earlier, but it is difficult to test younger children. The lateralization of speech processes, however, seems to be an adaptation which man's ancestors made to accommodate the increasingly complex linguistic code along with his other problem-solving abilities.

Vocal Tract Changes

The vocal tract has also changed during hominid evolution. The larynx has evolved from an organ adapted especially for respiration to one which, after other adaptations to such changes as erect posture, was finally uniquely adapted for sound production in human speech. The supralaryngeal area has also evolved because of several factors: the improvement of vision over olfaction as a means of gaining information about other animals, and the need to produce a wide variety of distinctive sounds. The final adaptation of the vocal tract for speech is unique in the Homo genus.

Negus, a British physiologist, was the first to systematically study the evolution of the larynx and the vocal tract. He illustrates how the simple sphincter of the lung fish, which was maximally efficient for respiration (it simply worked as a valve to open or close the access to the lungs), gradually changed during evolution to the complex arrangement of muscles which we find in the human larynx, differentiated to control the opening, closing, tension, and shape of the vocal folds, thus creating differences in voice quality and fundamental frequency (Fig. 7.11). The tract above the larynx, which in earlier species of mammals efficiently separated the digestive tract from the respiratory tract, was first adapted in man to his upright position. Vision replaced the sense of olfaction (smell) as the primary sense, freeing the epiglottis to lower and separate from the soft palate. In sheep dogs, for example, olfaction is primary, and the epiglottis is high, making contact with the soft palate to produce a discrete respiratory channel from the nose to the lungs. Dogs can smell danger while eating, for the oral cavity is separate, and the food goes down a channel at each side of the larynx to the esophagus leading to the stomach. Thus, there is no confusion of the two channels and no danger of food entering the lungs. This separation of the respiratory and digestive tracts is also present for human babies when they are nursing. The tongue and larynx of the baby elevate, the tongue to press against the nipple and the larynx to connect with the nasal passage so the baby can continue to breathe while feed-

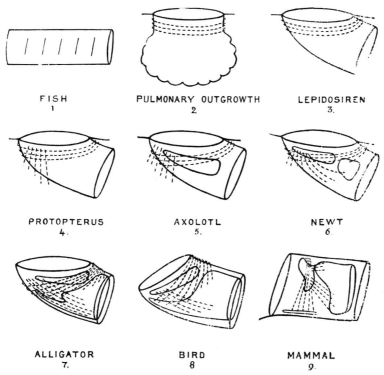

FISH
1

PULMONARY OUTGROWTH
2

LEPIDOSIREN
3.

PROTOPTERUS
4.

AXOLOTL
5.

NEWT
6

ALLIGATOR
7.

BIRD
8

MAMMAL
9.

Figure 7.11. Evolution of the larynx. Starting with the gill slits in the first stage, the sphincter muscle in *Stages 2* and *3* is combined with a dilator muscle in *Stage 4*, with the appearance of cartilages in *Stages 5–8*. The mammalian larynx is characterized by a separation of cartilages and the division of the sphincteric muscle into components. (Reprinted with permission from V. E. Negus: *The Comparative Anatomy and Physiology of the Larynx*, Hafner Publishing Co. © 1962.)

ing (Fig. 7.12). This arrangement is quickly lost as the baby develops, however, and young children and adults have larynges and tongues which have descended in the throat, producing a pronounced L-shaped vocal tract (Fig. 7.13). This arrangement is maximally efficient for producing the large variety of distinctive sounds used in human speech, but is less efficient for respiration and digestion since they share a common pathway, the pharynx. Not only is there danger of choking on food in the windpipe, but man cannot swallow and breathe at the same time as other creatures do.

It seems, then, that speech is not simply a function overlaid upon anatomical systems used for respiration and digestion, but that anatomical changes have taken place to tune the body especially for speech, even at some expense to the life-sustaining systems.

Information on the evolutionary nature of these changes has been provided by the

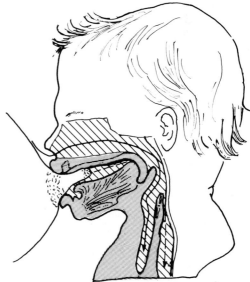

Figure 7.12. Respiratory and digestive tracts for a nursing baby. (Adapted from an original painting by F. H. Netter, M. D. in E. S. Crelin: *Clinical Symposia 28,* CIBA Pharmaceutical Co. © 1976.)

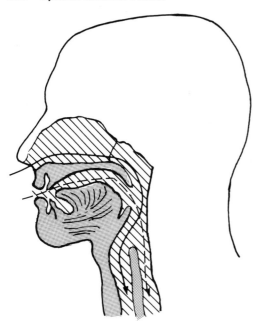

Figure 7.13. Respiratory and digestive tracts in an adult. (Adapted from an original painting by F. H. Netter, M. D. in E. S. Crelin: *Clinical Symposia. 28,* CIBA Pharmaceutical Co. © 1976.)

collaborative efforts of Crelin and Lieberman. Crelin, a physiologist at Yale specializing in neonatal anatomy and physiology, has made rubber silicone casts of the vocal tracts of newborn babies, modern chimpanzees, and human adults and has reconstructed probable vocal tract casts from fossil skulls of Neanderthal specimens. Vocal tract shapes were approximated by noting the angles of muscle facets in the skulls and comparing them to known vocal tracts, such as those of living apes and humans. Lieberman, a linguist with special training in the acoustics of speech, estimated the possible vocal tract areas which each specimen might assume and fed this information to a computer programmed to compute the formant frequencies (or resonances) of all possible speech sounds. The possible resonances were compared to those known to be produced by humans to evaluate how closely each type of vocal tract might approach the sounds of speech as we know them today.

The computer simulations for neonate humans and modern chimps resulted in resonance patterns which corresponded well with the actual sounds made by such vocal tracts, although the computer indicated that the chimp might be holding back. He may be able to produce a larger variety of sounds than he actually does. Greater apes and human babies produce more neutral vocal sounds such as /e/ or /æ/, usually quite nasal, and are incapable of the vocal tract adjustments necessary for the more extreme vocal sounds /i/ /ɑ/ or /u/. The simulations of vocal tract resonances which may have been possible for the 'classic' Neanderthal man and other hominids were determined in the same way.

Fig. 7.14 pictures the casts of a newborn baby, an adult chimpanzee, a reconstruction from a Neanderthal fossil (La Chapelle-aux-Saints), and an adult human. Figure 7.15 shows the vocal tract areas of the same specimens, with landmarks indicated, when drawn equalizing the size. Notice how close the epiglottis is to the soft palate in the baby, the chimp, and the Neanderthal examples. Note, too, that the foramen cecum of the tongue (the point where the large papillae begin) has descended into the pharynx of the adult human, producing a humped tongue capable of three-directional movement, housed partly in the oral cavity, partly in the pha-

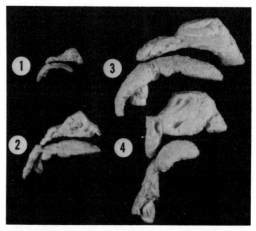

Figure 7.14. Casts of the nasal, oral, pharyngeal, and laryngeal cavities of (*1*) newborn modern man, (*2*) adult chimpanzee, (*3*) Neanderthal man, and (*4*) adult modern man. (Reprinted with permission from P. Lieberman, E. S. Crelin, and D. H. Klatt: *American Anthropologist. 74,* 1972, 291.)

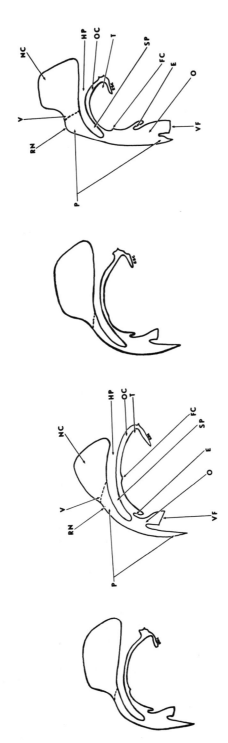

Figure 7.15. Diagrams of the air passages of a newborn human, adult chimpanzee, Neanderthal man, and adult human: Anatomical landmarks noted on the diagram of the chimpanzee and adult man are: *P*, pharynx; *RN*, roof of nasopharynx; *V*, vomer bone; *NC*, nasal cavity; *HP*, hard palate; *OC*, oral cavity; *T*, tongue; *FC*, foramen cecum; *SP*, soft palate; *E*, epiglottis; *O*, opening of larynx into pharynx; and *VF*, level of vocal folds. (Reprinted with permission from P. Lieberman, E. S. Crelin, and D. H. Klatt: *American Anthropologist 74*, 1972, 292.)

ryngeal cavity, in contrast to the flat, relatively more massive tongue which occupies the oral cavity of the other specimens. Finally, notice the long pharynx in the adult human, which along with the oral cavity, produces the two-chamber resonator distinctive in human adults.

The results of the computer simulations indicate that some of the fossil forms, Australopithecus and the classic Neanderthal, like modern chimps and babies, could have produced only a limited repertoire of sounds for communication, while other fossils could have produced a wider variety, some fossil hominids having vocal tracts which could presumably produce and resonate sounds similar to those produced by contemporary Homo sapiens. Steinheim man, a fossil found in western Germany, dating around 250,000 years ago, had the brain capacity and the necessary vocal tract shape for a fully developed linguistic code.

It is too bad that the finds of very early Homo fossils discovered by Leakey and by Johanson and Taieb have been so fragmentary, for if the cranial vaults and teeth more nearly resemble those of man than those of Australopithecus africanus, their contemporary, or the later Neanderthal, so too might the organization of facial bones, which would add evidence for the development of a vocal tract appropriate for speech 2 or 3 million years ago. Of course, speech depends on more than an appropriate vocal tract. Lieberman suggests that other important factors were automatization, cognitive ability, and the development of a speech code.

A LIKELY TALE

Incorporating some of the clues derived from considering speech evolution from the perspectives of social need, psychological studies of chimps, birds, babies, and of biological studies of the brain and vocal tract, we can make a guess as to how speech may have originated and evolved, and fashion a likely tale.

Millions of years ago, families of ape-men lived in the jungles of Africa, hunting for food in small groups or tribes. They communicated with one another by using a variety of body stances, gestures, facial expressions, cries, grunts, and comfort sounds. Like many animals living today, these creatures used sound in the same way that they used gesture. There was a simple relationship between a gesture and its meaning and between a sound and its meaning. As birds' cries of warning, wolves' calls of mating, and gorillas' screams of aggressiveness, these predecessors of man produced shrill cries of alarm and understood the meanings of many vocalized and gestural forms of communication—signs for food, mating, fear, excitement, hate, and contentment. Each gathered his or her own food, staying within close range of others in the group and thinking only of the present.

Gradually, some of the groups left the dense forest to search for food in the more open lands of the savanna (Fig. 7.16). They no longer needed to swing from trees but needed to roam further apart to find food, and the postural-gestural-cry mode of communication no longer sufficed. During the span of time that these ancestors of man were becoming more erect in their posture, they were increasingly using their hands to pick berries and to dig for roots. As they got progressively more adept at manipulating things with their hands, they found it efficient to use one hand to grasp and steady the object of their interest and the other hand to manipulate it. One hand developed the large muscle control needed to hold down a branch while the fingers of the other hand picked the berries using the more precise control afforded by the small digital muscles. Later on, when their descendants, who were hunters, began to fashion simple tools out of stone, they continued to use one hand to hold the stone and the other hand to chisel it. These tool-making ape-men developed a hand use preference which was unlike the tree-swinging apes who continued to use their hands interchangeably. Most ape-men came to use their right hands for operations which required precise movements, with the nerve fiber connections of the left cerebral hemisphere adapting themselves to these delicate maneuvers. Since these

Figure 7.16. A water hole; early man lived on such savannas. (Photograph courtesy of Stuart A. Altmann, University of Chicago.)

activities demanded care, concentration, and problem-solving abilities, it became efficient for the left hemisphere to dominate in the analytical processes associated with these activities. The right hemisphere, by contrast, was dominant in processes demanding synthesis, the ability to see the whole, and spatial-visual activities and perception. Once ape-men had lateralized brain function to a certain degree, their abilities increased rapidly. As hand use was frequently accompanied by meaningful vocalizations and noises, these sounds were gradually incorporated into the established left hemisphere network of associations which interrelated thought, sight, action, and sound.

By this time, perhaps 3 million years ago, early man stood fairly erect and became a tool user and an incipient speaker. He needed to name things because it was more productive to cooperate within the kinship group in obtaining and sharing food. Also, it became necessary to plan ahead and to divide the labor. His language

was restricted, however, by two factors: the anatomy of his vocal tract and his lack of a code. He simply made certain noises which carried meaning to his listeners. These noises always meant the same thing. He chose sounds which were perceived to be most contrastive to minimize confusion. He was also restricted in the number of sounds he could make, because his larynx was higher than modern man's and his tongue was more restricted in its mobility. He could make certain vowel sounds and some consonants. He could make nasal sounds, bursts, grunts, hissing sounds, and clicks. His inventory of possible messages was as limited as his inventory of sounds.

Gradually early man developed more messages by combining sounds. Discovering that he could use one sound in combination with other sounds for many meanings, man developed a code. As the code developed, so did the cognitive mechanisms with which to use it.

As emerging man become erect, his anatomy adapted to the gravitational pull upon his body. His larynx descended into his neck which was elongating. The increasingly fine motor demands put upon the tongue paralleled its increasing mobility and precision of movement. The oral cavity and the pharynx together created a longer resonating tube, and the increasingly flexible and mobile tongue could move in several directions, thereby enabling him to produce more sounds to use in his speech code.

As man began to think more abstractly, he began to use language both to express and to refine thought. The evolution of speech production took another leap forward when man realized that not only would changing the order of sounds in sound combinations give him more possible utterances (/am/ and /ma/), but changing the order of the combinations themselves could be used to further signal differences in meaning. The development of a syntax, or set of rules for word order, began what has turned out to be a remarkable display of inventiveness in finding many ways to signal changes in meaning.

'Is Tom ready' means something different from 'Tom is ready,' as do the utterances 'Tom hit Sam' as opposed to 'Sam hit Tom.' The words are identical in each case, but the changed syntax alters the meaning. It is more efficient to follow rules for such changes, so that one need not learn each instance but merely learn the rule which could be applied to other instances. Humans discovered additional ways to change meaning by adding, deleting, or changing a sound (run/ran, cat/cats), by changing stress (CONtract, 'a document'/conTRACT, 'agree'), by changing juncture ('a name'/'an aim'), or by changing intonation (She left?/She left.). Thus, the third stage in the development of language was a structure for linguistic expression. Anyone who knew the structural rules of a given language along with its lexicon, or store of words, could create sentences he had never heard or learned. In human language, the number of possible sentences is infinite, and there is a comprehensive semantic system or set of meaningful utterances. As the language load increased in complexity, so too did the cognitive mechanism to support its function.

Stage I	Sound = Meaning
Stage II	Sound combinations = Meaning
Stage III	Structured sound combinations = Meaning

Different tribes of early man roamed in different directions and the sound combinations or words which they developed differed. The particular structures of evolving languages differed also, although there were similarities in both structure and vocabulary when there was contact between people. The sounds of speech used by different language groups were fairly similar, however, because of the anatomical constraints and similarities of the human body, and men everywhere developed an oral language. Some of them put it into a written form. All languages operate by rules by which one organizes a complex code of meaningful utterances.

CONCLUSION

Two questions which pervade any discussion of the evolution of human language are (1) how can one explain the short span in an evolutionary time frame in which it is presumed to have evolved, and (2) how can one explain the genetic *versus* the learning factors involved in its origin and development. An explanation for the 'sudden' explosion of language evolution which is presumed to have taken place is that like the child who moves quickly from naming at 12 months to complex syntax by 24 months, early man proceeded quickly once the idea caught hold.

Another explanation may be that it was not an explosive development, but rather that it started much earlier than we have supposed, perhaps over 2 million years earlier, and that it developed gradually. This idea relates to the question of whether speech is innate or learned. Returning to Descartes and Locke, we may ask if man learns the language of his community entirely through his senses, as Locke might suggest, or if the fundamental understanding of language is based on man's innate competence as a reasoning creature, as suggested by Descartes. In terms of evolution, man had to reason well enough to develop the speech code in the first place, yet each person had to learn the particulars of the code anew. Natural selection has favored those best able to learn speech, so that the species we know as modern man is universally endowed with the ability to learn languages during childhood. Thus, the ability to learn languages and to speak is innate, whereas a particular language and actual speech is learned. Descartes and Locke would probably agree with this distinction, as would Skinner and Chomsky; the disagreement would be on where to place the emphasis.

And so we end this book on speech with a discussion of the beginnings of speech, and rightly so. The mind must move from the known to the unknown. Only through some knowledge of language systems, of the production of speech, and of speech perception can one hope to reconstruct the evolution of our language. As we discover more about the ways in which humans encode and decode linguistic messages, we will be better able to flesh out our admittedly distorted and overgeneralized theories.

The unanswered questions are numerous and provocative. How faithfully does the development of speech in a child mirror its evolutionary development? To what degree are infants tuned to perceive the auditory distinctions important in speech? How do the processes of speech perception and speech production interact during language learning? How does the brain control the parallel and overlapping motor commands during speech production? Which feedback mechanisms are necessary and under what circumstances? Speech science is a discipline of investigation at one of the important frontiers of human inquiry challenging us all.

BIBLIOGRAPHY

General

Harnad, S. R., Steklis, H. D., and Lancaster, J. (Eds.), *Origins and Evolution of Language and Speech*. *Ann. N. Y. Acad. Sci. 280*, 1976.

Negus, V. E., *The Comparative Anatomy and Physiology of the Larynx*. New York: Hafner, 1962. This book is a rewritten version of *The Mechanism of the Larynx* which Negus had published in 1928 in London by Heinemann Medical Books, Ltd.

Pfeiffer, J. E., *The Emergence of Man*, 2nd Ed., New York: Harper & Row, 1972.

Stam, J. H., *Inquiries into the Origin of Language: The Fate of a Question*. New York: Harper & Row, 1976.

A Sampling of Thoughts on Speech Origin and Evolution

Geschwind, N., The Neural Basis of Language. *Research in Verbal Behavior and Some Neurophysiological Implications*. K. Salzinger and S. Salzinger (Eds.) New York: Academic Press, 1967, pp. 423–427.

Hewes, G. W., Primate Communications and the Gestural Origin of Language. *Curr. Anthropol. 14*, 1973, 5–12.

Hockett, C. F., The Origin of Speech. *Sci. Am. 203*, 1960, 88–96.

Hockett, C. F., and Ascher, R., The Human Revolution. *Curr. Anthropol. 5*, 1964, 135–168.

Lamendella, J. T., Relations between the Ontogeny and Phylogeny of Language: A Neo-recapitulationist View. *Ann. N. Y. Acad. Sci. 280*, 1976, 396–412.

Lieberman, P., *On the Origins of Language: An Introduction to The Evolution of Human Speech*. Series in Physical Anthropology. New York: Macmillan, 1975.

Lieberman, P., Crelin, E. S., and Klatt, D. H., Phonetic Ability and Related Anatomy of the Newborn and Adult Human, Neanderthal Man, and the Chimpanzee. *Am. Anthropol. 74*, 1972, 287–307.

Mattingly, I. G., Speech Cues and Sign Stimuli. *Am. Sci. 60*, 1972, 327–337.

Fossil Hominids

Day, M. H., Leakey, R. E. F., Walker, A. C., and Wood, B. A., New Hominids from East Rudolf, Kenya, I. *Am. J. Phys. Anthropol. 42*, 1975, 461–476.

Holloway, R. L., The Casts of Fossil Hominid Brains. *Sci. Am. 231*, 1974, 106–115.

Johanson, D. C., Ethiopia Yields First 'Family' of Early Man. *Natl. Geogr. Mag. 150*, 1976, 791–811.

Leakey, R. E. F., Evidence for an Advanced Plio-Pleistocene Hominid from East Rudolf, Kenya. *Nature. 242*, 1973, 447–450.

Living Primates and Birds

Gardner, R. A., and Gardner, B. T., Teaching Sign Language to a Chimpanzee. *Science. 165*, 1969, 664–672.

Gardner, R. A., and Gardner, B. T., Comparative Psychology and Language Acquisition. In *Psychology: The State of the Art*. K. Salzinger and F. L. Denmark (Eds.) *Ann. N. Y. Acad. Sci. 309*, 1978, 37–76.

Marler, P., A Comparative Approach to Vocal Development: Song Learning in the White-crowned Sparrow. *J. Comp. Physiol. Psychol. 71,* 1970, 1–25.

Marler, P., On the Origin of Speech from Animal Sounds. In *The Role of Speech in Language.* J. F. Kavanagh, and J. E. Cutting, (Eds.) Cambridge, Mass.: M. I. T. Press, 1975, pp. 11–37.

Myers, R. E., Comparative Neurology of Vocalization and Speech: Proof of a Dichotomy. *Ann. N. Y. Acad. Sci. 280,* 1976, 7845–7857.

Premack, D., Language in Chimpanzee? *Science. 172,* 1971, 808–822.

Rumbaugh, D. M., Gill, T. V., and Von Glasersfeld, E. C., Reading and Sentence Completion by a Chimpanzee (Pan). *Science. 182,* 1973, 731–733.

Van Lawick-Goodall, J., *In the Shadow of Man.* Boston: Houghton Mifflin, 1971.

The Phonetic Alphabet for American English

Based upon the International Phonetic Alphabet

The Sounds of American English*

Vowel sounds	Key words	Consonant sounds	Key words
i	each, free, keep	ð	then, clothe
ɪ	it, bin	t	ten, it
e	ate, made, they		
ɛ	end, then, there	d	den, had
æ	act, man	n	no, one
		l	live, frill
a	ask, half, past	r	red, arrow
ɑ	alms, father	s	see, yes
ɒ	hot, odd, dog, cross	z	zoo, as
ɔ	awl, torn	ʃ	show, ash
o	obey, note, go	ʒ	measure, azure
ʊ	good, foot	j	you, yes
u	ooze, too	ç	huge, human
ə	alone, among circus, system	k	key, ache
ə, ɚ	father, singer	g	go, big
ʌ	up, come	ŋ	sing, long
ɝ, ɝ	urn, third	h	he, how

Consonant sounds	Key words	Consonant combinations (affricates)	Key words
p	pie, ape	tʃ	chew, each
b	be, web	dʒ	gem, hedge
m	me, am		

		Vowel combinations (diphthongs)	Key words
w	we, woe	eɪ	aid, may
ʍ	why, when	aɪ	aisle, sigh
f	free, if	ɔɪ	oil, joy
v	vine, have	aʊ	owl, cow
θ	thin, faith	oʊ	own, go

* Adapted from A. J. Bronstein: *The Pronunciation of American English.* New York: Appleton-Century-Crofts, Inc., 1960, pp. 28–30.

Cranial Nerves Important for Speech and Hearing

I Olfactory	Nose	
II Optic	Eye	
III Oculomotor	Eye	
IV Trochlear	Eye	
*V Trigeminal	Face	Motor to jaw muscles and to tensor palatini muscle. Sensory from anterior ⅔ of tongue.
VI Abducent	Eye	
*VII Facial	Face	Motor to lip muscles.
*VIII Auditory	Ear	Sensory from cochlea with some motor fibers.
*IX Glossopharyngeal	Pharynx	Motor to pharynx. Sensory from back of tongue.
*X Vagus	Larynx	Motor to laryngeal muscles.
*XI Accessory	Soft palate	Motor to levator palatini.
*XII Hypoglossal	Tongue	Motor to tongue muscles.

* Only functions related to speech and hearing are listed.

APPENDIX 3

Spinal Nerves Important for Speech

*C_1–C_8	Cervical	Neck	C_3–C_5 phrenic nerve to diaphragm.
*T_1–T_{12}	Thoracic	Chest	T_1–T_{11} to intercostal muscles. T_7–T_{12} to abdominal muscles.

* Only functions related to speech are listed. The dorsal roots (emerging from the back of the spine) are sensory. The ventral roots (emerging from the front of the spine) are motor.

Glossary

An informal reminder of the meaning of terms
COMPILED BY JOLIE BOOKSPAN

ABX TEST: Procedure for testing discrimination by requiring the listener to indicate whether the third stimulus presented sounds more like the first or the second.

ABDUCT: [L. 'ab' - away, off.] To move away from the mid-sagittal axis of the body or one of its parts.

ABSCISSA: The x coordinate of a point; its distance from the y axis measured parallel to the x axis (horizontal axis).

ABSOLUTE THRESHOLD OF AUDIBILITY: Magnitude of a sound detected by a listener 50% of the time.

ACCELERATION: The time rate of change of velocity.

ACOUSTIC REFLEX: A bilateral reflex of the middle ear in response to loud sounds which alters middle ear impedance.

ACOUSTIC RESONATOR: Something which contains air; air-filled structures designed to vibrate at particular frequencies.

ACOUSTICS: [Gk. 'akoustikos' - hearing.] The study of sound.

ADAPTATION: Variation in speech movements depending upon phonetic environment.

ADAPTATION STUDIES: Tests of speech identification and discrimination after the listener has been repeatedly exposed to a stimulus.

ADDUCT: [L. 'ad' - toward, to.] To move toward the mid-sagittal plane of the body or one of its parts.

AFFERENT: [L. 'ferre' - to bear.] Bringing to or into; in the nervous system, neurons conducting from the periphery toward the central nervous system.

AFFRICATE: A sound which combines a stop closure with a fricative release.

ALL-OR-NONE PRINCIPLE: When a single nerve or muscle fiber is stimulated at or above threshold, it will fire to its fullest extent regardless of intensity of stimulus.

ALLOPHONE: One member of the family of sounds functioning as a phoneme; [p^h] is an allophone of the phoneme /p/.

ALPHA (α) MOTONEURONS: Large efferent nerve fibers (9–16 μ in diameter) that innervate the skeletal muscles.

ALVEOLAR PROCESS: The inferior border of the maxillary bone or the superior border of the mandible which contains sockets holding the teeth.

AMPLITUDE: (Of a wave.) The absolute value of the maximum displacement from a zero value during one period of an oscillation.

AMPLITUDE SPECTRUM: (Pl. spectra.) A graphic representation of a vibratory event in which the ordinate (the vertical axis) represents the amplitude of the signal while the abscissa (the horizontal axis) represents the component frequencies.

ANALOG-TO-DIGITAL CONVERTER: Electronic device that transforms continuous signals into signals with discrete values.

ANALYSIS-BY-SYNTHESIS THEORY: A theory put forth by K. N. Stevens that speech analysis or perception involves some form of rudimentary reconstruction or synthesis of the acoustic signal.

ANTERIOR FAUCIAL PILLARS: (Also called the glossopalatine arch.) Arch-like downward continuations of the soft palate containing the glossopalatine muscles.

ANTIRESONANCE: A filtering effect of the vocal tract characterized by loss of acoustic energy in a particular frequency region.

APERIODIC: Pertains to vibrations with irregular periods.

273

APHASIA: [Gk. 'a' - not + 'phanai' - to speak.] A partial or total loss of the ability to use or to understand language following damage to the brain.

ARTICULATION: Movements of the vocal tract to produce speech sounds.

ARYTENOID: [Gk. ladle-shaped.] Triangular shaped cartilages to which the vocal folds attach.

ASPIRATE: A sound with friction produced at the glottis; /h/.

ASSIMILATION: [L. 'similis' - like, to become like.] A change in the features of a speech sound toward the features of neighboring sounds.

ATHETOSIS: [Gk. 'athetos' - without position or place.] A condition in which there is a constant succession of slow, writhing, involuntary motions of different parts of the body.

AUDITION: Hearing.

AUDITORY AGNOSIA: ['a' - not + Gk. 'gnosis' - knowledge.] Central auditory imperception of sound.

AUDITORY NERVE: VIIIth cranial nerve. A sensory nerve with two branches: the vestibular which carries information about bodily position and the cochlear which carries auditory information; also called the vestibulocochlear nerve and the acoustic nerve.

AURICLE: [L. 'auris' - ear.] The visible cartilage of the outer ear; also called the pinna.

AUTISM: [Gk. 'autos' - self.] A syndrome characterized by difficulty in forming interpersonal relationships and in developing language.

AUTISTIC THEORY: Mowrer's theory that children are internally rewarded for subvocal rehearsal of new words.

AXON: [Gk. 'axon' - axis.] The part of a neuron that carries impulses away from the cell body.

BABBLE: Variety of sounds without linguistic referents produced by infants.

BASAL GANGLIA: [Gk. 'ganglion' - knot.] A collection of several gray masses embedded in the white matter of each cerebral hemisphere (consisting of the corpus striatum, the claustrum, and the amygdaloid nucleus).

BASILAR MEMBRANE: Thin membrane forming the base of the Organ of Corti which vibrates in response to different frequencies of sound and stimulates individual sensory hair cells in the Organ of Corti.

BERNOULLI EFFECT: The pressure fall caused by increased velocity through a constricted passage.

BODY PLETHYSMOGRAPH: An instrument in the form of a sealed box used to measure air displacement produced by respiratory movements.

BRAINSTEM: The midbrain, pons, and medulla oblongata.

BUCCAL CAVITY: [L. 'bucca' - cheek, mouth.] Mouth cavity between the teeth and the cheeks.

CNS: See central nervous system.

CVA: See cerebral vascular accident.

CAROTID ARTERY: [Gk. 'karro' - sleep or stupor.] Principle artery of the neck supplying blood to the brain.

CATEGORICAL PERCEPTION: Speech sounds are perceived as belonging to groups with abrupt perceptual shifts between groups. Equal acoustic changes in speech-like stimuli are discriminated easily when assigned by the listener to different groups but are difficult to discriminate when assigned to a single group.

CATHETER: A slender tube inserted into a body passage or cavity.

CENTRAL NERVOUS SYSTEM: (CNS) The portion of the nervous system consisting of the brain and spinal cord.

CENTRAL TENDENCY: A value chosen as typical of a collection of measures.

CEREBELLUM: [L. diminutive of cerebrum.] A main division of the brain situated behind the cerebrum and above the pons; it is concerned with the coordination of movement.

CEREBRAL HEMISHERES: The two halves of the cerebrum; the main portion of the brain.

CEREBRAL PALSY: A name given to a group of disorders characterized by paralysis or muscular incoordination due to intracranial lesion at or near the time of birth.

CEREBRAL VASCULAR ACCIDENT: (CVA; stroke.) A clot or rupture of the blood vessels of the brain resulting in damage to the nervous system.

CERUMEN: [L. 'cere' - wax.] Ear wax.

CERVICAL NERVE: [L. 'cervix' - neck.] One of eight pairs of spinal nerves that arise from the segments of the spinal cord in the neck region.

CILIA: Hair-like processes (found in the external auditory meatus and in the cochlea).

CINEFLUOROGRAPHY: Motion pictures of X-ray images.

CLAVICLES: [clavicula' - bolt.] The collar bones.

CLEFT PALATE: Congenital fissure of the roof of the mouth (the palate).

CLOSED LOOP SYSTEM: A system operating under feedback control.

COARTICULATION: A temporal overlap of articulatory movements for different phones.

COCHLEA: The snail-shaped cavity of the inner ear that contains the sense organs for hearing.

COCHLEAR DUCT: The membranous labyrinth of the cochlea which contains the Organ of

Corti; also called cochlear partition and scala media.

COGNATE: (Voice.) A pair of sounds, identical in place and manner of articulation, which differ only in the presence or absence of voicing.

COLLECTIVE MONOLOGUE: Several people speaking monologues as if alone, but taking turns, as if in conversation.

COMMUNICATION: A giving or giving and receiving of information.

COMPLEX TONE: Sound having more than one sine wave component.

COMPRESSION: The reduction in volume and increase of pressure of a medium.

CONDITIONED RESPONSE: (CR) In classical conditioning, a response that comes to be elicited by a previously neutral stimulus; in Pavlov's experiment, the salivation that came to be elicited by the bell.

CONDITIONED STIMULUS: (CS) In classical conditioning, a previously neutral stimulus that comes to elicit a response; in Pavlov's experiment, the bell that came to elicit salivation.

CONTACT ULCERS: Points of erosion occurring in the cartilaginous portions of the vocal folds caused by forceful adduction.

CONTINUANT: A speech sound that can be sustained and retain its acoustic characteristics.

CONTROL: A group in an experiment that is the standard of comparison to other groups in the experiment; often the control group is considered to be normal relative to the experimental groups.

CONUS ELASTICUS: Membrane that continues the respiratory passageway upward from the cricoid cartilage to the vocal ligament which bounds the glottis.

CORTEX: [L. 'cortex' - bark.]. The outer or superficial part of an organ, as the outer layer of gray matter of the cerebrum.

COSTAL PLEURA: (Also called parietal pleura.) The membrane lining the walls of the thoracic cavity.

CRANIAL NERVES: The 12 pairs of nerves that emerge from the base of the brain. (See Appendix 2 for listing.)

CREAKY VOICE: See vocal fry.

CRICOID: [Gk. 'krikos' - ring + 'oid' - like.] The cartilage of the larynx which resembles a seal ring.

CRICOTHYROID MUSCLE: Intrinsic muscle of the larynx which tenses the vocal folds.

CRITICAL PERIOD: (For learning speech.) The period of life during which perception and production of a first language normally develop. It is believed that, after this period, development is difficult or impossible.

CYBERNETICS: [Gk. 'kybernetikos' - a pilot, to steer.] The study of self-regulatory systems.

DAF: See delayed auditory feedback.

DAMPING: The decay in amplitude of displacement over time.

DECIBEL: Unit of intensity; a ratio between the measured sound and a reference sound.

DELAYED AUDITORY FEEDBACK: (DAF) A delay in hearing one's own speech. Produced artificially.

DENDRITE: [Gk. 'dendron' - a tree.] The branching process that conducts a nerve impulse to the cell body.

DEPENDENT VARIABLE: The variable in an experiment which is observed and which changes as a result of manipulating the independent variable.

DEVELOPMENTAL APHASIA: Abnormal acquisition of speech and language in children due to central nervous system impairment.

DIAPHRAGM: The muscular and tendinous partition which separates the abdominal and thoracic cavities; used as a respiratory muscle.

DISCRIMINATION TEST: Type of test where stimuli are presented in ordered groups. The listener determines similarities and differences among the stimuli.

DYNE: A unit of force; the force required to accelerate during 1 second a 1-gram mass 1 cm per second.

DYSARTHRIA: A disorder of articulation due to the impairment of parts of the nervous system which control the muscles of articulation.

DYSLEXIA: Difficulty in learning to read.

ECHOLALIA: Automatic repetition of what is said by another.

EFFERENT: [L. 'ex' - out + 'ferre' - to bear.] Conducting from a central region to a peripheral region; refers to nerves which convey impulses from the central nervous system to the periphery.

EGOCENTRIC SPEECH: Talking aloud to oneself. (See monologue and collective monologue.)

ELABORATED CODE: Bernstein's term for the speech of those who do not assume that the listener knows the context; explicit. (See restricted code.)

ELASTICITY: Tendency to return to original shape after deformation under stress.

ELASTIC RECOIL: Return of a medium to its resting state due to its structural properties.

ELECTROMYOGRAPHY: Recording of muscle electrical potential by insertion of electrodes into the muscle fibers themselves or application on the skin surface.

EMPIRICIST: One who bases conclusions on experiment or observation rather than on reason alone.

ENCODED: (V., to encode.) Transformed in such a way that the original elements are no longer recognizable as discrete units.

ENDOLYMPH: The fluid in the membranous labyrinth of the inner ear.

EPIGLOTTIS: [Gk. 'epi' - on + 'glottis' - tongue.] A leaf-shaped flap of cartilage which closes the opening to the trachea preventing food and liquids from entering.

ESOPHAGUS: [Gk. 'eso' - within + 'phagus' - food.] The hollow muscular tube extending from the pharynx to the stomach.

EUSTACHIAN TUBE: [From Bartolommeo Eustachio, 16th century anatomist.] Narrow channel connecting the middle ear and the nasopharynx. Opening the tube allows for equalization of pressure on opposite sides of the eardrum.

EXPERIMENTAL: (Condition.) A set of circumstances under which observations are made.

EXTERNAL AUDITORY MEATUS: Canal leading from the eardrum to the auricle; part of the outer ear.

EXTERNAL FEEDBACK: A system's information about the consequences of its own performance; tactile and auditory feedback of speech. (See internal feedback and response feedback.)

EXTERNAL INTERCOSTAL MUSCLES: Muscles connecting the ribs and elevating them during inspiration.

EXTERNAL OBLIQUES: Muscles of the abdomen coursing downward and forward in the lateral walls.

FEATURE DETECTOR: A neural mechanism specialized to respond to acoustic or phonetic features in a signal.

FEATURES: Aspects of speech sounds that distinguish one from another.

FEEDBACK: Information about performance that is returned to control a system; negative feedback conveys error information, while positive feedback conveys the information that performance is as programmed.

FIBERSCOPE: A flexible bundle of optical fibers used for direct visual examination of interior of body cavities.

FISSURE OF ROLANDO: A groove which separates the frontal from the parietal lobes of the cerebral hemispheres.

FLUOROSCOPE: An instrument for direct visual observation of deep body structures by means of X-ray.

FORCED VIBRATION: Oscillation by an external force.

FORMANT: Vocal tract resonance; formants are displayed in a spectrogram as broad bands of energy.

FREE VIBRATION: Oscillation following displacement without further outside influence.

FREQUENCY: The number of cycles per second.

FRICATIVE: [L. 'fricare' - to rub.] High frequency sound produced by forcing the airstream through a narrow aperture.

FRONTAL LOBE: That part of either hemisphere of the cerebrum which is above the Sylvian fissure and in front of the Rolandic fissure.

FUNDAMENTAL FREQUENCY: The lowest frequency component of a complex tone.

GAMMA (γ) MOTONEURONS: Small motoneurons which transmit impulses to the intrafusal fibers of the muscle spindle.

GENIOGLOSSUS MUSCLE: An extrinsic tongue muscle which acts to bring the tongue body upward and forward.

GLIDE: Sound whose production requires the tongue to move quickly from one relatively open position to another in the vocal tract; /w/ and /j/ in English.

GLOTTAL ATTACK: A mode of initiation of voicing in which the vocal folds are tightly adducted at onset.

GLOTTIS: The space between the true vocal folds.

GLOTTOGRAPH: An instrument used to measure the relative amount of light transmitted through the glottis.

GRAPHIC LEVEL RECORDER: An instrument used to plot intensity as a function of time.

GRAY MATTER: Unmyelinated areas in the nervous system; such areas consist largely of cell bodies that contrast in color with the whitish nerve fibers.

HARD PALATE: The bony partition between the mouth and the nose; the roof of the mouth.

HARMONIC: An oscillation whose frequency is an integral multiple of the fundamental frequency.

HOMINIDS: Members of the family of modern and fossil man; does not include the apes.

HYOGLOSSUS MUSCLE: An extrinsic tongue muscle which can lower the tongue.

HYOID BONE: [Gk 'hyoeides' - U-shaped.] A horseshoe-shaped bone situated at the base of the tongue and above the thyroid cartilage.

HYPERNASALITY: A voice quality characterized by excessive nasal resonance.

HYPONASALITY: Voice quality characterized by inadequate nasal resonance.

IDENTIFICATION TEST: Perceptual test in which stimuli are presented separately to be labeled.

IMPEDANCE: Opposition to motion as a product of the density of the medium and the velocity of sound in it; the complex sum of reactances and resistances.

IN PHASE: Two signals with pressure waves that crest and trough at the same time.

INCISORS: The front teeth of the upper and lower jaw; eight teeth in normal dentition.

INCUS: [L. 'incus' - anvil.] The middle of the three ear ossicles; also called the anvil.

INDEPENDENT VARIABLE: The variable manipulated in the experiment.

INERTIA: The property of matter as a consequence of its mass by which it retains its state of rest or its velocity along a straight line so long as it is not acted upon by an external force.

INFERIOR CONSTRICTOR MUSCLE: One of the three pharyngeal constrictor muscles. Its fibers act as a valve separating the laryngopharynx from the esophagus.

INFERIOR LONGITUDINAL MUSCLES: Intrinsic tongue muscles which act to depress the tongue tip.

INTENSITY: Magnitude of sound expressed in power or pressure.

INTENSITY LEVEL: The power of the signal; decibels derived from a power ratio; the usual reference is 10^{-16} watts/cm^2.

INTERARYTENOID: Between the arytenoid cartilages; the transverse and oblique arytenoid muscles together compose the interarytenoid muscles. They function in adduction.

INTERCHONDRAL: Between cartilages; used to refer to the parts of the intercostal muscles running between the cartilaginous portions of the ribs.

INTERCOSTAL MUSCLES: Situated between the ribs; act in respiration.

INTERFERENCE PATTERN: Display of a complex wave.

INTERNAL AUDITORY MEATUS: The canal from the base of the cochlea which opens into the cranial cavity; a conduit for the VIIIth nerve, auditory veins and arteries, and the facial nerve (VII).

INTERNAL FEEDBACK: A system's information about its planned performance within the control center; the loops among the cerebrum, basal ganglia, and cerebellum during speech. (See response feedback and external feedback.)

INTERNAL INTERCOSTAL MUSCLES: Muscles connecting the ribs. Most act to lower the ribs during expiration.

INTERNAL OBLIQUES: Muscles of the abdomen coursing downward and posteriorly along the lateral walls.

INTERNAL PTERYGOID MUSCLE: See medial pterygoid muscle.

INTONATION: Perceived changes in fundamental frequency; pattern of modulation and inflection in connected speech.

INTRAORAL PRESSURE: Air pressure in the oral cavity.

INVERSE SQUARE LAW: Intensity of a sound varies directly as the square of the distance from the source.

JUNCTURE: The joining between words. Changing juncture signals differences in meaning; 'a name' and 'an aim' differ in juncture.

KINESTHESIS: [Gk. 'kinein' - move + 'aisthesis' - feeling.] Perception of one's own movement based upon information from proprioceptors.

LAG EFFECT: More accurate identification of the later stimulus presented in dichotic listening tests.

LAMINOGRAPHIC TECHNIQUE: A radiographic method in which X-rays from several sources are focussed in a plane yielding better definition of soft tissues; same as tomographic.

LANGUAGE: [L. 'lingua' - tongue.] The words, and rules for combining them, common to a particular group of people.

LARYNGEAL VENTRICLE: The space between the true and false vocal folds; also called the Ventricle of Morgagni.

LARYNGOGRAPH: An instrument used to measure impedance across the vocal folds.

LARYNGOSCOPE: A mirror and source of illumination for viewing the larynx from above.

LATERAL: A sound in which the phonated breath stream is emitted around the sides of the tongue; /l/.

LATERAL CRICOARYTENOID MUSCLES: Muscles which act to compress the medial portion of the glottis by rotating the arytenoid cartilages.

LATERAL INHIBITION: The isolation of a stimulus on the basilar membrane due to the inhibition of response in the nerve cells surrounding the point of maximal stimulation.

LATISSIMUS DORSI MUSCLE: Large broad muscle located on the back of the body on either side of the spine. It functions in forced respiration.

LAX: (Vowels.) Phonetic property of vowels that are produced with lower relative tongue height than tense vowels and with shorter durations.

LEVATOR PALATINI MUSCLE: Muscle running to and comprising most of the soft palate; its contraction elevates and backs the soft palate toward the pharyngeal wall.

LEVATORES COSTARUM MUSCLES: Twelve small triangular shaped pairs of muscles. They assist in inspiration by contracting and raising the ribs.

LINEAR SCALE: A scale in which each unit is equal to the next, permitting units to be summed by addition.

LINGUISTIC COMPETENCE: What one knows unconsciously about one's own language; the ability to understand and produce the language.

LINGUISTIC PERFORMANCE: How the knowledge of a language is used in expressive behavior such as speech or writing.

LIQUID: In English, /l/ and /r/, two of the semivowels produced with relatively prominent sonority.

LOGARITHMIC SCALE: [Gk. 'logos' - proportion + 'arithmos' - number.] A scale based on multiples of a given number (base).

LOMBARD EFFECT: The increased vocal intensity of a speaker who cannot hear himself.

LONGITUDINAL WAVE: [L. 'longitudo' - length.] Particle movement in the same direction as wave movement.

LOUDNESS: The subjective, psychological sensation of sound intensity.

MALLEUS: [L. 'malleus' - hammer.] The outermost and largest of the three middle ear ossicles; also called the hammer.

MANDIBLE: [L. 'madere' - chew.] The lower jaw bone.

MANNER: (Of articulation.) Classification of consonant sounds based on the strategy rather than the place of production; for example, the fricative /s/ differs from the stop /t/ in manner of articulation.

MANOMETER: An instrument for measuring the pressure of liquids or gases.

MANUBRIUM: The largest process of the malleus to which attaches the tympanic membrane.

MAXILLARY BONE: One of a pair of bones that form the upper jaw; the two together are often considered as one bone.

MAXIMUM EXPIRATORY PRESSURE: Combined active and passive forces available for expiration at a given lung volume.

MAXIMUM INSPIRATORY PRESSURE: Combined active and passive forces for inspiration at a given lung volume.

MEDIAL PTERYGOID MUSCLE: A muscle on the inner side of the mandible that acts in speech to close the jaw. (Also called the internal pterygoid.)

MEDULLA OBLONGATA: The portion of the brain which is continuous with the spinal cord below and the pons above; it lies ventral to the cerebellum.

MEL: Unit of pitch; value of $\frac{1}{1000}$ of the pitch of a 1000-Hz tone.

MENTAL RETARDATION: Condition in which inadequate brain development slows or prevents learning and adaptation.

METATHESIS: Interchange of sounds, syllables, or letters in a word.

MIDDLE CONSTRICTOR MUSCLE: The middle of three pharyngeal constrictor muscles which acts to narrow the pharynx in swallowing.

MIDDLE EAR: Small cavity containing three ossicles: the malleus, incus, and stapes; functions as an impedance matching transformer between air and cochlear fluid.

MONOLOGUE: [Gk. 'monos' - single + 'logos' - speech.] Speech by a lone person. (See collective monologue.)

MORPHEME: The smallest meaningful linguistic segment. The word 'books' contains two morphemes, 'book' and '-s' which means 'more than one.'

MORPHOLOGICAL: (Adj.) (Noun: morphology.) [Gk. 'morphe' - form + 'ology' - study.] Study of the form of words as affected by inflection or derivation.

MOTOR: A muscle, nerve, or center that effects movements.

MOTOR THEORY: A theory put forth by A. M. Liberman that speech perception makes reference to speech production.

MOTOR UNIT: The efferent nerve fiber and the muscle fibers that it innervates.

MUSCLE SPINDLES: Specialized muscle fibers with sensory innervation that signal muscle length and changes in length.

MYELIN: White fatty substance that sheaths many cranial and spinal nerves.

MYOELASTIC AERODYNAMIC THEORY OF PHONATION: Theory that holds that vocal fold vibration is primarily due to air pressure forces acting on the elastic mass of the folds.

NASAL SOUNDS: Those that are produced with an open velopharyngeal port.

NATURAL RESONANT FREQUENCY: That frequency at which a system oscillates with greatest amplitude when different frequencies are applied.

NEGATIVE FEEDBACK: See feedback.

NERVE: A bundle of neuron fibers that convey impulses from one part of the body to another.

NEURON: One of the cells of which the brain, spinal cord, and nerves are composed.

OBLIQUE ARYTENOID MUSCLE: Muscle which closes the glottis by approximating the arytenoid cartilages. Together with the transverse arytenoids, composes the interarytenoids.

ODDBALL TEST: Procedure for testing discrimination by requiring the listener to indicate which of three presented stimuli differs from the other two.

ONTOGENY: [Gk. 'ontos' - being + 'geneia' - origin.] The entire developmental history of an individual organism.

OPEN LOOP SYSTEM: A feedforward system without benefit of feedback on performance.

OPERANT CONDITIONING: A process by which the frequency of response is increased depending on when, how, and how much it is reinforced.

ORAL CAVITY: [L. 'oris' - mouth; L. 'cavus' - hollow.] The space inside the mouth.

ORAL SOUNDS: Sounds which are resonated in the mouth.

ORAL STEREOGNOSIS: The discrimination or recognition of object shapes by feeling them in the mouth.

ORBICULARIS ORIS MUSCLE: The sphincter muscle of the mouth which contracts to purse, protrude, or close the lips.

ORDINATE: The y coordinate of a point; its distance from the x axis measured parallel to the y axis (vertical axis).

ORGAN OF CORTI: The sensory organ of hearing which rests on the basilar membrane and contains sensory hair cells which are stimulated by movements within the cochlear duct.

OSCILLOSCOPE: An instrument which displays the magnitude of an electrical signal as a function of time; a cathode ray tube used to analyze waveforms.

OSSEOUS: [L. 'os' - bone.] Bony, or containing bones.

OSSICLES: Small bones; especially the small bones of the middle ear: the malleus, incus, and stapes.

OSSICULAR CHAIN: Composite of the three middle ear bones: the malleus, incus, and stapes.

OVAL WINDOW: Membrane between the middle and inner ear connecting and passing vibrations from the stapes to the cochlear fluids; also called the vestibular window and fenestra vestibuli.

PNS: See peripheral nervous system.

PALATOGLOSSUS MUSCLE: Extrinsic tongue muscle which raises the back of the tongue and can lower the soft palate; also called the glossopalatine muscle; the palatoglossus muscles form most of the anterior faucial pillars.

PALATOGRAPHY: A method of measuring points of contact between the tongue and palate.

PARALLEL PROCESSING: The coarticulation and adaptation of neighboring phones in speech production and the simultaneous decoding of neighboring phones in speech perception.

PARIETAL LOBE: A lobe in the upper center of the cerebrum behind the Fissure of Rolando and above the Fissure of Sylvius.

PARIETAL PLEURA: See costal pleura.

PECTORALIS MAJOR MUSCLE: The most superficial muscle of the chest. It functions in forced inspiration by elevating the ribs.

PECTORALIS MINOR MUSCLE: A thin, flat, triangular muscle which lies under the cover of the pectoralis major. With the scapula fixed, it may elevate the ribs for inspiration.

PERILYMPH: The fluid in the space between the membranous and osseous labyrinths of the ear.

PERIOD: The time taken for one cycle of vibration.

PERIODIC: Recurring at equal intervals of time.

PERIPHERAL NERVOUS SYSTEM: (PNS) Consists of the ganglia and nerves outside the brain and spinal cord.

PHARYNGEAL PLEXUS: [L. 'plexus' - a tangle.] A network of nerves through which the glossopharyngeal nerve supplies the mucous membranes of the pharynx with sensory branches and the accessory nerve supplies the levator palatini muscle with motor fibers.

PHARYNX: [Gk. 'pharynx' - throat.] The throat cavity made up of the nasopharynx, oropharynx, and laryngopharynx.

PHON: A unit of equal loudness.

PHONATION: Production of sound in the larynx.

PHONE: A particular speech sound; an allophone, or variant of a phoneme; the aspirated [t^h] and [t] are allophones of the phoneme /t/.

PHONEME: [Gk. 'phone' - sound.] A family of sounds that functions in a language to signal a difference in meaning.

PHONETIC: Representing speech sounds.

PHONOLOGICAL: (Adj.) (Noun: phonology.) Study of the system of sounds used in language; study of the history and changes in sounds of a language.

PHOTOELECTRIC: Electricity or electrical changes produced by light.

PHRENIC NERVE: Motor nerve to the diaphragm composed of several cervical nerves.

PHYLOGENY: [Gk. 'phylon' - race $^+$ 'geneia' - origin.] The entire developmental history of a race or group of organisms.

PINNA: See auricle.

PITCH: The subjective, psychological sensation of sound frequency; a low frequency sound produces a perception of low pitch.

PLACE OF ARTICULATION: Classification of speech sounds based on place of articulatory contact or constriction; for example, the bilabial /p/ and alveolar /t/ differ in place of articulation.

PLACE THEORY: Different frequencies activate the sensory nerve fibers at different places on the basilar membrane; higher frequencies closer to the base of the cochlea, lower frequencies toward the apical end.

PLOSIVE: [L. 'plaudere' - to clap.] A type of consonant sound made by sudden release of air impounded behind an occlusion in the vocal tract.

PNEUMOTACHOGRAPH: Instrument for measuring respiration.

POLES: An engineering term for resonances.

PONS: [L. 'pons' - bridge.] A large transverse band of nerve fibers in the hindbrain which forms the cerebellar stem and encircles the medulla oblongata.

POSITIVE FEEDBACK: See feedback.

POSTERIOR CRICOARYTENOID MUSCLES: (PCA) Muscles which separate the vocal folds by rotating and tilting the arytenoids, opening the glottis.

PRECATEGORICAL ACOUSTIC STORAGE: (PAS) Short-term auditory memory presumed to hold information during phonetic analysis.

PRESSURE: Force per unit area.

PRESSURE TRANSDUCER: A device that transforms relative pressure into an electrical signal.

PROSODY: (Adj., prosodic) [Gk. 'pros' - in addition to + 'oide' - song.] The description of the rhythm and tonal patterns of speech.

PULMONARY PLEURA: (Also called visceral pleura.) The membrane covering the lungs.

PURE TONE: A sound that consists of only one frequency of vibration.

PYRAMIDAL TRACT: (Corticospinal.) A major pathway for transmitting motor signals from the motor cortex.

QUANTAL THEORY: A theory put forth by K. N. Stevens that there are quantal discontinuities in the acoustic output of the vocal tract.

REA: See right ear advantage.

RAREFACTION: Area in a wave between compressions where the conducting medium is reduced in pressure.

RATIONALIST: One who bases conclusions on reason or intellect rather than on the senses.

REAL TIME SPECTRAL ANALYZER: An instrument that displays the frequency components of a complex signal.

RECENCY EFFECT: Subjects tend to remember the last item (most recent) on a list more readily than others on the same list.

RECTIFY: To reverse the direction of alternating impulses; transform an alternating current into a direct current.

RECTUS ABDOMINIS MUSCLE: Major muscle of the abdomen running vertically along the midline of the anterior wall.

RECURRENT NERVE: The branch of the vagus (Xth) nerve which innervates all intrinsic muscles of the larynx except the cricothyroid muscle; also called inferior laryngeal.

RELAXATION VOLUME: Amount of air in the lungs at the end of an exhalation during normal breathing; volume at which pressure inside the lungs is equal to atmospheric pressure, at about 40% vital capacity.

RESONANCE: Vibratory response to an applied force.

RESONATOR: Something which is set into vibration by the action of another vibration.

RESTRICTED CODE: Bernstein's term for the speech of those who assume that the listener knows the context. (See elaborated code.)

RETROFLEX: Retraction of the tongue tip; typical for production of /r/ in American English.

REVERBERATE: To be reflected many times, as sound waves from the walls of a confined space.

RIBS: Twelve pairs of bones extending ventrally from the 12 thoracic vertebrae and enclosing the thorax.

RIGHT EAR ADVANTAGE: (REA) In dichotic listening tests, subjects usually more correctly identify stimuli fed to the right ear than to the left.

SCALENUS MEDIUS MUSCLE: One of three pairs of muscles on each side of the neck which, acting from above, may elevate the first rib for inspiration.

SCAPULA: Flat triangular bone on the back of the shoulder. Also called the shoulder blade.

SECTION: A special form of spectrogram which shows the amplitude spectrum of a brief time segment of the signal.

SEMANTICS: [Gk. 'sema' - sign.] The study of meanings and the development of meanings of words.

SEMICIRCULAR CANALS: See vestibular system

SENSORY: (Nerve.) A peripheral nerve conducting impulses from a sensory organ toward the central nervous system; also called afferent nerve.

SERRATUS POSTERIOR SUPERIOR MUSCLE: Muscle extending obliquely downward and laterally from the upper portion of the thoracic region of the vertebral column to the superior borders of the upper ribs which they serve to elevate during inspiration.

SERVOMECHANISM: An automatic device which corrects its own performance.

SIBILANTS: [L. 'sibilare' - to hiss.] The high frequency fricative speech sounds of /s/ or /ʃ/ and their voiced cognates.

SIMPLE HARMONIC MOTION: Periodic vibratory movement where the amount of displacement from the position of equilibrium is proportional to the force that tends to restore it to equilibrium.

SINE WAVE: A periodic oscillation having the same geometric representation as a sine function.

SODIUM AMYTAL TEST: See Wada test.

SOFTWARE: Term for computer programs.

SONE: A unit of loudness equal to that of a tone of 1 kHz at 40 dB above absolute threshold.

SOUND: The sensation produced by stimulation of the organs of hearing by vibrations transmitted through the air or another medium.

SOUND PRESSURE LEVEL: (SPL) With reference to sound, the pressure of a signal; decibels derived from a pressure ratio; the usual reference is 0.0002 dynes/cm^2.

SOUND SPECTROGRAM: The hard copy produced by a sound spectrograph.

SOUND SPECTROGRAPH: An instrument that produces a hard copy display of a signal with frequency on the ordinate, time on the abscissa, and intensity as relative darkness.

SOUND WAVE: A longitudinal wave in an elastic medium; a wave producing an audible sensation.

SOURCE FUNCTION: The origin of acoustic energy for speech; for vowels at the vocal folds, for voiceless consonants in the vocal tract, and for voiced consonants both at the folds and in the tract.

SPASTICITY: Involuntary contraction of a muscle or group of muscles resulting in a state of rigidity.

SPECTRUM: See amplitude spectrum.

SPEECH PERCEPTION: Understanding speech.

SPINAL NERVES: The 31 paired nerves arising from the spinal cord which innervate body structures. (See Appendix 3 for listing.)

SPIROMETER: An instrument for measuring volumes of air taken in and expelled from the lungs.

SPOONERISM: A transposition of the initial sounds of two (or more) words in a phrase; named for William A. Spooner.

STAPEDIUS MUSCLE: Muscle which alters movement of the stapes in the oval window.

STAPES: [L. 'stapes' - stirrup.] The innermost of the three ear ossicles; also called the stirrup.

STERNOCLEIDOMASTOID MUSCLE: A paired muscle running diagonally across the neck which assists in forced inspiration by elevating the sternum.

STERNOHYOID MUSCLE: An extrinsic laryngeal muscle which depresses the hyoid bone and larynx; one of the strap muscles.

STERNUM: The breastbone.

STIMULUS ONSET ASYNCHRONY: (SOA) A time difference between the onsets of two dichotically presented stimuli.

STOP: See plosive.

STORAGE OSCILLOSCOPE: A cathode ray tube instrument that can maintain a display for a period of time.

STRAIN GAUGE: A transducer that converts movement patterns into patterns of electrical voltage.

STROBOSCOPE: A device that emits brief flashes of light at a controlled frequency.

STYLOGLOSSUS MUSCLE: One of the extrinsic tongue muscles; lifts the tongue upward and backward.

SUBCLAVIUS MUSCLE: A relatively small flattened muscle which lies beneath the clavicle and assists in inspiration by elevating the first rib.

SUBGLOTTAL AIR PRESSURE: Air pressure beneath the vocal folds.

SUPERIOR CONSTRICTOR MUSCLE: Uppermost of three pharyngeal constrictor muscles acts to narrow the pharynx in swallowing. May aid in velopharyngeal closure during speech.

SUPERIOR LONGITUDINAL MUSCLE: Intrinsic tongue muscle which acts to turn the tip of the tongue upward.

SUPRASEGMENTAL: Overlaid upon the segments of speech; meaning given by stress, juncture, and intonation.

SYLLABIC CONSONANT: A consonant that takes the place of a syllabic nucleus.

SYLLABIC NUCLEI: (Sing., syllablic nucleus.) The relatively steady-state vocalic portions of syllables.

SYLLABLE: A unit of speech consisting of a vowel alone or with one or more consonants.

SYNAPSE: The region of juncture between one nerve cell and other.

SYNTAGMA: The uninterrupted speech phrase.

SYNTAX: (Adj., syntactic) [Gk. 'syn' - together + 'tassein' - arrange.] Arrangement of the words of a sentence in their proper forms and relations.

TABULA RASA: Blank slate; referring to the theory that the mind is initially a blank slate upon which experiences imprint themselves.

TECTORIAL MEMBRANE: Gelatinous membrane overlying the Organ of Corti.

TEMPLATE: A pattern.

TEMPORAL LOBE: The lower, lateral portion of the cerebral hemisphere, lying below the Fissure of Sylvius.

TENSE: (Vowels.) Phonetic property of vowels that are produced with slightly higher relative tongue position than lax vowels and with longer durations.

TENSOR PALATINI MUSCLES: Muscles which open the eustachian tube and which may act to tense the soft palate.

TENSOR TYMPANI: Muscle which tenses the eardrum.

THALAMUS: [Gr. 'thalmos' - inner chamber.] A mass of gray matter situated at the base of the cerebrum; thought to be important to speech.

THORACIC NERVES: Twelve pairs of spinal nerves that arise from the segments of the spinal cord in the chest region.

THORAX: The part of the body between the neck and the abdomen separated from the abdomen by the diaphragm; the chest.

THYROARYTENOID MUSCLE: An intrinsic laryngeal muscle which shortens and tenses the vocal folds; consisting of external and internal parts (see vocalis); forms part of the vocal folds.

THYROID: [Gr. 'thyreos' - shield.] The large shield-shaped cartilage of the larynx.

THYROHYOID MUSCLE: A muscle originating on the side of the thyroid cartilage and inserting in the greater horn of the hyoid bone; it is innervated by the upper cervical nerves and acts to raise and change the shape of the larynx.

TIDAL VOLUME: The amount of air normally inspired and expired in a respiratory cycle.

TOMOGRAPHIC METHODS: See laminographic.

TORQUE: A rotatory force; used to refer to the untwisting of the cartilaginous portions of the ribs.

TRACHEA: The windpipe, a tube composed of horseshoe-shaped cartilages leading to the lungs.

TRAGUS: Small cartilaginous flap which shields the opening to the external auditory meatus.

TRANSFER FUNCTION: The contribution of vocal tract resonance of the source function to the resulting speech sound. (See source function.)

TRANSIENT: Not lasting; an acoustic event of brief duration.

TRANSILLUMINATION: A method of indirectly measuring glottal opening. (See glottograph.)

TRANSITION: A change in formant frequency.

TRANSVERSE ARYTENOID MUSCLE: See interarytenoid.

TRANSVERSE MUSCLES OF THE TONGUE: Intrinsic tongue muscles which act to narrow the tongue body.

TRANSVERSE WAVES: A type of wave where particle movement is perpendicular to wave movement.

TRANSVERSUS ABDOMINIS MUSCLES: Muscles of the abdomen coursing horizontally across the walls.

TRAVELING WAVE THEORY: Theory that the cochlea analyzes incoming auditory signals into component 'traveling waves.'

TWO-POINT DISCRIMINATION: The ability to perceive two discrete points in close proximity as such and not as a single point.

TYMPANIC MEMBRANE: The eardrum, a fibrous membrane at the end of the external auditory meatus; its response is transmitted to the middle ear ossicles.

ULTRASOUND: Ultrasonic waves (those above audible frequencies); a method of measuring movement is to bombard a structure with ultrasonic waves.

UNCONDITIONED STIMULUS: (UCS) In classical conditioning a stimulus that naturally elicits a response; in Pavlov's experiment, the meat powder that elicits salivation.

UVULA: [L. 'uvula' - little grape.] Small fleshy mass which hangs from the back of the soft palate.

UVULAR MUSCLE: The muscle within the uvula.

VELOCITY: Change of position in time.

VELOPHARYNGEAL CLOSURE: The closing off of the nasal passages from the oral cavity by raising the velum against the pharynx.

VELOPHARYNGEAL PORT: The passageway connecting oral and nasal cavities.

VELUM: The soft palate.

VENTRICULAR FOLDS: The 'false vocal folds;' the folds above the true vocal folds.

VERBAL TRANSFORMATION: Changes in the auditory perception of a repeated utterance.

VERTEBRAE: (Sing., vertebra.) The segments of the bony spinal column.

VERTICAL MUSCLES: Intrinsic tongue muscle fibers which act to flatten the tongue.

VESTIBULAR SYSTEM: Three canals in the inner ear containing the sense organs for equilibrium.

VESTIBULE: The cavity at the entrance to the cochlea which houses the utricle and saccule, sense organs responsive to linear acceleration.

VISCERAL PLEURA: See pulmonary pleura.

VITAL CAPACITY: The total volume of air that can be expelled from the lungs after maximum inspiration.

VOCAL FRY: (Creaky voice.) A vocal mode in which the vocal folds vibrate at such low frequency that the individual vibrations can be heard.

VOCAL TRACT: All the cavities superior to the larynx used as a variable resonator; includes the buccal, oral, nasal, and pharyngeal cavities.

VOCALIS MUSCLE: The internal portion of the thyroarytenoid muscle; the vibrating part of the vocal folds.

VOICE: (Verb form.) See voicing.

VOICE ONSET TIME: (VOT) The interval of time between the release of a stop-plosive, voiced or unvoiced, and the onset of voicing of the following vowel.

VOICING: The production of sound by the vibration of the vocal folds.

VOLLEY THEORY: Frequency information conveyed directly by the firing of neurons. At frequencies higher than the firing capacity of individual neurons, groups of neurons cooperate.

VOLTMETER: An instrument for measuring electromotive force in volts.

WADA TEST: (Sodium amytal test.) A procedure to establish which side of the cerebrum is dominant for language.

WATT: A unit of electric power equivalent to 1 joule per second.

WAVEFORM: A graphic representation of a vibratory event showing amplitude *versus* time.

WAVELENGTH: (λ) The distance in space occupied by one cycle.

WHITE MATTER: Myelinated areas in the central nervous system.

WHORFIAN HYPOTHESIS: The theory that language determines to some extent the way one thinks.

ZEROS: An engineering term for antiresonances.

Index

References to illustrations are in boldface type; titles of publications are in italics.

Abbs, J., 136, 159, 212, 242
Abdominal muscles, 70, **72**
Abduction of vocal folds, 78, 273
Abramson, A. S., 116, 118, 158, 181, 193, 210, 242, 243
Abscissa, 33, 35, 273
Absolute threshold of audibility, 273
ABX test, 273
Acceleration, 28, 30, 273
Acoustic adaptation, **126**
Acoustic cues in speech perception, 171–187, 205. *See also* Speech perception
Acoustic discontinuities, in speech perception, 208
Acoustic locus, 177, **180**
Acoustic reflex, 166, 273
Acoustic resonator, 44, 273
Acoustic signal, 11, 14, 33, 34. *See also* Amplitude; Frequency; Sound; Velocity; Vibration; Wavelength
Acoustic theory of vowel production, 95–107
Acoustical Society of America (ASA), 24; publication of, 24
Acoustically shielded booth, 216, **218**
Acoustics, 17, 18, 20, 22, 24, 27–45, 273
Active theories of speech perception, 204–206
Adam's apple, 77
Adaptation, 124–127, 197, 273
Adduction of vocal folds, 78–80, 273
Ades, A. E., 212
Aerodynamic forces, **83**. *See also* Myoelastic theory; Vocal fold vibration
Afferent neurons, 48, 273
Affricates, 91, 122–**123**, **125**, 182–183, 273
Agnosia, auditory, 57
Air pressure, measurement of, 69
Airflow, 228
Alaryngeal speech, 86–87
Ali, L., 174, 209
Allen, G. D., 242
Allophone, 8, 273
All-or-none principle, 49, **50**, 273

Alpha motoneurons, 135, 273
Alveolar fricative; *see* Fricatives
Alveolar nasal; *see* Nasal consonants
Alveolar process, 91, 273
Alveolar ridge, 93, **113**
Alveolar stops; *see* Stop consonants
Alveoli, 61, 63
American Association for the Advancement of Science, 25
American Association of Phonetic Sciences, 24
American Sign Language (Ameslan), 2–3, 251
American Speech-Language-Hearing Association (ASHA), 24; publications of, 24
Ameslan; *see* American Sign Language
Amplitude, 28, 29, 31, **33**, **34**, 35, 273
Amplitude spectrum, 35, 37, 273
Ampulla, **167**
Analog to digital converters, 241, 273
Analysis, auditory; *see* Auditory analysis
Analysis, phonetic; *see* Phonetic analysis
Analysis-by-synthesis theory, 204, 205, 273
Anarthria, **54**
Anderson, S., 211
Angel, R. W., 159
Anterior faucial pillars, **113**, 273
Anterior nasal spine, **92**
Anterior speech cortex, **56**; *see* Broca's area
Anticipatory assimilation, 127
Antiresonance, 114, 115, 273
Aperiodic vibration, 35, 37, 59, 273
Aphasia, 3, 52, **54**, 55, 274; developmental, 57, 162, 275
Architectural acoustics, 34–35
Artery, carotid, 56, 274
Articulation, 89–95, 174, 176, 183–186, 274
Articulatory adaptation, 124–127
Articulatory effort, and stress, 129
Artificial palates, 236
Arytenoid cartilages, **76**, **77**, 79, 274
ASA; *see* Acoustical Society of America
Ascher, R., 250, 265

ASHA; *see* American Speech-Language-Hearing Association
Aspirate, 121, 274
Aspiration, 116–117, 181, 182
Assimilation, 127, 274
Associate chain theory, 142
Athetosis, 57, 274
Atkinson, J. E., 86, 157
Audibility, 33; threshold of, 40, **41**, 273
Audiometers, 42
Audition, 162, 274·
Auditory agnosia, 57, 162, 200, 274
Auditory analysis, in speech perception, 196–197
Auditory cortex, 170
Auditory feature detectors, 207
Auditory feedback, 131–133
Auditory masking, 134
Auditory mechanism, 33, 38, 162, 169–171, 201, 208, 274
Auditory nerve, 52, 169–171, 201, 269, 274
Auditory property detectors, 207
Auditory template, 204, 206
Auditory theory, 140–141
Aungst, L. F., 199, 211
Auricle, 163, 274
Australopithecus, 262; A. africanus, 246, 247, 249, 256; A. robustus, 249
Autism, 57, 274
Autistic theory, 6, 274
Axon, 49, **50**, 274

Babbling, 4, 5, 203, 204, 255, 274
Backward masking, 202
Baddeley, A. D., 212
Bailey, P., 212
Baken, R. J., 242
Barney, H. L., 103, 104, 158, 173
Bartlett, F. C., 162, 209
Basal ganglia, 48, 57, 274
Basilar membrane, 167, **168, 169**, 274
Bastian, J., 134, 210
Bel, 39
Bell, A. G., 19, 20, 39
Bell, A. M., 19
Bell, C., 134
Bell, M., 19
Bell-Berti, F., 113, 114, 126, 128, 157, 158
Bell Telephone Company, 20, 21
Bell Telephone Laboratories, 22, 95, 138
Benade, A. H., 45
Berlin, C., 211
Berman, A. J., 160
Bernoulli, D., 81
Bernoulli effect, 80, 81, 274; principle, 75, **83, 84**
Bernstein, B., 5
Berti, F., 157
Bicuspid, **113**
Bilabial nasal; *see* Nasal consonants
Bilabial stops; *see* Stop consonants
Binaural hearing, 164
Binaural listening condition, 239

Bird song, 206, 253–254
Black, J. W., 158
Blind, reading machine for, 23
Blumstein, S., 212
Body plethysmograph, 229, **232**, 274
Bolinger, D. W., 210
Borden, G. J., 128, 158, 159
Borst, J. M., 174, 209
Bouhuys, A., 68, 157
Bowman, J. P., 159
Boyle's law, 60, 66
Brain, 5, 48, **49**, 256
Brain and Language, 25
Brain stem, 48, **49**, 274
Branch, C., 157
Breast bone; *see* Sternum
Breath group, 130
Breathing: clavicular, 73; negative pressure, 59–61. *See also* Expiration; Inspiration; Respiration
Breathy voice, 87
Bremer, C. D., 211
Broad Romic, 19
Broadbent, D. E., 173, 206, 209, 212
Broca, P., 52, 156
Broca's area, 52, **53**, 55, **56**, 57, 203, 247, 256
Bronchi, 61, 63, **65**
Bronchioles, 61, 63
Brown University, 194
Bruner, J., 3
Buccal cavity, 90, 274
Buchwald, S. E., 194, 210

Campbell, E., 157
Cardinal vowels, **106**
Carlson, R., 209
Carney, A. E., 197, 211
Carotid artery, 56, 274
Carryover assimilation, 127
Case Western Reserve University, 247
Cassette recorders, 218
Catania, A. C., 159
Categorical perception, 187–199, 254, 274
Catena, L., 159
Catheter, 228, 274
Cathode ray tube (CRT), 221
Cavity; *see* Buccal cavity; Nasal cavity; Oral cavity; Pharyngeal cavity; Pleural cavity
Cell body, of neuron, 48, **50**
Central incisor, **92**
Central nervous system (CNS), 48, 52–57, 274. *See also* Nervous system
Central tendency, 274
Centre National de la Recherche Scientifique, 247
Cerebellum, 48, **49**, 57, 274. *See also* Nervous system
Cerebral cortex, 48, **49**, 52, 53, **54**, 55, **56**, 57, 256, 275. *See also* Nervous system
Cerebral hemispheres, 274; *see* Cerebral cortex; Cerebral lateralization: Hemispheric dominance; Nervous system
Cerebral lateralization, 200–203, 204, 256–258, 262, 263. *See also* Hemispheric dominance

Cerebral palsy, 57, 74, 114, 274
Cerebral vascular accident (CVA), 52, 200, 274
Cerumen, 164, 274
Cervical nerve(s), 62, 274
Chadwick, L. E., 157
Chiba, T., 95, 97, 157
Child language, and speech evolution, 254–257
Chimpanzee language, 252–253, 254
Chimpanzee warning call, 250
Chinchillas, 254
Chistovich, L. A., 128, 143, 144, 158, 160, 205, 212
Chomsky, N., 2, 5, 7, 139, 160, 245, 265
Chomsky and Halle, 139
Cilia, 164, 274
Cinefluorography, 216, 234, 235, 274
Clavicles, 274
Clavicular breathing, 73, 74
Cleft palate, 114, 274
Closed loop system, 131, **132,** 274
Closed syllables, 107
CNS; see Central nervous system
Coarticulation, 127–128, 129, **251,** 274
Cochlea, **163, 167, 168, 169,** 274
Cochlear duct, **167,** 168, **169,** 274
Cochlear nerve, **163**
Cochlear partition, **168**
Cognate, 116, 275
Cole, R. A., 207, 212
Collective monologue, 4, 275
Columbia University, 247
Communication, 1, 275
Competence, linguistic, 2, 7
Complex tone, 35, **36, 37,** 84, 275
Complex vibration, 27, 35, 37
Complex waveform, 35
Compression, 32, **33,** 275
Concert halls, 34–35
Condillac, 245
Conditioned response (CR), 6, 275
Conditioned stimulus (CS), 6, 275
Conditioning, 6, 279
Consonants, 38, 78, 109–128
Contact ulcers, 87, 275
Context dependence, 187
Context effects, 130
Continuants, 91, 121–133, 275
Contrastive stress; see Stress
Control condition, 215, 275
Conus elasticus, 79, 86, 275
Cooper, F. S., 11, 22, 23, **23,** 140, 158, 160, 171, 174, 177, 209, 210, 212, 213, 243
Cooper, S., 159
Cooper, W. E., 212
Corbit, J. D., 197, 211
Cornua: of hyoid bone, 77; of thyroid cartilage, 77, **78**
Corpus, of mandible, **93**
Corpus callosum, 200
Cortex, cerebral; see Cerebral cortex
Cortico-spinal (pyramidal) tract, **55,** 57
Costal pleura; see Pleurae

CR; see Conditioned response
Crandall, I. B., 95, 157
Cranial nerves, 48, 52, 78, 85, 112, 114, 117, 120, 121, 166, 169–171, 201, 269, 274, 275
Creaky voice, 87, 275
Crelin, E. S., 260, 265
Cricoid cartilage, **76, 77,** 79, 275
Cricothyroid membrane, **76**
Cricothyroid muscle, **85,** 130, 275
Critchlow, V., 136, 159
Critical period, 204, 275
Crowder, R. G., 203, 212
CRT; see Cathode ray tube
CS; see Conditioned stimulus
Cuspid, **113**
Cutting, J. E., 196, 202, 211
CVA; see Cerebral vascular accident
Cybernetics, 131, 144, 275
Cycles per second; see Hertz

DAF; see Delayed auditory feedback
Damping, 28, 275
Daniloff, R. G., 128, 158, 159, 174, 209
Darwin, C. J., 197, 203, 209, 211, 212
David, E. E., Jr., 45, 209
Davis, H., 209
Day, M. H., 265
Day, R. S., 202, 211, 212
Deaf speech, 3, 73, 109, 114, 133, 162
Decibel, 39–41, 275
De Clerk, J. L., 125, 158, 160
Deep structure, 11
Delattre, P., 22, 23, 171, 174, 177, 209, 210
Delayed auditory feedback (DAF), 131, **133,** 138, 275
Dendrite, 49, **50,** 275
Denes, P., 45, 157, 162, 182, 209, 210, 242
Dependent variable, 215, 275
Descartes, R., 245, **246,** 264, 265
Desensitization, 215
Determining tendency, 142
Development, of language and speech; see Language and speech development
Developmental aphasia, 57, 162, 275
Diaphragm, 61, **62, 63, 65,** 70, **72,** 275
Dichotic listening, 200, 201, 239
Dichotic stimuli, 201
Dickson, D. R., 156
Diehl, R. L., 194, 210
Digastric muscle, **95, 117**
Diphthongs, 90–91, 107–109, 173; synthetic, see Speech synthesis
Discrimination, tactile, 134
Discrimination function, 190, **193**
Discrimination test, 189, **190,** 275
Displacement, 29, **30, 33**
Distinctive features, 139, 206
Dolphins, 252
Dominant hemisphere, 52, 55, **56**–57. See also Cerebral lateralization
Dorman, M. F., 158, 159, 183, 205, 210, 212

Dorsum, of tongue, **94**
Draper, M. H., 70, 157
Dudley, H. W., 21
Dunn, H. K., 242
Duration, 128–130
Durrant, J. D., 209
Dyne, 39, 40, 275
Dysarthria, 55, 275
Dysfluency, and delayed auditory feedback, 131
Dyslexia, 57, 275

Ear, 33, 38, 39, 45, **163, 164**
Ear canal, **163, 164**
Eardrum, **164**. See also Tympanic membrane
Eccles, J. C., 57, 156, 160
Echolalia, 4, 275
Edman, T. R., 173, 209
Efferent neurons, 48, 275
Egocentric speech, 4, 275
Eimas, P. D., 193, 194, 197, 210, 211, 254
Elaborated code, 5, 275
Elastic recoil, 28, 66, 67, 70, 275
Elasticity, 27, 28, 30, 31, 275
Electrical potential, 233
Electrodes, 233, **236**, 238; insertion of, 234
Electromyography, 233, 234, **237**, 238, 275
Ellman, S. J., 160
Elman, J. L., 194, 210
EMG; see Electromyography
Empiricism, 245
Empiricist, 276
Endolymph, 167, 276
Endolymphatic duct, **167**
Epiglottis, **65**, 75, **76**, 276
Equal loudness contours, **41**
Equilibrium, **33**
Esophagus, 75, **90, 92**, 276
Esthesiometer, 134
Eustachian tube, **112, 163, 164**, 166, 276
Evans, E. F., 213
Evarts, E. V., 160
Evolution of language and speech, 245–266
Experimental condition, 215, 276; method, 215
Expiration, 66–74
Expiratory pressure curve, 67–**68**
External auditory meatus, **163, 164**, 276
External feedback, 134, 276
External intercostal muscles, 62, **64**, 69, 70, 276
External oblique muscle, **66**, 70, **72**, 276
Exteroceptors, 135
Extrafusal fibers, 135
Extrinsic muscles of tongue, **94**

F_1 cutback, 178, **180**, 181, 182
Faaborg-Andersen, K., 157
Facial muscles, **95**
Facial nerve, 114, 120, **163**, 269
Fairbanks, G., 108, 144, 146, 158, 159, 160
False vocal folds; see Ventricular folds
Falsetto voice, 81, 85

Fant, G., 95, 98, 106, 139, 157, 160, 173, 206, 209, 212, 242
Feature detector, 197, 206, 207, 276
Feature detector theory, 207
Features, phonetic, 11, 276
Fechner, G., 39
Feedback, 131–138, 143, 274, 276, 277, 278, 279, 280
Fenn, W. O., 157
Fiberoptic endoscope data, **237**
Fiberscope, 230, **233**, 276
Fissure of Rolando, **53, 54**, 276
Fissure of Sylvius, **53**, 258
Fitzgerald, M. J. T., 159
Flanagan, J. L., 138, 157, 242
Fletcher, H., 41, 45, 209
Fletcher, S. G., 242
Fluoroscope, 234, 276
Folia Phoniatrica, 25
Folkins, J. W., 159
Forced choice, 190
Forced vibration, 44, 276
Formants, 100, 102–111, 171, 173, 226, 276
Fossil hominids, 246–247
Four-interval forced choice procedure, 197
Fourcin, A. J., 211, 242
Fourier, J. B. J., 35, 45
Fourier analysis, 98; by cochlea, 168–169
Free vibration, 43, 276
Freeman, F. J., 158
Frequency, 27, 28, 29, **31**, 33
Frequency analysis, by cochlea, 168–169
Frequency, fundamental; see Fundamental frequency
Frequency, natural resonant, 43–44
Frequency range, of ear, 38
Fricatives, 91, 119–122, **123, 124**, 182–183, 276
Frick, J. V., 199, 211
Fritzell, B., 113, 157
Fromkin, V. A., 11, 58, 156, 159
Frontal lobe, 52, **53**, 276
Fry, D. B., 157, 158, 187, 193, 209, 210
Fujimura, O., 115, 157, 210, 242
Fujisaki, H., 210
Fundamental frequency, 35, 38–39, 43–44, 75, 84–86, 88, 105, 129, 276
Furth, H., 3

Gallagher, T., 174, 209
Gamma motoneurons, 135, 276
Gammon, S. A., 159
Ganglia, basal; see Basal ganglia
Garber, S. F., 133, 159
Garcia, M. P. R., 229, 230
Gardner, B. T., **252**, 265
Gardner, H., 211
Gardner, R. A., 252, 265
Gay, T., 79, 87, 128, 157, 158, 173, 209, 242
Gazzaniga, M. S., 200, 211
Geldard, F. A., 209
General Electric Research Laboratories, 23
Genioglossus muscle, **94, 95, 100**, 108, 109, 121, 126, **127**, 276

Geniohyoid muscle, **86, 94, 95,** 108, 121
Gerstman, L. J., 171, 173, 174, 209, 210
Geschwind, N., 200, 211, 256, 265
Gestural language, 251
Gill, T. V., 266
Glides, 276. *See also* Semivowels
Glossary, 273–283
Glossopalatus muscle; *see* Palatoglossus muscle
Glottal area, 23
Glottal attack, 87, 276
Glottal fricative, 121
Glottal stop, 117
Glottis, 76, **77,** 78, **79,** 276
Glottograph, 231, 276
Godfrey, J. J., 211
Goehl, H., 199, 211
Goff, W. R., 202, 212
Golden, S. A., 199, 211
Goldstein, J., 174, 209
Goodglass, H., 200, 211
Goodwin, G. M., 136, 159
Goto, H., 199, 211
Granstrom, B., 209
Graphic level recorder, 221, **223,** 276
Gray matter, 51, 276
Green, H. C., 157
Griffith, B. C., 189, 210
Guttman, N., 158

Habituation, 194
Hadding-Koch, K., 210
Hair cells, 168, 169
Halle, M., 139, 160, 204, 212
Hamlet, S. L., 159
Hammarberg, R. E., 158
Hand preference, 262
Hard copy, 216, **221**
Hard palate, 92, **93, 113,** 276
Hardcastle, W. J., 159
Harmonic motion, simple; *see* Simple harmonic motion
Harmonics, 19, 35, **84, 96,** 276
Harnad, S. R., 265
Harris, K. S., 126, 128, 156, 158, 159, 182, 189, 209, 210, 213, 242
Harrison, E., Jr., 242
Harvard Medical School, 256
Harvard University, 245
Haskins Laboratories, 22, 172, 176, 178, 204
Hearing, 40, 41, 162–171; theories of, 168, 169, 280, 282, 283
Hebb, D. O., 140, 160
Heinz, J. M., 122, 158
Helmholtz, H. L. F., 209. *See also* Von Helmholtz.
Helmholtz model of vocal tract, 95
Helmholtz resonators, **18**
Hemispheres, cerebral, 274; *see* Cerebral cortex; Cerebral lateralization; Hemispheric dominance; Nervous system
Hemispheric dominance, 52, 55, **56,** 57. *See also* Cerebral lateralization

Henke, W., 142, 160
Hertz (Hz), 18, 27, 28, 29, 38
Hertz, H., 18
Hewes, G. W., 265
Higgins, J. R., 159
Hirano, M., 242
Hirose, H., 79, 87, 157, 242
Hixon, T. J., 156, 157
Hoarse voice, 87
Hockett, C. F., 250, 254, 265
Hoffman, H. S., 189, 210
Holbrook, A., 108, 158
Holloway, R. L., 247, 256, 265
Hominids, 246, 276
Homo erectus, 247, 254, 256
Homo sapiens, 5, 7, 245, 249, 262
Horii, Y., 159
House, A. S., 95, 98, 158, 159, 160, 176, 209, 212
Huggins, A. W. F., 242
Husson, R., 75, 157
Hutchison, J. M., 159
Hyoglossus muscle, **94, 102,** 276
Hyoid bone, 75, **76, 86, 94,** 276
Hypernasality, 114, 276
Hypoglossal nerve, 117, 120
Hypokinesis, 57
Hyponasality, 114, 276
Hz; *see* Hertz

Identification function, 190, **192**
Identification test, 189, **190,** 277
IL; *see* Intensity level
Impedance, 165, 166, 277
Imprinting, 254
Incisive foramen, **93**
Incisor, 91, **92, 113,** 277
Incus, **164,** 165, 277
Independent variable, 215, 277
Inertia, 28, 30, 31, 277
Inferior constrictor muscle, 91, **92,** 277
Inferior longitudinal muscle, **94, 95,** 277
Innateness hypothesis, 7
Innateness, of speech perception, 198
Inner ear, **163,** 166–169
Inner speech, 4
Inspiration, 61–**68,** 70, **71**
Instrumentation, in speech science, 216–242
Intensity, 33, 39, 40, 41–42, 70, 72–73, 129, 277
Intensity level, 277
Interarytenoid muscle, 79, **80,** 82, 277
Intercostal muscles, 62, **64,** 69–70, 276, 277
Interference pattern, 33–35, 221, 277
Internal auditory meatus, 170, 277
Internal feedback, 136–137, 277
Internal intercostal muscles, 62, **64,** 70, 277
Internal oblique muscle, 70, **72,** 277
Internal pterygoid muscle, 277
Internal response, 6
International Congress of Phonetic Sciences, 24
International Phonetic Alphabet (IPA), 8, 19, 267
Intonation, 11, 85, 128, 129–130, 186, 187, 277

Intrafusal fibers, 135
Intraoral pressure, 113, 277
Intrinsic duration, 130
Intrinsic muscles of tongue, 94, **95**, 121
Invariant cues, in speech perception, 207
Inverse square law, 42, 277
IPA; see International Phonetic Alphabet
Irwin, J. V., 156

Jakobson, R., 139, 160
JASA (Journal of the Acoustical Society of America), 24
Jenkins, J. J., 194, 210
Johanson, D. C., 247, 262, 265
Joos, M., 106, 158, 209
Journal of the Acoustical Society of America (JASA), 24
Journal of Phonetics, 24
Journal of Speech and Hearing Disorders (JSHD), 24
Journal of Speech and Hearing Research (JSHR), 24
JSHD (Journal of Speech and Hearing Disorders), 24
JSHR (Journal of Speech and Hearing Research), 24
Juncture, 128, 130, 187, **188,** 277
Jusczyk, P., 194, 195, 210

Kajiyama, M., 95, 97, 157
Kawashima, T., 210
Keller, H., 3
Kent, R. D., 158, 242
Kiang, N. Y. S., 209
Kim, C. W., 159
Kimura, D., 201, 204, 211, 258
Kinesthesis, 134, 277
Kiritani, S., 242
Klass, V. A., 205, 212
Klatt, D. H., 198, 211, 265
KNM-ER 1470, 247, **248**
Koenig, W., 242
Koenig scale, 106
Koenigsknecht, R. A., 198, 211
Kohn, J., 199, 211
Kopp, G. A., 157
Kornfeld, J. R., 199, 211
Kozhevnikov, V. A., 128, 143, 144, 158, 160
Kuhl, P. K., 195, 196, 210
Kuhn, G. M., 158, 178, 209–210
Kutz, K. J., 199, 211
Kuzmin, Y. I., 205, 212

Labiodental fricatives; see Fricatives
La Chapelle-aux-Saints, 250, 260
Lacy, L. Y., 242
Ladefoged, P., 45, 70, 87, 106, 142, 157, 158, 159, 160, 173, 209
Lag effect, 202, 277
Lambda, 42
Lamendella, J. T., 256, 265
Laminographic technique, 277
Laminography, 234
Lana, 252, **253**

Lancaster, J., 265
Lane, H. L., 159, 212
Language, 1–2, 4–7, 55, 277. *See also* Speech and language development
Language and speech; *see* Speech and language
Laryngeal endoscope, 230
Laryngeal function, study of, 229–235
Laryngeal ventricle, **76,** 277
Laryngitis, 87
Laryngograph, 232, 233, **234, 235,** 277
Laryngology, 230
Laryngopharynx, 91
Laryngoscope, 229, 277
Laryngoscopy, 230
Larynx, 61, 63, **65,** 74–75, **76, 77,** 78, 258, 260, 263–264
Lashley, K. S., 142, 160
Lateral, 277. *See also* Semivowels
Lateral cricoarytenoid muscle, 79, **81, 87,** 277
Lateral incisor, **92**
Lateral inhibition, 170, 277
Lateral pterygoid muscle, **121**
Lateral semicircular canal, **167**
Lateralization; see Cerebral lateralization
Latissimus dorsi muscle, 63, **66,** 277
Law, M. E., 159
Lawrence, M., 209
Lax (vowels), 107, 277
Lazarus, J. H., 197, 211
Leakey, R. E. F., 247, 262, 265
Leanderson, R., 159
Learning disabilities, 57
Lee, B. S., 131, 159
Lee, C. Y., 160
Left cerebral hemisphere, **56,** 200–203, 263
Left hemisphere; *see* Left cerebral hemisphere
Lehiste, I., 108, 157, 158, 210
Lenneberg, E. H., 7, 204, 211
Levator palatini muscle, 93, **112,** 113, 120, 277
Levatores costarum muscles, 63, 278
Lever principle, of ossicles, 165
Lexicon, 264
Li, K.-P., 159
Liberman, A. M., 11, 22, 23, 128, 140, 141, 158, 160, 171, 174, 177, 187, 189, 193, 204, 205, 207, 209, 210, 212, 251
Lieberman, P., 130, 156, 158, 173, 209, 260, 262, 265
Lindau, M., 160
Lindblom, B. E. F., 127, 140, 142, 158, 173, 209
Line spectrum; *see* Amplitude spectrum
Linear scale, 39, 278
Linguadental fricative; *see* Fricative
Linguistic competence, 2, 7, 278
Linguistic determinism, 4
Linguistic performance, 2, 7, 278
Linguistic Society of Paris, 245
Lip rounding, 104
Lips, 95
Liquid, 278. *See also* Semivowels
Lisker, L., 118, 158, 166, 174, 181, 209, 210, 242
Listening station, 239, **240**

Localization of function (in brain), 52. *See also* Cerebral lateralization; Hemispheric dominance
Locke, J., 245, **247**, 264, 265
Locke, J. L., 159, 199, 201
Locus principle, **180**
Logarithmic scale, 39, 278
Lombard effect, 133, 278
Longitudinal wave, 32, 278
Loudness, 39, 41–42, 278
Lovrinic, J. H., 209
Lubker, J. F., 113, 158, 242
Lung volume changes, **67**, 68, **69**, 70, **72**, **73**, 228
Lungs, 33, 61, **62**, **65**, 66, **67**
Luschei, E. S., 159

MacKay, D. G., 138, 157
MacNeilage, P. F., 14, 124, 125, 140, 141, 142, 156, 158, 160
Malécot, A., 174, 210
Malleus, **164**, 165, 278
Mandible, 91, **92**, 93, **95**, 278
Manner of production, 116, 176, **181**, 182, 183–186, 278
Manometer, **228**, 278
Manubrium, 164, 278
Marler, P., 206, 212, 253, 266
Martin, J. G., 142, 143, 160
Masking, auditory, 134
Massachusetts Institute of Technology (MIT), 139, 204, 245
Mathematical model, of speech production, 142
Matthews, P. B. C., 136, 159, 160
Mattingly, I. G., 13, 242, 251, 265
Matz, B. J., 242
Maue, W. M., 156
Maxilla, **92**, **93**
Maxillary bone, 91, 93, 278
Maximum expiratory pressure, 278
Maximum inspiratory pressure, 278
McCloskey, D. I., 136, 159
McCutcheon, M. J., 242
McGill University, 57
McNabb, S. D., 202, 211
McReynolds, L. V., 199, 211
Mead, J., 68, 70, 157
Medial pterygoid muscle, **121**, 278
Medulla oblongata, 48, **49**, 61, 278
Mel, **38**, 278
Membrane, basilar, 274
Membranous labyrinth, **167**
Memory, and speech perception, 203
Mental retardation, 57, 278
Menyuk, P., 211
Mermelstein, P., 174, 210
Metathesis, 128, 278
Microphone, 218
Middle constrictor muscle, 91, **92**, 278
Middle ear, **163**, **164**–166, 278
Miller, G. A., 176, 182, 210
Miller, J. D., 196, 210

Milner, B., 57, 157, 211
Minifie, F., 156, 158
MIT; *see* Massachusetts Institute of Technology
Miyawaki, K., 210
Models of speech production, 12, 13, 59, 138–144, 146, **155**
Molar, **113**
Moll, K. L., 113, 128, 158, 242
Monaural listening, 239
Monologue, 278; collective, 4, 275
Monophthongs, 109
Moore, G. P., 242
Morpheme, 8, 278
Morphology, 7
Morphophonological rules, 7
Morse, P. A., 196, 210
Morton, J., 203, 206, 212
Motion, simple harmonic; *see* Simple harmonic motion
Motoneurons, 239; alpha, 135, 273; gamma, 135, 276
Motor cortex, 57
Motor equivalence, 140
Motor nerve, 48
Motor strip, 53, **54**, **55**, **56**
Motor unit, 238–239, 278
Motor theory of speech perception, 204, 205, 278
Mott, F. M., 160
Mowrer, O. H., 6
Moxon, E. C., 209
Müller, J., 75, 157
Munson, W. A., 41, 45
Muscle action potentials, 238
Muscle activity, study of, 238–239
Muscle spindles, **135**, 278
Muscles: of expiration, 70–72; of inspiration, 62–66; of phonation, 78–80. *See also* specific muscle names
Muscular process, of arytenoid cartilage, **77**
Myelin, 51, 278
Myers, R. E., 254, 266
Mylohyoid muscle, **95**, **117**
Myoelastic aerodynamic theory of phonation, 74–75, 278

Nakatani, L. H., 243
Narrow band spectrogram; *see* Sound spectrogram
Nasal; *see* Nasal consonants
Nasal bulb, **229**
Nasal cavity, 63, **65**, **90**; evolution of, **260**
Nasal consonants, 90–91, 114–115, 174, 176; syllabic, 109; synthetic, *see* Speech synthesis
Nasal murmur, 115, 174, 176
Nasal notch, **92**
Nasal resonance, 114–115
Nasal sounds, 112, 278. *See also* Nasal consonants
Nasality, 11
Nasopharynx, 91, **163**
Natural resonant frequency, 43–44, 278
Neanderthal man, 250, 260, 262
Negative feedback; *see* Feedback
Negative pressure breathing, 59–61

Negus, V. E., 157, 258, 265
Nerve block, effects on speech, 134
Nerve impulse, 49–51
Nerves, 278; auditory, 52, 169–171, 201, 269, 274; cervical, 62, 274; cochlear, **163;** cranial, 48, 52, 78, 85, 112, 114, 117, 120, 121, 166, 169–171, 201, **269**, 274, 275; motor, 48; phrenic, 62, **279;** recurrent, 78, **80, 81,** 85, 280; spinal, 48, 70, 271, 281; superior laryngeal, 85; thoracic, 62, 70, 282; trigeminal, 117, 121, 269; vagus, 78, 85, 269; vestibular, **163**
Nervous system: all-or-none-principle, 49, **50;** auditory cortex, 170; control of speech, 48–58; divisions of, 48, **49;** gray matter, 51, 276; myelin, 51; pyramidal tract, **55,** 57; in speech perception, 200–204; synapse, 51; white matter, 51. *See also* Broca's area; Cerebellum; Cerebral cortex; Nerves; Wernicke's area
Netsell, R., 72, 157
Neurochronaxic theory of phonation, 75
Neuron, 48–49, **50,** 51–52, 278
Neurophysiology, of speech perception, 200–204
Neutralization, of vowels, 109, 127, 173
New York Academy of Science, 245
Newman, E. B., 45
Nicely, P. E., 176, 182, 210
Nodules, vocal, 87
Non-acoustic cues, in speech perception, 162
Non-speech stimuli, perception of, 191
Nooteboom, S. G., 11, 141, 142, 160
Nordström, P. E., 173, 209
Norman, D. A., 212

Oblique arytenoid muscles, 79, **80,** 279
Occipital lobe, **53**
O'Connor, J. D., 174, 209
Oddball method, 197
Oddball test, 279
Ohala, J., 242
Öhman, S. E. G., 128, 142, 158, 210
Oliver, W., 159
Ontogeny, 256, 279
Open loop system, 131, **132,** 279
Open syllable, 107
Open tube, resonance of, 95
Operant conditioning, 6, 279
Operant response, 6
Oral anesthetization, 215
Oral cavity, 59, **90,** 91–93, **113,** 279; evolution of, **260,** 279
Oral sounds, 112, 279
Oral stereognosis, 134, 279
Orbicularis oris muscle, **95, 102,** 109, 114, 117, 120, 279
Orbital surface, **92**
Ordinate, 33, 35, 279
Organ of Corti, 168, **169,** 279
Oropharynx, 91
Oscilloscope, 32, 220, 279
Oshida, H., 242
Ossicles, **163, 164,** 165, 279
Ossicular chain, 279. *See also* Ossicles
Otis, A. B., 157

Outer ear, **163**–164
Output spectrum, **99**
Oval window, **163, 164,** 165, 166, 167, **168,** 279
OVE synthesizer, 191
Oya, N., 158

Palatal consonants, 109, 114, 116, 120–121
Palatal prostheses, 236
Palate, **65,** 92–93, 276; cleft, *see* Cleft palate; soft, *see* Velum
Palatine bone, **93**
Palatine process, **93**
Palatoglossus muscle, **112,** 113, 117, 279
Palatography, 236, 279
Papçun, G., 160
Paragrammatism, 200
Parallel processing, 128, 140, 279
Paralysis, vocal fold, 86
Parietal lobe, **53,** 279
Parietal pleura; *see* Pleurae
Parkinson's disease, 57
Particle motion, 29, 32, **33**
Particle movement; *see* Particle motion
PAS; *see* Precategorical acoustic storage
Passive theories, of speech perception, 206–208
Pattern Playback, 22, **23,** 24, 104, 171, 172, 174, 176, 181, 189
Pavlov, I. P., 6
Pavlov Institute, 143
Pectoralis major muscle, 63, **66,** 279
Pectoralis minor muscle, 63, 279
Penfield, W., 6, 53, 55, 57, 157, 200, 204, 211
Perception, categorical; *see* Categorical perception
Perception and psychophysics, 25
Perception, speech; *see* Speech perception
Performance, linguistic, 2, 7
Perilymph, 166, 167, 168, 279
Period, 28, 279
Periodic vibration, 29, 35, 37, 59, 74, 84
Peripheral nervous system (PNS), 48, 279
Perkell, J. S., 128, 156, 158, 208, 213, 242
Persson, A., 159
Peters, R. W., 159
Peterson, G. E., 103, 104, 108, 124, 139, 158, 160, 173
Peterson and Shoup, 139
Pfeiffer, J. E., 265
Pharyngeal cavity, 59, **90;** evolution of, **260**
Pharyngeal constrictor muscles, **92**
Pharyngeal muscles, **112**
Pharyngeal plexus, 112, 279
Pharynx, 63, **65,** 75, 91, 279; evolution of, 264
Phase, **34,** 35, 277
Philological Society (London), 19
Phon, 41, 42, 279
Phonation, 74–89, 279. *See also* Vocal folds; Voicing
Phone, 8, 279
Phoneme boundary, 190, 193
Phoneme identification, 203
Phoneme reversals, 57–58
Phonemes, 8, 11, 24, 279

Phonemic contrasts, 199
Phonetic alphabet; see International Phonetic Alphabet (IPA)
Phonetic analysis, in speech perception, 196–197
Phonetic feature detectors, 197, 207
Phonetic features, 11, 207
Phonetic transcription, 11
Phonetica, 25
Phonological rules, 7
Phonology, 7
Phrase groups, 73
Phrenic nerve, 62, 279
Phylogeny, 256, 279
Piaget, J., 4
Pick, H. L., Jr., 159
Pierce, J. R., 45, 209
Pinna, 163, 279
Pinson, E. N., 45, 157, 162, 209
Pisoni, D. B., 196, 197, 202, 207, 211, 212
Pisoni and Sawusch, 207
Pitch, 38–39, 191, 280
Pitch rise, 130
Place of articulation, 11, 117, **118, 120,** 174, 176–177, **181,** 182, 183–186, 202, 280
Place of production; see Place of articulation
Place theory, 280
Plethysmograph, body; see Body plethysmograph
Pleurae, 61, **62,** 275, 279, 280, 283
Pleural cavity, **65**
Plosive(s), 91, 280. *See also* Stops
Plotter, 221
Pneumotachograph, 228, **230,** 280
PNS; see Peripheral nervous system
Poles, 280
Pons, 48, **49,** 280
Positive feedback; see Feedback
Posterior cricoarytenoid muscle, 78, **80,** 82, 280
Posterior faucial pillar(s), **113**
Posterior semicircular canal, **167**
Posterior speech cortex, **56**
Potter, R. K., 22, 157
Power, 33, 39, 40
Precategorical acoustic storage (PAS), 203, 280
Premack, D., 252, 266
Premaxilla, **93**
Pressure, 39, 40, 280
Pressure transducer, 228, **229,** 280
Pressure-velocity relationship, **98**
Pressure-volume relationship, 67–**69,** 70, **72**
Pribram, K. H., 157
Print-through, 219–220
Proctor, D. F., 68, 157
Production of a sentence, 145–155; *chart,* **148–154**
Proprioception, 134–136
Prosek, R. A., 159
Prosody, 11, 128, 280
Pulmonary pressure, **68**
Pure tone, 27, 29, 31, **33, 34,** 35, **36,** 280
Putnam, A. H. B., 159
Pyramidal (cortico-spinal) tract, **55,** 57, 280

Rahn, H., 67, 157
Ramus, of mandible, **93**
Raphael, L. J., 158, 181, 183, 205, 210, 212
Rarefaction, 32, **33,** 280
Rasmussen, T., 157
Rate, of speech, 173
Rationalism, 245
Rationalist, 280
Rayleigh, J. W. S., 45, 95, 158
REA; see Right ear advantage
Real time spectral analyzer, 221, **223,** 280
Recency effect, 203, 280
Receptors, touch, 48
Recording speech, 216, 218–220
Recording tape, signals on, **219**
Rectus abdominis muscle, **66,** 70, **72,** 280
Recurrent nerve, 280
Reflex, acoustic, 273
Reinforcement, 6
Reissner's membrane, **169**
Relative loudness; see Loudness
Relaxation pressure curve, 67–**68,** 70
Relaxation volume, 68, 280
Research tools, in speech science, 215–243
Residual air, 67
Residual volume, 67
Resistance, 28
Resonance, 18, 20, 43–45, 89–90, 95–**96, 97,** 98–**99,** 102, 280
Resonant frequency, natural, 43–44
Resonator, **44,** 45, 59, 115, 273, 280
Respiration, 58–74
Respiratory analysis, 227–229
Response, conditioned, 6, 275
Resting volume, 67
Restricted code, 5, 280
Retroflex, 110–111, 280
Reverberation, 34–35, 280
Reversals, phoneme, 57–58
Reversals, word, 57–58
Rhesus monkey, 254
Rhythm, 128, 142
Ribs, 61, 280; elevation of, 62–63, **64, 65, 66**
Riesz, R., 22
Right ear advantage (REA), 201, 202, 204, 280
Ringel, R. L., 134, 158, 159
Roberts, L., 53, 55, 57, 157, 200, 204, 211, 212
Rockefeller University, 253
Rolando, Fissure of; see Fissure of Rolando
Rosner, B. S., 196, 211
Round window, **163, 164**
Rumbaugh, D. M., 265

Saccule, **167**
Sapir, E., 4
Sarah, 252
Sawashima, M., 242, 243
Sawusch, J. R., 207, 212
Scala tympani, 168, **169**
Scala vestibuli, 168, **169**

Scale, linear vs logarithmic, 39
Scalenus medius muscle, 63, 280
Scapula, 280
Schulman, S., 212
Schvey, M. H., 242
Science, 25
Scott, B., 207, 212
Scott, C. M., 159
Section, on sound spectrogram, 225, 280
Semantics, 2, 3, 7, 11, 264, 280
Semicircular canals, **163, 167,** 169, 280
Semivowels, 90–91, 109–111, **147,** 174; synthetic, *see* Speech synthesis. *See also* Glide; Liquid
Sentence, production of, 145–156; *chart,* **148–154**
Serratus anterior muscle, 63, **66**
Serratus posterior superior muscle, 63, 281
Servomechanism, 131, 144, **146,** 281
Shadowing experiments, 205, 206
Shankweiler, D. P., 140, 158, 160, 173, 202, 209, 211, 212
Sherrington, C. S., 134, 160
Shipp, T., 157
SHM; *see* Simple harmonic motion
Short-term memory, 203
Shoup, J. E., 124, 139, 158, 160
Sibilants, 120, 281
Siegel, G. M., 159
Sign; *see* American Sign Language (Ameslan)
Simon, C., 211
Simple harmonic motion (SHM), 27, 28, 29, **30, 31, 32,** 35, 42, 281
Sine wave, 28, 32, **33,** 34, 35, 281
Siqueland, E. R., 194, 210
Skinner, B. F., 245, 265
Slips of the tongue, 11
Smith, P. J., 159
Smith, T. S., 160
Snowden, C. T., 196, 210
SOA; *see* Stimulus onset asynchrony
Social releaser, 251
Sodium amytal, 56, 57
Sodium amytal test; *see* Wada test
Soft palate; *see* Velum
Software, 281
Sone, 42, 281
Sound, 27–45, 281. *See also* Amplitude; Frequency; Velocity; Vibration; Wavelength
Sound cancellation, 35
Sound influence, 124–128
Sound level meter, 41
Sound pressure, 39
Sound pressure level (SPL), 39, 40, 41, 281
Sound spectrogram, 22, 100, **119, 123, 125, 147, 225, 226, 237,** 281; section, 225, 280
Sound spectrograph, 22, 23, 222, **224,** 281
Source function, 98, **99,** 281
Spasticity, 57, 281
Spectral analysis, 24, 221–227
Spectrogram, sound; *see* Sound spectrogram
Spectrograph, sound; *see* Sound spectrograph
Spectrum, 281

Spectrum, amplitude, 35, 273
Spectrum, line; *see* Amplitude spectrum
Speech acquisition; *see* Speech and language development
Speech and Language, 25
Speech and language development, 5–7, 204, 257, 264; evolution of, 245–266
Speech chain, 162
Speech code, 140, **141,** 265
Speech cortex, 55, **56, 57**
Speech errors, 57–58
Speech journals, 24, 25
Speech, language, and thought, 1–15
Speech, nerve block effects on, 134
Speech, neurophysiology of, 48–58
Speech perception, 14, 22–25, 161–213, 281; acoustic cues, 171–187, 205; categorical, 187–199; innateness of, 207; neurophysiology of, 200–204; nonlinearity of, 176; redundancy in, 176; research, instrumentation for, 239; theories of, 204–208, 280
Speech processor, 202, 205
Speech production, 12, 22, 47–160; models of, 12, 13, 59, 138–144, **146, 155;** neurophysiology of, 48–58; and perception, 198–199; preplanning in, 57–58; research, instrumentation for, 216, 217; role of left hemisphere in, 200–201; syllable commands, **143, 144, 145.** *See also* Affricates; Diphthongs; Fricatives; Manner of production; Nasal consonants; Place of articulation; Semivowels; Sentence; Stop consonants; Suprasegmentals; Vowels
Speech rate, 173
Speech recognition machines, 187
Speech rhythm, 128, 142
Speech science, 14, 17–25; instrumentation in, 215–242
Speech sounds, 90–91, 124–130
Speech synthesis, 24, 171–173; by computer, 241; of diphthongs, 173; of nasals, 174, 176, **181;** by rule, 241–242; of semivowels, 174, **175, 177, 192;** of stops, 176–**177, 178, 179, 180, 181.** *See also* Speech synthesizers
Speech synthesizers: circuit diagram, **241;** OVE, 191; Pattern Playback, 22, **23,** 24, 104, 171, 172, 174, 176, 181, 189; Vocoder, 22; Voder, **21,** 22. *See also* Speech synthesis
Sperry, R. W., 200, **201,** 211
Spinal cord, **49**
Spinal nerves, 48, 70, 271, 281
Spiral ligament, **169**
Spirometer, 229, **231,** 281
SPL; *see* Sound pressure level
Split brain experiment, 200, **201**
Spooner, W. A., 57
Spoonerism, 57, 281
Stam, J. H., 265
Stapedius muscle, 166
Stapes, **163, 164,** 165, 167, **168,** 281
Steinheim man, 262
Steklis, H. D., 265
Stelmach, G. E., 160
Stephens, R. W. B., 45

Stereognosis, oral, 134, 279
Sternocleidomastoid muscle, 63, 281
Sternohyoid muscle, **86,** 281
Sternothyroid muscle, **86**
Sternum, 61, **63,** 281
Stetson, R., 70, 157
Stevens, K. N., 95, 98, 122, 158, 160, 193, 198, 204, 208, 210, 211, 212, 213
Stevens, S. S., 38, 45, 159, 209
Stimulus: conditioned, 6, 275; unconditioned, 6, 282
Stimulus onset asynchrony (SOA), 202, 281
Stop consonants, 91, 116–**118, 119,** 176–177, **178, 179,** 180–182, 202, 281
Stops; see Stop consonants
Stops, synthetic; see Speech synthesis
Storage oscilloscope, **220,** 222, 281
Strain gauge, 235, **238,** 281
Strange, W., 173, 194, 197, 209, 210, 211
Strap muscles, **86**
Stress, 11, 70, 72–73, 128–129, 187
Stress-timing, 142
Stroboscope, 230, 281
Strome, M., 242
Stromstra, C., 159
Studdert-Kennedy, M., 140, 150, 158, 202, 203, 209, 210, 211, 212, 213
Stuttering, 74, 88
Styloglossus muscle, **94, 102,** 110, 117, 281
Stylohyoid ligament, **92**
Stylohyoid muscle, **94**
Styloid process, of temporal bone, **94**
Stylopharyngeal muscle, **94**
Subclavius muscle, 63, 281
Subglottal air pressure, **69,** 70, 72–73, 80–81, 281
Subsonic vibration, 38
Subtelny, J. D., 158
Subtelny, J. D., 121, 122, 158, 243
Sulcus terminalis, **113**
Summation waveform, 34
Superior constrictor muscle, 91, **92, 112,** 281
Superior longitudinal muscle, 94, 95, 117, 120, 281
Superior speech cortex, 55, **56**
Suprahyoid muscles, 86
Supralaryngeal movement, study of, 235–238
Suprasegmentals, 128–130, 186–187, 281
Surface structure, 11
Sussman, H. M., 212
Sweet, H., 19
Syllabic consonant, 109, 117, 281
Syllable, 129, 281
Syllable nucleus, 109, 281
Sylvian fissure; see Fissure of Sylvius
Sylvius, Fissure of; see Fissure of Sylvius
Synapse, 51, **52,** 281
Syntagma, 143, 281
Syntax, 2, 7, 11, 256, 264, 281
Synthetic speech; see Speech synthesis

Tabula rasa, 245, 282
Tactile feedback, 133–134
Taieb, 247, 262

Tape recorder, **219,** 239
Tape recording, 216, 218
Tape-splicing, 239
Target, of diphthongs, 109
Target theory, 140–142
Taub, E., 160
Tectorial membrane, 168, 282
Teeth, 91–92, **95**
Template hypothesis, 206, **255,** 282
Temporal bone, 166, 170
Temporal lobe, 52, **53,** 170, 282
Temporoparietal area, 52, 55, 200, 256, **258**
Tense (vowels), 107, 282
Tensor palatini muscle, **112,** 282
Tensor tympani muscle, 164, 166, 282
Terminal arbor, **50**
Thalamus, 48, 282
Theories of hearing, 168, 169, 280, 282, 283
Theories of speech perception, 204–208, 280
Third formant, in semivowels, 110
Thoracic nerves, 62, 282
Thoracic volume, 62, 66, 70
Thorax, **61, 62, 66**
Thought, 1–15. See also Language; Speech and language development; Speech, language, and thought
Threshold of hearing; see Hearing
Thyroarytenoid muscle, **76, 77,** 79, 282. See also Vocalis muscle
Thyrohyoid membrane, **76, 92**
Thyrohyoid muscle, **86,** 282
Thyroid cartilage, 74, **76, 77, 78,** 92, **94**
Thyroid notch, 77, **78**
Tidal volume, 66–67, 282
Timing, models of, 142, 143
Tomographic methods, 234, 282
Tones: complex, 35, **36, 37;** periodic, 35, **36, 37;** pure, 27, 29, 31, **33, 36, 37.** See also Amplitude; Frequency; Sound; Velocity; Vibration; Wavelength
Tongue, 65, 94–95, 104, 110, 264
Tonsils, **113**
Torque, 66, 282
Touch receptors, 48, 133–134
Trachea, 61, 63, 65, 75, **76, 92,** 282
Tracheal puncture, 228
Tragus, 163, 282
Tranel, B., 159
Transcription, phonetic, 11
Transfer function, **99,** 282
Transient, 37, 282
Transillumination, 231, 282
Transitions, formant, 282; in diphthongs, 109; as perceptual cue, 174–176; in semivowels, 109–111; in stops, 118
Transverse arytenoid muscle, 78, **80,** 282
Transverse muscles of tongue, 94, **95,** 282
Transverse wave, 32
Transversus abdominis muscle, 70, **72,** 282
Traveling wave theory, 168, 169, 282
Tuning forks, 27, **28,** 35
Two-formant patterns: CV syllable, **189;** stops, **179;** vowels, 103, **104**

Two-point discrimination, 134, 282
Tympanic membrane, **164,** 166, 282

UCLA; see University of California at Los Angeles
Uldall, E., 122, 158
Ultrasonic vibration, 38, 43
Ultrasound, 235, 282
Unconditioned stimulus, 6, 282
Universal features, of language, 5
University of California at Los Angeles, 58
University of California at Santa Barbara, 252
University of Nevada, 252
University of Washington, 195
Unmarked breath group, 130
Utricle, **167**
Uvula, 93, 112, **113,** 282
Uvular muscle; see Uvula

Vallate papillae, **113**
Vallbo, Å. B., 160
Van Bergeijk, W. A., 45, 209
Van den Berg, J., 75, 85, 157
Van Lawick-Goodall, J., 250, 266
Van Riper, C., 156
Variable: dependent, 275, independent, 277
Velar adjustment, and voicing, 114
Velocity, 28, **30,** 42, 96, 282; of nerve impulse, 50–51
Velopharyngeal closure, 94, 112, 113, 120, 282
Velopharyngeal port, 111–114, 282
Velum, 93–94, 112, **113,** 282
Ventricular folds, **76,** 282
Verbal transformation, 200, 282
Verbrugge, R. R., 173, 209, 210
Vertebrae, 61, **63,** 282
Vertical muscles of tongue, 94, 282
Vestibular nerve, **163**
Vestibular organs; see Vestibular system
Vestibular system, **163, 167,** 282
Vestibule; see Vestibular system
Vibration, 27–29, 33–35, 38; forced, 44, 276; free, 44, 276. See also Amplitude; Frequency; Simple harmonic motion; Sound; Vocal folds
Vigorito, J., 194, 202, 210, 211
Visceral pleura; see Pleurae
Visible Speech, 19, 20
Visicorder, 221, **222**
Vital capacity, 66–**67,** 73, 283
Vocal abuse, 87
Vocal attack, 87
Vocal folds, 74–75, **76,** 77–79, **90;** abduction of 78; adduction of, 78–80; adjustments during speech, 78–80; false, see Ventricular folds; length, 75; paralysis of, 86; vibration of, 33, 38, 59, 67–70, 80–**83, 84, 88,** 114, 116
Vocal fry, 87, 282
Vocal ligament, **77,** 79, 86
Vocal nodules, 87
Vocal play, 255
Vocal process, of arytenoid cartilage, **77,** 79
Vocal tract, 5, 11, 18, 20, 45, 59, **90,** 91, **92–96, 97,** 98–99, 102, **103,** 106, 115–123, **238,** 283; evolution of, 258–260, **261,** 262
Vocalis muscle, 75, 82, 282. See also Thyroarytenoid muscle
Vocoder, 22
Voder (Voice Operation Demonstrator), **21,** 22
Voice; see Vocal folds, vibration of; Voicing
Voice bar, 178, 182, 186
Voice disorders, 73
Voice onset time (VOT), 116, 118, 181, 193, 194, 197, 282
Voice Operation Demonstrator; see Voder
Voice quality, 86–87
Voicing, 78–80, 114, **119,** 282; perception of, 181, 182, 183–186. See also Vocal folds, vibration of
Volkmann, J., 38, 45
Volley theory, 283
Volta Bureau, 20
Voltmeter, 239, 283
Volume: of lungs, 66–**67,** 68, **69,** 70, 72; thoracic, 62; tidal, 66–67
Von Békésy, G., 138, 159, 169, 209
Von Euler, C., 136, 159
Von Glasersfeld, E. C., 266
Von Helmholtz, H., 17, 75, 95, 157. See also Helmholtz
Von Leden, H., 242
VOT; see Voice onset time
Vowels, 18, 19, 20, 90–91, 99–**100, 101, 102, 103,** 104, **105, 106, 107, 108,** 111; neutralization of, 173; perception of, 171–173, 193, 202; synthetic, see Speech synthesis
Vowel quadrilateral, 102, 104, **106**
Vowel triangle; see Vowel quadrilateral
VU meter, 218
Vygotsky, L., 4

Wada, J., 157
Wada test, 56, 57, 283
Wakita, H., 242
Walker, A. C., 265
Warren, R. M., 212
Washoe, **252**
Waters, R. S., 196, 210
Wathen-Dunn, W., 160
Watkin, K. L., 242, 243
Watt, 39, 40, 282
Wave: longitudinal, 32, 278; transverse, 32
Waveform, 11, 29, 30, **31,** 32, **33, 34,** 35, **36,** 37, **98,** 208, 221, 283
Waveform analysis, 220–221. See also Fourier analysis
Wavelength, 42–**43,** 283
Weber, E., 39
Webster, R. L., 159
Weiner, N., 131, 144, 158
Weiss, M., 212
Wernicke, C., 52, 157, 200, 212
Wernicke's area, **53,** 55, 57, 200, 203
Wever, E. G., 169, 209
Whitaker, H. A., 203, 212

White, F. D., 242
White-crowned sparrow, 254
White matter, 51, 283
Whitfield, I. C., 213
Whitteridge, D., 70, 157
Whorf, B., 4
Whorfian hypothesis, 4, 282
Wide band spectrogram; see Sound spectrogram
Widin, G. P., 197, 211
Williams, F., 156
Williams, G. C., 211
Williams, L., 198, 199, 211
Wilson, W. A., Jr., 196, 210
Windpipe; see Trachea
Wolf, M. B., 242
Wood, A., 45

Wood, B. A., 265
Wood, C. C., 202, 212
Word order, 11
Word reversals, 57–58
Wrenn, C., 19

X-ray microbeam system, 238

Yates, A. J., 159
Yerkes Regional Primate Research Center, 252

Zagzebski, J. A., 243
Zaidel, E., 201, 212
Zemlin, W. R., 156
Zeros, 283
Zlatin, M. A., 198, 211